W9-DIH-629

JUN 1 8 2010

NO LONGER THE
PROPERTY OF
ELON UNIVERSITY LIBRARY

Introduction to e- Supply Chain Management

Engaging Technology to Build Market-Winning Business Partnerships

David F. Ross

Introduction to e- Supply Chain Management

Engaging Technology to
Build Market-Winning
Business Partnerships

S^t_L

ST. LUCIE PRESS

A CRC Press Company
Boca Raton   London   New York   Washington, D.C.

Library of Congress Cataloging-in-Publication Data

Ross, David Frederick, 1948-
    Introduction to e-supply chain management: engaging technology to build
market-winning business partnerships / by David F. Ross.
       p. cm.
    Includes bibliographical references and index.
    ISBN 1-57444-324-0 (alk. paper)
    1. Business logistics—Data processing. 2. Information technology. 3. Internet. I. Title.

HD38.5 .R6753 2002
658.7'0285—dc21

2002031711
CIP

This book contains information obtained from authentic and highly regarded sources. Reprinted material is quoted with permission, and sources are indicated. A wide variety of references are listed. Reasonable efforts have been made to publish reliable data and information, but the author and the publisher cannot assume responsibility for the validity of all materials or for the consequences of their use.

Neither this book nor any part may be reproduced or transmitted in any form or by any means, electronic or mechanical, including photocopying, microfilming, and recording, or by any information storage or retrieval system, without prior permission in writing from the publisher.

The consent of CRC Press LLC does not extend to copying for general distribution, for promotion, for creating new works, or for resale. Specific permission must be obtained in writing from CRC Press LLC for such copying.

Direct all inquiries to CRC Press LLC, 2000 N.W. Corporate Blvd., Boca Raton, Florida 33431.

Trademark Notice: Product or corporate names may be trademarks or registered trademarks, and are used only for identification and explanation, without intent to infringe.

Visit the CRC Press Web site at www.crcpress.com

© 2003 by David F. Ross
St. Lucie Press is an imprint of CRC Press LLC

No claim to original U.S. Government works
International Standard Book Number 1-57444-324-0
Library of Congress Card Number 2002031711
Printed in the United States of America 2 3 4 5 6 7 8 9 0
Printed on acid-free paper

Dedication

My loving thanks to my wife Colleen and my son Jonathan, who had to bear, yet again, the burden of lost afternoons and long evenings, but who receive little of the rewards.

Preface

The first years of the twenty-first century have been dramatic ones indeed. The new century began with unprecedented prosperity, record employment, relative security from war, and massive governmental surpluses at all levels. The business and financial communities and, indeed, almost all aspects of life from entertainment to shopping were caught up in the excitement of a computerized tool called the Internet that was cast as the destroyer of the old industrial economy, the harbinger of a whole "new economy," and the digitization of all forms of human endeavor. By the middle of 2002 the good times had not only soured, but the specter of financial recession, massive layoffs, and corporate scandal had rocked the U.S. economy. The over-hyped e-business revolution fizzled into bankruptcy, ruined stock portfolios, and disillusionment when the dot-com bubble burst. The computer software/hardware industry saw sales plummet as companies looked inward to cost-cutting initiatives and to conserve cash. A vicious and deadly terrorist attack on 11 September, 2001 reminded the country that the world was not rational and peaceful after all, that there was a specter that could with one blow topple what had been considered a rock solid and prosperous economic environment. And, finally, corporate greed, arrogance, abuse of power, and lack of stewardship — the dark side of management that, in the hands of morally weak and intellectually dishonest corporate executives, destroys businesses and human lives — just about applied the knockout blow as the Dow dropped below 8000 and the NASDAQ sank to around 25 percent of its former highs.

While traumatic, the new realities of the economic environment have served to reveal not how over-hyped, although a good deal was indeed just vapor, but how important the effective convergence of technology and the supply chain are to corporate survival. The plummeting economy and the disruptions to the supply chain, while negatively impacting business, have simply accelerated the changes to how companies were internally organized and measured, how they dealt with each other, how assets were to be transacted through the supply pipeline, and what was to be the role of technology, which were already in the works without the intervention of the folks at al-Qaida and WorldCom. The Kmart bankruptcy, for example, illustrated that the company's inability to master supply chain technology and, consequently, benefit from supply chain efficiencies, could cause disaster to even the largest of companies. Far from causing executives to place *supply chain management* (SCM) and Internet concepts and technologies on the back burner as they rode out the decaying economic times, the tightening of the economy and heavier restrictions and security measures placed on channel flows have rendered access to real-time, accurate supply chain information more critical than ever. Connectivity, messaging, and collaboration have become today's foremost buzzwords, as companies compete for survival in an environment where cycle times and permissible margins of error continue to shrink.

According to an Accenture survey (March 2002) on the impact of SCM and the Internet on the worsening economy and restrictions in the supply chain, SCM/Internet initiatives were credited with cost reductions, improved efficiencies, better customer service, more revenue, and greater competitiveness by over 80 percent of the companies responding. Also, more than 70 percent felt that the application of Web-based applications providing end-to-end visibility to the supply chain were the single most important enabler of collaboration with top trading partners. While the survey indicated that the prime reason why companies increasingly were turning toward supply chain partners to outsource functions was to cut costs in the short run, 70 percent of executives saw the long-term creation of partnering agreements as a major strategy in achieving corporate objectives.[1]

The mission of this book is to provide a window into the concepts, techniques, and vocabulary of the convergence of SCM and the Internet so that companies can continue to leverage and expand on these exciting business tools to maintain, in these uncertain times, the momentum in supply chain savings and competitive advantage detailed in the Accenture survey. As will be detailed in the pages to follow, what is termed e-SCM provides today's enterprise with the business concepts and technical toolsets to activate supply chain capabilities that will enable executives to architect:

- Process-centered, technology-enabled organizations composed of networks of knowledgeable and highly skilled teams capable of assembling the competencies and resources to be found within the business and outside among trading partners into "virtual organizations" focused on activating strategies designed to continuously pursue total customer satisfaction.
- Collaborative communities of supply chain partners integrated together by concurrent access to databases and information flows that permit them to closely synchronize day-to-day operations and long-term strategies, so that they appear as if they were a single logical enterprise providing seamless, optimized capabilities to the customer.
- Inter-enterprise, Web-based technologies engineered to provide cross-channel teams access to interoperable computerized business components that empower them to interweave common and specialized knowledge to form collaborative supply chain nodes capable of integrating and networking channel processes to achieve optimal productivity.

Today's computer architectures and business applications are truly exciting, and they do portend the coming of a new age of business-to-customer connectivity based on the communication and enrichment of digital information. While the shape of these architectures is still in the process of development, one conclusion, however, is clear: the actual practice of SCM today has moved far beyond its original definition as a technique for optimizing a collection of logistics operations. Today, SCM is a dynamic, evolutionary concept that encompasses not only operational objectives but also inter-enterprise strategies determining how the whole supply chain will compete in the twenty-first century.

Each chapter in this book attempts to explore and elaborate on the many different components of the combination of SCM and today's Internet technologies. The first chapter focuses on defining Web-enabled SCM and detailing its essential elements. The argument that unfolds is that e-SCM is a management model that conceives of individual enterprises as nodes in a supply chain web, digitally architected and collectively focused on the continuous evolution of new forms of customer value. Among the topics discussed will be the function of Internet-based information in e-SCM, the utilization of supply chain trading partners, and understanding the role of supply chain synchronization.

Chapter 2 is devoted to a detailed discussion of the economic "revolution" driven by the Internet. The analysis begins with a review of the business dynamics of what is being termed the first stage of the "new economy." Among the areas explored are the changes brought about by the Internet to customer management, product cycle management, the basis of information technology, the creation of global businesses, and logistics management. After, the discussion centers on the fundamental principles of e-business: e-collaboration, the rise of new forms of e-business, and the impact of the Internet on human resources. The chapter concludes with a review of the major trends impacting the development of e-business, ranging from the continued migration from vertical to virtually integrated enterprises to the changed role of logistics.

In Chapter 3, the systems foundation of e-SCM will be explored. Discussion begins with an overview of the enterprise systems governing internal computing. Following, the analysis shifts to a review of business-to-business computing, beginning with *electronic data interchange* (EDI) and continuing with a review of the four phases of Internet commerce. Key topics detailed are utilization of the Internet for marketing and sales, Web applications targeted at activating e-commerce possibilities with customers and integrating supplier networks, and the possibilities inherent in e-collaboration and the generation of real-time, agile, and scalable supply chains. The chapter concludes with a brief review of the integrative architectures necessary to assemble into a single framework the mixture of *enterprise resource planning* (ERP) applications, *business-to-business* (B2B) and *business-to-customer* (B2C) point solutions, and business processes and work flows.

Chapter 4 seeks to explore how companies can build effective market-winning business strategies by actualizing the opportunities to be found in SCM and the Internet. Structuring effective business strategies requires companies to closely integrate the physical capabilities, knowledge competencies, and technology connectivity of their supply chain networks alongside company-centric product, service, and infrastructure architectures. Building such a powerful e-SCM strategy requires strategists to carefully craft a comprehensive business vision, assess the depth of current e-SCM trading partner connectivity, and identify and prioritize what initiatives must be undertaken to actualize new value chain partnerships. The chapter concludes with a detailed discussion of a proposed e-SCM strategy development model.

Defining the concepts and computerized toolsets associated with *customer relationship management* (CRM) will be explored in Chapter 5. The chapter begins with an attempt to define CRM, detail its prominent characteristics, and outline its primary mission. Next, the discussion shifts to outlining a portrait of today's customer. The profile that emerges shows that customers are value driven, that they are looking for strong partnerships with their suppliers, and that they want to be treated as unique individuals. Effectively responding to today's customer requires a customer-centric organization. The middle part of the chapter attempts to detail the steps for creating and nurturing such an organization. The balance of the chapter is then focused on the e-CRM technology applications, such as Internet sales, sales force automation, service, partnership relationship management, electronic billing and payment, and CRM analytics.

Chapter 6 is concerned with exploring the application of e-SCM practices and Web-based tools to the management of manufacturing. The discussion begins by reviewing the role of manufacturing in the "age of e-business." Of particular interest is the availability of an almost bewildering array of technology tools to assist in the management of almost every aspect of manufacturing from transaction control to Internet-enabled B2B exchanges. The chapter discusses one of today's most important drivers of productivity — the ability of manufacturing firms to architect collaborative relationships with business partners to synchronize, through the Internet, all aspects of product design and time-to-market. The chapter concludes with an analysis of today's advanced manufacturing planning functions that seek to apply the latest optimization and Web-based applications to interconnect and make visible the demand and replenishment needs of whole supply network systems.

In Chapter 7, the functions of purchasing and *supplier relationship management* (SRM) will be explored. A critical observation is that the strategic importance of SRM is not to be found in the optimization and automation of purchasing functions, but rather in the nurturing of buy-side partner relationships. The application of Web-based functions have opened an entirely new range of SRM toolsets, enabling companies to dramatically cut costs, automate functions, such as sourcing, *request for quotation* (RFQ), and order generation and monitoring, and optimize supply chain partners to achieve the best products and the best prices from anywhere in the supply network. The chapter concludes with a full discussion of the anatomy of today's e-SRM system followed by an exploration of the e-SRM exchange environment, today's e-marketplace models, and the steps necessary to execute a successful e-SRM implementation.

Chapter 8 is concerned with detailing the elements of logistics management in the Internet Age. The discussion begins with a review of the function of logistics and its evolution to what can be called *logistics resource management* (LRM). After a detailed definition of the structure and key capabilities of LRM, the chapter proceeds to describe the different categories of LRM available today and the array of possible Web-based toolsets driving logistics performance measurement and warehouse and transportation management. Afterwards, strategies for the use of third-party logistics services are reviewed. The different types of logistics service providers, the growth of Internet-enabled providers, and the challenges of choosing a logistics partner that matches, if not facilitates, overall company business strategies are explored in depth.

Grappling with the content and selection decisions surrounding today's Web-enabled technologies is the subject of the last chapter. Discussion opens with a review of the internal, interorganizational, and technology architecture requirements for implementing e-SCM. Converging SCM and the Internet will require companies to make the transition from company-centric to supply chain process-centric organizations that are customer-focused, flexible, and capable of metamorphosing to be more responsive to the needs of trading partners and customers, and that they are driven by an empowered cross-functional, cross-enterprise work force. The analysis next moves to the construction of inter-enterprise architecture. The argument voiced is that internal organizational reengineering is insufficient, and that the only way in today's business environment to build sustainable competitive advantage is to architect a collaborative community of trading partners collectively driven to deliver the highest level of customer service possible. The discussion of the third area, technology architecture, attempts to describe the hardware and software frameworks necessary to ensure the interoperability and integration of the business applications found at each trading partner node in the supply channel. The chapter ends with a review of the future of e-SCM, new technology developments, and the steps necessary to transform the organization to the e-SCM environment.

ENDNOTES

1. "SCM is Key to Improvement, Accenture Poll Finds," *Global Logistics and Supply Chain Strategies*, 6, 3, 2002, 16.

Acknowledgments

Writing a book on today's business environment is like trying to hold quicksilver. Today's technology and business environment is changing so quickly that concepts and applications at the forefront of thought are often passé or even obsolete when the book hits the general marketplace. Doubtlessly, many of the ideas and the relevancy of the resources used to create this book are destined, with alarming quickness, to be out-of-date as the book moves past its publication date. Still, to begin with, I would sincerely like to express my sincere thanks to the many students, professionals, and companies that I have worked with over the past several years, who have contributed their ideas and experience. I would also like to thank my colleagues and friends at Intentia, whose expert knowledge on today's suite of collaborate business software contributed significantly regarding the many technical aspects of the book.

The author would especially like to thank the executive and editorial staff at CRC Press for so eagerly welcoming the project. I would like to thank Ms. Pat Roberson for her kind help in processing the manuscript through to completion. The author would also like to thank the entire staff at the University of Chicago Library for their help. Finally, I would like to express my thanks to my wife Colleen and my son Jonathan for their support, encouragement, and understanding during the many months this book was written.

About the Author

A distinguished educator and consultant, **David F. Ross**, Ph.D., CFPIM, has spent over 25 years in the fields of production and distribution management. During his 13 years as a practitioner, he held several line and staff positions. For the past 15 years, Dr. Ross has been involved in ERP and e-Business education and consulting for several software companies. Currently, he is Education Business Group Manager for Intentia–Americas and is located in the corporate offices in Schaumburg, IL (e-mail: david.ross@intentia.com). He has taught operations management at Eastern Illinois University and Oakton Community College. He is also an instructor in the APICS practitioner education program.

Introduction to e-Supply Chain Management is Dr. Ross's third book in the field of distribution and supply chain management. His first book, *Distribution: Planning and Control* (Kluwer, 1996), has been used as a standard logistics management text by several universities and is on the required reading list for the APICS's "Detailed Planning and Scheduling" CPIM exam. His second book, *Competing Through Supply Chain Management* (Kluwer, 1998), was one of the first texts on the science of supply chain management and it also has been on the reading lists at several universities for courses in logistics management.

Acronyms

3PL	Third Party Logistics
4PL	Fourth Party Logistics
ABC	Activity-Based Costing
ABCM	Activity-Based Cost Management
ABM	Activity-Based Management
ACM	Advanced Customer Management
AEI	Automatic Equipment Identification
AIDC	Automatic Identification and Data Collection
AIM	Automatic Identification Manufacturing
ALM	Asset Lifecycle Management
AMHS	Automated Material Handling Systems
ANSI	American National Standards Institute
ANX	Automotive Network Exchange
APICS	American Production and Inventory Control Society
APS	Advanced Planning and Scheduling
ASN	Advanced Shipping Notice
ASP	Application Service Provider
ATP	Available to Promise
B2B	Business-to-Business
B2C	Business-to-Customer
BI	Business Intelligence
BOM	Bill of Materials
BPM	Business Process Management
CAD	Computer Aided Design
CAM	Computer Aided Manufacture
CAM	Collaborative Asset Management
CBCs	Collaborative Business Communities
CIC	Customer Interaction Center
CLM	Council of Logistics Management
CMC	Collaborative Manufacturing Commerce
CMS	Customer Management Strategies
CMMS	Computerized Maintenance Management System
CORBA	Common Object Request Broker Architecture
CPC	Collaborative Product Commerce
CPFR	Collaborative Planning, Forecasting, and Replenishment
CPD	Collaborative Product Development
CPG	Consumer Packaged Goods
CRM	Customer Relationship Management
CRP	Continuous Replenishment Programs

CSM	Customer Service Management, or Component and Supplier Management
CTP	Capable to Promise
CTX	Consortium Trading Exchange
DCS	Design Collaboration Software
e-BPO	Electronic Business Optimization
e-SCM	Electronic Supply Chain Management
EA	Enterprise Application
EAI	Enterprise Application Integration
EAM	Enterprise Asset Management
EBO	Equipment Brand Owner
EBPP	Electronic Bill Presentment and Payment
EBS	Enterprise Business System
ECM	Enterprise Commerce Management
ECR	Efficient Customer Response
EDI	Electronic Data Interchange
EMA	Enterprise Marketing Automation
EMS	Enterprise Management Strategies
EPM	Enterprise Performance Measurement
EPS	Earnings Per Share
ERP	Enterprise Resource Planning
EVA	Economic Value Added
FGI	Finished Goods Inventory
FMS	Freight Management System
GLS	Global Logistics System
GUI	Graphical User Interface
HCM	Human Capital Management
HRMS	Human Resources Management System
HSC	Hosted Supply Chain Services
IBPP	Internet Bill Presentment and Payment
ICO	Inventory Chain Optimization
ICT	Information and Communications Technology
IES	Inter-Enterprise Solutions
ISO	International Standards Organization
ISP	Internet Service Supplier
IT	Information Technology
ITE	Internet Trading Association
ITX	Independent Trading Exchange
JIT	Just-In-Time Manufacturing and Distribution
KPI	Key Performance Indicator
LAN	Local Area Network
LLP	Lead Logistics Provider
LLS	Lead Logistics Supplier
LP	Linear Programming
LSP	Logistics Service Providers
LTL	Less Than Truckload

MRO	Maintenance, Repair, and Operations Supplies
MRP	Material Requirements Planning
NAPM	National Association of Purchasing Management
NPV	Net Present Value
OEM	Original Equipment Manufacturers
OLAP	Online Analytical Processing
ORM	Operational Resource Management
OSB	Order, Shipping, and Billing
P2P	Peer-to-Peer
PDM	Product Data Management
PIM	Product Information Management
PLM	Product Lifecycle Management
PMI	Performance Measurement and Improvement
POD	Bill of Lading and Delivery Receipt
POS	Point-Of-Sale
PPE	Plant, Property, and Equipment
PRM	Partner Relationship Management
PSO	Professional Services Organization
PTX	Private Trading Exchange
QFD	Quality Functional Deployment
QR	Quick Response
RFID	Radio Frequency Identification
RFQ	Request for Quotation
ROA	Return on Asset
ROACE	Return On Average Capital Employed
ROI	Return on Investment
ROIC	Return On Invested Capital
ROLAP	Relational Online Analytical Programming
SCCI	Supply Chain Council International
SCE	Supply Chain Execution
SCEM	Supply Chain Event Management
SCM	Supply Chain Management
SCOR	Supply Chain Operations Reference model
SCP	Supply Chain Planning
SCS	Supply Chain Synchronization
SCVA	Supply Chain Value Assessment
SEM	Strategic Enterprise Management
SFA	Sales Force Automation
SKU	Stock Keeping Unit
SMEs	Small and Medium Size Enterprises
SPA	Specialty Apparel Business
SPC	Statistical Process Control
SRM	Supplier Relationship Management
SSM	Strategic e-Sourcing Management
T&A	Time and Attendance
T&E	Time and Expense

TCM	Total Cost Management
TCO	Total Cost of Ownership
TOC	Theory Of Constraints
TL	Truck Load
TMS	Transportation Management System
VAN	Value-Added Network
VMI	Vendor Managed Inventory
VPN	Virtual Private Networks
VSP	Vertical Service Provider
WAN	Wide Area Network
WERC	Warehousing Education and Research Council
WIP	Work-in-Process
WMS	Warehouse Management System
WRM	Workforce Relationship Management
XML	Extensible Markup Language

Table of Contents

1 The Advent of Supply Chain Management: Architecting the Supply Chain for Competitive Advantage

Over the past decade, companies spanning a wide spectrum of industries have been focusing their competitive strategies on leveraging the competencies and innovative capabilities to be found in the clusters of customers and suppliers constituting their business supply chains. While it is true that during the same period much effort had been invested in quality management models, the application of information technologies, and process and organizational reengineering, today's best enterprises have increasingly looked toward *supply chain management* (SCM) to provide fresh vistas for new sources of competitive advantage.

This is not to say that in the past companies were unmindful of the importance of the relationships that existed between themselves and their trading partners. Businesses had always looked to their channel partners for opportunities to apply organizational techniques and technologies that could accelerate transaction and information transfer speed and cement channel loyalties. Today academics, consultants, and practitioners alike have come to understand that the capacity of companies to continuously reinvent competitive advantage depends on the ability to look *outward* to their supply chains in the search for resources to engineer the right blend of competencies that will resonate with their own organizations and core product and process strategies. In fact, perhaps the *ultimate* core competency an enterprise may possess today is not to be found in a temporary advantage it may hold, for example, in an area of product design or market brand, but rather in the ability to continuously assemble and implement market-winning capabilities arising from collaborative alliances with supply chain partners. Competitive advantage in tomorrow's environment will go to those enterprises that can consistently anticipate and implement customer-winning supply chain competencies, while discarding those that have become commodities or easily copied by the competition.

This opening chapter is focused on defining SCM and exploring the competitive challenges and marketplace opportunities that have shaped and continue to drive its development. The chapter begins with an examination of why SCM has risen to be perhaps today's most critical business strategic paradigm. Next, a short description of the evolution of Internet-enabled SCM will be explored. Once the broad contours of SCM and its merger with e-business are detailed, a concise definition of *e-SCM* will be offered. The argument that unfolds is that e-SCM is a management model that conceives of individual enterprises as nodes in a supply chain web, digitally architected and collectively focused on the continuous evolution of new forms of customer value. Once a working definition of e-SCM has been established, the balance of the chapter will detail the characteristics of the e-SCM concept. Among topics discussed will be the function of Internet-based information in e-SCM, the utilization of supply chain trading partners, and understanding the role of supply chain synchronization.

I. THE RISE OF SUPPLY CHAIN MANAGEMENT

In today's business environment, no enterprise can expect to build a successful product, process, or service advantage without integrating their strategies with those of the supply chain systems in which they are inextricably entwined. In the past, what occurred outside of the four walls of the business was of secondary importance in comparison to the execution of strategies designed to effectively manage internal engineering, manufacturing, marketing, sales, and finance activities. In contrast, a company's ability to look *outward* to its channel alliances to gain access to sources of unique competencies, physical resources, and marketplace value is now the measure of success. Once a backwater of business management, creating "chains" of business partners has become one of a successful company's most powerful competitive strategies.

What has caused this awareness of the "interconnectiveness" of once isolated and often adversarial businesses occupying the same supply chain? What forces have obsoleted long-practiced methods of ensuring corporate governance, structuring businesses, and developing strategies? What will be the long-term impact on the fabric of business ecosystems of an increasing dependence on channel partnerships? What are the possible opportunities as well as the liabilities of channel alliances? How should information technology tools like the Internet be integrated into supply chain management, and what new sources of market winning product and service value will be identified?

The supply chain focus of today's enterprise has arisen in response to several critical business requirements.[1] To begin with, companies have begun to extend the tools of modern enterprise management to their supplier and customer channels in the search for additional sources of cost reduction and process improvement. Over the past decade, businesses have been assiduously applying to internal functions computerized techniques and management methods, such as *Enterprise Resource Planning* (ERP), *total quality management* (TQM), and *business process reengineering* (BRP), in an effort to optimize organizations and activate highly agile, lean manufacturing and distribution functions capable of superlative quality and service. As this movement toward *internal* cost reduction and process optimization has moved to its ultimate conclusion, today's best companies have sought to apply the same management and technology paradigms *outward* to their supply chains. The goal is to relentlessly eradicate all forms of waste where supply chain entities touch, such as logistics, inventory, procurement, customer management, product development, and financial functions.

Second, over the past several years, companies have all but abandoned strategies based on the vertical integration of resources. On the one side, businesses have continued to divest themselves of functions that were either not profitable or for which they had weak competencies. On the other side, today's market-leading enterprises have found that, by closely collaborating with their supply chain partners in developing such cross-channel functions as product development, forecasting, inventory management, and logistics, new avenues for competitive advantage can be uncovered. Achieving these advantages can only occur when entire supply chains work seamlessly to leverage complementary capabilities. Collaboration can take the form of outsourcing operations functions to permit channel specialists to leverage their core competencies to supplement an internal functional weakness. Channel partnering can also take the form of strategic collaboration regarding product development, sourcing, marketing, production and capacity management, information technology, and distribution and delivery.

Third, the explosion in global trade has opened up new markets and new forms of competition virtually inaccessible just a few years ago. Leveraging the interactive power of today's Internet technologies and breakthroughs in international logistics, companies are no longer limited to selling and sourcing within their own national boundaries. Recently, global enterprises, fostered by international bodies and regional trade agreements, have been on a frantic search for business partners that will provide them not only with cost reductions but also access to resources and markets previously beyond their reach. Finally, e-business technologies have enabled even the smallest of companies to assemble closely networked global supply chains, empowering them with the capability to implement competitive business models previously possessed by only the largest of corporations.

Fourth, today's marketplace requirement that companies be agile as well as efficient, in order to meet consumer demand for shorter time frames in terms of services, product mixes, and volume and variety changes, has spawned the engineering of virtual organizations and interoperable processes impossible without supply chain collaboration. The conventional business paradigms assumed that each company was an island and that collaboration with other organizations, even direct customers and suppliers, was self-defeating. In contrast, market-leading enterprises depend on the creation of panchannel integrated processes that require the generation of organizational structures capable of merging similar capabilities, designing teams for the joint development of new products, productive processes, and information technologies, and structuring radically new forms of vertical integration. Today's most successful and revolutionary companies, such as Wal-Mart, Amazon.com, Intel, W.W. Granger, and others, know that continued market dominance will go to those who know how to harness the evolutionary processes taking place within their supply chains.

Finally, the application of breakthrough information technology tools centered on the Internet has enabled companies to look at their supply chains as a revolutionary source of competitive advantage. Before the Internet, businesses used their supply chain partners to realize tactical advantages, such as passing documents through *electronic data interchange* (EDI) and integrating logistics functions. With the advent of e-commerce, these tactical advantages have been dramatically enhanced with the addition of strategic capabilities that enable whole supply chains to create radically new regions of marketplace value virtually impossible in the past. Enterprises are recognizing that the transfer of all functions of SCM to the Web will provide for the true integration of the customer value-enhancing capacities found among allied channel partners. As companies implement Internet technologies that connect all channel information, transactions, and decisions, whole channel systems will be able to continuously generate radically new sources of competitive advantage through cyber-collaboration, enabling joint product innovation, on-line buying markets, networked planning and operations management, and customer fulfillment.

For over a decade, market leading companies have been learning how to leverage the competitive strengths to be found in their business supply chains. Enterprises, such as Sun Microsystems, Microsoft, Siemens, Amazon.com, and Barnes & Noble.com, have been able to tap into the tremendous enabling power of SCM to tear down internal functional boundaries, leverage channel-wide human and technological capacities, and engineer "virtual" organizations capable of responding to new marketplace opportunities. With the application of e-business to SCM, these and other visionary companies are now generating the agile, scalable organizations capable of delivering to their customers revolutionary levels of convenience, delivery reliability, speed to market, and product/service customization impossible without the Internet. Without a doubt, the merger of the SCM management concept and the enabling power of the Internet are providing the basis for a profound transformation of the marketplace and the way business will be conducted in the twenty-first century.

II. EVOLUTION OF SUPPLY CHAIN MANAGEMENT

Although the concept of SCM has only just appeared, its development can be traced back to the rise of modern logistics. In fact, SCM is closely connected with and in many ways is the product of the significant changes that have occurred in logistics management. Over the past 30 years logistics has progressed from a purely operational function to a key strategic component. As logistics has evolved through time, the basic features of SCM can also be identified. Logistics has always been about managing the synchronization of the needs of individual companies for product and service acquisition with the resources available from suppliers, on the one side, and distribution functions to meet the demands of the customer, on the other. The SCM concept, enhanced by the power of Internet technology, is the maturation of these basic value-added functions. This section seeks to explore briefly the origins of SCM and sets the stage for a full definition of e-SCM value chains to follow.

A. HISTORICAL BEGINNINGS

For centuries, enterprises have been faced with the fundamental problem that demand for goods and services often extended far beyond the location where products were made. It had always been the role of the *logistics* functions within the company to fill this gap in the marketing, distribution, and procurement systems by providing for the efficient and speedy movement of goods and services from the point of manufacture to the point of need. The critical dynamics of this process consist of time to delivery, cost, and ease of exchange. Companies that have been able to effectively leverage the supply channels linking them with their customers and suppliers are able to more profitably operate and focus their productive functions, while extending their reach to capture marketplaces and generate demand beyond the compass of their physical locations. When viewed from this perspective, the supply chain system concept can be described as a network of interdependent partners, who not only supply the necessary products and services to the channel system, but who also stimulate demand and facilitate the synchronization of the competencies and resources of the entire supply chain network to produce capabilities enabling a level of operational excellence and marketplace leadership unattainable by each business operating on its own.

B. STAGES OF SUPPLY CHAIN MANAGEMENT DEVELOPMENT

Historically, synchronizing the supply chain has always occupied a central position in the management of the enterprise, linking business marketing and sales strategies with manufacturing, inventory, and service execution. As far back as the beginning of the twentieth century, economists considered the activities associated with effectively managing business channels to be the crucial mechanism by which goods and services were exchanged through the economic system. However, despite its importance, this concept, first termed *logistics*, was slow to develop. Most business executives considered the channel management function to be of only tactical importance and, because of the scope and lack of integration among supply network nodes, virtually impossible to manage as an integrated function. In fact, it was not until the late 1960s, when cost pressures and the availability of computerized information tools enabled forward-looking companies to begin to dramatically revamp the nature and function of the supply chain, that the strategic opportunities afforded by logistics began to emerge.

The SCM concept could be said to consist of five distinct management stages. The first can be described as the era of internal logistics departmentalism. In the second stage, logistics began the migration from organizational decentralization to centralization of core functions driven by new attitudes associated with cost optimization and customer service. Stage three witnessed the dramatic expansion of logistics beyond a narrow concern with internal warehousing and transportation to embrace new concepts calling for the linkage of internal operations with analogous functions performed by channel trading partners. As the concept of channel relationships grew, the old logistics concept gave way, in stage-four, to full supply chain management. Today, with the application of Internet technology to the SCM concept, we can describe SCM as entering into stage five, e-SCM. These stages are portrayed in Table 1.1. A short discussion of each stage is as follows.

TABLE 1.1
SCM Management Stages

SCM Stage	Management Focus	Organizational Design
	Stage 1 to 1960s	
Warehousing and Transportation	Operations performance	Decentralized logistics functions
	Support for sales/marketing	Weak internal linkages between
	Warehousing	logistics functions
	Inventory control	Little logistics management authority
	Transportation efficiencies	
	Stage 2 to 1980	
Total Cost Management	Logistics centralization	Centralized logistics functions
	Total cost management	Growing power of logistics
	Optimizing operations	management authority
	Customer service	Application of computer
	Logistics as a competitive advantage	
	Stage 3 to 1990	
Integrated Logistics Management	Logistics planning	Expansion of logistics functions
	Supply chain strategies	Supply chain planning
	Integration with enterprise functions	Support for TQM
	Integration with channel operations functions	Expansion of logistics management functions
	Stage 4 to 2000	
Supply Chain Management	Strategic view of supply chain	Trading partner networking
	Use of extranet technologies	Virtual organization
	Growth of coevolutionary channel alliances	Market coevolution
	Collaboration to leverage channel competencies	Benchmarking and reengineering
		Supply chain TQM metrics
	Stage 5 2000+	
e-Supply Chain Management	Application of the Internet to the SCM concept	Networked, multi-enterprise supply chain
	Low-cost instantaneous sharing of all databases	.coms, e-tailers, and market exchanges
	e-Information	Organizational agility and
	SCM synchronization	scaleability

1. First Stage — Logistics Decentralization

Historically, the first stage of SCM occurred in the period extending from the late 19th century to the early 1960s. During this era logistics was not perceived as a source of significant competitive advantage. Viewed essentially as an intermediary function concerned with inventory management and delivery, it was felt that logistics could not make much of a contribution to profitability and, therefore, was not worthy of much capital investment. It was accorded little management status, and assigned less qualified staff. For the most part, companies segmented logistics activities, dividing them among operations functions, such as sales, production, and accounting. Not only were activities that were naturally supportive, such as procurement management, inbound transportation, and inventory management, separated from one another, but narrow departmental performance measurements also pitted logistics functions against each other. The result was a rather disjointed, relatively uncoordinated, and costly management of logistics activities.

In an era when process and delivery cycle times were long, global competition practically non-existent, and the marketplace driven by mass production and mass distribution, logistics decentralization was a minor problem for most companies. By the early 1960s, however, changes in the business climate were forcing executives to rethink their logistics strategies. To begin with, expanding product lines, demand for shorter cycle times, and growing competition had begun to expose the dramatic wastes and inefficiencies of logistics decentralization. Second, executives were finding themselves handcuffed by the lack of a unified logistics planning and execution strategy. Logistics responsibilities were scattered throughout the organization, and no single manager was responsible for integrating channel management activities with the rest of the business. Finally, logistics decentralization had made it impossible to pursue effective cost trade-off strategies. Logistics performance was often caught in a performance measurement paradox. For example, transportation might seek to reduce costs by requiring a higher payload-to-cost ratio, even if the decision resulted in higher inventories.

By the mid-1960s it was clear that the existing structure and purpose of logistics and channel management functions were in need of serious revision. As late as 1969, Donald Bowersox, the dean of modern logistics management, lamented that the management science of logistics was still in its infancy. There was no standardization of terms or a commonly accepted vocabulary. No one was quite sure what form a revamped logistics function should look like. Should it be attached to the firm's marketing function? Should it be attached to manufacturing? Should it be a department on its own? What would be the impact on logistics of the growth of computerized technology?[2]

2. Second Stage — Total Cost Management

The second stage in the evolution of SCM can be said to revolve around two critical focal points. The first can be described as the concerted effort made by companies to centralize logistics functions into a single management system. By merging what previously had been a series of fragmented functions into a single department, it would be possible to decrease individual costs associated with transportation, inventory, and physical distribution, while simultaneously increasing the productivity of the logistics system as a whole. Second, it was hoped that centralization would facilitate the application of the *total cost concept* to logistics. The objective of this strategy is to strive to minimize the total cost of logistics, rather than focus on reducing the costs of one or two specific logistics functions, such as transportation or warehousing. A much larger assumption was that, because logistics costs and customer service were reciprocal, it would be easy to calculate the cost trade-offs necessary to balance total logistics costs with marketing and sales objectives.

The movement toward logistics centralization was driven by three converging factors. To begin with, as the economic and energy crises of the mid-1970s dramatically drove up inventory carrying costs, the marketplace began to demand smaller order quantities and more frequent deliveries from their supply partners. Second, explosions in product lines during the period required everyone in the supply channel to deliver products on time, avert obsolescence, and prevent channel inventory imbalances. Finally, new concepts of marketing, pricing, and promotion facilitated by the computer necessitated a thorough change in the cumbersome, fragmented methods of traditional channel management.

In addition to the operational demands driving reinvention of the logistics, a number of new ideas regarding the strategic place of logistics in the enterprise were emerging simultaneously. The first was the growing realization that, instead of a disconnected series of functions, logistics should rather be considered as a single integrated supply system. Complementary to this new idea of logistics was the application of new computerized technologies and management methods. During this period, computers became much more sophisticated, less costly, and more accessible. Also, new management methods centering on *just-in-time* (JIT), zero inventories, and quality management permitted companies to be more flexible and responsive, further eroding the old logistics model. Finally, logistics centralization was further accentuated by the realization that effective execution of logistics functions was critical to expanding customer service. As the era of mass production and mass distribution faded, companies found themselves looking to logistics capabilities to assist in gaining and sustaining competitive advantage through the coordination of channel resources.

3. Third Stage — Integrated Functions

During the 1980s, enterprise executives became increasingly aware that focusing solely on the total cost of logistics represented a passive approach to channel management. This awareness was driven by the radical changes occurring in what was rapidly becoming a global marketplace. If the decade could be compressed into two quintessential catchwords, they would be *competition* and *quality management*. Competition came in the form of tremendous pressure from global companies, often deploying radically new management philosophies and organizational structures that realized unheard-of levels of productivity, quality, and profitability. The threat also came from a new view of the place of quality and how it could be implemented to capture marketplace advantage. Management concepts, driven by JIT and *total quality management* (TQM) philosophies, were providing competitors with tools to compress time out of development cycles, engineer more flexible and "lean" processes, tap into the creative powers of the workforce, and generate entirely new forms of competitive advantage.

Businesses responded to these challenges by focusing, first of all, on revamping their organizations, either through corporate restructuring or by searching for methods to achieve cost reductions, work-force retraining, the application of technology to improve productivities, more careful use of fixed and variable assets, strategic outsourcing, and identification of customers, products, and markets providing the greatest potential for competitive advantage. Second, companies began to understand that logistics and other channel management functions could be leveraged as a dynamic force capable of winning customers beyond the execution of traditional marketing objectives. Competitive values, such as speed of delivery, value-added services, development time to market, materials acquisition, and product availability, could be realized when the entire organization worked together, both internally and in close collaboration with supply chain trading partners.

One of the most significant results of the challenges of the 1980s was the recognition that logistics itself constituted a significant competitive weapon. Up to this period, most executives had viewed logistics as playing a tactical role, with little impact on corporate strategic planning. By the mid-1980s, however, companies began to understand that, by enabling organizations to pursue both cost/operational and service/value advantages through continuous process improvement and closer integration with channel partners, logistics could provide enormous strategic value. By enabling trading partners not only to integrate their logistics functions but also to converge supporting efforts occurring in marketing, product development, inventory and manufacturing capacity planning, and quality management, companies could tap into reservoirs of "virtual" resources and competencies unattainable by even the largest of corporations acting independently. The realization of this opportunity is the subject matter of stage-four SCM.

4. Fourth Stage — Supply Chain Management

During the mid-1990s, companies began to expand the concepts of integrated logistics and supply channel management to embrace the new realities of the marketplace. The acceleration of globalization, the increasing power of the customer demanding ever higher levels of service and supplier agility, organizational reengineering, third-party outsourcing, and the growing pervasiveness of information technologies had forced businesses to look beyond the integrated logistics paradigm in the search for new strategic models. The pressure of responding to these new challenges compelled organizations to implement what only can be called a dramatic paradigm shift from stage-three logistics to SCM. As discussed above, the fundamental feature of the integrated logistics model was the merger of channel management functions with those of trading partners targeted at improving customer service and total cost reduction across whole channels. In contrast, at the core of phase four organizations is a distinct recognition that competitive advantage can only be built by optimizing and synchronizing the productive competencies of each channel trading partner to realize entirely new levels of customer value.

Using the *supply chain operations reference* (SCOR) model as a benchmark, the differences between stage-three logistics and stage-four SCM can be clearly illustrated.

- *Plan.* In stage-three logistics, most business functions were still inward looking. Firms focused their energies on internal company scenario planning, business modeling, and corporate resource allocation management. ERP systems and sequential process management tools assisted managers to execute channel-level inventory flows, transportation, and customer fulfillment. In contrast, stage-four SCM companies began to perceive themselves and the supply networks to which they belonged as "value chains." Knowing the total cost to all network partners and optimizing the customer-winning velocity of collective supply channel competencies became the central focus. Companies began to deploy channel optimization software and communications enabling tools like EDI to network their ERP systems, in order to provide visibility to requirements needs across the entire network.

- *Source.* Companies with stage-three sourcing functions utilize the integrated logistics concept to merge their procurement needs with the capabilities of their channel suppliers. The goal is to reduce costs and lead times, share critical planning data, assure quality and delivery reliability, and develop win-win partnerships. In contrast, stage-four SCM sourcing functions perceive their suppliers as extensions of a single supply chain system. Besides achieving the benefits of integrated logistics, a critical goal of SCM-driven companies is to utilize channel data to execute volume purchasing to benefit all network trading partners. When possible, computerized extranet technologies are used to assemble channel collaborative relationships pointing toward consortia buying. Transportation and warehousing costs are reduced by the joint utilization of outsourcing opportunities, thereby reducing the overall assets invested in channel inventories.

- *Make.* Stage-three organizations resist sharing product design and process technologies. Normally, collaboration in this area is undertaken in response to quality management certification or when it is found to be more economical to outsource manufacturing. There is minimal networking between trading partners when it comes to *computer aided design* (CAD) and ERP manufacturing databases. Stage-four companies, on the other hand, seek to make collaborative design planning and scheduling with their supply chains a fundamental issue. When possible, they seek to closely integrate their ERP systems to eliminate time and cost up and down the supply channel. SCM firms also understand that speedy product design-to-market occurs when they seek to leverage the competencies and resources of channel partners to generate "virtual" manufacturing environments that are capable of being as agile and scaleable as necessary to take advantage of every marketplace opportunity.

- *Deliver.* Customer management in stage-three companies is squarely focused on making internal sales functions more efficient. A heavy priority is placed on basic available-to-promise functionality, finished goods management, and determining the proper timing of distribution channel differentiation. While there is some limited sharing of specific information on market segments and customers, databases are considered proprietary, and pricing data is rarely shared. In contrast, stage-four SCM firms are focused on reducing logistics costs and channel redundancies by converging channel partner warehouse space, transportation equipment, and delivery capabilities. Customer management looks toward automation tools to facilitate field sales, capability to promise tools, *customer relationship management* (CRM) software, mass customization, and availability of general supply chain repositories of joint trading partner market and customer data.

Stage-four SCM organizations possess the power to move beyond a narrow focus on channel logistics optimization to one where channel partners strive to identify the best core competencies and collaborative relationships among their trading partners in the search for new capabilities to realize continuous breakthroughs in product design, manufacturing, delivery, customer service, cost management, and value-added services before the competition. Through the application of SCM tools that seek to network whole supply channels, enterprises have the capability to view themselves and their channel partners as extended "virtual organizations" possessed of radically new methods of creating marketplace value.

5.   Fifth Stage — e-Supply Chain Management

Today, the application of Internet technology has propelled the SCM concept to a new dimension. Originating as a management method to optimize internal costs and productivities, SCM has evolved, through the application of e-business technologies, into a powerful strategic function capable of engendering radically new customer value propositions through the architecting of *external,* Internet-enabled collaborative channel partnerships. Actualizing e-SCM is a three-step process. Companies begin first with the integration of supply channel functions within the enterprise. An example would be integrating sales and logistics so that the customer, rather than departmental measurements, would receive top attention. The next step would be to integrate across trading partners channel operations functions, such as transportation, channel inventories, and forecasting. Finally, the highest level would be achieved by utilizing the power of the Internet to synchronize the channel functions of the entire supply network into a single, scaleable "virtual" enterprise, capable of optimizing core competencies and resources from anywhere at any time in the supply chain to meet market opportunities.

Although the remainder of this book will concentrate in detail on the enormous changes to SCM brought about by the application of e-business tools, the high-points of these changes are as follows:

Product and Process Design

As product life cycles continue to decline and development costs soar, firms have been quick to utilize Internet enablers to link customers to the design process, promote collaborative, cross-company design teams, and integrate physical and intellectual assets and competencies in an effort to increase speed to market and time to profit. In the past, efforts utilizing traditional product data management systems and exchange of design data had been expensive, cumbersome, and inefficient. Internet technologies, on the other hand, now provide interoperable, low cost, real-time linkages between trading partners. For example, Adaptec, a semiconductor manufacturer, is connected through its Web-based network to its manufacturing and assembly partners in Taiwan, Hong Kong, and Japan. During product development, chip designers send designs and diagrams through the network to their partner counterparts for review, simulation, and real-world testing. Test outcomes are immediately communicated to Adaptec for redesign or approval. Since the entire process can be performed in real time, product design and market introduction have been dramatically cut.[3]

e-Marketplaces and Exchanges

Sales and procurement have traditionally been concerned with proprietary channels characterized by long-term relationships, negotiation over lengthy contracts, long lead times, and fixed margins. Today, the Internet is completely reshaping this environment. Companies can now buy and sell across a wide variety of Internet-enabled marketplaces ranging from independent and private exchanges to auction sites. As an example, Ingersoll-Rand has launched a business-to-business (B2B) service provider unit designed to help companies with annual sales of under $900 million who purchase similar types of products as Ingersoll-Rand. The goal is to get participators from the bottom tier of the supply base to outsource their purchasing effort to the site. In addition, the site plans to give smaller suppliers a chance to participate in collaboration, program development, problem solving, and design issues.

Collaborative Planning

Historically, enterprises were averse to sharing critical planning information concerning forecasts, sales demand, supply requirements, and new product introduction. Such information was considered proprietary and strictly reserved for internal strategic planning functions. Today, as many organizations increasingly outsource non-core functions to network partners, the ability to transfer planning information on-line and real-time to what is rapidly becoming a "virtual" supply chain has become a necessity. The challenge has become how to transfer product and planning information across the business network to achieve the two-way collaboration necessary for joint decision-making. Fujitsu Computer Products of America, Inc. (FCPA), San Jose, CA, responded to the need for greater planning collaboration with their trading partners' data by implementing state-of-the-art supply chain planning software. The system provides FCPA employees with the ability to access and manage information about product forecasting, availability, and deployment throughout various stages in the supply chain process. The result is that FCPA can track inventory levels and sources of supply, evaluate options and make decisions quickly, and refresh the supply chain database as needed.

Fulfillment Management

The collapse of the dot-com era in 2000 revealed one of the great weaknesses of e-business. Customers may have access to product information and can place orders at the speed of light, but actual fulfillment is still a complex affair that occurs in the physical world of materials handling and transportation. Solving this crucial problem requires the highest level of supply chain collaboration and takes the form of substituting, as much as possible, information for physical flows of inventory. Some of the methods incorporate traditional tools, such as product postponement, while others utilize Web-based network functions, providing logistics partners with the capability to consolidate and ship inventories from anywhere in the supply network and generate the physical infrastructures to traverse the "last mile" to the customer. An example would be the strategic partnership between Ford Motor Company and UPS Logistics' Auto-gistics. Using real-time Web-based technologies with leading edge distribution network design and execution, the alliance is designed to reduce by up to 40% the time required to deliver vehicles from Ford plants to the customer. The system provides pinpoint network operations capability through real-time reporting by Auto-gistics people at every node in the delivery channel.

As this section concludes, it is clear that channel management is no longer the loose combination of business functions characteristic of stages one and two logistics. New Internet-enabling technologies and management models have not only obscured company functional boundaries, they have also blurred the boundaries that separate trading partners, transforming once isolated channel functions into unified, "virtual" supply chain systems. Today's top companies are using Internet connectivity to reassemble and energize supply chain management processes that span trading partners to activate core competencies and accelerate cross-enterprise processes. They are also using Web technologies to enable new methods of providing customer value by opening new sales channels as they migrate from pure "bricks-and-mortar" to "click-and-mortar" business architectures. The next section will continue this discussion by offering a detailed definition of e-SCM that will serve as the cornerstone for the rest of the book.

III. DEFINING e-SUPPLY CHAIN MANAGEMENT

The immense changes brought about by the dynamics of today's global marketplace and the breakthroughs occurring in Internet-based technologies have elevated the effective management of the supply chain to new levels of importance. As companies find themselves under constant pressure to develop fast, flexible, scalable product and service capabilities that empower customers to choose and transact the product/service solutions they value the most, digitally and in real time, they have been increasingly turning to their business trading partners for sources to enrich their competitive competencies. Increasingly, it has become apparent that traditional business paradigms centered solely on closed, internal performance metrics are rapidly being replaced by new models coalescing around the recognition that, to continuously recreate competitive advantage, companies must work together across enterprise boundaries and optimize interchannel processes and innovative capabilities. Effectively defining SCM is, therefore, the first step in understanding these basic business environmental issues.

A. SCM DEFINITIONS

SCM can be viewed from several perspectives. Like most management philosophies, definitions of SCM must take into account a wide spectrum of applications incorporating both strategic and tactical objectives. A sample of definitions currently being offered will reveal this point. Handfield and Nichols[4] define SCM by breaking the concept into two terms, *supply chain* and *supply chain management*. The *supply chain* is defined as encompassing

> all activities associated with the flow and transformation of goods from the raw materials stage (extraction), through to the end user, as well as the associated information flows. Material and information flow both up and down the supply chain.

Following, *supply chain management* is defined as

> the integration of these activities through improved supply chain relationships to achieve a sustainable competitive advantage.

In a similar vein Ayers[5] defines the *supply chain* as

> life cycle processes comprising physical, information, financial, and knowledge flows whose purpose is to satisfy end-user requirements with products and services from multiple linked suppliers.

Ayers then defines supply chain management as the

> design, maintenance, and operation of supply chain processes for satisfaction of end user needs.

While these definitions provide for a generalized understanding, they are inadequate to describe the depth and breadth of both the theory and practice of SCM. As illustrated in Figure 1.1, SCM can be approached from three perspectives, one tactical, one strategic, and finally, one Web-enabled. The *tactical* perspective considers SCM as an operations management technique that seeks to integrate and optimize the capabilities of all internal enterprise operations — finance, marketing/sales, manufacturing, procurement, and logistics — and then to direct them to continuously search for opportunities for cost reduction and increased channel throughput by working with the matching functions to be found in supply chain customers and suppliers. The mission of SCM at this level is focused on synchronizing day-to-day operations activities with those of channel partners in an effort to streamline process flows, reduce network costs, and optimize productivity and delivery resources centered on conventional channel relationships. Finally, SCM in this area is dominated by a *sequential* view of the flow of supply chain materials and information.

Tactical SCM can be broken down into four key value-enhancing activities. The first set of activities, *channel supplier management*, involves optimizing the inbound movement of inventories and includes supplier management, sourcing and

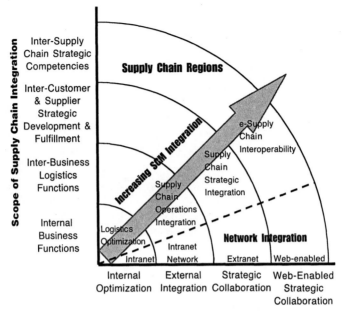

FIGURE 1.1 SCM definitions.

negotiation, forecasting, purchasing, transportation, and stores receipt and disposition. After inventory receipt, companies can begin executing the second major channel activity, *product and service processing*. In this group of functions can be found efforts to involve channel partners in product engineering, product manufacturing, product costing, and service wrap development. The third group of activities, *channel customer management,* includes finished goods warehousing, value-added processing, customer order management, channel fulfillment, and transportation. The final group of activities, *channel support activities*, focuses on utilizing channel partners to facilitate financial transactions, marketing information flows, electronic information transfer, and integrated logistics. The objective of operational SCM is to engineer the continuous alignment of internal enterprise departments with the identical functions to be found in supply chain partners. Channel operations synchronization will accelerate the flow of inventory and marketing information, optimize channel resources, and facilitate continuous channel-wide cost reduction efforts and increased productivity.

The second perspective of a comprehensive definition of SCM expands SCM beyond a concern with merely interfacing channel functions on an operational level to the generation of *strategically integrated* supply chains (see Figure 1.2). The principle characteristic of strategic SCM can be found in the transition of channel members away from a supply chain model that is interfaced, sequential, and linear to one whose prime value is centered on functional and strategic *interoperability*. The mission of SCM at this level is to propel channel trading partners beyond a concern with purely logistics integration to the establishment of collaborative partnerships characterized by the architecting of cross-channel correlative processes,

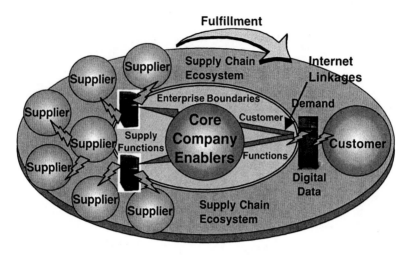

FIGURE 1.2 e-Supply chain system.

which create unique sources of value by unifying the resources, capabilities, and competencies of the entire network ecosystem to enhance the competitive power of the network as a whole, and not just an individual company.

The impact of strategic SCM can be recognized in the heightened level of channel connectivity of the four key supply chain value-enhancing activities. *Channel supplier management* migrates from a focus on achieving company-centered value-added sourcing and negotiation, procurement, order entry, and payment cost reduction through supplier logistics integration to a strategic perspective that utilizes collaborative processes directed at merging interchannel procurement volumes, quality, and transaction costs reductions that benefit the individual company as well as the entire supply chain. *Product and service processing* is enhanced from a position of searching for channel competencies that can be imported to assist in proprietary product development, manufacturing, and service wrap functions to the application of technology tools that activate opportunities for shared product design, the networking of local ERP systems to facilitate channel-wide inventory planning and scheduling, and the seamless integration of necessary core competencies from all points in the supply channel. The third group, *channel customer management*, moves beyond a limited sharing of customer databases, applying best practices to improve internal order fulfillment, managing fixed product lines, and pursuing average service for average customers to facilitating supply channel fulfillment by merging customer databases and service options that activate the close matching of customer requirements with finished goods to be found on all levels in the supply chain, cataloging customer needs as they impact everyone in the supply channel, and providing fulfillment functions that enable the supply chain to treat each customer's product/service needs as unique. Finally, *channel support services* are elevated from a concern with company-centric transaction management and financial measurements, internal logistics capabilities, and sequential pipeline information flows to the utilization of methods that seek to *unify* not only basic logistics functions, such as inventory planning, purchasing, and transportation, but also financial, sales, and product development by converging interchannel process competencies in an effort to remove the encumbrances of traditional serial hand offs of critical marketing and fulfillment information.

The above *tactical* and *strategic* perspectives of SCM are focused on the continuous coevolution of seamless networks of businesses capable of generating exceptional product and service innovation, new processes and technologies, increased reliability and speed, and new forms of channel vertical integration and mass-customization economies. Although these new perspectives have constituted a revolution in business management in and of themselves, today's merger of SCM and the Internet has added a radically new dimension that has changed completely the nature of supply chain theory and practice. The driver of this dramatic change, which some have described as a virtual "tsunami-like change,"[6] is to be found in the Internet's capability to act as an effective medium enabling the integration and synchronization of all supply chain information and processes. Such a breakthrough is possible because of the ease and low cost of Internet technology. According to one estimate, Web-based applications permit a wide range of transactions at roughly 20% of the private network cost.[7] In addition, the presence of universal standards for e-commerce and the application of Web technologies, such as *extensible markup language* (XML) and Java, have the potential to enable the low-cost integration of information from channel partners of all sizes, the communication of all types of documents in real time, and the ability of all channel nodes to perform some transactions never before standardized.

The application of the Internet is such a radical enhancement to the SCM concept that it deserves to be relabeled *e-SCM*. This new view of SCM is radical because it enables companies to use the Internet to develop new methods of integrating with their customers, suppliers, and support partners. e-SCM extends channel management systems beyond traditional boundaries to integrate, in real time, the customer/product information and productive competencies to be found in customers' customers and suppliers' suppliers channel systems. As illustrated in Figure 1.3, e-SCM facilitates the transfer of multiple levels of product and service data that simultaneously generate value for customers as well as for each node in the supply chain network. The synergy created enables companies to dramatically improve revenues, costs, and asset utilization beyond a dependence on internal capabilities and resources.

Finally, e-SCM provides today's supply chains with the means to realize the strategic possibilities of the original SCM model. By the end of the 1990s, companies had come to realize that they were not simply isolated competitors struggling on their own for survival, but were, in reality, part of a much larger matrix of intersecting business systems composed of intricate, mutually supporting webs of customers, products, and productive capacities played out on a global scale. What had been missing in the past was an effective mechanism to enable the intense networking of commonly shared strategic visions and mutually supportive competencies among channel partners. Technologies such as ERP and EDI imposed severe limits to the range of information communication and erected unscalable barriers limiting participation. The merger of the Internet and SCM, on the other hand, offers whole supply chains the opportunity to create value for their customers through the design

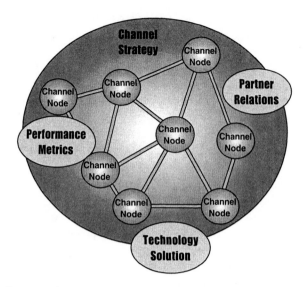

FIGURE 1.3 Elements of e-supply chains.

of agile, flexible systems built around dynamic, high performance networks of Web-enabled customer and supplier partnerships and critical information flows.

B. e-SCM DEFINITION

The emerging strategic capabilities of SCM and the empowering technologies to be found in the Internet provide the central themes of this book. Any definition that does not include these twin pillars of e-SCM would be wide of the mark. Based on these factors, it is possible to construct a meaningful definition of e-SCM. The definition is as follows:

> e-SCM is a tactical and strategic management philosophy that seeks to network the collective productive capacities and resources of intersecting supply channel systems through the application of Internet technologies in the search for innovative solutions and the synchronization of channel capabilities dedicated to the creation of unique, individualized sources of customer value.

The changes to former definitions of SCM brought about by the application of Internet technologies have also fundamentally changed the definition of the *supply channel*. In the place of a preoccupation with optimizing and accelerating the flow of material and information up and down the supply chain, Web-based channel management is concerned with the creation of new forms of customer *value* for both the internal and external customer. The Web-enabled supply channel can be defined as

> The application of Internet technologies focused on the continuous regeneration of networks of businesses empowered to execute superlative, customer-winning value at the lowest cost through the digital, real-time synchronization of product/service transfer, service needs and demand priorities, vital marketplace information, and logistics delivery capabilities.

The elements constituting this definition are revealing. The concept, *continuous regeneration of networks of businesses,* implies that successful supply channels are constantly mutating to respond to the dynamic nature of today's ceaseless demand for new forms of customer/supplier collaboration and scaleable product and information delivery flows. This element defines how supply channels will organize to compete. *Customer-winning value* refers to the marketplace's need to continuously reinvent unique product and service configuration and agile delivery capabilities. This element defines the mission of the channel. And finally, *digital, real-time synchronization,* refers to the application of technology process enablers that network internal enterprise systems, decision support tools, and data warehouses. Java, XML, and other Internet and e-commerce technologies have now made it possible to transcend extranet enterprise integrators with low cost, inclusive Web-enabled tools that merge, optimize, and effectively direct supply channel competencies. This element describes the mechanics of how e-nabled supply chains will compete.

IV. CHARACTERISTICS OF e-SCM

The merger of SCM and the Internet calls for a transvaluation of former perspectives of the tactical and strategic importance of the supply chain. Past definitions of SCM were more or less preoccupied with attempts to extend the concepts of supply channel integration to the performance of operations activities associated with optimizing manufacturing and logistics processes and accelerating the flow of inventory and information through the network system. Laboring under the limitations of intranet and extranet technology tools, such as EDI, the best companies could hope to accomplish was to structure private value-added networks (VANs) that permitted the transmission of a narrow band of information from a narrow group of supply partners. With the emergence of Internet technologies, the concept of supply channel management has moved to a whole new dimension. In the past, the primary problem inhibiting full activation of the SCM model was the *mechanism* that would provide the interlocking connectivity between business systems. The Internet solves this gap in SCM collaboration. Today's Web applications provide whole supply chains with the capability to instantaneously share databases, forecasts, inventory and capacity plans, product information, financial data, and just about anything else companies may need for effective decision-making. And the integration can be global, $24 \times 7 \times 365$, with 100% accuracy. Enabling the full power of e-SCM requires an understanding of the following principles.

A. e-SCM Enables a Whole New View of the Function of Information in the Supply Chain

The prime attribute of Internet information is *speed*, and speed is today's most crucial competitive advantage. Klaus Schwab, head of the World Economic Forum, summarized best this attribute of *e-information* when he said: "We are moving from a world in which the big eat the small to a world in which the fast eat the slow." The spread of technology tools for the networking of all forms of computerized devices, integrated operating platforms, and the development of global standards for the

Internet have enabled forward-looking enterprises to be able to effectively accumulate, track, and monitor e-information from anywhere in the supply chain in real time. The challenges associated with accessing and harnessing e-information are at the heart of e-SCM and can be summarized as follows:

1. Utilization of e-Information

Today's best companies are able to capitalize on e-information by architecting systems that permit real-time, simultaneous, rather than serial, use of supply chain data. FedEx, for example, uses e-information to manage the real-time data transmission for the daily routing and tracking of 2.5 million packages, remote bar-code scanning that updates a centralized database, transmission bandwidth enabling concurrent rather than serial processing of transaction events driven by nearly 400,000 daily service calls, the evolution of new e-businesses, as in the case of FedEx's alliance with Proflowers.com (a dot-com company operating a portal for ordering fresh flowers), and a total company dedication to continuously accelerating the speed of e-information and logistics flows. Cisco Systems is dedicated to using the Internet to continuously reengineer processes to achieve a truly global networked organization. Each critical node in Cisco's supply chain, from Web-enabled order entry (50% of orders received) and customer service (inquiry, pricing, configuration, validation, product catalogue) to software distribution download, is executed through Internet-based processes. In addition, Web-enabled *collaborative planning, forecasting, and replenishment* (CPFR) applications permit Cisco to communicate demand changes with suppliers and distributors. Finally, Cisco's e-procurement programs provide on-line access to purchasing/marketplaces exchanges. Cisco's e-strategy has enabled the company to reduce costs by $560 million per year during the late 1990s, while spearheading an annual growth rate of 400% for the past five years (Figure 1.4).

2. Supply Chain Event Management

Agile and flexible supply chains occur when companies can effectively respond to both planned and unexpected events. The ability of e-information to extend visibility and a degree of control throughout the supply chain has been facilitated by the growth of a number of real-time software applications, called *supply chain process management* (SCPM) and *supply chain event management* (SCEM), that combine supply chain visibility, out-of-bounds alerts, alert resolution logic, and workflow-enabled business rules. The goal of SCPM/SCEM is to empower companies with more effective methods of managing supply chain processes and providing managers with a window into key events and metrics in time to make corrective action. Event-driven information provides supply chain planners with the following tools to ensure the continuous effectiveness of their supply chains.[8]

- Measure, compare, and report on supply channel performance over time.
- Monitor channel events in real time, from the flow of customer demand into the supply channel to inventory levels and shipments.

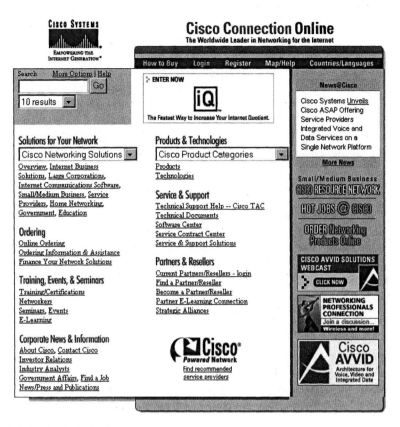

FIGURE 1.4 Cisco's Web site.

- Proactively notify a channel decision maker, through e-communications technologies, that an action might have to be taken as a result of transactions occurring somewhere in the supply network.
- Perform simulation, or what-if scenarios, based on current or expected events occurring in the supply chain.
- Enable decision makers to collectively control the entire supply network by making timely decisions.

3. "Real Options" Management

To use a concept originated by Stewart Myers of the Sloan School of Management, effective channel event management arising from e-information metrics provides "Real Options" for companies in the supply chain to use time-based information to mitigate risks in designing channel processes or collaborative efforts. For example, by having a real-time handle on the channel demand pull, network trading partners can strategically plan and deploy safety stocks, determine the optimal point for product postponement, allocate capital, and minimize the impact of volume variances due to forecast error. On the customer services side, e-information enables companies to integrate customers directly into their business systems, while at the same time enabling the application of performance tools necessary to provide a perfect order every time, including the execution of all value-added services and billing. On the shop floor, e-information improves planners' forward visibility into supplier capacities to smooth capacity spikes and improve throughput. In the supply channel, e-information provides the bridge between company-level optimization planning and the global demand pull of the entire business network.

e-Information enables the generation of what one writer has described as "a portfolio of triggerable decisions with options to proceed or abandon by milestone."[9]

4. Supply Chain Systems Integration

The impact of e-SCM is measured by the depth and breadth of connectivity existing among channel members. Integrative IT tools such as XML, Java, integrated operating platforms, component-based e-business applications, wireless communications, and others, are now providing leading-edge companies with the real-time information and interoperable networks necessary to eliminate channel inventory buffers and improve customer service.

5. Collaborative Relationships

Beyond transaction efficiencies, e-information provides for new avenues for the development of collaborative strategies and networked business planning. The goal is to facilitate channel collaboration on all levels, from product design to customer service, by exploiting real-time data through enter-enterprise Internet-enabled networks.

B. e-SCM Enables Enterprises to Form Customer-Winning Relationships with Supply Chain Partners

What has made e-SCM such a potent marketplace force today is its ability to leverage digital technology to provide a seamless channel structure, which is physically dispersed and consists of different competencies, yet functions as a coherent customer-satisfying resource whose boundaries appear invisible to the customer. The more tightly information is synchronized among network business partners, the more the entire channel is enabled to act as if it were a single company. For example, Cisco Systems' e-planning applications automatically alert suppliers when actual customer demand deviates from forecasts, thereby reducing inventory imbalances throughout the entire supply channel. As Cisco is able to include more suppliers in the planning system, their ability to be more flexible to meet any customer order exponentially grows. The validity of this proposition is based on the e-business postulate known as "Metcalf's Law." The hypothesis of the law asserts that capabilities for value generation grow exponentially with the number of nodes added to an Internet-enabled value chain. The power of Web-enabled supply chains can be described as follows:

- The Internet allows companies to electronically connect all facets of their businesses, from product development to order fulfillment, with every trading partner in the supply chain matrix cheaply and quickly.
- e-SCM enables the execution of cross-enterprise processes and the integration of trading partner operations, moving companies from an enterprise-centric supply channel driving multiple processes to synchronized, Web-enabled supply networks driven by a single process, real-time and on-line, dedicated to a single objective: superior customer service.
- The ability of a company to communicate electronically will enable it to develop supply networks with traditional players, such as suppliers, manufacturers, distributors, and retailers, as well as the new breed of dot-com intermediaries, such as virtual/contract manufacturers, service providers, fulfillment specialists, and on-line trading exchanges.
- Electronically connected supply chains provide the ability to enhance and coordinate SCM processes across trading partners. Examples include Cisco Systems and Solectron Corporation (Milpitas, CA), which have leveraged their SCM operations to build successful virtual manufacturing and distribution models.
- Utilization of the Internet to realize totally new methods of selling and new sales channels. Examples include W.W. Grainger and Barnes and Noble who opened successful Web sites to augment their positions of leadership in MRO distribution and retail.

Detailing the structure of the Internet-enabled supply chain provides an insight into the radical difference between e-SCM and business models of the past. Today's e-supply chain is focused around the customer. The mission of the channel ecosystem that emerges is to utilize e-information to capture, in real time, not only customer sales but also planned and unplanned requirements and transmit this data digitally to the supply chain network. The goal is to align the core capabilities of available channel partners with the product and service needs and priorities of customers anywhere in the supply chain. Bovet and Martha[10] have termed such a channel focus a "value net" and characterize the customer-supplier relationships that emerge as "symbiotic," in that customer choices trigger a reaction in network sourcing, manufacturing, delivery, and information transfer necessary to meet demand needs, "interactive," in that the channel collaboratively assigns aspects of customer demand to the partner best able to perform the requirement, and "value-enhancing," in that both the customer and the entire supply channel ecosystem receive total value either through the streamlining of costs or flawless execution of customer product and service needs.

Succeeding in tomorrow's business environment means that companies today must embrace the following new postulates of supply chain collaboration:

1. Establish a Web-Enabled Network of Channel Partners

For today's most forward-looking companies, the key to success is managing a network of partners. Fundamentally, this proposition means that effective e-SCM comes down to execution: generating an environment of trust between trading partners, establishing well-defined expectations of value up and down the supply chain, and then carefully tracking results to ensure value propositions are being realized. It also means that partnerships are true "partnerships," in that each party receives shared value from the arrangement and that safeguards are in place to ensure that the partnership matures through time.

Dell Computer Corp., best known for its success in selling computers via the Web, has been enormously successful in engineering a build-to-order manufacturing model, while pursuing zero inventories by utilizing supply partners. Once an order is taken, Dell's supply chain partners spring into action. While Dell does some of the work itself, third-party suppliers do a significant amount of the manufacturing and distribution. As a result, Dell's inventory turns are more than once a week (60 times a year), thereby enabling the company to escape from being stuck with excess inventories of short-lived electronic components. Part of this "zero inventories" model is achieved by requiring suppliers to hold consignment inventories close to its manufacturing plants. One logistics partner, Ryder Integrated Logistics, Inc., warehouses critical inventories in facilities located within a 15-minute drive of Dell's plants. Customer orders received by Dell are routed via the Web every two hours to the warehouse for final assembly or for component delivery to another assembly plant within two hours.

2. Network-In Customers

While Internet-linked suppliers provide e-commerce businesses with the products and services necessary to remain competitive, it is the customer that is the focus of an enterprise's particular Internet solution. In the past, companies met customer demand by offering fixed product lines, standardized prices, and relatively undifferentiated, one-size-fits-all solutions determined by the needs of the average customer. In today's value-driven supply chain, every customer is considered as unique. Individual customers come to a supplier expecting to receive customizable, personal product/service solutions that embody the attributes they value the most. And more and more customers are expecting to increase the velocity of the manufacturing, fulfillment, and associated services by utilizing the Internet.

Marshall Industries, one of the world's largest wholesale distributors of industrial electronic components, was an early leader in establishing a Web site providing $7 \times 24 \times 365$ customer service. The company began by linking its backbone systems to its Web site, thereby providing customers with the ability to search on line for critical information regarding unallocated inventory status, order history information, and design support. Logistics carriers were then networked into the system to provide pinpoint tracking of shipments. In addition to facilitating customer service, the Internet tools dramatically impacted Marshall's operations. The Web site soon replaced handwritten sales reports, paper-based catalogs, and phone calls. Similarly, W. W. Grainger, one of the world's largest distributors of *maintenance, repair, and operations* (MRO) equipment, moved beyond its traditional model of doing business through over-the-counter sales at branch locations, with the establishment of a one-stop on-line trading exchange called OrderZone.com. The site provides customers with the ability to place orders involving multiple vendors and receive a single invoice. The on-line site electronically sends orders to respective suppliers for fulfillment.[11]

3. Accelerate and Improve Decision-Making by Integrating Business Partners

In a competitive environment, where your best customers are only a click away from your competitor, speed of response is critical. "Speed" in this context, however, is not about just doing things faster: it is also about doing them better. With the use of the Internet, customer order information can move at the speed of light to each member of a supply network. If, say, an inventory shortage appears at the prime distribution center in Chicago, the information is transmitted both to the customer and cascades through the supply channel. The goal is then to decide how the requirement should best be delivered from alternate inventory stocking centers before the customer clicks over to a competitor. This kind of total channel response can only occur when network partners utilize real-time e-information to respond to any possible situation as a single customer fulfillment team.

The ability to quickly respond to customer demand is at the heart of retail giants Home Depot Inc. and GE Appliances. Both companies recently created a network of Internet kiosks that enable prospective customers to research product specifications and costs, place orders for home appliances, and schedule deliveries. In addition, the on-line catalog provides customers with the ability to explore a much wider range of product features and options than would be possible if they where to simply be browsing among display models at a storeroom. The impact of this joint excursion into Web-based sales has permitted Home Depot to reduce retail display and storage costs, while enabling GE Appliances to reduce inventories and better plan for production.[12]

4. Meeting Customer Expectations

In the past, companies developed their response to the marketplace by focusing on set offerings of products, options, and service features driven by a standardized price for all customers. But, according to a recent A.T. Kearney–sponsored survey of critical issues driving retail customers, the issue of price placed third among consumer requirements. The survey showed that the number one factor influencing consumer purchase decisions was the robustness of the bundle of services surrounding the product. These services included everything from in-store assistance, to the availability of customer service Web sites, 800 numbers, and product assembly and integration services. The second most critical factor was product quality. In third place was price. But even in this category, the element of price was seen in its broadest sense, as part of an entire process that encapsulated other elements, beginning with actual product purchase, through the product use lifecycle, to replacement, and finally, repeat sales.

An open extended enterprise network assumes companies can respond to the virtually infinite ways that products and services can be combined to achieve customer satisfaction. For example, configuring an effective e-supply channel driven by Internet-based customer management is at the heart of Lanier Worldwide, Inc.'s business strategy. Lanier, the world's largest private-label distributor of copiers, needed to construct an e-business system that would enable the company to both view global supply chain operations and at the same time provide pinpoint visibility to customer orders across the fulfillment channel. According to Bill Cook, vice president of logistics, "Every one of our customers has a unique set of needs in terms of information, delivery commitments, even product mix." Customers span a wide variety of businesses, including an extensive dealer network, aftermarket customers, and a direct sales force. Lanier's e-business software solution empowers both customers and staff to resolve customer order problems, while assembling e-information for trend analysis, performance tracking, and quality control for the company's supply chain.[13]

C. SUPPLY CHAIN SYNCHRONIZATION: TIMING IS EVERYTHING!

The ability of businesses to utilize e-information and leverage the productive capabilities of their supply chain partners constitutes only two of the three components of the e-SCM concept. The ability to transmit and share supply channel information electronically is simply not enough. In fact, companies have always had that capability with their EDI systems. The problem is that tools like EDI send information over proprietary networks to trading partners in batches of messages, which are, in reality, electronic versions of paper documents. Hours, even days, can transpire between the time of data receipt and the availability of the data for channel decision-making. Take, for example, California-based Aspect Communications Corp., which manufactures communications and call-center equipment. The company outsources much of its manufacturing to multiple trading partners. Because of the nature of the complex systems sold by Aspect, a single customer order might be manufactured and delivered from four different supply locations. Successfully executing such a strategy means that Aspect must be able not just to transmit e-information, but also to perfectly integrate that information across manufacturing processes owned by supply chain partners. In such an environment, the value of the information is as important as the actual manufacture and delivery of the product.[14]

To meet the challenges of doing business in today's marketplace, companies like Aspect have been engineering new methods for linking together real-time e-information. The result of this effort is the concept of *e-supply chain synchronization* (e-SCS), and it is about transmitting e-information as fast as possible through the supply channel and interlinking all network nodes to achieve a seamless supply chain response to the customer. The obvious goal of e-SCS is to utilize technology to achieve a direct linkage between demand and supply at all points in the channel network. The value of such synchronization is obvious: minimization of work-in-process inventories, elimination of the "bullwhip" effect through the distribution channel, overall reduced costs, and the perfect matching of customer requirements with available product.

Perfect e-SCS is obviously a goal that is almost impossible to achieve in today's business environment. In the real world, the broadcast of demand through the supply chain system is limited by the technology capacities and capabilities of channel trading partners. Capacity anywhere in the supply channel is expensive and finite. Networked computer systems are equally expensive to implement and have as yet to reach critical mass. Safety stocks and lead times cannot be eliminated, only reduced. Companies still run their businesses by selecting the best trade-offs between inventory, service, and costs and can only hope to extend competitive advantage by persuading channel partners to collectively optimize resources and costs. Still, e-SCS enables whole supply chains to concurrently manage the ever-increasing complexity of today's e-business and collaborative relationships and can provide the following advantages:[15]

- Ability to network companies in a supply chain community, in order to manage channel complexities by engineering enhanced planning and decision-making capabilities, starting with internal ERP systems, and extending connectivity to Internet-linked channel trading partners.
- Ensuring that supply channel costs are minimized and that they are, as much as possible, the most competitive across geographies and companies.
- Capturing the most profitable customers, on a global basis, by creating more compelling, value-based relationships than other supply chain networks.
- Securing access to the most value-added suppliers, on a global basis, by establishing superior Internet-enabled supply chains that offer business-to-business technology and trading partner relationships.
- Engineering flexible, agile organizations and supply networks that can leverage an array of Internet technologies, ranging from collaborative product commerce to multi-channel e-information visibility to capitalize on changes to customer demand and shifts in supply-side dynamics.

Establishing effective e-SCS in a supply channel ecosystem will require network trading partners to create channel structures, integrated planning and control, and information architectures capable of promoting continuous channel synchronization through collaborative design. A successful e-SCS channel will contain the following key components: a market-winning strategy, synchronized relations with partners, technologies that enable channel synchronized e-information, and performance metrics that assist cross-channel teams to continuously review channel capabilities and reformulate channel decisions (see Figure 1.5).

1. Develop a Supply Chain Strategy that Provides for Avenues of Ongoing Supply Chain Synchronization

An effective e-SCS strategy requires that channel trading partners begin by defining the objectives to be pursued by each individual channel node as well as the entire supply chain acting as a unified market-satisfying force. The majority of the time, companies find that individual and supply chain strategies are focused on the same goals and are mutually supportive. As such, the process of e-SCS strategy formulation

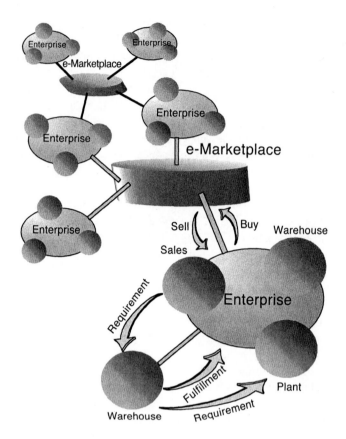

FIGURE 1.5 e-Supply chain channels.

extends far beyond company borders and should be regarded as an inter-enterprise exercise. The results of an effective e-SCS strategy can be seen in the identification of two critical objectives. The first consists in the determination of the best options necessary to cost-effectively deliver the product to the customer by leveraging the entire supply chain. The second objective coalesces around identifying which supply network trading partners are most capable of designing and executing optimal delivery processes at specific points in the supply channel.

For example, in designing an effective e-SCS strategy for the personal computer, supply chains could choose from several channel models. One way to design the supply network would be to concentrate on a *compression* strategy. In this scenario, a single company could pursue final PC configuration at the distribution-center level. Second, an intercompany postponement strategy could be chosen, where final assembly is performed by a downstream channel partner, such as a distributor, reseller, or retailer. Finally, the manufacturer could be responsible for fulfillment, thereby removing all inventories from the channel, with downstream distributors/resellers shouldering the responsibility for sales and order management.[16]

TABLE 1.2
e-SCS Enablers and Channel Benefits

Channel Function	Technology Enabler	Channel Benefit
Channel Supply Management	Multipartner ERP data integration EDI, Web-driven synchronized channel requirements Collaborative supplier base B2B exchanges e-Logistics/4PL services	Reduced inbound channel inventories and total costs Alignment of channel demand/supply Direct feed of requirements data into ERP backbone Metrics for event notification and exception management
Product and Service Processing	Collaborative product and service wrap design Collaborative planning, CPFR initiatives Collaborative supplier base e-Procurement initiatives	Capacity optimization Flexible/agile manufacturing Alignment of demand with material planning Supply chain visibility Minimize channel inventories
Channel Customer Management	e-CRM Data Warehousing e-Service/Call centers Marketplace metrics Real-time, digital customer demand feedback	Proactive e-Relationships Market of one Responsive and reliable fulfillment channel functions Mass customization Channel demand transparency
Channel Support Activities	e-Logistics/4PL services Customized delivery channels "Real options" management XML, Java, wireless communications technologies Interoperable IT platforms	Better utilization of channel assets Effective channel decision-making Responsive and reliable fulfillment channel functions Scaleable channel aligned with actual customer demand

2. Provide for the Establishment of Avenues for e-SCS Operations Excellence

The foundation for effective e-SCS is constructed on the ability of entire supply chain networks to achieve superlative levels of collaborative operations excellence. As discussed here, e-SCS operations excellence, however, is more than establishing transactional relationships between network supply nodes or sharing some information to be used for joint planning and decision-making. Real collaborative operations excellence requires trading partners to develop technology and organizational methods to coordinate jointly high levels of channel fulfillment and performance target complexity, while at the same time managing multiple levels of external relationships. Establishing both the framework and content of such a robust level of channel synchronization requires deep commitment, trust, and the willingness and capacity to acquire and expand new skills. Table 1.2 highlights some of the benefits whole supply chains can gain through e-SCS.

While still in their infancy, e-SCS tools and management methods are already being employed by today's most forward-looking supply chains. For example, TradingProduce, an internet-based exchange, sells food produce, meats, and flowers to its customers, such as Global-NetExchange's worldwide produce arm, Sears Roebuck, and Kroger, utilizing state-of-the-art e-SCS methods. According to TradingProduce's CEO Ron Bonavito, the goal of the partnerships is to "synchronize data, so that you create a seamless and paperless workflow all the way through your accounting system." e-SCS responds to channel requirements very differently than the traditional sequential, linked supply chains of the past. e-SCS attempts to move from a one-to-many, to a many-to-many approach, where issues can be addressed simultaneously. "We look," according to Gregory Cronin, president and CEO of synchronization technology supplier, Viewlocity, "at it not as a linked process any more. We look at it as a supply web composed of two things — collaboration and synchronization. The collaboration is really an ability to share. The synchronization is the intelligence of being able to know how to move the goods to satisfy orders." Such statements reinforce the view that e-SCS is not just enabling trading partners to employ synchronization tools — it is demanding that companies up and down the supply chain embrace the accompanying cultural and organizational changes as well.[17]

3.   Identify and Implement the Right Enabling Technologies

The basis of effective e-SCS can be found in the ability of trading partners to synchronize their business systems, normally ERP, first through extranets and now through the Internet. Utilizing technology tools to achieve channel synchronization has always been the objective of the logistics function, long before today's focus on e-commerce. In the past, it was telephone calls and faxes. Today, e-SCS is driven by a number of new technology toolsets that provide for radically different levels of cooperation, automation, and productivity. These tools can be described as EDI, the Internet, XML programming, workflow management solutions, and new hardware and software architectures providing real-time processing for such capabilities as forecasting, advanced planning, optimization, and rapid order configuration and order promising. The challenge to today's supply chain systems is to effectively manage the implementation of these technologies, as they evolve through time, across multiple partners, countries, alternate supply chains, and technology applications.

Home Depot's commitment to synchronizing demand and supply can be seen in its constant search to utilize technology to improve the integration between its supply chain and customer relationship management applications. Recently, the company expanded its capabilities by signing agreements to use third-party software and middleware to replace its homegrown supply chain and customer management systems. Previously, sales-transaction data were posted to a central database, and resulting product updates and prices were transmitted to stores in batches each night. The new system will enable the transmission of two-way data, in real time, and expand access to information for store managers and supply chain trading partners. This means that customers and suppliers, whether on the phone or at the Web site, will know exact inventory statuses and have access to store-based databases that include information on everything from delivery and installation schedules to tool rentals, promotional events, and details on 1 million products in 1,220 stores. In addition, Home Depot's commerce Web site technologies have enabled the company to entertain over 30,000 customer visits each week with a projected growth of 20% a year.[18]

4. Design and Implement New Forms for Organizational Relationships

Beyond all the discussion about technology, perhaps the most important element driving e-SCS can be found in the willingness of trading partners to adapt their organizations to leverage the advantages to be found in cross-supply chain collaboration. Some of the issues revolve around understanding that, since all nodes in the channel network are now collectively responsible for revenue growth, asset utilization, and customer service, there must be, correspondingly, an equitable sharing of the rewards as well as the risks. Second, company senior management must understand that the level of e-SCS success directly depends on their ability to foster business strategies that cultivate a supply chain culture among employees throughout the supply network. Lack of common values, behaviors, and beliefs will drain the high level of trust and collaboration necessary for success. Finally, e-SCS might mean that traditional functions performed by trading partners might change as the supply channel looks for ways to accentuate the various strengths and capabilities possessed by individual companies constituting the supply network. This often will mean that real data, often thought of as proprietary, be available to decision-makers outside company boundaries. Like natural ecosystems that unceasingly must adapt to environmental forces, winning supply chains must also ensure the companies populating a network at any given moment must possess the proper blend of capabilities, business philosophies and vision, institutional values, and commitment to success.

Achieving such levels of collaboration is not easy, and many companies today are reluctant to share critical information. Research has found that channel partners are most willing to exchange information that past business practices have forced companies to cooperate on, while more proprietary data is religiously withheld. According to an *"Information Week's* Research Information Sharing and Collaboration Study" (May 2001), about half of business-to-business (B2B) and business-to-customer (B2C) companies were willing to share marketing information, monthly/quarterly sales reports, collaborative planning data, and aggregated consumer data with their e-channel partners. In contrast, only about 30% of B2B and B2C companies were willing to share financial data. Eighty-four percent of B2C companies were reluctant to share individual customer sales data, and only about twenty-five percent of both B2B and B2C companies were willing to impart cost structures. The report did conclude with a survey of how positive supply chain collaboration had been. About 28% of both B2C and B2C businesses felt the effort to be "highly positive," almost 50% "somewhat positive," and only about 2% "somewhat negative" or "highly negative."[19]

Despite the hurdles, companies that have successfully shared data with their trading partners have shown significant success. Home Depot, for example, is extremely aggressive in their efforts to share information in order to drive sales and cut costs. Although, in the Business Week Survey, only 13% of companies shared real-time sales data, Home Depot will do it when company management feels that it will pay off. To get the data, channel suppliers have to demonstrate that receiving it will result in lower prices and fewer item stock-outs. Once authorized, "Then," according to CIO Ron Griffin, "we'll allow them whatever information they want — sales by store, geography, day of the week, whatever."[20]

V. SUMMARY AND TRANSITION

Today, even the best run organizations have begun to feel the strain of successfully responding to the realities of the twenty-first century marketplace. New concepts of what constitutes customer value, requirements for more agile, flexible product designs and manufacturing processes, the growth of "virtual" companies and collaborative processes, and the continuous fragmenting of marketplaces demanding customized products and services to satisfy a "marketplace of one" have rendered obsolete past organizational models and partnerships with trading partners. In addition, the ubiquitous presence of the computer, the ultimate enabler promising the real-time synchronization of information with anyone, anytime, anywhere, has reshaped the very nature of business and altered fundamental thinking about the way companies market, sell, buy, and communicate with their customers and suppliers.

Of these changes occurring in what has been problematically labeled the "new economy," perhaps the most pertinent has been the realization that to survive in this new environment, companies, whether large or small, must perceive themselves not as self-contained competitive entities, but rather as nodes in a much larger network of intersecting business systems, composed of intricate, mutually supportive webs of customers, products, competencies, resources, and information played out on a global scale. The best enterprises understand that to thrive in today's marketplace, it is imperative that they continuously activate the synergies that occur when they bypass the limitations of traditional internally focused business models, leverage capital and human capabilities wherever they can be found in the supply chain, and merge channel trading partner centers of expertise to establish virtual, scaleable organizations capable of responding decisively to any marketplace challenge.

Over the past half decade, the principles supporting this nascent management paradigm have gathered around the term *supply chain management* (SCM). SCM provides today's enterprise with the strategic vision, as well as the operational principles, necessary to integrate once isolated companies into unified supply chain value-generating networks. Although SCM constitutes a virtual revolution in business management in and of itself, the merger of SCM with the enabling power of the Internet has propelled SCM to a new level by linking the concept with powerful networking tools, enabling the real-time integration and synchronization of channel-wide processes and databases and the tight linking of trading partners. The application of the Internet to SCM is such a radical enhancement to the SCM concept that it deserves to be relabeled *e-SCM* and can be defined as follows:

e-SCM is a tactical and strategic management philosophy that seeks to network the collective productive capacities and resources of intersecting supply channel systems through the application of Internet technologies in the search for innovative solutions and the synchronization of channel capabilities dedicated to the creation of unique, individualized sources of customer value.

Enabling the full potential of e-SCM requires that companies, first of all, understand the function of Internet-driven information in the supply chain. e-SCM enables the real-time connectivity of all trading partners and provides for the instantaneous visibility of events and decision-making across the global supply chain. Second, e-SCM provides companies with the ability to leverage digital technology to structure close, collaborative partnerships with their supply chain partners. The goal is to provide for the execution of cross-enterprise processes and the integration of trading partner operations, moving companies from an enterprise-centric supply channel driving multiple processes, to Internet-synchronized supply networks focused on a single objective: superior customer service. Finally, e-SCM enables whole supply chains to synchronize information arising from all network nodes to achieve a seamless supply chain response to the customer. Transmitting channel information electronically is simply not enough. Customer event-driven data must be available in real-time across the supply network, thereby enabling not sequential but concurrent decision-making, as information is broadcast to the supply chain system.

e-SCM has become today's most important management concept, because it enables enterprises organized along supply network systems to exploit the new realities transforming the marketplace. Investigating in greater detail the content of these marketplace challenges that are fueling the growth of e-SCM is the subject of the next chapter. The discussion will focus on five marketplace dynamics and how e-SCM and individual companies can leverage their supply chains to master each challenge.

ENDNOTES

1. This section has been summarized in part from Ross, David F., *Competing Through Supply Chain Management*, Chapman & Hall, New York, 1998, ix–xi.
2. Bowersox, Donald J., "Physical Distribution Development, Current Status, and Potential," in *Readings in Physical Distribution Management: The Logistics of Marketing*, Bowersox, Donald J., LaLonde, Bernard J., and Smykay, Edward W., Macmillan, London, 1969, 3–8.
3. For more on this topic see Anderson, David L. and Lee, Hau, "New Supply Chain Business Models — The Opportunities and Challenges," in *Achieving Supply Chain Excellence Through Technology*, 3, Anderson, David L., ed., Montgomery Research, San Francisco, 2001, 12.
4. Handfield, Robert B. and Nichols, Ernest L., *Introduction to Supply Chain Management*, Prentice Hall, Upper Saddle River, NJ, 1999, 2.
5. Ayers, James B., *Handbook of Supply Chain Management*, St. Lucie Press, Boca Raton, 2001, 4–5.

6. Poirier, Charles C. and Bauer, Michael J., *E-Supply Chain*, Berrett-Koehler Publishers, Inc., San Francisco, 2000, ix.
7. Costello, Daniel, "Reach Out and Touch Somebody's Brand," *Customer Relationship Management*, 5, 8, 2001, 58.
8. Trebilcock, Bob, "Welcome to e-World," *Supply Chain Yearbook 2001*, Cahners, 92.
9. Reary, Rob and Springer, Alicia, "Return on Relationship: a Different Lens on Business," in *Achieving Supply Chain Excellence Through Technology*, 3, Anderson, David L., ed., Montgomery Research, San Francisco, 2001, 41.
10. Bovet, David and Martha, Joseph, *Value Nets: Breaking the Supply Chain to Unlock Hidden Profits*, New York: John Wiley & Sons, 2000, 4.
11. These and other company stories can be seen in Lapide, Larry, "The Innovators Will Control the e-Supply Chain," in *Achieving Supply Chain Excellence Through Technology*, 3, Anderson, David L., ed., Montgomery Research, San Francisco, 2001, 186.
12. Morehouse, James and Morales, José, "New Rules for the Extended Enterprise," *Supply Chain Technology News*, 3, 6, 2001, 47.
13. Harps, Leslie Hansen, "Lanier Gains Visibility Across the Supply Chain," *Inbound Logistics*, 20, 1, 2000, 108.
14. Seideman, Tony, "Supply-Chain Synchronization: Timing is Everything," *Supply Chain e-Business*, 2, 1, 2001, 32.
15. Some of these points can be found in Gattorna, John L. and Berger, Andrew J., "The eSynchronized Supply Chain," *Supply Chain Management Review Global Supplement*, 5, 1, 2001, 22.
16. Anderson, David L. and Lee, Hau, "Synchronized Supply Chains: the New Frontier," in *Achieving Supply Chain Excellence Through Technology*, 1, Anderson, David, L., ed., Montgomery Research, San Francisco, 1999, 12.
17. These comments can be found in Seideman.
18. Rosen, Cheryl, "Home Depot Spiffs Up CRM and Supply Chain," *Information Week*, July 2, 2001, 24.
19. D'Antoni, Helen, "Data Exchanges Permeate Supply Chains," *Information Week*, May 7, 2001, 159.
20. Gilbert, Alorie, "Collaborative Business," *Information Week*, May 7, 2001, 43.

2 The e-Business Economic Revolution: The Components and Impact of e-Business

During the last two decades of the twentieth century, companies became aware that, to survive and flourish in the marketplace, they needed to expand their business strategies and operations processes beyond the parochial borders of their own individual enterprises to their trading partners out in the supply chain. Emphasis gradually shifted from a long-time concern with managing fairly static internal organization structures, cost and performance measurements, product design and marketing functions, and a localized view of the customer to a realization that new marketplace and technological forces and the accelerating speed of everything, from communications to product life cycles, were driving companies to look beyond their firms to their supply chains for sources of competitive advantage. By the end of the 1990s it was widely perceived that only those companies that could effect the collaboration of product resources and value-generating competencies with those of their supply network partners would be able to successfully take advantage of the new global marketplace. The management philosophy that was developed to flourish in this new economic environment was *supply chain management* (SCM), and it quickly was adopted as the core strategic model for most enterprises.

At the same time that supply chain optimization was emerging, radical breakthroughs in Internet technologies were providing the communications and transaction mediums that enabled the *connectivity* of SCM to move from a decoupled, serialized flow of interbusiness competencies to the real-time integration and synchronization of every process and relationship occurring in the supply network. In the 1990s, companies used business process reengineering, *total quality management* (TQM), *enterprise resource planning* (ERP), *just-in-time* manufacturing and distribution (JIT), and intranet and extranet models to create more competitive, channel-oriented strategies. Today, the Internet has propelled SCM to an entirely different dimension, by enabling a global ability to pass information and transact business friction-free anywhere, anytime, to customers, suppliers, and trading partners. The application of Internet technologies requires a transformation of tradition business focusing on:

- The *end-to-end integration* of all supply chain functions from product design, through order management, to cash. This integration encompasses the activities of customer management on the delivery end of the supply channel, technologies connecting individual firms with trading partner competencies on the supply end of the channel, and internal transaction management associated with orders, manufacturing, and accounting on the inside of the business.
- The development of *end-to-end infrastructures* that facilitate real-time interaction and fuse together the synchronized passage and convergence of network information. Internet knowledge requires the transformation of infrastructures and technologies from a focus on internal performance measurements and objectives to organizations and information tools that engender unique interconnected networks of value-creating relationships and possess the agility and scalability to meet the constantly changing objectives of today's economic environment.

In this chapter, the basis of the economic "revolution" driven by the Internet and e-business will be explored. The chapter begins with a review of what is being termed the first stage of the "new economy." Following, the chapter will detail the five business dynamics driving the transformation to the e-business economy. Among the areas explored are the changes brought about by the Internet to customer management, product cycle management, the basis of information technology, the creation of global business, and logistics management. After, the discussion centers on the fundamental principles of e-business: e-collaboration, security, trust and branding, the rise of new forms of e-businesses, and the impact of the Internet on the human side of business. A definition of key e-business terms is offered. The chapter concludes with a review of five major trends impacting the development of e-business, ranging from the continued migration from vertical to virtually integrated enterprises to the changed role of logistics.

I. RISE OF THE "NEW ECONOMY"

Prophets have always regarded the birth of a new millennium as heralding a new age of radical change from what had gone before. Often, the words of prophets seek to engender apocalyptic visions rendering what had seemingly stood the test of time, guiding the thoughts, passions, and actions of communities and nations, no longer possessed of value and demanding that all must be swept away before a new, but still unfolding reality. The head-on collision of what has been termed the "old economy" of the twentieth century with the world of e-business of the twenty-first has propagated such an eschatology. During the first years of the new millennium, enthusiastic economists, academics, and technology visionaries earnestly, fervently proclaimed the birth of the "new economy," dismissing as irrelevant the traditional economic rules of the past. There were to be no limiting walls of factories, archaic concerns with structured business organizations, wasted preoccupations with internal performance metrics, messy business practices driven by the ugliness of haggling and compromise — just a seamless interplay of Web-enabled buyers and sellers uninhibited by boundaries of corporate will or global time and space.

Trade journals and think-tanks like Forrester Research, Gartner Group, AMR, and others warned that companies taking a wait-and-see attitude to e-business adoption would be left dramatically behind the competition as the decade moved forward. The numbers projected for the new e-economy were nothing short of spectacular. The research firm Dataquest projected that the $33 billion in revenues transacted for *business-to-consumer* (B2C) in 1999 would top $380 billion by 2003. On the *business-to-business* (B2B) side, the Gartner Group calculated that the value of B2B Internet commerce sales transactions in 2000 had surpassed $433 billion, a 189% increase over 1999 figures. Despite the economic downturn beginning in 2001, they forecasted that B2B commerce would reach $919 billion, followed by $1.9 trillion in 2002, $3.6 trillion in 2003, and rising to $8.5 trillion in 2005.[1] Running this explosion in technology would, according to AMR, cost companies nearly $1.7 trillion to acquire workable Internet solutions. "By 2002," according to the Gartner Group's Karen Peterson, "channel masters not investing in collaborative technologies will see their agility and market share decrease significantly." "What we've been saying is that e-business is business-as-usual," said John A. White, of supply chain software supplier Manugistics. "It's not this animal you can tackle as time permits. Companies that don't jump on-board may look up and realize that they're losing customers, especially when it comes to participating in trading exchanges and the like. The Internet is changing everything."[2]

Today, the hype and euphoria of the first years of the e-business craze have all but faded away in the hard reality of the marketplace. Most of the host of profitless dot-coms that had been begun their existence as hot IPOs with stratospheric valuations have been relegated to the graveyard with other bubble schemes of history that were too good to be true. Just as vigorously as trade publications had proclaimed the new era of the dot-com and the irrelevancy of the stodgy old Dow Jones club, by mid-2001 they were as gleeful in exposing the painful death of unfortunate NASDAQ wunderkind who had, alas, been conceived without even a trace of how they were to become profitable enterprises. For example, the headlines for *Computerworld* on April 9, 2001, declared "Confidence in B2B Sinks to a Major Low." One *InformationWeek* lead article for June 25, 2001, entitled "Failed Marketplaces Keep Piling Up" started ominously, "Just when you thought it couldn't get any worse, it looks like the bottom is falling out of the B2B e-commerce market." On the cruel side, *InternetWeek* had a column entitled "As E-Business Turns" which paraded for all the buyouts, shutdowns, and general wacky ups-and-downs of the current week's episode of the "Days of Dot-Com Lives." Even nastier were the Web sites that had been started just to document the bust. Names like *www.dotcomfailures*, *www.thecompost*, and the descriptive *www.techdirt* listed the losers and provided insights into what had gone wrong. *InternetWeek* for July 16, 2001, produced its own line item "Grocery Bill" for the Webvan liquidation sale:

Estimated Capital Invested	$1.2 Billion
Fixed Asset, Equipment, and IT	$357 Million
Cost of Developing and Maintaining Web Software	$44 Million
Average Cost of Building Each Distribution Center (7 established)	$39 Million

The Webvan failure was the most spectacular dot-com disaster so far, surpassing the closure of eToys, which burned through nearly $500 million.

With all the volatility associated with e-business ventures described above, what is the place of the Internet in today's business environment? Is it really just a lot of hype, wishful thinking, and espousal of business models that are fundamentally unsound? Can the technology really be developed that is cost-effective and easy to implement to make e-business practices a reality? Will real businesses, the kind that are more concerned with P2P ("path to profitability") than B2C and B2B, adopt e-business technologies? What can be learned from the failures and successes of e-businesses over the past couple of years? Is the "new economy" really new at all, and can the Internet bring anything of value to today's business environment?

As the dust settles on the first years of the "Internet Revolution," it is clear that, while the period of business and economic excess and experimentation is definitely over, the advent of e-business technologies has forever changed the landscape of the business environment. Some critics have contended that the entire array of Web-based initiatives is based on grossly inflated expectations, faulty business practices, and invalid business models. But while such "Luddites" do have a point, it is clear that Web technologies have engendered a whole new way of conducting business. What is needed now are not vague revolutionary proclamations, such as "bricks and mortar companies are moribund," "everything is different," "ERP is dead," and others, but a deliberate and reasoned application of sound management and operations principles to actually *running* enterprises using e-business technologies. Taylor and Terhune have succinctly summarized this point: "What the past three years [writing from early 2001] of furious technology and economic experimentation have done is form the basis for the next 20 years of business value."[3] The trick will be for firms to manage and exploit real *value*, as e-business tools and the economic climate emerge and transform through time.

Companies that have effectively integrated e-business tools with a sound management strategy are, indeed, not only surviving the dot-com storm but are actually achieving radical competitive breakthroughs. For example, Intel Corporation has been aggressively pursuing becoming an *e-corporation*, not only to capture market share, but also to shield the company from the economic downturn of 2001–2002. According to chief e-strategist Christopher S. Thomas, Intel was generating $2 billion a month in income using the Web in the first quarter of 2001. Internet initiatives have also provided the company with the ability to offer 24 × 7 customer support coverage, while processing 40% more orders in the same amount of time. Almost 93% of Intel's customers are ordering on-line, and order errors are down by 75% since the project's inception. At the same time, said Thomas, Intel has learned some important lessons. These include the need to design Web systems for maximum ease of use, streamline business processes, allow for rapid process change, and standardize many services and platforms "so we don't reinvent the wheel." Future efforts are expected to tackle personalized browsing for customers, event-driven activation to assist in order monitoring, peer-to-peer collaboration, and dynamic links between businesses.[4]

Other industries — high tech, chemical, apparel, pharmaceutical — are equally enthusiastic about the prospect of Web markets. And why not! They promise to give buyers access to new, less expensive sources of supply and a global customer base driven by the ability to share data and plans in real time. While there is a lot of vapor-ware and hype about e-markets that still goes on unabated in the press, e-business is for real, and a number of large manufacturers have invested big money in Web markets and are using them to make multimillion-dollar deals. For example, Covisint, the giant automotive exchange being built by General Motors, Ford, and DaimlerChrysler, has already been the site for the purchase of millions of dollars' worth of direct materials via on-line markets. Together, the exchange expects to be transacting billions of dollars' worth of goods each year. "This is the largest business-to-business electronic network that has been announced so far, that will link not only the $80 billion Ford supply chain but the automotive supply chain around the world," says Jack Nassar, Ford's CEO. "This will mean quicker decisions, less inventory, lower cost, and better production for Ford and its suppliers. It's a ground-breaking move in the auto industry."[5]

Overall, there is ample evidence that revenues attained through electronic commerce have been rising despite the economic slowdown beginning in 2001. In 1999, *InformationWeek* Research's semiannual E-Business Agenda study reported that the average company received 10% of its revenue electronically. A year later that figure had risen to 14%. In 2001 it was projected at 17%. In addition, electronically received revenue was up year after year in four of five sectors (see Table 2.1). While financial services showed a slight gain, technology suppliers have seen the electronic portion of their total revenue increase by 43% compared with 2000 figures. Such revenue growth has spurred on technology suppliers to aggressively shift revenues to more efficient digital mediums such as supply chains, e-commerce direct sales, and exchange marketplaces.[6]

The bottom line is that e-business, regardless of the hype and the financial disasters, is here to stay. One way or another, companies both large and small are going to have to come to terms with e-business and map out a strategy that utilizes Internet technologies. What has and will divide successful adopters of e-business will be not only those companies that see that their future includes the Internet, but also those that recognize that they must be positioned as *viable businesses*. In the words of Rob Hirschfeld, "The traditional economy is run by the rule that businesses exist to make money. Unfortunately, most dot-com businesses followed the new economy rule: *Businesses exist to get market share*. This paradigm led these dot-com companies to focus more on hype, discounts, and marketing than creating profitable products and services."[7] Surviving in the world of the Internet economy means that companies must not only thoroughly understand the optimal application of e-business tools but also the basis of the Internet business landscape. Grasping the realities of the later is the topic of the next section.

II. UNDERSTANDING THE INTERNET BUSINESS ENVIRONMENT

There can be little doubt that the Internet has dramatically changed forever the way both individuals and companies approach not only the processes of buying and

TABLE 2.1
Percent of Industry Total Revenue Received from e-Commerce

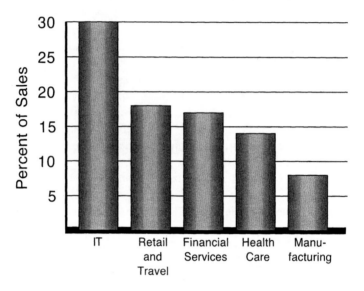

Data from InformationWeek Research e-business agenda study, June 2001.

selling products and services, but also how they communicate with each other, the mediums by which knowledge is transferred, even how they will be entertained. Already, in the late 1990s, the marketplace had become aware of a definite acceleration in the speed of change shaping the business environment. Management buzzwords, such as agile enterprises, virtual organizations, total quality management, business process engineering, and lean manufacturing, all focused on a common theme: how to eliminate time and costs from the process while providing new levels of customer satisfaction across whole supply channels. Today, the development and utilization of the Internet as the global standard for both communications and commerce has so dramatically increased the velocity of change that it has produced a virtual inflection point obsoleting previously accepted norms of how the marketplace works. What capabilities does the Internet offer enterprises that they did not have before? How does the Internet fundamentally change the business landscape? In answering these questions, several points can be detailed. To begin with, the Internet provides an example of what Downes and Mui[8] term a "disruptive technology." According to the Law of Disruption, changes in the social, political, and economic environment occur incrementally, while changes in technology are exponential in nature and cause order-of-magnitude shifts in the environment that negate past rules of engagement. For example, the enabling power of the Internet inaugurated a change in the way business is conducted that was on another level in comparison to the incrementalist strategies of process management tools such as *business process management* (BPR), ERP, TQM, and JIT.

Why the Internet has been so disruptive to what now is termed the "old economy" is simple, yet at the same time, profound. According to Fingar, Kumar, and Sharma,[9] "The Internet enables *business ubiquity*, allowing a company to conduct business everywhere, all the time. e-commerce eliminates the constraints of time and distance in operating a business.... Just as the computer itself demarcated the end of the Industrial Age and heralded in the Information Age, e-Commerce heralds a new age of ubiquitous business." The Internet has not only increased the ability for companies to network databases and information, it has also enhanced the very nature of information itself. The Internet enables companies not only to communicate globally, but also to broadcast business rules and processes in real time. The Internet enables the shift from focusing on optimizing individual channel components to optimizing the performance of the entire supply chain. Finally, the Internet enables the activation of networks of cross-channel knowledge repositories that permit agents anywhere, at anytime, to access data and execute transactions with customers, suppliers, or channel partners.

In this section, five key business dynamics driven by the Internet will be detailed. Collectively, the changes attributed to each of the dynamics represent a radical departure from the past and a roadmap to the future. Understanding today's *customer* is the first dynamic. The key to this dynamic is charting the immense power e-business has given to customers in their search for unique value and a solution to their buying needs. The second business dynamic, *product cycle management*, is characterized by the ability of companies to construct product design and roll-out competencies enabling rapid first-to-market capabilities, coupled with agile processes that provide superior product and service quality, configurability, and superb delivery mechanisms. The explosion in *information technologies* constitutes the third dynamic. Growing marketplace connectivity depends on the continued development of devices, such as network servers and browsers, wireless technologies, WebTV, and future Internet-compatible devices. Leveraging the productive competencies to be found in the opening of the *global marketplace* and the establishment of *networks of collaborative trading partners* constitutes the fourth dynamic. Finally, the last dynamic can be seen in the impact of the Internet on *logistics functions*.

A. Customer Management Dynamics

The ability to provide pinpoint solutions to customer requirements has for over a decade been the driving force of business. In the past, businesses competed by marketing product lines consisting of standardized, mass-produced products. Today, customers are demanding to be treated as unique individuals and expecting their suppliers to provide configurable, solutions-oriented bundles of products, services, and information capable of evolving through time as their requirements change. In addition, with their expectations set by "world class" companies across global marketplaces, customers are demanding that their supply channels provide the highest quality for the lowest price, quick response deliveries, and ease of order management and customer service. This new business mission is perhaps best summarized by Kent Mahlke, supply chain manager at NCR. "I see," he states, "NCR's evolution as one from being product focused to solutions focused. We no longer supply just products to customers; we are actually providing solutions — a set of hardware, software, and services that solve a particular business problem for that customer."[10]

This migration of marketplace power from producers and sellers to buyers and consumers is being accelerated and amplified by the Internet revolution. Today's e-customer is demanding that suppliers provide Web-based capabilities, and because of the ubiquitous use of the Internet, there can be little doubt that most of tomorrow's customers will be e-customers. As Celia Fleischaker points out, e-customers are different from traditional customers. "They are entrepreneurial and independent and often prefer to transact business on their own terms. They value the self-service model." In addition, they want access to information at any time, from anywhere. They are more apt to work with their suppliers using the Internet and e-mails than telephones and faxes. They expect a higher level of collaboration when it comes to pricing, promotions, and changes to product lines. Because e-customers work in a fast paced environment, they are less tolerant of missed delivery dates, inaccurate invoices, and other impediments that retard the pace of business. "In short," says Fleischaker, "e-customers expect much more from their business relationships, and these expectations are growing."[11]

The use of Web technologies has added several new dimensions to the equation that has virtually reengineered the customer satisfaction processes. To begin with, e-commerce implies that suppliers are expected to provide all-around $24 \times 7 \times 365$ business coverage. This means that e-enterprises must be able to construct systems that are not only technically available and reliable, but also dynamically scalable to service spikes in demand without going off-line. Second, e-customers expect their suppliers to expand their Web capabilities by integrating new technologies. As Fingar, Kumar, and Sharma point out, "The continuous stream of innovation in electronic devices and gadgets will continue: the palm top, the lap top, the cell phone, the PDA, the fax, the pager, IP telephony, e-mail, digital mail, kiosks, and so on."[12] Today's fast-paced and increasingly Internet-enabled customer demands access devices to conduct e-business regardless of the medium. Third, the Internet provides companies with unparalleled opportunities to customize product and service offerings to match the individual needs of each customer. By assembling demand pattern portfolios, businesses can develop tailored marketing presentations to their customers that zero in on their buying requirements, while simultaneously eliminating the time customers must search for the right solution. Driven by the communications power of the Internet, marketers can engage in a variety of cross-selling and up-selling opportunities, while reaching each customer in real time, one-to-one. In addition, Web functions enabling the customer to access a company's service resources, so that they can self-service their product questions and order queries, further increases customer management of the buying experience. While company resources become more visible and accessible through self-service, the overall cost to provide quality service will also decline. Finally, the emergence of e-customers has resulted in a new form of *customer relationship management* (CRM) — e-CRM. The goal is to utilize the Internet to cement new customer loyalties through the digitized care and feeding of the marketplace. At Rockwell International (Milwaukee, WI), a B2B portal termed SourceAlliance.com and several on-line Web stores were created to provide customers a seamless one-stop shopping experience, where they can buy hardware needed to connect control hardware and software to plant floor networks. Customers can take advantage of account personalization, flexible ordering and shipping options, and customized, Web-based reporting of contracts. According to Rod Michael, e-business solutions manager, customers can also link their procurement systems directly to Rockwell's Internet CRM system, enabling Rockwell "to integrate right into their workflow and not just be an add-on."[13]

The e-CRM concept has provided today's customer with radically new sources to demand the highest quality, configure products that fit their individual needs, and service themselves, all at the lowest cost possible. For suppliers, the Internet has provided unprecedented opportunities to leverage software applications and processes that enable sales, marketing, and service to engineer strong relationships with their customers. By permitting them to reach through the Web into their supplier's market-facing functions to place an order, view inventory status, check on a delivery, and perform a host of other e-nabled functions, customers are empowered and will want to repeat the personalized experience. In this sense, the Internet provides them with the necessary feeling of having received superior value and a stronger sense of commitment to the supplier — all critical marketplace attributes in an environment where dissatisfied customers are merely a click away from the competition.

B. PRODUCT CYCLE MANAGEMENT DYNAMICS

In order to meet the requirements of providing products and service bundles at Internet speed, producers have had to revolutionize the way they previously designed, manufactured, and distributed products to the marketplace. In the past, companies competed by selling standardized, mass-produced products based on the lowest cost and possessing standards of average quality and availability. Pricing was fixed, and the relationship with the customer was one-dimensional. Today, the old paradigms driving production and distribution have been obsoleted by the ability of the Internet to leverage the collaborative capabilities of channel trading partners to accelerate the speed by which products and service values are generated and distributed. Marketplace leaders must be able to tap into the competencies of their channel networks if they expect to continuously produce and deliver products and services capable of the rapid development, deployment, and configurability that add customer value and secure competitive survival.

Materializing Internet-driven expectations about this new view of products and services is e-collaborative *product lifecycle management* (PLM). Activated by the Internet, PLM requires producers and suppliers to think of the entire process of conceiving, designing, planning, procuring, producing, and selling a product as a closely integrated activity in which collaborative commerce systems hold the post position. Although integrating such systems is still on the horizon, the applications are being assembled today that will permit many-to-many B2B synchronization, expose constraints as they emerge across the supplier network, alert the appropriate product life cycle teams, and synchronize the workflow. The benefits of such integration are obvious — reduced product design time through producer/supplier collaboration, reduced costs for procurement, and faster time to market. c-Commerce

PLM rests upon three critical components: product development, planning, and procurement. Collaborative product development requires designers and engineers to be able to communicate *product data management* (PDM) in an interactive, real-time manner. The goal is to use the Internet to provide portals synchronizing producers, suppliers, and customers, where such data as bills of material, outsourcing information, CAD drawings, design updates, and build schedules can be interactively shared among diverse development teams. This piece permits the PDM engineer, whether that person is within the plant or outside of it, to see the impact of a particular design or a change to be made, and possibly even to suggest a superior alternative.

To make PDM activities really work, however, it is essential that the effort also includes extensive use of collaborative planning, not only for traditional supply chain demand, replenishment, and capacity planning, but also for new product design. The objective is to integrate collaborative planning, forecasting, and replenishment (CPFR) technologies with e-collaborative PDM systems. A merger of both technologies would provide engineers and suppliers with the visibility to determine the best time to make a design change or, perhaps, make no change at all. In addition, to manage design content and engineering changes, designers will be able to source and procure materials directly through a virtual manufacturing network. Finally, by providing real-time information about supply network constraints, such as capacity bottlenecks or critical material shortages, PDM design teams up an down the supply chain can make more effective decisions early in the design process. While there are many obstacles to realizing such a level of cooperation, from reshaping market exchanges to tackling the issue of combining and converging so many different types of software, forward-looking companies are already diving straight in. For example, Chris Edwards, CIO for Group Dekko (North Webster, IN), a manufacturer of wire harnesses, feels that manufacturers need collaborative commerce systems. "The ability to collaborate on the Web," he says, "will be a matter of competitive advantage."

C. Information Technology Dynamics

A decade ago technologists hailed the end of the Industrial Age and the birth of the Information Age. As the twentieth century came to a conclusion, it was asserted that it was *information*, rather than productive assets, materials, and labor, that constituted the fundamental source of wealth. The capture, compilation, and communication of information could provide companies with radically new avenues to generate wealth by reaching previously inaccessible markets, providing revolutionary mediums for the transfer of goods and services, enabling new ways to capture customer loyalty, and enabling innovative companies to do things they never dreamt they could do. What this meant for business was that technology would be perceived not only as an effective management tool that shortens cycle times and increases productivity through automation but also as a key enabler, providing companies with the opportunity to activate highly competitive organizations and channel networks that engendered radically new markets and breakaway businesses models.

Today, the effective management of information has been propelled to a new dimension by the integrative power of the Internet. And what is at heart of the

Internet revolution is "ubiquity (existing or apparently existing everywhere at the same time), an attribute that can transform the very fabric of society and commerce."[14] The Internet enables companies to transform not just internal processes but whole industries — customers, suppliers, and trading partners who inhabit intersecting value chain communities. Today's most forward-looking companies understand that the World Wide Web is not simply a technical mechanism that facilitates communication; it is now the nervous system of a new business infrastructure that will profoundly affect the organization of work, the mediums by which enterprises respond to each other, and the way global economies will be conducted.

Constructing the global knowledge network and engineering new digital enterprise models has already begun. According to Raisch,[15] the emerging knowledge network began "first with the foundation of a standardized global telecommunication network, followed by a universal data and rich media network that is provided via the global Internet, and finally via communication, collaboration, and *enterprise application integration* (EAI) solutions, which are being introduced at a breakneck pace." Despite the disappointments of the dot-com crash and the tremendous difficulties in overcoming technical and trust issues, companies all along the value chain are recognizing that information collaboration, ranging from marketing information, to inventory, to product design and forecasting, enables enterprises to structure powerful knowledge networks to engineer new competitive space that transcends the limitations of time, geography, and talent.

Constructing the Internet knowledge network consists of a matrix of business system architectures that enable the convergence of virtual teams to focus on the collaborative identification, linking, sharing, and evaluation of entire value chain information assets. As illustrated in Figure 2.1, knowledge networks are composed of "knowledge hubs," consisting of individual enterprises ringed by internal information entities. Connectivity of knowledge hubs is made possible by Internet technologies, which provide a virtual workspace for collaborative communication and workflow. Evolving e-marketplaces will seek to leverage this information to drive reconfigured processes targeted at offering new products, services, and information back through the channel network. To materialize networking tasks, Internet systems must possess the following characteristics:

1. They must have the capability to span inter-enterprise functional boundaries and enable the structuring of true global channel-wide information networking. This capability should span the information resident in marketing and sales, design and production, materials procurement and storage, and distribution and logistics channel nodes.
2. They must be based on communications technologies, such as satellite, broadband, and wireless devices, that seek to make Internet connectivity ubiquitous.
3. They must be based on distributed open systems that enable applications to be free of past proprietary operating system architectures and offer the capability of digital devises to "talk" with one another.

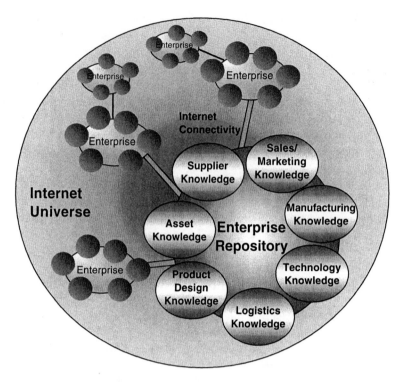

FIGURE 2.1 Internet knowledge connectivity.

4. They must be based on distributed relational database technology. Today's computing environment requires databases that are transparent to users both within the enterprise and anywhere around the globe.

5. They must provide for new ways of sharing information. The availability of cable modems, DSL, and wireless devices provides continuous connection through the Internet along with the capability of allowing virtually everyone to be a source of information storage and computing power to virtually everyone else.[16]

D. GLOBAL CHANNEL DYNAMICS

One of the key components in the development of today's e-business environment is the emergence of the global economy. During the concluding decades of the twentieth century, the end of the Cold War, the opening of markets in Eastern Europe and Asia, the proliferation of communications technologies, the speed of transportation, and the virtual integration of the world's economic activities have propelled companies, large and small, into the global marketplace at a dizzying pace. This explosion in international trade has been spurred on by a number of factors. To begin with, the maturing of global economies has enabled companies to view the remotest places on earth as potential areas for market development. The general growth of global wealth, the establishment of workable distribution systems, and the speed of communications have increased the world's appetite for products and services and spawned new market opportunities. In addition, strategies focused on leveraging the core competencies of business partners across the globe have provided radically new opportunities to expand processes and opportunities unreachable for individual companies confined within national boundaries. Finally, the emergence of the World Wide Web has enabled anyone, from anywhere, at any time, to access information and transact business without regard for the limitations of time or geography.

The potential impact of the Internet on global commerce is immense. According to Gartner Group estimates (May 2001), global B2B Internet commerce is on pace, despite the economic slowdown of 2001–2002, to total $8.5 trillion by 2005. In 2000 the value of worldwide B2B transactions surpassed $433 billion, a 189% increase over 1999 sales figures. Worldwide B2B Internet commerce is projected to reach $919 billion in 2001, followed by $1.9 trillion in 2002, $3.6 trillion in 2003, and $6 trillion by the end of 2004. While much smaller, the size of B2C revenues are still astonishing. According to the *Industry Standard*, global e-tailing is projected to reach $1.3 trillion by 2003. The magnitudes of such numbers indicate that global e-business is an irresistible force in today's increasingly Internet-based economy.

Based on such expectations, the world's leading enterprises are aggressively seeking to carve out their own space in the burgeoning global Internet economy. Some companies are trying to gain recognition as early leaders in global Internet business as part of their overall corporate strategies. Similar to the rush to establish bricks-and-mortar businesses in foreign lands, characteristic of the past, today's firms are eager to leverage e-business to lower procurement and inventory costs while tapping into new sources of revenue. And as global companies of the past have experienced, setting up assets is one thing: marketing to different cultures, understanding local political economies, developing structural and organizational backbones, and working with country-specific commerce and regulatory practices necessary to realize a global Internet strategy is another. Activating global Internet commerce will require close attention to the following points:

1. *Building effective channel alliances.* While the Internet renders a company vulnerable to competition from anywhere on earth, it also provides tremendous opportunities to implement collaborative e-business strategies to leverage the intellectual, material, and marketing resources of business partners worldwide to render penetration into far-flung markets easier and more cost-effective.
2. *Building global collaboration.* As the Internet links global resources closer together, Web-enabled companies are finding it increasingly easier to coordinate design, product manufacture, marketing, and distribution processes with international partners to establish "virtual" global enterprises capable of responding to any customer opportunity.
3. *Globalizing Internet Content.* Globalizing the Internet means being able to provide presentational content that is localized and personalized to meet the cultural, language, currency, commercial practices, local laws, and tastes of the customer. While e-commerce mediums originally were developed to be any-to-any, it has become increasingly clear that increased localization will be required to respond to global needs.

4. *Responding to national governments.* Changing economies and drawing the world closer together requires responding to various governmental and environmental issues. Commerce bodies like the World Trade Organization (WTO), the Global Trading Web, and others will have to assist governments to find consensus on global e-business trading practices. Governing bodies will have to arrive at policies that are consistent with national objectives, while at the same time provide international rules that foster the flourishing of the Internet economy.

5. *Development of global strategies.* No matter a company's size, the capability of the Internet to dramatically increase supply chain connectivity and radical improvements in logistics systems have enabled the prospect of a single, globally networked supply system that welds together Web-linked trading partners to generate the emergence of Internet *vortexes* pulling products and services from sources everywhere to fill the needs and desires of customers everywhere.

E. Logistics Dynamics

The pace of change driven by the expectations of the customer, the speed of product and service innovation, the emergence of global marketplaces, and the radical opportunities for collaboration and connectivity offered by the Internet have dramatically altered the structure and mission of logistics. In the past, logistics was perceived principally as an operations function concerned with warehousing, transportation, and finished goods management. In contrast, today's enterprise views logistics as a competitive weapon activating strategies that not only achieve delivered service and quality at the lowest cost but also enable enterprises to synchronize materials and information from one end of the supply network to the other. With the application of the Internet, logistics becomes *e-logistics*, and its role expands from a linear, serial transfer of products and information to the generation of single, scalable "virtual" supply networks capable of responding to dynamic sourcing, dynamic deployment, and real-time fulfillment by optimizing competencies and resources from anywhere in the supply chain.

e-Logistics can be described as a critical enabler of both e-business and e-commerce. Because it utilizes the integrative and collaborative capabilities found in the Internet to manage processes, e-logistics can be said to be directly a component of e-business. Because it can provide the technologies to execute Web-generated requirements for product fulfillment and supply channel information, e-logistics is a fundamental driver of e-commerce. e-Logistics provides today's Internet-enabled enterprise with the capabilities to cope with the following marketplace dynamics.

- *Fulfillment.* While Internet presentational content will grab the customer's attention and facilitate the buying experience, true loyalty can only be won when the product/service solution is delivered to meet expectations. The primary function of e-logistics is to synchronize supply channel resources to realize, as close as possible, immediacy of product/service delivery.

- *Visibility.* Supply network visibility enables real-time analysis and event management to direct the flow of materials and information up and down the value network. The goal is to provide channel logistics functions with a system to predict fulfillment process flow disruptions and offer corrective solutions.
- *Globalization.* Responding effectively to the requirements to produce and market goods on a global scale requires new logistics challenges. Applying Web-based solutions to logistics enables global companies to deploy resources from anywhere in the world to meet delivery expectations.
- *Supply Channel Optimization.* Perhaps the most critical objective of e-SCM is transforming efforts focused on optimizing a single node within the supply network to optimizing the network as a whole. By applying e-information enablers to logistics functions, virtual supply channels will be able to respond to market requirements at Internet speed.
- *Product Life Cycle Management.* As producers seek to reduce the time-to-market for new products, time-to-delivery for these products takes on added importance. e-Logistics provides value chain marketers with the capability to leverage Web-linked information to dramatically decrease the time between product development and market introduction.
- *Fixed Asset Reduction.* Today's enterprise is continually seeking to cut investment in distribution assets and reduce the proliferation of inventory throughout the supply channel. A fundamental objective of e-logistics is to utilize information about demand and supply dynamics whenever possible, as a substitute for inventories and physical handling.
- *Outsourcing.* Today's enterprise is constantly reviewing internal processes in an effort to eliminate non-core competency functions. e-Logistics facilitates business collaboration by linking enterprise requirements to alternative resources and competencies from anywhere in the supply network.
- *Value-Added Automation.* By providing for the real-time linkage of nodes of information across the supply channel, e-logistics decreases response times so fewer special shipments are needed, decreases work-in-process (WIP) costs, increases the velocity of time fulfillment, reduces returns, and lowers labor requirements.

While the objective of the old view of logistics was to ensure marketplace fulfillment for individual customer–company transactions, the goal of Internet-enabled logistics is to provide entire channels with marketplace knowledge exchanges that will facilitate joint decision making. As Web technologies proliferate, the real value in e-logistics will move away from the physical aspects of delivery mechanisms, to linking sources of network competencies to meet the heightening of customer expectation, product development, global trade, and supply chain collaboration.

III. PRINCIPLES OF THE e-BUSINESS AGE

Although the first euphoric phase of the "e-business revolution" has ended with not a few bankruptcies and a faltering economy, there can be little doubt that the realities of today's business environment will compel companies to renew their original e-business assumptions. What the shape of this deconstruction and reconstruction of e-business will be is, at this point, unclear. However, certain basic tenets are beginning to emerge. To begin with, there can be little doubt that the focus of e-business will migrate from building dot-com companies to measuring real profits from investments made in Internet applications. Second, the shakeout of B2Bs and B2Cs begun in 2001 will continue. Cybermediaries incapable of delivery and the growing reluctance of companies to participate in independent exchanges will doom all but the most solid of e-businesses. Third, companies are becoming more pragmatic in using trading exchanges. The somewhat idealistic view that companies would freely and openly collaborate with cybermediaries has given way to private exchanges dominated by the coercive power of mega-companies such as Wal-Mart, Target, and General Motors. Finally, on the positive side, there can be little doubt that e-business will expand. It will be more pragmatic and more centered on solving the real problems of businesses, rather than the original "seismic" revolution originally predicted. A few of the pivotal "principles" of the next round of e-business change are detailed below, beginning with definitions of some key terms.

A. DEFINING TERMS

The vernacular of today's Internet-enabled technical, infrastructure and strategic environment suggests that operating business in the twenty-first century will be significantly different in scope and management approach than what had come before. Over the past couple of years, business literature and discussion has been flooded by a host of new words and concepts that come not from new management methodologies but rather from the Internet. Terms such as ASP, B2B, B2C, CMC, dot-com, PTX, XML, and a host of other acronyms have now become part of the business vocabulary. The speed at which these terms and phrases have invaded and now permeate all serious discussion indicates how quickly and how decisively the power of Internet technologies has altered forever the traditional methods by which executives had organized the running of business. The list of acronyms at the front of this book provides an exhaustive list of the current acronyms in use today. Considering the seismic changes that continue to shake the technology and business environment, it can be safely said that this list will probably double in the next few years.

While it is beyond the scope of this work to provide a concise definition of all of today's Internet-driven acronyms and phrases, it might be useful to pause and define the major terms. Such an effort will clarify understanding and assist in understanding the body of the text to come.

1. e-Business

This term has become an inclusive phrase used to describe all of the business relationships that exist between trading partners driven by and operating with the Internet. This term includes all electronic-based transactions, documents, and fulfillment functions transferred through *electronic data interchange* (EDI) or Web-based mediums. The range of e-business content is almost unlimited and consists of activities that span the spectrum, beginning with market research, through collaborative product development, and ending with billing, payment, and channel transaction and data analytics.

2. e-Commerce

In the strict sense, this term refers to the process of performing transactions utilizing the Internet. It involves such actions as placing and receiving orders over the Web, as well as applications that provide visibility to what is happening in the supply channel. Once this data has been assembled, it would then be possible to both share data and execute decisions that would impact channel plans and execution activities.

3. e-Fulfillment

This term refers to the activity of physically delivering products and services placed in the network supply system through e-commerce transactions. Failure to execute on fulfillment was one of the most critical contributing factors to the destruction of most dot-coms during the years 2000–2001. Today, supply networks are expending considerable effort to perfect their Web-based service and delivery systems, to ensure that each Internet order is converted into a real profit. e-Fulfillment can be broken down into four critical elements. First, e-commerce customers expect on-line visibility of channel inventories and e-mail $24 \times 7 \times 365$ notification of order status. Second, personalization of the ordering process is important. Customers still want the same kind of services, such as gift wrapping, greeting cards, etc., they have come to expect from the retail environment. Third, faster cycle times are a given. Customers expect the same speed in delivery as they enjoyed during order entry. And, finally, e-fulfillment changes the traditional order profile. Instead of case lots and full pallets, piece picking is the norm.

4. Business-to-Business (B2B)

The use of the Internet applications that enable companies to sell goods and services to other businesses on the Net is referred to as *business-to-business* (B2B) e-commerce. There are several characteristics of B2B commerce. To begin with, B2B utilizes virtual marketplaces or clusters of buyers and sellers who gravitate together through targeted Web sites. The goal is to utilize a many-to-many approach to matching suppliers and customers that results in increased revenues and decreased costs while improving the customer buying experience. Second, the objective of a B2B marketplace is procurement and resource management, where companies use Web technology to streamline the buying process for production and nonproduction goods and services. Finally, B2B provides enterprises with the capability to integrate isolated supply chains to create extended collaborative e-business value networks that provide for a spectrum of functions, from one-to-one customer service, to joint product development, to order fulfillment and payment.

5. e-Procurement

This term refers to the automation and integration of the purchasing process by the application of e-procurement software and the growth of B2B trading exchanges. B2B exchanges, enabled by ERP or *application service provider* (ASP) exchange platforms, provide firms with the capability to implement new methods of ordering that have been able to reduce inventories and shrink costs by 50 to 70%. Exchanges enable select groups of trading partners to bid on goods and services, a method most appropriate for the liquidation of excess inventories and used equipment. e-Procurement is also facilitated by B2Bs reverse auctions and on-line catalogs, tools useful for commodity-type purchasing and MRO materials.

6. Business-to-Customer (B2C)

The use of a variety of Internet applications that enable companies to sell goods and services directly to the end-customer on the Net is referred to as *business-to-customer* (B2C) e-commerce. B2C consists of several dovetailing objectives: generating revenue by selling goods and services, building customer loyalty by offering consumers an individual, customized shopping experience, and developing repositories of customer data. Some B2C Web sites do not sell products at all. Their goal is to provide content and services that derive earnings from advertising and subscription fees. Finally, other B2C companies provide services that facilitate transactions between buyers and sellers. For example, UPS derives revenue from its Web site by providing logistics services that enable shipment and electronic bill payment between suppliers and customers. Today's most profitable B2C e-businesses seek to simultaneously sell products and services, build on-line content and communities, and reduce the overall cost of channel transactions.

7. Collaborative Commerce (c-Commerce)

c-Commerce is a termed coined by Gartner, the consulting and research group. c-Commerce is defined as a business strategy that seeks to utilize Internet technologies to enable closer collaboration of channel network partners. While consulting groups, software companies, and business seminars on c-commerce abound, the concept is still in its introductory stage. Today, the amount of collaborative activities is relatively small and the vision of a fully synchronized network of customers, manufacturers, suppliers, and service providers transferring critical supply chain information in real time is clearly years away. Still, the benefits of c-Commerce — closer and timelier contact with the customer, better channel inventory management, faster time-to-market, improved supplier synchronization, and increased revenues — have been realized by early adopters like Dell, Wal-Mart, and Hewlett-Packard.

8. Trading Exchanges

Trading exchanges provide for the creation of Internet portals combining transactions, content, and services focused on optimizing, synchronizing, and automating selling, buying, and fulfillment. There are two types of trading exchange. *Independent, public exchanges* are Web sites where buyers congregate to seek out the best deals for a specific industry from a wide range of suppliers. *Private exchanges* perform the same functions as public, with the exception that they are proprietary, driven by a single host or "hub," and membership is usually closed to trading partners. Recently, groups of large companies have organized themselves and their trading partners into *Consortium exchanges*. These large exchanges are private in that only members can participate, and, at the same time, are public in that members can freely trade with each other inside the exchange.

B. e-COLLABORATION IS AT THE HEART OF e-BUSINESS

Beyond all the hype of e-business models, today's Web-based technologies are truly enabling companies to enrich, to a degree never before possible, the relationships they have historically formed with their customers, suppliers, and business partners. e-Business tools have provided thousands of companies with the ability to remove unnecessary redundancies and costs from their processes, while permitting them to realize dramatic benefits in customer service and supply chain integration. However, similar to all techniques and management methods that focus solely on reengineering processes and promoting infrastructure optimization, the benefit is short-lived — as the value of the improvement slowly diminishes as competitors adapt to and copy the method — thereby neutralizing what once had been a source of competitive advantage. What many companies have come to realized is that, while driving short-term cost benefits, the real advantage of e-business applications is to be found in the dramatic opportunities the Web provides for the closer integration of supply network trading partners. Today, industry experts and business practitioners alike have come to see that the real value of e-business is not to be found in *automation*, but rather in the dramatically increased opportunities it provides for business *collaboration*.

1. Defining e-Business Collaboration

The term *collaboration* has become business's newest buzzword, in much the same fashion that JIT and quality management dominated discussion in the past. No one will disagree that collaboration is not a new idea, that collaboration among supply chain partners is necessarily good, and that enterprises simply cannot hope to be competitive without positioning collaboration at the heart of their business strategy. Problems arise, however, when an attempt to define collaboration is made. Like defining *quality*, collaboration can mean many things, depending who is saying it and the context in which it is being used. While the term describes an activity pursued jointly by two or more entities to achieve a common objective, it can mean anything from transmitting raw data by the most basic means, to the periodic sharing of information through Web-based tools, to the structuring of real-time technology architectures that enable partners to leverage highly interdependent infrastructures in the pursuit of complex, tightly integrated functions ensuring planning, execution, and information synchronization.

While the concept and content of collaboration is still in its infancy, companies have become keenly aware that pursuing closely integrated supply chain partnerships is critical to survival. The following points have surfaced as the main drivers.

- The relentless acceleration in the forces changing today's business environment — the power of the customer, global trade, Internet enablers, deregulation, emerging markets, rapidly diminishing product life cycles, and others — require all categories of business to be able to leverage these changes to increase competitive advantage. The faster the growth, the more dependent firms have become on utilizing the resources and core competencies of channel network partners to stay ahead, if not drive the power curve.
- Companies have always known that the more integrated and efficient the passage of information and the performance of transactions, the less the cost. As the level of collaboration technologies, even as simple as the facsimile, increases between trading partners, the more the cost of business declines and the capacity to respond to marketplace needs increases.
- The changes impacting today's marketplace have increasingly obsoleted the old strategies for creating value. Companies simply cannot remain inward-focused and dependent on historically successful product and service offerings. Business strategists must look to merge existing marketplace leadership with continuous innovation to enlarge the scope and scale of competitive reach or generate new competitive opportunities. Succeeding in this agenda means quickly gaining new efficiencies and capabilities possible only by collaborating with channel network partners.
- The increasing customer-centricity of the marketplace is obsoleting previous response strategies. Connectivity tools providing for the real-time visibility of market channel functions, such as forecasting, inventory availability, transportation capacities, and supply channel-driven capability-to-promise, will enable manufacturers to configure products and supply nodes quicker to respond more accurately to reduce supply chain waste and shorten lead-times. It once took 120 days to deliver a custom automobile. Today, thanks in large measure to its collaborative capabilities, Toyota can deliver the same car in three days.
- Finally, the assets and material, financial, and intellectual capital required of each business today to meet the needs of an increasingly global and volatile marketplace are gradually outstripping the capabilities of even the largest of companies. World-class human capital, as well as productive assets, may be far cheaper to locate out in the supply chain through collaboration than to develop internally.

While the above points emphatically reveal that businesses must diligently pursue collaborative relationships, it still leaves a precise definition of collaboration unformulated. The Gartner Group defines collaborative commerce as "the set of electronically enabled collaborative interactions between an enterprise, its suppliers, customers, trading partners, and employees" and divides the concept into three converging components: *business elements* consisting of bargaining power, ROI, relationship management, and complementary benefits; *technology elements* consisting of Internet and ERP/Relationship applications; and *human elements* consisting of trust, communication, and personal gain.[17] According to La Londe,[18] collaboration contains the following six elements: (1) mutual trust between each business partner; (2) sharing of information; (3) sharing of knowledge; (4) relatively long planning horizon; (5) multiple-level relationships; and (6) process for sharing benefits and burdens. Treacy and Dobrin,[19] on the other hand, divide collaboration into two spheres of ascending collaboration intensity. In the first can be found *technical* collaboration. Collaboration in this sphere ranges from no electronic connectivity, to EDI and Internet tools providing visibility to data across supply networks, to server-to-server links, and finally, to process management applications that enable true real-time channel information and transaction synchronization. In the second sphere can be found *business* collaboration. On the low end, forms of collaborative practices are at a bare minimum, and traditional competitive values dominate. From this level the degree of collaboration intensifies, beginning with increasing communication to facilitate joint operations, to coordination where companies in the supply chain use the competencies of network partners, to cooperation where channel partners work together as if they were a single company.

Prahalad and Ramaswamy[20] feel that the content of collaborative relationships exists on several levels as illustrated in Figure 2.2. In the first level, *internal focus*, companies may intermittently engage in collaborative relationships, when it improves cost and time or enhances customer satisfaction, but have minimal desire for sharing information with trading partners. Firms may utilize EDI or Internet tools for data transmission, but technology is not perceived as an enhancer to competitive advantage. Companies at level two, *transactional/informational collaboration,* understand that working closely with channel partners can dramatically shrink costs, improve cycle times, and enhance customer satisfaction by linking interchannel processes. Businesses at this level regard more complex applications of technology as essential, in order to network information about orders, forecasts, inventory levels, and capacities. In level three, *shared processes and codevelopment*, channel network partners seek to integrate individual resources and competencies to synchronize competitive functions, such as product design, demand planning and forecasting, and total channel customer management, to remove redundancies and rapidly deploy new customer-winning values. Participating firms will look to advanced technology capabilities to provide for real-time, integrating collaboration applications permitting the utilization of a common distributed database of channel knowledge. Finally, in the fourth level, *linked competitive vision,* collaborating partners will move into new dimensions of joint marketplace development, shared resources, and trust, to architect a common channel structure that is focused around the pursuit of a common strategic vision. At this level, companies will leverage highly integrated, complex technologies that provide for common applications and infrastructures, unified information access, and rapid knowledge creation and deployment,

As companies ascend the collaboration-intensity continuum, the level of cooperation and the deployment of technology tools become geometrically more complex,

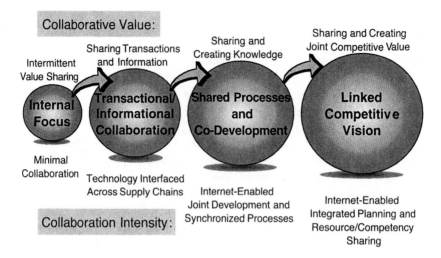

FIGURE 2.2 Collaborative levels. (Adapted from note 20.)

but so does the capability to jointly generate new forms of competitive advantage. Prahalad and Ramaswamy conclude their analysis by pointing out that each level of collaboration generates value through four critical drivers.

- The collaborative capacity of intra-company management teams grows in proportion to the level of collaboration intensity.
- As collaborative intensity grows, there is an exponential growth in the need for more complex technical and business infrastructures to create and extract value.
- While unifying intra-channel business processes are critical in effecting collaborative value, they are just the beginning of the possible collaborative opportunities.
- Strategic planners must constantly search for and implement new technologies and management methods if supply network collaboration is to continue to provide useable knowledge and new competitive insights.

2. c-Commerce at Manco

c-Commerce is a business strategy that does not have to be costly or highly computerized to succeed. Often the best approach to enrich existing business partner relationships is by applying e-SCM tools. Manco, a manufacturer of duct tape and other adhesives, embarked on a c-commerce program by selecting Ace Hardware, one of its best and largest customers and one with which they had a long-standing *vendor managed inventory* (VMI) program. In 1999 Manco leveraged its VMI program with Ace to pursue an initiative to determine whether the hardware giant would permit them access to their computerized inventory management system. According to Brian Bastock, supply chain director, Manco "approached Ace and asked if there was a way we could dial into their system so that we would all be looking at the same information, without it having to be translated from one system to another." After a short discussion, the idea was readily accepted by both parties. Ace agreed to set up Manco to view only inventory positions and forecasts, while Manco agreed to pay a license fee to the software supplier for the right to use the system. This straightforward c-commerce initiative has been a huge success. "Today," states Bastock, "we dial into their system through the Internet to receive forecast information, resolve exceptions, and plan promotions. It used to be that we learned about promotions when we got the purchase order, which often was too late to do any real effective cost-conscious planning." Besides sales events like promotions, the two companies also are collaborating on determining optimal product mixes and economic order quantities, while taking into account logistics costs. Recently, Manco has sought to broaden their c-commerce strategy by initiating a similar program with another large customer, Tru Value. Overall, Manco management is looking to expand their collaborative partnerships with other retailers and is counting on its ERP supplier to provide a framework for future expansion. According to Bastock, "We believe that collaborative initiatives have become a permanent part of how we go to market."[21]

3.   Working with the Realities of Supply Chain Collaboration

Despite the obvious need for supply chain partners to seek closer relationships with their network trading partners, often the best-intended efforts at collaboration fail or are blocked before they even have had a chance to start. While the popular press and scholarly articles extol the benefits of collaboration and describe the many advantageous forms it can take, in reality few businesses, let alone entire supply chains, have developed working collaborative agendas. According to Thomas Speh, a logistics professor from Miami University, companies seem willing to share information about long-term strategies, but are reluctant to share information at the operational, day-to-day level. "There is," he states, "a high degree of commitment but low scores on the trust factor." The successful collaborative programs that do exist are being driven by major companies whose revenues top $20 billion. "I'm waiting," continues Speh, "to hear about companies with $5 million and their commitment to collaboration." Donald Bowersox, a professor at Michigan State University, places a lot of blame on disorganization within companies. Many managers want to collaborate but do not know how or are uncertain about the legalities of information sharing. "Most corporations," comments Speh, "can't even integrate their own functions."[22]

According to *Industry Week's Fourth Annual Census of Manufacturers*, these sentiments appear to be painfully accurate. When a group of executives was asked if collaboration with suppliers and customers was considered in their businesses to be a critical factor driving competitive advantage, only half replied in the affirmative. As detailed in Table 2.2, the collaborative initiatives ranged from continuous replenishment to participation in new product development. Even more revealing were the technologies the respondents reported they used to support their collaborative agendas. When it came to the customer side, only 10% utilized Internet tools, 31% EDI, with a dramatic 61% reporting communication by nonelectronic means. The supply

TABLE 2.2
Collaborative Practices Implemented

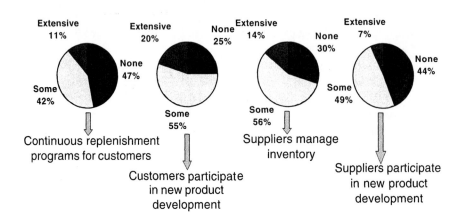

side faired even worse. Only 7% utilized Internet tools, 25% EDI, and 69% reported communications by nonelectronic means.[23]

Why is collaboration having such a difficult time being moved to the forefront of enterprise competitive strategy? Several reasons inhibiting the growth of collaboration can be detailed.

1. *Technology barriers.* There can be little doubt that the incompatibility of information systems across company and supply chain boundaries is a serious deterrent to shared communication. Without a means to effectively transact, view, and manipulate database information, even the simplest forms of collaboration can be frustrating at best. While technologies like EDI and open-systems tools like Java and XML can help to remove the barriers, most companies are miles away from legacy system conversions that will enable collaboration to become a strategic alternative.

2. *Security.* One of the constant objections to collaboration revolves around the issue of security. Much of this fear stems from the concern that channel partners might pass on valuable information to competitors. However, beyond real safeguards that need to be in place to protect computer systems and databases from unwanted intruders, this issue is largely a phantom. Companies have always transferred data among partners and there have been policies and standards governing document handling and intellectual property in place for decades. The real issue that renders today's collaborative initiatives so threatening is not the access to content but rather the *speed* by which information can be communicated. Releasing collaboration from the security threat can be solved by implementing the following process controls: confidentiality, integrity, authority, authenticity, and accountability.[24] Further, application-driven functionality providing traceability and tolerance compliance can also help in limiting

security breaches. After the terrorist attacks of September 11, 2001, observers predicted that the concept of collaboration would be severely set back as companies focused on securing their IT environments. Instead, the logistics disruptions and a weakening economy drove home even deeper the message that collaboration is critical to business survival.

3. *Trust.* The development of effective collaborative relationships normally takes years of good will and considerable investments in resources. Generating trust in collaborative initiatives requires business partners to set expectations up front about the dynamics of the relationship. The promise of collaboration is that trading partners will be able to leverage repositories of knowledge, competencies, and capital assets that will permit them to realize complex market opportunities. Still, despite the apparent advantages of collaboration, not all channel partners are ready to throw open their databases to even their best customers. For example, when R.R. Donnelley & Sons Co. developed a collaborative on-line system that permitted the company to integrate data from supply chains, customer inventories, design tools, and project-management software, subcontractors were more than suspicious. "They were concerned," felt David Oberst, director of Web applications, "we were creating a system to beat them down on price." It took time before contractors became comfortable with the system. In other words, Donnelly's trading partners had to learn to trust the intentions of their partner's on-line collaboration initiative. In many ways activating collaboration will require companies to change their business practices — and beliefs — before the full advantages of today's leading-edge collaborative tools can be seen as mainstream.

4. *Return on investment.* Too often managers confuse collaborative initiatives with process reengineering. Many attempt to determine the value of collaborative efforts by attempting to calculate cost and cycle-time reduction. Whether their collaborative effort has any value is measured up against the yardstick of increased *efficiencies.* Unfortunately, such performance standards lead to an under-leveraging of the true value of collaboration. According to Prahalad and Ramaswamy, such limited thinking results in companies missing the "biggest benefits of collaboration: elimination of redundancies, leveraging best practices from within, and innovation. Collaboration isn't constrained by lack of knowledge about strategic benefits, then, but internal IT limitations, managerial culture, and the nature on managerial performance-measurement systems within the company."[25]

5. *Corporate cultures.* Perhaps the biggest impediment to collaboration is corporate cultures. Forger[26] feels that managers and the workforce can be divided into four distinct camps regarding collaboration. In the first can be found the *Not-Nows,* who have made a conscious decision to ignore and mistrust collaboration. In the second camp can be found the *Nevers.* These types of managers are embedded deep in their departmental silos, have learned to survive by avoiding sharing information with anyone, and feel that collaboration is just another fad that will soon evaporate. The *Pretenders* can be found in the third camp. This group actually is

practicing some forms of collaboration, but sees it as a tool to wrench concessions out of partners. In the final camp can be found the *Real Deals*. These companies understand collaboration as a channel business process that benefits all network trading partners and not just an individual company. Creating a positive collaborative culture can be, for most enterprises, a massive uphill climb where some of the most cherished ways of doing business are challenged.

The implementation of collaborative commerce is a complex and open-ended process, in that the term spans a broad spectrum of management initiatives, technical communications standards, and various levels of trading partner capabilities and business processes. Effective c-commerce relationships must be able to utilize channel-wide customer relationship skills and technologies capable of supporting simultaneously multiple business models and communications media characteristic of trading relationships spanning supply chain systems. The goal is to achieve collaborative relationships that provide a seamless end-to-end process that can meet the business and technological requirements of each respective network partner. Table 2.3 details a variety of possible c-commerce initiatives.

C. Security, Trust, and Branding: Keys to c-Commerce Success

Collaborative e-business consists of an ever-increasing operations tool box that will reduce transaction costs, such as invoicing, bill payment, and general accounting, change the procurement of blue and white collar MRO inventories as well as production materials, revolutionize the placement of customer orders and the collection of analytics for market research, and transform human capital management. e-Marketplaces also have the capability to more efficiently match buyers and sellers, speed inventory transfer through the supply network system, and engineer new types of trading partner relationships. But realizing such opportunities will require a dramatic change in the way companies have traditionally managed often decades-old relationships and hard-earned feelings of trust and security in regards to sharing information, pursuing quality and conformance in the products and services transacted, and confirming the financial and competitive plans that lie at the core of every business.

The capability of supply chain partners to transition their often long-held, trusted business relationships from the "physical world" to the cyber-world of the Internet is perhaps one of the foremost challenges of e-business. In the past, trust and security were found in the depth of the relationships between trading partners whose physical manifestation is to be found in product/service branding. Branding is a marketing attribute that develops over time and consists of the continuous fulfillment of explicit and implicit claims of overall quality and usability of the product/service offerings made to buyers. Ford's automotive product lines guarantee their customers quality products that have stretched from generation to generation of car buyers. Home Depot's wide selection of high quality products and services make it the natural choice for the professional as well as the amateur house and garden enthusiast.

TABLE 2.3
Varieties of c-Commerce Initiatives

Area	Initiative
Demand Management	Configuration Management
	Catalogue Management
	Customer Relationship Management
	Contract Adherence
	Promotions Management
Channel Management	Vendor-Managed Inventories
	Collaborative Planning, Forecasting & Replenishment
	Scan-Based Trading (POS)
	Inventory Visibility
Demand Fulfillment	Third-Party Logistics
	Transportation Management
	Electronic Payment Processing
Manufacturing Management	Collaborative Product Commerce
	Product Data Management
Procurement	e-RFP/e-RFQ
	Catalogue Procurement
	Auctions
	Order Documentation Transfer

Amazon.com has built its branding image by providing e-shoppers with an exciting experience, a wide range of products, and high customer service. Historically, buyers have identified and certified products and suppliers by using a variety of information tools. When planning purchases, buyers normally consulted preferred supplier lists, directories, supplier marketing materials, market research reports, trade magazines, and industry conferences. It was the role of the buyer to organize this information into a useable database that could guide the sourcing, negotiating, pricing, purchase, and delivery process.

Today, the Internet has made accessible virtually every supplier and product from across the global. Unfortunately, e-buying exchanges have not only deluged buyers with a mass of information that often lacks timeliness, usefulness, and validity, but the sheer volume and the wide-range of trading conditions offered by e-suppliers has often threatened to destroy decades of patiently cultivated and negotiated relationships existing between buyers and suppliers. It has been stated earlier that one of the salient points of e-business is the change from one-to-many supplier relationships to many-to-many virtual trading communities. While e-business can thusly provide a more comprehensive trading environment, it has also accelerated competition as well and increased the likelihood of supplier substitution. As trading partners increasingly participate in e-markets and Internet tools improve interoperability, dependence on long-established trading relationships correspondingly will decrease. In fact, transactional parties may never have even heard of each other, much less have conducted business in the past.

While the lure of on-line markets seems to promise buyers access to an almost limitless reservoir of new, less expensive sources of supply and the capability to reach customers worldwide, there is also a dark side. The utilization of tools like shopping agents or "bots" that facilitate comparative e-market searches tend to commoditize products and services and promote price as the fundamental criteria in a trading occasion. The results can be disastrous. For example, thanks to an on-line auction, Ensign Corp. (Bull Ridge, IL) lost a bid for a contract with an established customer to whom Ensign had delivered about a quarter of a million transformers with near-perfect quality and on-time delivery for two years running. When the customer decided to put its contracts for bid on-line, Hugh Arnold, Ensign's president, sat with dismay at his computer on the day of the auction and watched as a stream of low-ball bids dropped from boarder line to the absurd. The bidding frenzy had degenerated solely into a battle about price in which Ensign's exemplary past performance had absolutely no impact. The bids that came in "were half of what the customer was already paying," stated Arnold. "I was shocked. I couldn't believe that anyone could manufacture things for that price or live up to the commitment. It became almost comical."[27]

Sorting out these types of issues will be critical for the e-markets of the future. Today's largest corporations are attempting to solve the problem by establishing private e-markets where they can act as the "channel master," inviting their direct suppliers to participate. Large companies such as Wal-Mart and Dow Chemical have established *private trading exchanges* (PTXs) where past relationships built on quality and delivery standards are seen as critical elements. However, all analysts are predicting that this is a temporary stage in e-business evolution, whose power will continually erode as more and more companies participate in greater numbers of e-markets. In any case, future e-procurement markets will have to include all the elements of traditional supplier buyer relationships — quality, service, support, trust — and not solely the criterion of price.

D. Rise of New Forms of e-Business

Traditionally, the supply channel has been perceived as consisting of three basic entities (Figure 2.3). The first component, *manufacturers*, is focused primarily on the development and creation of products to be used by industry or by the end consumer. Occupying a gateway position in the supply channel process, it is manufacturing's responsibility to make available those products demanded by the marketplace at the right time and in the right quantities. Somewhere between

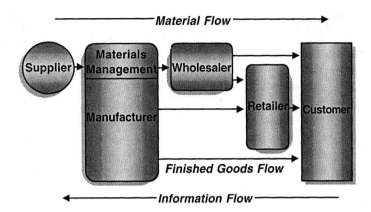

FIGURE 2.3 Supply channel structure.

manufacturers and retailers can be found the *wholesaler*. The traditional function of this component has been to serve as intermediaries, providing retailers with products originating from the manufacturer or providing direct sales to the end-customer. Wholesalers exist because of their ability to act as aggregators, assembling and selling merchandise assortments in varying quantities originating from a number of manufacturers. Finally, *retailers* can be considered as occupying a position at the terminal point in the supply channel. The essential function of retailing is to sell goods and services directly to the customer.

It has long been said that the channel entity that is most closely linked to the customer would be known as the "channel master" and exercise dominant control over the supply channel. In the past, supply channel power resided with retailers in consumer goods and the end-user in industrial goods. With the advent of e-business, this trend has within a few short years undergone a significant turnabout. The catalyst driving this dramatic reversal in channel power is, of course, the Internet. By combining the advertising and ordering capabilities of the Web, even the smallest of companies can present its products and process orders from anywhere in the world without the intervention of an intermediary to shoulder the cost of marketing, sales, and distribution. In addition to the growth of direct sales, the Internet has provided the opportunity for the birth of the electronic marketplace, which brings buyers and sellers together through auction sites, private exchanges, buyer/seller matching, and other functions. The Internet has provided all companies with the power to continuously reconfigure their supply networks, adding value and gaining dominant roles by leveraging the capabilities of radically new e-SCM business models.

Although this process of supply channel "disintermediation" has been identified as signifying the coming end of the traditional broker, distributor, and freight-forwarder, such prognostications have proven to be premature. While some are doomed, forward-thinking channel intermediaries have been building new competencies by using the Internet to "re-intermediate" themselves at critical points in their supply channels. According to AMR Research, the traditional linear, sequential supply channel will give way to the evolution of real-time, electronically connected networks, composed of the traditional players described above, joined by a number of nontraditional intermediaries. In the past, companies used vertically integrated business models to cut costs from the channel system, speed transaction throughput, and connect directly with the customer. In the "Internet Age," savvy entrepreneurs will utilize the Web to transfer non-value-added functions to channel partners, while continuing to cut costs and tightening their connection to the marketplace.

In contrast to traditional supply chains, where inventory flows down through the pipeline, node by node, and information from each node moves back up the channel, the new Internet-enabled cybermediaries may never own or physically inventory the product. Their role in the supply network will be to leverage the Internet, to perform matching of products and buyers or coordinating marketing and transaction processes among network trading partners. Take, for instance, the partnership announced in mid-August 2001 between Amazon.com and Circuit City. The partnership is designed to provide shoppers with the option of buying electronics from the Amazon Web site and then picking them up at one of 600 Circuit City stores or, by early 2002, having them sent directly to consumers' homes. Amazon, who will never touch the product, will be able to increase its consumer electronics inventories by several thousand items and will receive a percentage of the sales originating from the Web site.

According to AMR Research[28] at least four new e-SCM business cybermediary models are emerging today:

- *Virtual Manufacturers.* This channel component actually does not physically manufacture any products. Its role is to control product development, marketing, and sales, as well as coordinate customer service for its products. An example is Sun Microelectronics, which outsources the manufacturer of its electronic boards, while retaining control of all product designs.
- *Virtual Distributors.* This channel component neither owns any warehouses nor does it physically distribute any products. Its role is to control marketing and sales and to coordinate order management by using contract manufacturers, third-party logistics, and fulfillment service providers.
- *Virtual Retailers.* This channel component does not own any "brick-and-mortar" stores, but rather, utilizes the Internet to present to customers products displayed in on-line catalogs and other Web mediums. e-Tailers, like Barnes and Noble.com and Grainger, control the order management process, while relying on their own distribution capabilities, or those of partners, to execute order fulfillment.
- *Virtual Service Providers.* This channel component provides channel services without possessing any physical assets. Examples would include *lead logistics providers* (LLPs), that perform contract logistics functions, or *logistics exchanges* (LX), which provide exchanges for purchasing and monitoring logistics functions.

As time moves forward, it can be expected that new e-business models will appear. The goal of all such virtual business models is the ability to leverage the Internet to enable channel partners to eliminate non-core functions, while linking supply networks closer together by providing for the sharing of real-time information and decoupling the flow of goods and information from traditional supply chain flows.

E. IMPACT OF e-BUSINESS ON HUMAN RESOURCES

The birth of the "e-Age" was greeted by technologists as one of those rare events, an "inflection point," in the history of the world. The logic and possibilities of the Internet seemed to promise to all disciplines a world where information about anything could be accessed without the age-old constraints of space and time. As more than one technologist has pointed out, the dramatic explosion in Internet use appears to have validated this exponential explosion in communications. Previous breakthrough communications technologies had taken decades to reach critical mass. The typewriter was not commonly used for at least 29 years after its invention. The telephone, perhaps the twentieth century's single most important communications invention, took 35 years to reach 50 million people. By contrast, it took only four years for the Internet to reach the same number of users.[29]

However, as was the case with past technologies, drastic changes in individual usage do not axiomatically guarantee that the wider context of human society can change as fast. People can adapt to change more readily than institutions, like governments, education institutions, and companies. Internet usage may be expanding every day, but the ability of businesses to act on such an opportunity is limited by the capabilities of real companies to effectively utilize it. According to David Perry, CEO of Ventro, a company that builds and runs on-line exchanges, "It's a chicken and egg problem. Companies are, by definition, late adopters. In the case of B2B, there's all this work to do first. You need to make a machine-to-machine connection. You go to a rational buyer who says 'I love what you're doing here, this sounds great, come back and see me in twelve months when you've got all my suppliers on board.' And the supplier says the same thing." The bottom line is that few companies today have been willing to commit the millions it would take to retool their business for e-business. One analyst even felt that the 2001 recession actually gave CEOs the opportunity to postpone e-business initiatives while technology-related issues played themselves out.

The gulf that exists between the hype surrounding e-business and actual application can be seen in the 2000 PulseMark survey conducted by RSM McGladrey, Inc. and the National Association of Manufacturers (NAM). A sample of the findings is revealing. The survey found that 11.9% of manufacturers responding report purchasing MRO material from the Internet, while only 5.5% report purchasing direct raw materials, and 14.7% said they presently conduct Internet sales transactions. Finally, 12.7% of manufacturers report sharing new product development, production data, sales forecasts, inventory data, and other metrics across the Internet with their trading partners. Another survey conducted by NAM and Forester Research, Inc. detailed similar findings.

- Most manufacturers are in the early stages of on-line purchasing.
- Few organizations have seen cost savings from buying on the Internet, with only 26.6% of respondents reporting cost savings.

- Few organizations (7.7%) have seen the Internet significantly change their procurement processes.
- Only 9.4% of respondents felt that their preferred suppliers' on-line capabilities were satisfactory.[30]

Although it can be argued that manufacturing is perhaps the slowest business sector to adopt Internet practices, such surveys confirm that most organizations are in the early stages of leveraging the Internet for competitive advantage. As such, during the next couple of years the use of Web technologies will only appear to be driving seismic changes in business practice. In reality, the vast majority of Internet applications will be used to streamline existing processes and business models. Still, savvy executives will have to continually prepare their organizations to remain flexible and focused on wider e-business strategies, while providing a sense of real purpose and structure. The following principles should guide today's executive in planning and executing effective Internet-enabled strategies:[31]

1. *Continuously review the business landscape.* Periodically review the topology of both supply trading partners and the competition. Anticipate new collaborative relationships and identify possible strategic partners. Chart changes in competitors' business alliances, shifts in outsourcing strategies, participation in cybermediary activities, and adoption rates of Internet technologies.
2. Be prepared for competitive challenges from new business models. While remaining vigilant regarding e-business adaptations made by traditional competitors, executives will have to keep a sharp lookout for the rise of cyber-challengers, who can suddenly appear from unexpected quarters and wreak havoc on long-established supply chains. The fear of being "Amazoned" has kept many a CEO awake through the night.
3. Be prepared to venture into radically new organizational models. Threats from cybermediaries must be quickly countered by adoption of competitive e-business models. Many companies have counterattacked on-line challengers by buying, spinning off, or investing in an e-business.
4. *Plan for strategic e-business visions, execute tactical initiatives.* While it is critical that businesses begin the process of formulating strategic approaches to e-business opportunities, most companies simply do not possess the resources, executive leadership, or corporate cultures to materialize those plans. Instead, companies should focus on implementing limited, tactical Web technology tools that will enhance existing processes without requiring initially radical changes to the business.

IV. e-SUPPLY CHAIN BUSINESS TRENDS

Historically, the role of supply chains was to create value by providing product availability, broad product assortment, low price fulfillment, and marketplace information and financial flows. Today, enterprises of all sorts are recognizing that simply facilitating product delivery and accommodating customer requirements for greater configurability, flexibility, and choice are insufficient. Satisfying the customer also means that businesses must understand that e-business technologies have provided the marketplace with greater capabilities to control the buying process, alternative, nontraditional methods to make choices, and a variety of ways to meet requirements for goods and services that fit their individual business environments. Understanding this dramatic shift in the way business is to be conducted from an industrial to an information technology-driven marketplace can be distilled down to several critical "trends" impacting supply chain management. Responding to each of these changes constitutes the fundamental challenge to today's supply chain network, as businesses struggle to establish efficient, effective, and relevant product/service solutions for their customers.

What will be the landscape of tomorrow's e-business driven marketplace? An effective answer to that question, as witnessed by the dramatic convulsions in e-business marking the early years of the twenty-first century, is, at this point, unclear. However, the following trends can be said to be shaping the future of tomorrow's "e-world."[32]

A. CONTINUED MIGRATION FROM VERTICAL TO VIRTUALLY INTEGRATED ENTERPRISES

In the past, companies focused their efforts on structuring closely knit vertical organizations. It was reasoned that process value could be best attained when production and distribution functions were within the same corporate entity. The goal of the strategy was to maintain marketplace flexibility, while retaining industry independence and safeguarding product and process competencies that were considered as proprietary. All management activities focused inward and were designed to increase a firm's ability to be competitive on its own. However, during the past two decades or so, the following problems of the vertical integration model slowly began to emerge:[33]

   a. *Reliance on "fixed" industry structures.* Historically, companies tended to perceive the marketplace as composed of immutable industries. These closed business systems were inhabited by narrow customer definitions that, in turn, were closely contested for by bitterly opposed rivals who struggled against each other for local supremacy.
   b. *Presence of internal organizational functionalism.* According to prevailing organizational theory, companies were composed of narrowly defined functional "silos." Such organizations tended to focus on local performance measures and competitive values and resisted attempts to establish intra-enterprise cooperation.
   c. *Focus on economies of scale and scope.* In the past, businesses were structured to exploit the economies of scale and scope made possible by vertical integration and centralized hierarchical management methods. The objective was to engineer processes that produced low-cost, standardized products and services for a mass market.

d. *Narrow view of customer service.* Customers were dependent on their suppliers. Customers had little choice but to pick from a narrow range of product and service offerings with little configurability and had minimal impact on design and delivery utilities.

The problem with the vertically integrated business model is that it assumes that each company is an isolated, self-sufficient competitive entity and that forms of partnership with customers and suppliers are actually destructive to competitive health. In contrast, today's market-winning companies have come to understand that collaboration with supply chain members, sometimes even including competitive channels, is the only pathway to respond to the demands of the customer and the need for product and service agility and flexibility. Furthermore, as companies employ the widening band of Internet technologies to coordinate and enrich processes across trading partners, older business models fostering supply chain disengagement and independence have become obsolete. Whether it is designing a customer relationship management system or establishing Web-based trading exchanges, today's Internet-enabled enterprises have acquired tremendous advantage over their conventional industry rivals.

The truth of the matter is that the proprietary, linear supply chain systems of the past simply cannot provide the bandwidth necessary to enable the new world of electronic marketplaces and the explosion in products, dot-com cybermediaries, and facilitators, the way the Internet can and the world of e-business demands. Instead of a *physical* channel network system, governed by time and space, the *virtual* supply chain, driven by Internet technologies, provides channel trading partners with the ability to view events and pursue opportunities in real time, from anyplace on the globe. Using the Internet to build ad hoc collaborative communities of customers, suppliers, and support cybermediaries, today's e-business enterprise has become a network player, sometimes contributing core competencies, and at other times assembling the necessary capabilities from across the supply channel to meet marketplace expectations.

Instead of concentrating on incremental improvements in costs and market share, the virtual organization enables the development of channel-facing strategies that redefine fundamental assumptions about who customers are and how internal and channel partner competencies are to be shaped to preemptively seize competitive leadership. The ability to fully leverage the Internet-enabled organization resides around four basic premises:

a. *Executing Effective e-Business Strategies.* In today's widening Internet-enabled global marketplace, only those trading partners that can develop superbly executed collaborative e-business strategies will be able to hold onto the shifting sands of market leadership. Although core operations strategies will remain as essential barometers of internal enterprise performance, those companies able to muster the foresight, structure, and competitive will to constantly shape and reshape the supply chain network will be able to continue on the path to competitive survival.

b. *Building Effective e-Supply Chains.* The Internet has rendered obsolete the vertical organization and made it possible for companies to achieve a level of marketplace advantage only possible when webs of channel partners leverage the competitive strengths of each other for mutual advantage. In fact, it has become evident that market leadership belongs to those who are better than their competitors at creating and competing through closely linked networks of channel partners despite potential rivalries. On any given day, for example, Microsoft might find Intel to be a supplier, a buyer, a competitor, and a partner. The goal is not to dictate terms to channel partners through closed information systems and proprietary exchanges, but rather to develop unbeatable alliances linked by technologies that provide real-time visibility to joint sourcing and fulfillment needs and facilitate supply-web intelligence by increasing the speed of response, efficiency, and reliability of chains of collaborative businesses.

c. *Continuously Creating Product/Service Wrap Innovation.* As product life cycles decrease, the flood of new products explodes, and requirements for configurable goods and services increase, companies will migrate from a parochial concern with internal product/cost hurdles to a position that seeks, by closely collaborating with network partners, to tap regions of expertise to realize radically short development time-to-market strategies. Networked supply chains must continually focus their efforts on pursuing bold, trans-enterprise innovation that is targeted at providing customers superior solutions unattainable elsewhere in the marketplace.

d. *Engineering Competitive e-Supply Chains.* Conventional supply chain systems are unable to meet the demands of today's customers and deprive network partners of valuable efficiencies. For the most part, they can be described as slow, expensive, inaccurate, inconsistent, inflexible, non-scalable, and plant-centric. Conversely, Internet-enabled supply chains are capable of delivering superior customer service in ways that conventional supply chains cannot. Agile, Web-savvy businesses have been able to generate seamless coalitions of partners, that permit them to change the rules of engagement in mature industries (as Amazon.com has done in the book trade), redraw traditional industry boundaries (as W.W. Grainer has done in MRO equipment distribution), and invent whole new industries and marketplaces (as Microsoft has done in PC software).

Driving today's e-supply chain is the ability of trading partners to utilize information technologies to quickly create agile organizations capable of seizing marketplace initiative swiftly, decisively, and without notice to the competition. Such virtual value-added networks create havoc with their competitors who fear being "Amazoned" from unexpected quarters. They generate confusion and chaos, producing paralysis, shattering cohesion, and effecting the collapse of rival organizations who, though possessed of superior resources and initial marketplace advantage, cannot match the speed at which they effect change, exploit competitive weaknesses, and steal market advantage. Such is the strength of today's Internet-enabled supply chain and the capability of trading partners to vision opportunities for markets that do not as yet exist, rapidly converge resources and competencies as needed, and drive and sustain innovation before the competition.

B. e-Business Expansion Will Continue

In the years surrounding the turn of the new century, business readers were swamped with literature, from books and popular articles to scholarly case studies, declaring a virtual revolution caused by the rise of e-business. By mid-2001, as recession gripped the economy, the promise of a new business millennium had to undergo significant downward modification. The virtual destruction of many of the B2B *independent trading exchanges* (ITXs), the death of many upstart and promising dot-coms like Webvan, and the dramatic withdrawal of capital funding seen in the drop of the NASDAQ from highs in the 5000 range to the 1100s gave the whole e-business initiative the aura of unreality — a "bubble" frenzy that had burst. In reality, the hyperactivity that characterized that period was simply the opening phase of the introduction of e-business. That there were excesses and significantly unfounded assumptions cannot be denied. Equally, however, there can be no denying the fact that the Internet has changed forever the way business is to be conducted. Participating in the evolution of e-business and how it is to be utilized in their enterprise is now one of the fundamental tasks of every executive.

When the dot-com bubble burst, companies rediscovered the importance of developing and executing sound business principles. Success in e-business is more than just purchasing the newest Web software and setting up shop on the Internet. According to Mark B. Hoffman, chairman and CEO of Commerce One, "Long-term success in the New Economy requires a discerning approach to business management that combines sound business, IT, and supply chain strategies. The solutions you choose must enable your business model."[34] Companies espousing e-business must be prepared to reinvent their internal and supply channel environment as rapidly as e-business models themselves change. Often, experimentation will be necessary to identify the optimal business models, and how quickly organizations can adapt to change will dictate how successful they will be.

Achieving e-business success as the decade moves forward will require executives to scrupulously follow the following principles:

- *Understand customer needs.* Companies must be sure that the e-business solution they decide upon is in alignment with the needs (and networking capabilities) of their customers. Offering products and marketplace connections beyond the interest of the customer base is a sure way to ensure the e-business initiative will be stillborn.
- *Focus on the largest and most profitable customers.* Successful dot-coms have found that not all customers are equal. Expensive blanket marketing and service efforts focused on the general customer base have been found to be of little value in gaining and protecting customers from the competition. All e-business strategies need to start by identifying the narrow band of customers that constitute the highest percentage of sales. Make

sure that Web-based solutions start by focusing on optimizing and synchronizing business with these companies.

- *e-Business is a collaborative partnership.* An effective e-business strategy is, in essence, an on-line partnership. Companies must understand both their customers and their supply network systems to ensure they are adopting the right solution, which meets the immediate objectives of trading partners and also provides for continuous increase in value for the entire e-business community.
- *Track e-business performance.* An effective e-business strategy must be measured. This implies that Web-enabled companies must have the organization, processes, and systems in place to measure performance. Metrics associated with tracking total supply chain sales, shipments, stock-out, success of promotions, service call resolution, invoicing and payments, and ease of doing business are examples of critical metrics.
- *View the Internet as more than simply a method to perform electronic exchange.* While e-business functions do significantly simplify and automate transaction exchange, the real value of the Web is to be found in the collaborative relationships they make possible. Today's Internet solutions hold out the opportunity to streamline product time to market through collaborative design, remove inefficiencies from the channel network by shrinking inventories and facilitating throughput, and provide access to global suppliers. Internet-enabled enterprises and supply channel systems have the capability to create value by continuously aggregating content, buying power, transaction processing capabilities, and business processes and services that, in turn, attract more trading partners, expand channel value propositions, assemble critical mass, and generate profitability.
- *Simplify pricing and deal structures.* As Internet commerce takes hold, pricing will gradually migrate from fixed structures to price determined exclusively by supply and demand. In an e-market, in contrast to a physical market, all information about goods and services is available to all potential buyers instantaneously, with response measured in hours or days, not weeks or months. Competition for the customer will be played out through increased frequency of promotions, as supply networks go on-line, real-time, to counter pricing competition. Still, companies must be careful to temper the potential complexities in pricing by understanding that easy communication and information exchange, rather than dramatic promotions, will gain the highest customer loyalty.
- *Leverage new e-business services.* The expansion of e-business beyond transaction management will also foster the seamless integration of new business services, such as credit management, payment services, taxation, import/export documentation, shipping, and logistics. There are several challenges to this initiative. To begin with, many closed markets cannot use each other's services. Second, most enterprises operate business systems that are incompatible or cannot interoperate with each other. Finally, there is today a discontinuous collection of transmission standards and protocols further delaying e-information collaboration. e-Markets must

search for the proper mechanisms necessary to integrate information and services between each other.

- *e-Business success requires continuous breakthrough thinking.* The relentless speed of technological change requires today's market-winning supply network to continuously reinvent trading partner competencies, if they are to successfully respond to the constant morphing of customer needs. The best companies will look to the exciting opportunities offered by Internet technologies that allow whole supply chains to develop unique linkages with the marketplace. For example, consider the radical opportunities for competitive advantage offered by wireless devices for sales contact and analysis, order management, and information transfer.

Recently, industry analysts have projected the growth of e-commerce transactions to be enormous as the Internet becomes the technology of choice to do business. Gartner Group, for example, projects the figure to reach over $7.3 trillion worldwide by 2004. Whether these numbers have any reality is not important. What is significant, however, is that e-business will continue to grow and eventually dominate all marketplaces.

C. EXPANDING CUSTOMER RELATIONSHIP MANAGEMENT

Earlier in this chapter, the shift from measuring customer service by referencing internal corporate metrics to the engineering of supply chain configurations that fulfill the unique value propositions of each customer was documented. Supply networks possessed of the ability to convert product/service bundles into value-added solutions, through the application of e-business enablers that are simultaneously effective, efficient, and relevant, were seen as the competitive leaders dominating tomorrow's marketplace. The ability of supply chains to deepen and broaden relationships with their customers through e-business can, therefore, be established as perhaps the single most important trend guiding tomorrow's enterprise. Realizing greater levels of customer intimacy and collaboration requires each trading partner in a networked supply chain to be able to configure their collective resources relative to the requirements of each *individual* customer.

Supply chains capable of realizing these dramatic changes to customer management must be able to execute three fundamental objectives. To begin with, companies must recognize that the development of closely integrated relationships with customers takes place on several levels. Not all customers want or deserve the same overall level of service. Individual firms and their supply channel partners must be able to identify those core customers that closely match product and service offerings, and then configure nimble processes that enable the delivery of unique value-added solutions. By reviewing changing customer requirements and understanding their ability to utilize e-business techniques to search the marketplace to satisfy those needs, supply chains can ensure that they can continually match both their product/service offerings and their e-business capabilities to stay ahead of the competition.

Second, whole supply chain networks must be able to continuously enhance their customer relationship strategies by developing agile operations management techniques that enable them to anticipate and not simply to react to marketplace needs. This objective can only be realized when trading partners closely link customer information as it occurs at each point in the supply channel. Channel mastery will occur when the entire supply network can effectively respond to ordinary, unique, as well as unexpected demand circumstances. Such capabilities enable enterprises to capitalize on serviceability uncertainty to retain existing customers and to win new business. Some examples of operations enhancement necessary to achieve such objectives would be the empowerment of customer service functions to make spot decisions regarding product pricing, requirements for special configuration, and shipment from multiple nodes in the supply channel. Another example would be the strategic deployment of form and time postponement to enable supply networks to delay final product differentiation, in order to control inventory deployment and ensure the agility to satisfy customer-unique product configurations.

Finally, meeting the needs of today's customer requires that supply chains architect the blend of e-business techniques that best suites the needs of their marketplace. Building a strong sense of relationship, commitment, and involvement through the Web enables companies to understand the basis of gaining and retaining customer loyalty in a marketplace, where the competition is just a mouse click away. This objective can be attained by providing a quality product/service package, personalizing and humanizing Web-based interaction, revamping the service organization, and providing effective electronic linkages between the demand and the supply side of the channel network. Internet tools necessary to achieve these points consist of the following:

- Implementation of e-service functions that permit the customer to enter, review, and maintain order status and delivery.
- Close integration of Web sites with business system transaction back-bones.
- Product configurations that allow customers to automate the request-for-quote process, so they can easily pick the options they want on complex make-to-order and engineer-to-order products.
- Implementation of Web-based filtering techniques that permit companies to continually provide feedback regarding product/service quality as well as Web-site content.
- Utilization of electronic devices that provide customers with the ability to access the information they want without a PC. Futuristic options include cell phones, PDAs, pagers, smart cards, PC tablets, and even wireless laptops equipped with microphones and cameras.

Configuring robust relationships with customers is essential in surviving the potentially dangerous world of e-business. Competitors can appear out of nowhere with Internet-enabled tools that can rapidly deconstruct what was once a stable channel environment. Learning how to adjust to the changing competitive landscape driven by the potential destabilization of Internet commerce is the single most important requirement of today's executive. The goal will be to architect Internet environments that cause customers to build up dependencies on the Web-based solutions of their suppliers that can withstand the onslaught of incentive programs, price bidding, and radically new forms of convenience from upstart dot-coms.

D. INCREASED EMPHASIS ON BUSINESS COLLABORATION

Earlier in this chapter, the concept of *c-commerce* was introduced. Although it was stated that this strategic business model was still in its formative stage, there is no denying that utilizing c-commerce as the way to leverage supply chain partners will continue to grow. Although dramatic c-commerce paradigm shifts are unlikely in the next few years, research has indicated that companies have already begun implementing small collaborative projects to great effect. In a recent study performed in mid-2001, Jupiter Media Metrix revealed that company IS executives over the course of the next few years will be purchasing less B2B software and more collaborative-based software focused on facilitating such functions as CPFR, inventory level monitoring, and product design. Similarly, a survey conducted by Deloitte Consulting indicated that 60% of global business executives feel that c-commerce will become critically important to their firms for the immediate future. Table 2.4 illustrates the detailed findings from the Deloitte research survey.

Achieving c-commerce will require companies to achieve the following paradigm shifts. To begin with, c-commerce requires trust, convergence of strategic vision, and clearly defined objectives concerning the extent of interdependency and

TABLE 2.4
Survey of c-Commerce Initiatives

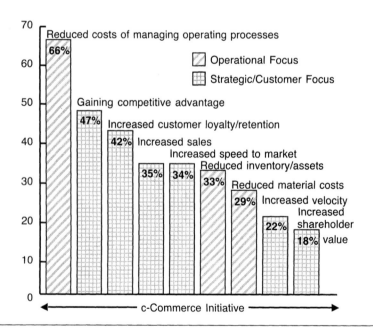

just what each party can expect from the collaborative initiative. For example, Janet Suleski from AMR Research cites an instance where a retailer asked a supplier to share information about production costs. What the supplier feared was the possibility that the retailer would use the information to squeeze margins even tighter. To avoid such fears, collaborative initiatives must preserve the delicate balance between partnerships that provide benefits to both parties and those that are decidedly one-sided. c-Commerce provides an opportunity for trading partners to optimize their supply networks and partner relationships to realize market-winning value, regardless of where the key competencies exist along the supply chain.

The second paradigm shift involves the establishment of business structures, cooperative values, and metrics that foster collaboration. Trading partner collaboration poses significant challenges, because of the wide spectrum of possible collaborative initiatives available, the variety of communications standards to be used, and the often uneven levels of competency and effectiveness of business processes found in the supply network. c-Commerce partners will need to define the rules and agreements specifying operational, informational, and financial linkages as well as responsible roles. In addition, while risk taking should be encouraged, the collaborative initiative will need to clearly define how benefits and penalties are to be apportioned across trading partners. One software firm[36] has developed a kind of rough value calculus that helps companies to identify high-return collaborative opportunities. The formula reads: "trust + communication + action = value, and value creates motivation for more trust." The goal is that, if firms can quantify what they are receiving from a c-commerce initiative, they will be more encouraged in their efforts to seek new collaborative partnerships with supply network partners.

The final paradigm shift requires companies to be prepared to be flexible in designing collaborative initiatives with their partners. Firms are often involved in managing multiple supply networks with multiple levels of relationships, ranging from individual buyers to strategic partnerships. As c-commerce initiatives mature, often the relationship between partners will accordingly change, driving the formation of new collaborative business models. A negative aspect of such changes is that firms might have to "de-construct" a partnership. It is advised, even though all collaborative partnerships are voluntary, that each e-commerce initiative contains a provision for a smooth and orderly exit from partnerships spinning in contrary directions.

In conclusion, while c-commerce can be a complex maze embodying organizational and structural change as well as evolving standards, tactical processes, and computerized software, it is clear that the marriage of e-business and collaborative partnership techniques is critical to sustain competitive leadership. Consulting firms and business analysts are as one in advising companies to minimize potential shocks to organizational and channel cultures, as well as budgetary hurdles, by first identifying a collaborative opportunity and working with network partners to define the goals, measurements, and technologies necessary to realize the greatest return on investment. In a marketplace still reeling from the damaging burst of the dot-com bubble and the after shocks of 9/11, enterprise executives must be careful to take steps toward c-commerce now to fight off potential challengers in the short run and to prepare for strategic utilization of e-business technologies as the decade progresses.

E. INCREASED IMPORTANCE OF LOGISTICS

As today's enterprise fights to utilize the Internet to transform the old concept of the supply chain to tomorrow's Web-enabled value chain, the importance of effective logistics functions will be dramatically increased. In fact, it can be argued that, as technological innovation expands, frontline companies will increase their lead over competitors by developing new e-SCM models that utilize radically new and differentiating logistics concepts to transform functions ranging from the acquisition of raw materials and services to final consumption, return, and recycling of product waste and obsolescence. Such models will trans-value the way orders are fulfilled in the supply network and optimize the emerging connectivity among supply chain suppliers, manufacturers, and consumers. What is certain is that, as written on the tombstone of many a consumer-facing dot-com, even the best engineered e-business can be disrupted, paralyzed, and even destroyed by logistics problems.

One thing is clear: companies that do not heed the requirements for revamped logistics functions are destined for failure. Take, for example, the very real crisis that was presented by a promising dot-com to North Carolina-based Tompkins Associates consulting firm. The company had estimated, in the autumn of 1999, that their Web site would be able to bring in 3,000 orders a week during the holiday rush, and that it could handle the load. By January 2000 the actual orders placed on the site were more like 3,000 a day, and company fulfillment had grinded to a virtual halt. Tompkins began to reverse the landslide into chaos by convincing management that the core competency of the company was not the Web front-end, but rather distribution's capability to ship each order when the customer wanted it. Instead of a Web-centric company, the dot-com was in reality the driver of a distribution-centric supply chain that depended on a convergence of technology and the cooperation of channel partners to remain competitive.[37]

The advent of e-business will dramatically reshape the way logistics management has been traditionally conducted and can be seen in the below four critical movements:

- *Deconstruction.* The requirements for increased logistics agility to meet the needs of e-fulfillment systems will require the reformulation of traditional logistics and the creation of radically new products and services. Transportation selection and routing will increasingly depend on real-time pan-channel information systems with the goal being the nearly 100% utilization of supply network assets. Overall, logistics systems will become leaner, with assets such as tractors, trailers, rail systems, air transport, and warehouses functioning at optimum capacity.
- *Dematerialization.* The speed, accuracy, and availability of e-information will similarly increase the throughput of inventories through the supply chain. The widening utilization of SCM systems, collaborative forecasting and planning, automated *point-of-sale* (POS), and *advanced planning*

systems (APS) will enable a close linkage of demand and supply that will drive down inventory levels and reduce the need for warehouse space. The result will be logistics systems capable of handling shorter cycle times, smaller orders, and more responsive supply networks.

- *Disintermediation.* As the Internet and more agile logistics systems enable manufacturers to get closer to their customers, traditional channel intermediaries will be eliminated from the supply chain. As the supply chain is gradually delayered, those "cyber-intermediaries" that survive will focus on utilizing Internet capabilities to perform matching of products and buyers and executing marketing and inventory transaction functions for network trading partners. Traditional *third-party logistics service providers* (3PLs) will transition from a focus on reducing their customers' costs to value creation through the use of Internet technologies. In fact, 3PLs will gradually metamorphose to *dot-com lead logistics providers* (.comLLPs) capable of performing not only traditional functions, but also collaborative demand planning, network logistics capacity optimization, e-fulfillment, e-logistics sourcing, and B2B mediation.

- *Deverticalization.* As logistics functions are increasingly globalized, sourced, and optimized, from the standpoint of the entire supply channel network, logistics as a core competency will increasingly migrate from the preserve of individual companies to outsourced functions. Logistics objectives centered on the perspectives of a single network player will no longer be sufficient for supply channel success. The Internet-enabled supply chain will only be as nimble and agile as its slowest-moving networked business node.

V. SUMMARY AND TRANSITION

When future business historians look back to the early years of the twenty-first century, they will undoubtedly characterize the period as one of radical change in the way companies were run, how products were developed, produced and distributed, and how they communicated information and collaborated with one another. When they turn to investigate the guiding management principles of business, they will unquestionably point to the fusion of SCM and the collaborative power of the Internet. Previously, enterprises had focused their energies on organizing and optimizing the functions to be found *within* the organization. SCM, on the other hand, provided enterprises with a management method to work with their supply chain partners who existed *outside* of the business. SCM enables whole supply networks to respond to the dynamics detailed above, by providing the management strategies necessary to transform individual companies from isolated, internally focused producers of goods and services to active participants in value chains, capable of providing uniquely configured solutions through agile, scalable productive functions capable of evolving as the needs of the marketplace change.

When combined with Internet technologies, the capabilities of SCM were radically transformed. e-SCM has enabled companies to engineer agile organizations that are capable of utilizing the competencies and resources of supply partners everywhere, at any time, through the establishment of Web-based systems that provide for the real-time connectivity and instantaneous visibility of events and decision-making across the global network. e-SCM enables whole channel systems to develop true collaborative relationships and synchronize the entire channel network into a single marketplace resource providing a seamless response to the customer.

Making e-SCM happen requires companies to keep the following principles of the Internet-business age in mind:

1. *Understand the culture and mechanics of today's e-business-driven environment.* Simply put, what does e-business enable enterprises to do today that they could not do in the past? Solving this problem requires knowledge of both today's business environment and the capabilities of current technology.

2. *The continuing shift to buyer power will drive the evolution of e-business.* The Internet puts the buyer in control of the process by allowing customers to conduct business anywhere, all the time. By eliminating the constraints of time and place, e-business provides any buyer, whether large or small, with an ever-widening array of choices, access to more information, and greater power over the transaction.

3. *Business collaboration is the key to the new economy.* Companies acting on their own cannot possibly meet the competitive challenges of today's marketplace. Supply chain collaboration provides the ability to integrate what the market values most with the productive resources of supply partners to create — quickly and with total quality — the configured, personalized product/service solutions demanded by the customer. How companies are able to utilize new on-line business models and leverage collaborative relationships is essential to doing e-business.

4. *The development of e-business requires thoughtful strategies.* When the dot-com craze of the early 2000s struck, it was perplexing to understand how whole companies were founded (and stratospherically financed!) on a strategy that sought purely to gather databases of customers. Quality was measured only in terms of Web site design and the volume of traffic. Failure occurred because e-business is more than just owning the whole customer — it is also satisfying the customer by meeting their expectations for products and services.

In the next chapter the discussion shifts to detailing the architecture of e-SCM systems. Much has been said about the importance and management philosophies of e-SCM and e-business. Chapter 3 will attempt to outline a functional model that will assist in delayering today's e-SCM business systems. The goal is to depict the convergence of e-business capabilities with the system elements of enterprise management and to offer a working model of e-business processes described in the remainder of the book.

ENDNOTES

1. Quoted in "Research Indicates That…," *Integrated Solutions,* May 2001, 30.
2. Trebilcock, Robert, "Welcome to e-World," *Supply Chain Yearbook, 2001,* Cahners, 2001, 87.
3. Taylor, David and Terhune, Alyse, *Doing E-Business: Strategies for Thriving in an Electronic Marketplace,* John Wiley, New York, 2001, 1.
4. Editors, "Ideas & Trends in Supply-Chain Management," *Global Logistics and Supply Chain Strategies,* 5, 4, 2001, 14.
5. Callaway, Erin, "B2B Exchange Mania!," *Managing Automation,* 15, 5, 2000, 29.
6. Weston, Rusty, "E-Business Revolution: The Battle Rages On," *InformationWeek,* June 11, 2001, 136.
7. Hirschfeld, Rob, "Where Have All the Dot-Coms Gone?," *Midrange Enterprise,* 5, 4, 2001, 42.
8. Downes, Larry and Mui, Chunka, *Unleashing the Killer Apps: Digital Strategies for Market Dominance,* Harvard Business School, Boston, 1998.
9. Fingar, Peter, Kumar, Harsha, and Sharma, Tarun, *Enterprise E-Commerce,* Meghan-Kiffer Press, Tampa, Florida, 2000, 23.
10. Quoted in Murphy, Jean V., "Customer-Driven Supply Chains Begin with Real-Time Visibility," *Global Logistics & Supply Chain Strategies,* 5, 3, 2001, 41.
11. Fleischaker, Celia, "e-Customers: How the Internet is Changing the Way you Do Business," *Midrange ERP,* 4, 5, 2000, 46.
12. Fingar, Harsha, and Sharma, 27.
13. Paul, Lauren Gibbons, "The E-Business Frontier, " *Managing Automation,* 15, 8, 2000, 34.
14. This point is stressed by Fingar, Harsha, and Sharma, 65.
15. Raisch, Warren D., The E-Marketplace: Strategies for Success in B2B Commerce, McGraw-Hill, New York, 2001, 166.
16. See the discussion in Taylor and Terhune, 248.
17. Sgarioto, Mary Stearns, "Trust Drives c-Commerce," *Manufacturing Systems,* 19, 6, 2001, 14.
18. La Londe, Bernard, "Connectivity, Collaboration, and Customization: New Benchmarks for the Future," in *Achieving Supply Chain Excellence Through Technology,* 3, Anderson, David L., ed., Montgomery Research, San Francisco, 2001, 168.
19. Treacy, Michael and Dobrin, David, "Make Progress in Small Steps," *Optimize Magazine,* December 2001, 53–60.
20. Prahalad, C.K, and Ramaswamy, Venkatram, "The Collaboration Continuum," *Optimize Magazine,* November, 2001, 31–39.
21. Murphy, Jean V., "Forget the 'E'! C-Commerce is the Next Big Thing." *Global Logistics and Supply Chain Strategies,"* 5, 8, 2001, 32.
22. These comments regarding the state of SCM collaboration were made by a panel of experts at the October 2001 Council of Logistics Conference.
23. The results of the survey were published in "Rocky Road to Collaboration," *Supply Chain Technology News,* 3, 5, 2001, 55.
24. For more information consult Fodor, George M., "Global Collaboration: Untying the Regulatory Knot," *Software Strategies,* 6, 7, 2001, 18–21.
25. Prahalad and Ramaswamy.
26. Forger, Gary R., "The Problem with Collaboration," *Supply Chain Management Review,* 5, 6, 2001, 90–91.

27. This story is found in Callaway, 32.
28. Larry Lapide, "The Innovators Will Control the e-Supply Chain," in *Achieving Supply Chain Excellence Through Technology*, 3, Anderson, David L., ed., Montgomery Research, San Francisco, 2001, 186.
29. These facts are detailed in Taylor and Terhune, 115–116.
30. The two survey have been detailed in Briscoe, Scott, "Industry Watch," *APICS: The Performance Advantage*, 11, 3, 2001, 2.
31. These points have been summarized from Taylor and Terhune, 120–123.
32. Some of these trends were identified by Bowersox, Donald J., Closs, David J., and Stank, Theodore P., "Ten Mega-Trends that will Revolutionize Supply Chain Logistics," *Journal of Business Logistics*, 21, 2, 2000, 1, PriceWaterhouseCoppers, "Supply-Chain Management is in the Chips," *Supply Chain e-Business*, 12, 1, 2001, 14, and Edmonds, David B., "Supply Chain Revolution is in Your Hands," *Inbound Logistics*, 20, 11, 2000, 70.
33. This section has been summarized in part from Ross, David F., *Competing Through Supply Chain Management*, Chapman & Hall, New York, 1998, 18 – 19.
34. Nittler, Mark L., "Get Ready for an e-Marketplace Explosion," *Supply Chain Management Review Global Supplement*, July/August 2001, 5.
35. These factors have been identified by Taylor and Terhune, 21.
36. This management formula is detailed in *Ibid.*, 40.
37. Scarborough, Jennifer, "Information is Money," *Transportation and Distribution*, 41, 5, 2000, 25.

3 Constructing the e-Business Model: Exploring the Anatomy of Today's e-Business Solutions

The origins and continuous development of the electronic supply chain management (e-SCM) concept are directly dependent on the enormous breakthroughs that have occurred in *information and communications technologies* (ICT) over the past decade. While it is true that commercial computer systems have been available for over 40 years, it has only been in the past 15 years or so that computers have been able to expand beyond the boundaries of their own architectures to literally "talk" with one another. Until fairly recently, programs, data, and information were confined to the four walls of the business. Today, radical advancements in hardware architecture, programming languages, and communications devices have enabled enterprises to engineer systems that allow business partners to peer, as if through a portal, into once inaccessible databases, pass documents freely back and forth without concern for the constraints of time and distance, and interactively enter data, verify information, and assemble real-time networks unencumbered by proprietary systems and software.

In fact, the mechanics of almost all of the management and operational aspects of e-SCM discussed in this book — the ability to network geographically dispersed productive and information generating processes, the integration of supply chain strategies and operations, communications technologies providing connectivity between enterprises, planning systems that facilitate the transfer of demand and inventory data across the channel pipeline, and others — would be impossible without the enabling capabilities of today's ICT systems. SCM, coupled with the power of connective technologies, is such a potent competitive and productive force because it is inherently intertwined with the networking power of today's information and communications systems. e-SCM and ICT are technology correlatives: as management applications and ICT tools expand, there can be little doubt that the integrative and informational capabilities of each will be reciprocally enhanced, providing ever fresher application and strategic perspectives.

In this chapter the systems foundation of e-SCM will be explored. The chapter begins with an overview of the enterprise systems governing the *internal* transactional and reporting functions residing at the core of the business. Following, the discussion shifts to a review of business-to-business computing, beginning with *electronic data interchange* (EDI) and continuing with an in-depth review of the four phases of Internet commerce. Beginning with the utilization of the Internet for marketing, the chapter goes on to detail Web applications targeted at activating e-commerce possibilities with customers and integrating supplier networks and reviewing the enormous possibilities available for e-collaboration and the generation of real-time, agile, and scalable supply chains. The chapter concludes with a brief review of the integrative architectures necessary to assemble into a single framework the mixture of ERP-type applications, *business-to-business* (B2B) and *business-to-customer* (B2C) point solutions, and business processes and workflows.

I. ENTERPRISE SYSTEMS FOUNDATIONS

Since the early 1950s, companies have looked to the computer to drive the collection, computation, dissemination, and decision-making power of business information. The requirement was straightforward and clear: how to capture and utilize the information that is generated by the interplay of demand and supply, as it flows through the enterprise out to the customers and suppliers, who operate on the borders of the business. In the beginning, the first computerized applications for such areas as payroll, general ledger, customer billing, and inventory, were stand-alone systems, each having its own application logic, database, and user interface. While automating time-consuming clerical tasks, the value of these systems was limited to the specific business areas they were designed for. They were useless when it came to coordinating activities across different departmental functions.[1]

By the late 1970s, business system software companies began to offer solutions that increasingly focused on linking departmental functions around a common database. Beginning first as *manufacturing resource planning* (MRP II) and then *enterprise resource planning* (ERP), these systems were an adaptation and refinement of earlier computerized applications. Today, the theory and practical use of ERP-type systems have so transcended their origins that it would be more appropriate to call them *enterprise business systems* (EBS). Whether "homegrown" or purchased from a software developer, applications originating in these systems support a wide spectrum of businesses, from manufacturers to nonprofit organizations, from universities to government agencies.

According to one group of experts,[2] the most significant aspect of an effective EBS can be found in its ability to "organize, codify, and standardize an enterprise's business processes and data." The goal of the EBS is to optimize an enterprise's *internal* value chain by integrating all aspects of the business, from purchasing and inventory management to sales and financial accounting. By providing a common database and the capability to integrate transaction management processes, data is made instantaneously available across business functions, enabling the visibility necessary for effective planning and decision-making. In addition, by providing for information commonality and integration, an EBS eliminates redundant or alternative information management systems and reduces non-value-added tasks, thereby dramatically impacting a company's productivity.

There are several other benefits gained by implementing an EBS. As companies continually grapple with engineering continuous change, many project strategists are looking to the suite of "best practice" process designs embedded in today's EBS business function work flows. While the software should be flexible enough to fit the business, often existing operating processes are ill-defined or obsolete, and the construction of new processes are facilitated by building them around the capabilities of resident business applications. Finally, as the basis of business changes to meet new challenges, companies with standardized processes driven by an EBS are more adaptable to change. Paradoxically, as Davenport points out,[3] "Standardization can lead to increased flexibility." A single, logically structured, and common information system platform is far easier to adapt to changing circumstances than a hodgepodge of systems with complex interfaces linking them together.

A. EBS: THE "BACKBONE" OF THE ENTERPRISE

While it is true, as will be discussed later, that today's EBS architecture has been expanded to include *customer relationship management* (CRM), *supply chain management* (SCM), and Web-based tools either embedded in the software or capable of "bolting" to best-of-breed point solutions, its primary role is to serve as the hub or the "backbone" of the enterprise's information infrastructure. An effectively implemented and utilized EBS links the different functions of the business, drives continuous improvement and process efficiency and effectiveness, provides the mechanism to support company strategies, and enables the pursuit of e-business technologies.

As illustrated in Figure 3.1, an EBS can be described as having two major elements: the system architecture and up to eight tightly integrated business modules. The system architecture determines the technical component of the system. In the narrow sense, EBS architecture refers to the hardware configuration, programming languages, graphic presentation, document output capabilities, and database designs available in the system. In a wider sense, architecture refers to the choice of how the EBS is assembled. It can be composed of a homogenous, fully integrated business software system that, in today's software environment, will include PC-based, memory-resident tools, such as *advanced planning and scheduling* (APS) and *supply chain management* (SCM), as well as e-commerce functions. Or, companies may elect to assemble a best-of-breed portfolio model linking third-party point solutions, such as *customer relationship management* (CRM), to a homegrown or previously implemented packaged solution.

The second element of an EBS is the array of eight possible business applications that an enterprise might deploy. The eight applications are described as follows: customer management, manufacturing, procurement, logistics, product data, finance, asset management, and human resources. Depending on the nature of the business, an enterprise may utilize some or all of the modules. For example, the EBS of a manufacturing company that performs distribution functions will have all eight modules activated. A wholesaler would have all except for manufacturing related

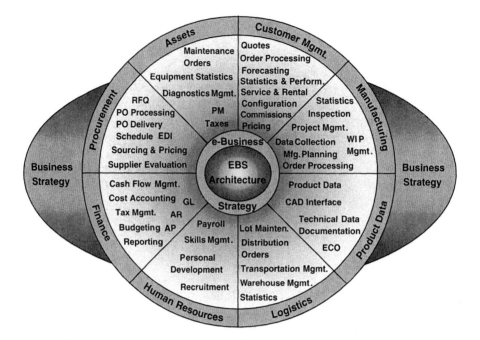

FIGURE 3.1 EBS backbone.

functions. A dot-com catalogue business would most likely have customer management, asset, human resources, finance, and perhaps procurement and logistics functions. Regardless of the business environment, every company will at least have to
install customer service, finance, and asset modules. These core functions would be
difficult to outsource without losing corporate integrity. A description of each of the
eight modules is as follows:

- *Customer management.* The primary role of this module in an EBS is to
  provide access to the presentation screens that enable order entry, order
  promising, and open order status maintenance. Order entry and ongoing
  service maintenance is the gateway to the sales and marketing database.
  Second, this module should provide the data necessary to perform real-
  time profitability analysis to assist in calculating costs, revenues, and sales
  volumes necessary for effective quotation and ongoing customer maintenance. Third, a well-designed EBS will provide marketers with tools to
  design sophisticated pricing schemes and discount models. In addition,
  the software should permit the performance of miscellaneous functions
  such as order configuration, bonus and commissions, customer delivery
  schedules, global tax management, customer returns, and service and
  rental. Finally, the customer database should be robust enough to permit
  the generation of sales budgets for forecast management and the generation of statistical reporting illustrating everything from profitability to
  contributing margins analysis.

- *Manufacturing.* Functions in this module comprise most of the foundation applications in the suite of a modern day EBS. Originating as a bill of material (BOM) processor, this module has been enhanced over the decades to include MRP processing, manufacturing order release, work-in-process (WIP) management, cost reporting, and overall shop floor control. A critical integrative aspect is the real-time linkage of demand to supply management facilitating order-to-production and WIP modeling while promoting real-time available-to-promise (ATP) to assist in customer order management. In addition to these basic tools, today's EBS manufacturing module also contains functionality for activities such as inspection, project management, capacity/resource management, and the compilation of production statistics. Finally, advances in technology have enabled the configuration of basic EBS applications with "bolt-on" data collection devices and advanced planning and optimizing software.

- *Procurement.* In today's business climate the ability to effectively integrate procurement requirements with a variety of supplier management concepts and technology tools is one of the most important components of an effective EBS. Although much press has been given to Web-based B2B technologies, basic management of procurement requires a close integration with internal MRP and *maintenance, repair, and operations* supplies (MRO) systems. Today's EBS contains robust functionality to facilitate purchase order processing, delivery scheduling, open order tracking, receiving, inspection, and supplier statistics and performance reporting. In addition, detailed *requests for quotation* (RFQs) must be available that tie back to customer demands and extend out to supplier management, negotiation, and pricing capabilities. Finally, the system architecture must include *electronic data interchange* (EDI) capabilities.

- *Logistics.* The ability to link in real-time logistics functions to sales, manufacturing, and finance is fundamental to competitive advantage in the twenty-first century. Today's EBS must provide the mechanism to run the internal supply chain of the business as well as provide the necessary connectivity to remote trading partners located on the rim of the supply network. Critical tools in the module center on distribution channel configuration, warehouse activity management, channel replenishment planning and distribution order management, and the generation of distribution, asset, and profitability reporting. Also, of growing importance is the integration of EBS functions with "bolt-on" warehouse and transportation management systems, as well as applications supporting Web-based customer and supply chain management systems.

- *Product data.* At the core of manufacturing and distribution information systems reside the databases describing the products that they build and distribute. Often considered highly proprietary, these databases contain data ranging from engineering descriptions to details concerning cost, sources of acquisition, planning data, and product structure details. Besides obvious uses for inventory and manufacturing planning and shop floor management, these databases are critical for marketing product life cycle management analysis and costing, engineering product introduction, and financial reporting and analysis. As the speed of time-to-market and ever shortening product life cycles accelerate, progressive companies have been looking to channel partners to implement collaborative technologies through the Internet that can link in real-time *computer-aided design* (CAD) and design documentation in an effort to compress time out of development, introduction, and phaseout of products and services.

- *Finance.* Without a doubt, one of the strong-suites of an EBS is its ability to support effective management accounting. In fact, one of the criticisms leveled at EBS is that it is really an accounting system, requiring everyone in the business to report on an ongoing basis each transaction they perform with 100% accuracy. Today's financial applications provide for the real-time reporting of all transaction information originating from inventory movement, accounts receivable, accounts payable, taxes, foreign currency, and journal entries occurring within the enterprise. The more timely and accurate the posting of data, the more effective are the output reports and budgets that can be used for financial analysis and decision-making at all levels in the business.
- *Assets.* Effective control of a company's fixed assets is essential to ensuring continuous planning of the productive resources necessary to meet competitive strategies. EBS databases in this module center on the establishment of equipment profiles, diagnostics and preventive maintenance activities, and financial tracking.
- *Human resources.* The final module composing a modern EBS is the management of an enterprise's people resources. Functions in this area can be broken down into two main areas. The first is concerned with the performance of transaction activities, such as time and attendance reporting, payroll administration, compensation, reimbursable expenses, and recruitment. The second is focused on the creation of databases necessary to support employee profiles, skills and career planning, and employee evaluations and productivity statistics.

B. CRITICISMS OF EBS

Over the past couple of years, much criticism has been leveled at the EBS concept. Some of the arguments center on the disruptive impact of Internet technologies. It is argued that the Internet signals a categorical inflection point in business computing, and what has come before it is by definition obsolete. It is envisioned (because it does not yet exist!) that Internet applications will become powerful enough not only to provide for external connectivity, but also to drive transactions to another application that, in turn, will drive it to the next, and so on, negating EBS's prime role as an enterprise information integrator.

Such arguments, however, flounder on several counts. To be begin with, even pure-play dot-coms know that at the bottom of the transaction chain lie the business functions that must produce, inventory, cost, warehouse, and transport product. The transaction side of the business is what today's EBS does the best, and companies that feel they can do without it will suffer the fate of so many dot-coms during the early 2000s that forgot that the attribute that wins the customer is delivery of the product, and not the elegance of the ordering process. A company may take the alternative of outsourcing EBS functions, but they can not outsource them all! Managing core functions will require even the most "virtual" of enterprises to maintain some EBS functionality.

Despite the obvious benefits, implementing an EBS is not without risk. Over the past 25 years both the popular press and business system folklore are replete with horror stories of EBS implementation failures. While offering a broad band of opportunities, unprepared companies have encountered a host of problems.

- *Change management.* Perhaps the most difficult aspect of implementing a full or partial EBS is the dramatic element of organizational and cultural change that many companies must undergo on the road to installation. Old work habits, timeworn organizational rules, departmental turfs, and other workday patterns are severely stressed as the entire enterprise must learn how to work as a single team, utilizing a single data base to make decisions impacting each area of the business. One consultant called an EBS implementation nothing less than a "skeletal transplant," where the backbone of the organization is removed and a new one forced down the limp cavity of the tissue and muscle of the old corporate body. Hardly an appealing metaphor for today's workforces, already stressed to the breaking point.
- *Cost.* The costs associated with an EBS implementation can be staggering. The cost of just the hardware and software can be enormous. It is estimated that spending in this area in 2000 was in excess of $15 billion worldwide. Professional services fees for the same period were well over $10 billion. To this cost must then be added expenditures for Internet, Web site, and electronic commerce initiatives.
- *Inflexibility.* Many companies argue that they are forced to change operating processes unduly, just so they can use EBS applications. What is even worse, once installed, the EBS is difficult to change as the nature of the business changes. Although today's best packages enable the software and not the company to adapt to the operating environment, often the requirement to migrate, even to a "best practices" process, can cause considerable alarm in even the best-run organization.
- *Extended implementation cycle.* Regardless of the depth of project scope, which will add to the cycle time, implementing an EBS takes time. Fully installing most EBS software can occur within a few days. The hard part is not the software but identifying and making desired changes to business processes. Again, an EBS is a *people* and not a technical project.
- *EBS is dead!* Over the past couple of years pundits have quite wrongfully proclaimed that EBSs are based on obsolete technology and are no longer of relevance in today's Internet environment. As will be described later, current EBS architectures are undergoing metamorphosis as they migrate from inward-focused transaction management systems to outward-focused

Internet-enabled technologies providing connectivity up and down the supply chain. Simply put, while tomorrow's EBS may be radically different architecturally, nevertheless, the backbone business functionality will still be that of today's EBS.

Despite the tremendous planning and control opportunities an EBS provides for the typical enterprise, doing business in today's Internet world has imposed a number of critical requirements that EBS architectures and founding concepts were never designed to address. This does not mean, however, that EBS is obsolete. Companies of the future will still have to manage sales, perform transactions, cost inventory, pay personnel, and a host of other functions that are simply a part of doing business, and that is what an EBS does best. However, as will be detailed in the next section, the needs of collaborative business, Web-based technologies, synchronized supply chains, and other issues are requiring businesses not to abandon, but to extend basic EBS, by incorporating today's newest technologies and thinking. Such an enterprise is what can be seen as a permanent attribute of EBS architecture: it has been and continues to be preeminently an adaptive technology capable of changing and merging with breakthroughs occurring both in business management and application hardware and software.

II. THE RISE OF INTERNET COMMERCE

Up until the late 1980s, limitations in computer architecture and communications devices forced even the most technically savvy companies to remain fairly concentrated on streamlining and integrating *internal* business functions. Although tools fostering business-to-business connectivity, such as EDI, were slowly growing, the enterprise-centric and proprietary nature of computing in this period was often suboptimized by the inability of systems to interconnect with vital information occurring out in the business network. Even simple data components, like inventory balances or forecasts, were communicated with great difficulty to sister warehouses or divisions, let alone to trading partners whose databases resided beyond the barriers of their own information systems.

The idea that companies depended on their customer and suppliers, that considerable competitive advantage could be gained by working in closely structured collaborative partnerships, was always part of the business landscape far before the World Wide Web was even dreamt of. As illustrated in Figure 3.2, companies recognized that the span of their business universe extended beyond the range of their immediate planning and control systems to their customers, trading partners, suppliers, and distribution channel networks. The problem was that the mechanism necessary to generate the gravitational pull binding the outside spheres to a single supportive system consisted, for the most part, of handshakes revolving around formal or implied contracts. Data transmission was purely a manual affair, and because of the nature of the business philosophies of the time, shared only with the greatest reluctance.

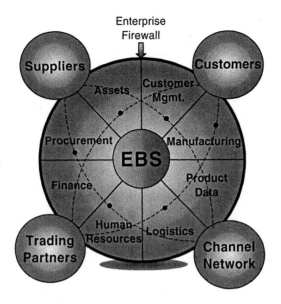

FIGURE 3.2 Basic business universe.

A. ELECTRONIC DATA INTERCHANGE (EDI): FIRST CONTACT

The first major technology breakthrough providing companies to link with other companies was EDI. Despite the recent rise in Internet-enabled data transmission capabilities, EDI constitutes today's most widely used method of supply chain connectivity. EDI provides for the computer-to-computer exchange of business transactions, such as customer orders, invoices, and shipping notices. As illustrated in Figure 3.3, EDI is an *extranet* system and consists of a set of transactions driven by a mutually agreed upon and implemented set of data transfer standards usually transmitted via private *value-added networks* (VANs). The critical importance of EDI is that the transacting companies can be using EBSs that run on different software systems and hardware. The EDI standards act as a "translator" that utilizes the agreed-upon transmission protocols to take the data residing in the computer format of the sending company and convert it into the data format used by the business system of the receiving company.

There are essentially two forms of EDI data transfer.

1. *Computer to Computer.* This method enables the computer system of one company to "talk to" the computer of a trading partner and transfer agreed-upon documents, such as purchase orders or payments, directly into each other's databases.
2. *Third-Party Linkage.* In this method, a third party indirectly links trading partners. This technique enables a single company's computer to interface with multiple supplier computers in any format, with any communications protocol. The third party performs the interfacing tasks for a fee.

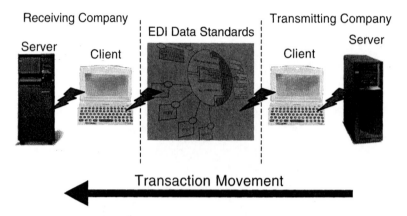

FIGURE 3.3 EDI environment.

As is the case with the implementation of any information technology tool, the ultimate value of an EDI system is only as good as the implementation effort and the ability of the channel information nodes to adapt to new organizational structures and values provided by the sharing of data throughout the channel network. The various benefits of EDI are as follows:[4]

- *Increased Communications and Networking.* By enabling channel partners to transmit and receive up-to-date information regarding network business processes electronically, the entire supply chain can begin to leverage the productivities to be found in information networking.
- *Streamlining Business Transactions.* By eliminating paperwork and maintenance redundancies, EDI can significantly shrink cycle times in a wide spectrum of transaction processing activities.
- *Increased Accuracy.* Because transactions are transferred directly from computer to computer, the errors that normally occur as data is manually transferred from business to business are virtually eliminated.
- *Reduction in Channel Information Processing.* EDI provides for the removal of duplication of effort and the accelerating of information flows that can significantly reduce time and cost between supply channel partners.
- *Increased Response.* EDI enables channel members to shrink processing times for customer and supplier orders and to provide for timely information that can be used to update planning schedules throughout the channel.
- *Increased Competitive Advantage.* EDI enables the entire supply network to shrink pipeline inventories, reduce capital expenditure, improve return on investment, and actualize continuous improvements in customer service.

While providing an effective method to perform data exchange between businesses, there are a number of drawbacks to EDI. To begin with, EDI is expensive and time consuming to implement. Companies must either agree on or use a recognized standard, often a daunting task in itself. Next, companies must shoulder the initial costs of purchase and implementation for VANs and translation/mapping software, and then begin the process of data-mapping and architecture design. Once the EDI structure has been put in place, parties to the EDI system must shoulder the recurring costs of VAN bills, software maintenance on translators and mappers, and efforts of full- and part-time EDI workers across the organization. Depending on the depth and complexity of the undertaking, an EDI implementation can cost millions. For example, according to Smeltzer,[5] Campbell Soup is said to have spent $30 million in 1996 to implement their EDI solution for order processing. Such obstacles keep EDI centered on the transmission of relatively simple data packets, like the exchange of purchase orders and invoices. The cost and effort to develop EDI for more complex, strategic functions, such as customer relationship management, collaborative manufacturing, and buying exchanges, are simply beyond the financial and operation capacities of most organizations.

In addition, there are other critical issues that directly impact EDI's capability to support the real-time processing of information needed by today's collaborative supply chains. The basic data elements of the EDI transaction are centered on transmitting whole packets of information that must be sent, translated, and then received through trading partner systems. The time it takes, often several days for processing, militates against the real-time flow of information and decision-making necessary for today's business environments. Furthermore, the proprietary nature and cost of EDI renders it a poor supply chain enabler. EDI is focused on eliminating operational costs that, by their very nature, have a law of diminishing returns. To be effective, EDI technology needs to enable the generation of data that could be used for strategic planning. Gaining such a perspective, however, requires that every member of the supply chain participate. Unfortunately, because of the high costs, EDI success stories are mostly confined to giant players like General Electric, Ford, and Wal-Mart who have not only the internal resources but also the power to dictate that channel partners use their system.

What was always needed was a way to make information available to the entire supply network at a very low threshold of cost and effort, but which, at the same time, enabled channel partners to use it to execute strategic decisions. This requirement for low cost and dramatically simple connectivity burst upon the scene in the late 1990s in the form of the Internet.

B. RISE OF INTERNET CONNECTIVITY

Sometime in the mid-1990s, technologically savvy companies began to explore the use of a new computerized tool that held out the potential to drastically alter forever the way firms fundamentally advertised their products and conducted business. That tool was the Internet. Fueled by the explosion in PC ownership, advancements in communications capabilities, and the shrinking cost of computer hardware and software, companies became aware that a new medium for exchange was dawning, a new medium that would sweep away the traditional channels governing the flow of products and information, in favor of a way of interacting with the customer that

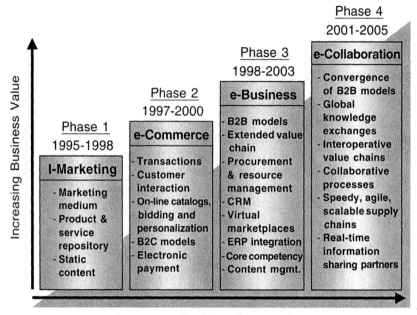

FIGURE 3.4 Four phases of Web-enabled e-business.

had not been seen since the days of the general store: personalized, one-to-one marketing, buying, and selling relationships between individual suppliers and consumers. Web-enabled e-business can be said to consist of four definite phases, as portrayed in Figure 3.4.

1. I-Marketing

Throughout history, businesses have been faced with the fundamental problem of identifying effective mediums to provide the marketplace with information about their identities and their product and service offerings. In the direct marketplace, the producer presents physically to perspective buyers available goods and services. Everything depends on the immediacy of availability and the personal relationship existing between buyer and seller at the moment of exchange. However, as businesses move beyond the physical marketplace, they are immediately confronted with the problem of how potential customers, separated by space and time, can find out about the company and its range of goods and services. In the past, firms attempted to solve this problem by utilizing marketing tools such as advertising, printed matter, such as catalogs and brochures, trade shows, industry aggregation registers, promotions and pricing, and direct sales force contact. The goal was to reach a marketplace with a matrix of information enablers that would act as a substitute for direct face-to-face product and service selection and exchange.

Despite the sophistication of the traditional techniques, there were a number of problems with the approaches. To begin with, by their very nature, space and time fragment markets. The ability to inform and communicate with customers, both beyond local markets and across vertical and horizontal industries, was a conundrum traditional marketers never really solved. Mass media advertising, direct marketing, and a host of other methods resulted in silo customer segmentation and hit-or-miss approaches that attempted to provoke a wide band of prospect interest or inform the existing client base. Second, the traditional marketing approaches represented a basically passive approach on the part of customers to search for and learn about new companies and their product/service mixes. Buyers tended to avoid the difficult task of sourcing and comparison in favor of purchasing based on branding and proven personal relationships.

In addition, information about new products or changes to existing company offerings was hard to communicate to the market without considerable expense, and even then the message often missed its mark. Furthermore, companies also had very limited ways of communicating promotional and pricing initiatives that could impact marketplace behavior. Also, because the content of traditional marketing was often limited by time and space, printed documentation, automation, and even language, globalization was rendered almost impossible. Firms focused their energies on supporting existing market positions, preferring to keep international initiates in the background. And finally, even heavily branded firms lacked the means to communicate with their customers concerning fundamental changes to business philosophies, goals, and strategies for the marketplace.

The advent of the Internet and the World Wide Web enabled companies to finally escape from the limitations of traditional marketing, by providing a revolutionary medium to communicate to customers, not only regionally and nationally, but also anywhere, at anytime, around the world. Originating as a communications tool designed to network scientific and academic information, the Web became, by the mid-1990s, a key medium for marketing that provided both domestic and global companies with a low-cost medium to convey product and service information. The use of the Web to market products and services was nothing short of explosive. For example, Forrester Research reported that by the end of 1995, around 34% of Fortune 500 companies had established a Web site. A year later, this figure had skyrocketed to nearly 80%.[6] Today it would be difficult to find a corporation that does not have a Web site informing browsers about information ranging from company goals to detail product categories.

The first phase of e-business has been termed *Internet Marketing* (I-Marketing), because it is almost exclusively limited to the presentation of documentation about companies and their products and services, utilizing relatively simple Web-based multimedia functions. Customer use of I-Marketing browsing is essentially restricted to searching, viewing graphical presentations, and reading static text. I-Marketing Web sites actually are little more than on-line repositories of information and are often termed 'brochureware" because of their similarity to traditional catalogues and other printed product/service publications. Due to their limited functional architectures and business purpose, I-Marketing Web-sites do not provide for the entry of transactions or the ability of companies to interact with existing customers or prospects using the site.

Despite the deficiencies, the use of I-Marketing signaled an order of magnitude departure from traditional marketing techniques. To begin with, the ubiquitous use of the Web meant that companies were no longer circumscribed by time and space. A firm's mix of goods and services could be accessed by anyone, anytime, anywhere on earth. This meant that all enterprises across the globe, both large and small, now had a level playing field when it came to advertising their businesses, their products, and their services. I-Marketing also changed dramatically the role of the customer who moved from a passive recipient of marketing information to an active participant in the search for suppliers that best matched a potential matrix of product, pricing, promotional, and collaborative criteria. Finally, I-Marketing enabled companies to aggregate marketing data from multiple vendors into a common catalogue, thereby creating an early version of electronically linked communities of buyers and sellers.

2. e-Commerce Storefront

While I-Marketing did provide companies with the capability to open exciting new channels of communication with the marketplace, technologically savvy executives soon realized that what was really needed was a way to perform transactions and permit interactions between themselves and the consumer over the Internet. During the second half of the 1990s, a new kind of Internet capability and a new kind of business model, the pure-play Internet storefront designed specifically to sell and service the marketplace on-line, emerged. Soon companies like Amazon.com, eBay, and Priceline.com were offering Web-based storefronts that combined I-Marketing on-line catalogues and advertising techniques with new technology tools such as Web-site personalization, self-service, interactive shopping carts, bid boards, credit card payment, and on-line communities that permitted actual on-line shopping. According to Hoque,[7] the new e-business storefronts spawned a whole new set of e-application categories and included the following:

- *e-Tailing and Consumer Portals*: These are the sites today's Internet shopper normally associates with Web-based storefront commerce. The overall object of enterprises in this category is to enable Web-driven fixed-price transactions, centered on products and services aggregated into catalogues and sold to aggregated groups of consumers.
- *Bidding and Auctioning*: Sites in this category perform two possible functions. Some sell products and services through auction-type bidding using bid boards, catalogue integration, and chat rooms. Others, like eBay, ONSALE, and uBid perform the role of third-party cybermediaries who, for a service price, match buyers and sellers.
- *Consumer Care/Customer Management*: These applications provide a wide range of customer support processes and functions focused on enabling a close relationship-building experience with the consumer. These applications include customer profile management, custom content delivery, account management, information gathering, and interactive community building.

- *Electronic Bill Payment* (EBP): These applications assist customers to maintain accounts and pay bills electronically. For example, large companies such as AT&T and MCI WorldCom have made conscious efforts to move their billing on-line, while a number of smaller EBP dot-coms have surfaced on the Web devoted to bill aggregating, payment, and personal finance management. Typical EBP features include Internet banking, bill consolidation, payment processing, analysis and reporting, and integration with biller accounting systems.

For many in both the marketplace and the investment community, this new brand of electronic business-to-consumer enterprise seemed to offer a path to a whole new way of selling and servicing in what was being termed the 'new economy.' The advantages of the e-business storefront over traditional "bricks-and-mortar" firms were obvious. A single seller could construct a Web storefront that could reach a global audience that was open for business every day of the year, at any hour. By aggregating goods and deploying Web-based tools, this new brand of marketer could offer customers a dramatically new shopping experience that combined the ease of shopping via personal PC with an immediacy, capability for self-service, access to a potentially enormous repository of goods and services, and information far beyond the capacities of traditional business models.

The goal of storefront e-commerce is nothing less than the reengineering of the traditional transaction process by gathering and deploying all necessary resources to ensure that the customer receives a complete solution to their needs and an unparalleled buying experience that not only reduces the time and waste involved in the transaction process, but also generates communities-of-interest and full service consumer processes. Take for instance Amazon.com., whose goal is not just to sell products, but to create a shopping "brand" where customers can log-on to shop for literally *anything*. In such a culture, the real value of the business is found in owning the biggest customer base, that contains not only their names and addresses but also their buying behaviors, opinions, and desires to participate in communities of like consumers.

3. e-Business Marketplaces

e-Business Marketplaces differ from e-Commerce Storefronts in several ways. The most obvious is that the former is concerned with the transaction of products and services between businesses (B2B) while the latter is between consumers and various types of e-Tailer. Also, the focus of the business relationship is quite different. By definition, e-Commerce is concerned with consumer-type buying, where the shopper searches electronically from storefront to storefront, often ignoring previous allegiances to store branding. In contrast, e-Business Marketplaces resemble traditional business purchasing: it is often a long-term, symbiotic, and relationship-based activity where collaboration between stakeholders directed at gain-sharing is critical.

e-Business Marketplaces can be divided into three separate types. The selection of a type depends on the overall strategy of the business and how it wants to compete in the marketplace. The e-marketplace types can be described as follows:

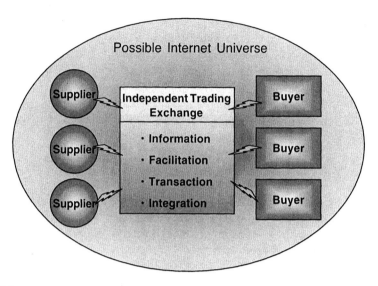

FIGURE 3.5 Independent Trading Exchange Model.

a. Independent Trading Exchanges (ITXs)

ITXs can be defined as a many-to-many marketplace, composed of buyers and sellers networked through an independent intermediary (Figure 3.5). Successful ITXs today operate in industry marketplaces that are highly fragmented and have a considerable level of product or service complexity. In this context, *complexity* is defined as requirements for special user needs, time-sensitive products, geographical limitations, volatile market conditions, and non-standardized manufacturing or channel delivery processes.

ITXs can essentially be divided into two types. The first, *independent vertical exchanges,* attempt to facilitate trade in order to make a vertical industry more efficient. ITXs in this group address industry-specific issues and provide industry-specific applications, services, and expertise without significant investment from existing industry players. Examples include CheMatch, e-STEEL, and Sci-Quest. The second type of ITX has been termed *independent horizontal exchanges.* ITXs in this group facilitate procurement economies, products, and services to support business processes that are common across multiple industries. ITXs are primarily used for managing spot buys, disposing of excess and obsolete inventory, and procuring noncritical goods and services.[8]

ITXs are operated by a neutral third party, which utilizes strong industry and domain expertise to manage relationships and vertical-specific processes. Their business plan is remarkably simple. ITXs offer a neutral site where purchasers and suppliers can buy and sell goods and services. In turn, the ITX operators collect user fees or transaction commissions for their web development, promotion, and maintenance efforts. According to AMR Research,[9] ITXs provide four major levels of functionality:

- *Information*. Perhaps the major function of ITXs is their ability to provide special assistance to industry verticals by leveraging a high level of industry expertise and information in the form of specialized industry directories, product databases and catalogs, discussion forms and billboards, and professional development.
- *Facilitation*. On this level, ITXs facilitate the matching of specific needs of buyers with the capabilities of suppliers, typically through an auction or chat room. The actual transaction is normally completed offline.
- *Transaction*. Besides matching buyers and sellers, ITXs on this level can conduct the transaction on-line. The ITX often takes title of the goods and corresponding responsibility for accounts payable and receivable. Besides pricing and terms management, the ITX can also provide shipping and order status information.
- *Integration*. On the highest level, ITXs provide integration functionality permitting trading exchange services to fit into a larger supply chain and application integration strategy. ITX services greatly increase their value to companies if they can help leverage investment in installed applications and established relationships.

As the dot-com craze swept through business at the beginning of 2000, industry analysts predicted that independent e-marketplaces would be the wave of the future. Between 1998 and 2000, ITXs grew by 1000% and analysts estimated that by 2004 there would be as many as 10,000 e-market sites. Almost every narrowly defined vertical market had one or more B2B sites to call its own. By mid-2001, however, the bottom had fallen out of the ITX marketplace, as sites ran out of money before they could attract enough participants or, recognizing there were too many sites chasing the same industries, merged with stronger competitors.

Beginning in 2002, ITXs are expected to see modest growth. AMR projects that ITXs will become progressively more specialized in function, as well as focused on a vertical marketplace. In addition, companies will increasingly view ITXs as a complement to the horizontal approach of private exchanges. Survivors can be expected to follow five strategies: ally with consortia players, merge with or acquire traditional businesses, provide specialty capabilities, serve niche marketplaces, or merge with other independent trading exchanges. Among today's major ITXs can be found CheMatch and ChemConnect in chemicals and plastics, e2open and Partminer in high-tech electronics, Agribuys, RetailExchange, and Redtagbiz in retail, and Enermetrix and Altra Energy Technologies in utilities.[10]

b. Private Trading Exchanges (PTXs)

The trouble with the ITX craze of 2000 was that they were "hyped" to satisfy expectations that they were never designed to fulfill. Companies soon realized that their initial step into the e-marketplace was first, to leverage Web-based tools to define unique opportunities for improving their own internal value chain performance and, secondly, to create similar integrated networks with their trading partners. ITXs provided simple buy-and-sell capabilities. What many companies realized is that what they really wanted from their B2B e-marketplace was not only ease of doing

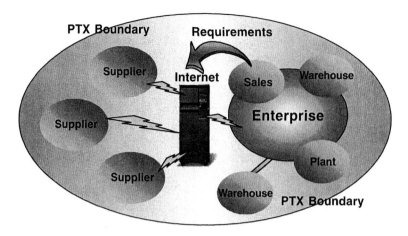

FIGURE 3.6 Private Trading Exchange Model.

business, but also one-to-one collaborative capabilities with network partners, total visibility throughout the supply chain, seamless integration of applications, and tight security.

By mid-2001, many companies interested in Web-driven marketplaces were creating private exchanges. The objective was to form an enterprise's internal business units and preferred business partners into a closed e-marketplace community linked by a single point of contact, coordination, and control. Such a strategy required the establishment of what has become known as a PTX. A PTX can be defined as a Web-based trading community hosted by a single company that requires or recommends trading partners, usually suppliers, participate in as a condition of doing business. Often this type of e-marketplace is driven by a large market-dominant company that seeks to facilitate transactions and cut costs while also cementing the loyalties of their own customers and suppliers. Figure 3.6 provides an illustration of the PTX concept.

According to Accenture,[11] the decision to construct a PTX is based on three fundamental criteria.

1. *Companies with exclusive products, processes, or market position.* Firms with proprietary product/service offerings often feel that a PTX would allow them to use e-business tools, while avoiding ITX comparison shoppers, as well as protect the product's unique value and brand.
2. *Companies possessing special process capabilities.* Businesses possessing special processing competencies in areas such as customization or flexible manufacturing are excellent candidates for a PTX.
3. *Companies with dominant market position.* PTXs are a logical choice for companies whose products hold a dominant position in the market. PTXs may also be the choice of companies that have little to benefit from the aggregation capabilities of an ITX or Consortium. A company like Wal-Mart has little to gain, and a lot to lose, in an open trading exchange.

Beside product, process, and market reasons, companies may choose a PTX over an ITX or a Consortium for other reasons. To begin with, a PTX provides companies with enhanced privacy and security regarding exchange pricing and volumes. Second, a PTX facilitates linkages across exchange partner EBS and SCM systems that can assist in passing information regarding inventory and capacity statuses. Next, unlike most ITXs, which focus either on the customer or the supplier side, a PTX enables companies to build e-business capabilities on both sides simultaneously. Fourth, a PTX offers firms the ability to move beyond mere transaction management and build network collaborative capabilities in such areas as inventory management and planning, product design, production planning and scheduling, and logistics. Finally, because PTXs help build among channel partners a sense of collaboration and trust, they can extend a greater level of competitive advantage than can participants in an open exchange.

A PTX provides a range of other services as well. According to an AMR report,[12] today's PTX provides the following key services:

- *Identity Management:* PTXs provide the ability for internal and external customers to establish and manage the identity of the transaction mediums and people executing the exchange.
- *Content Management:* PTX content ranges from relatively *static* functions, such as catalogs and service capabilities, to *dynamic* functions, such as pricing or product availability, to *interactive* functions, such as purchase order or ASN. Content management can also consist of unstructured content, such as multimedia and business rules. Functionality must include the ability to define and manage exchange content schemas and descriptions.
- *Integration:* An effective PTX must be fully integrated with the enterprise EBS back-office functions of trading partners. As this integration deepens, synchronization and collaboration with supply chain partners becomes more robust.
- *Process Management:* Effective PTXs must have functions including dynamic pricing, negotiation, returns, promotion management, or other collaborative applications.
- *Analytics:* Warehousing the vast amounts of data generated by PTX transactions is critical. Analysis of such data enables measurement of the effectiveness of the supply network relationships enabled by the PTX.

According to Forrester Research, about 42% of the companies it surveyed were using PTXs, versus 11% that were involved in ITXs. By 2003, those figures will be 53 and 19%, respectively. Also, during this period, EDI usage will fall to second place behind PTXs, to about 29% of respondents. While Forrester Research estimates that the companies they studied using PTXs are expected to save more than 10% in costs by 2003, there are drawbacks. The same report showed that effective PTXs are not built in a day, and that the price tag of anywhere from $.5 million to $55 million can be overwhelming for medium to small companies. Forester concluded their report by strongly recommending that businesses embarking upon a

PTX initiative match their requirements and expected benefits to the right PTX model.[13]

i. Case Study: Carpenter Technology Corporation
When *Carpenter Technology Corp.*, a 113-year old, 1.1 billion dollar steel maker in Wyomissing, PA, decided to create a PTX for its material purchase, it came as a natural progression from the company's desire to increase its footprint in the marketplace. Carpenter sells bars, rods, and wire products to aerospace and automotive companies, where product quality is a requirement. They categorize themselves as a specialty manufacturer geared toward metallurgists and applications engineers and, according to their general business manager of e-business, Scott Myers, are definitely "not a commodities company."

Although Carpenter had a functional extranet system linking them to their large customers, the company's difficulty in responding to the needs of a multitude (as many as 40,000) of smaller machine shop customers drove them to explore a PTX solution. Such customers "did not have time," says Myers, "for reverse auctions on public exchanges. They needed product ASAP." The result was the launch in October 2000 of Carpenterdirect.com. Within 6 months of launch, Carpenter has attracted 12,000 unique visitors and 2,000 registered customers, some 14% above the average.

Carpenterdirect.com provides over 100 search criteria and is rich with technical information on the properties of the materials it sells: tensile strength, corrosion, resistance, and chemistry. In fact, Carpenter's $10 million site is so popular that a number of related alloy companies have elected to post their inventories on the Web-exchange. The benefits have been worth the effort. Of the 2,000 registered site users, 60% are new customers. Myers expects the PTX to generate 10% of the company's total sales, making the site the largest contributor to Carpenter's growth. Although a number of ITXs have been trying to get Carpenter to join them, Myers feels that at the present time "there's no strategic reason to go with them now."[14]

c. Consortia Trading Exchanges (CTX)
As the ITX craze began to fizzle in 2000, another form of exchange, the industry consortium, began to emerge. A CTX can be defined as a *some-to-many* network consisting of a few powerful companies organized into a consortium and their trading partners. For the most part, the CTXs being formed are led by very large corporations in highly competitive industries such as automotive, utilities, airlines, high-tech, and chemicals. The goal of a CTX is simple: to combine purchasing power and supply chains in an effort to facilitate the exchange of a wide range of common products and services through the use of Web-based tools, such as aggregation and auction, between vertically-organized suppliers and a few large companies. The CTX model can be seen in Figure 3.7.

Functionally, CTXs utilize elements of both private and independent exchanges. Similar to a PTX, a CTX offers the critical elements of control over membership, security, and, most importantly, the ability to build and maintain collaborative capabilities. On the other hand, CTXs also enable opportunities for individual members to access each other's trading partners. In addition, consortia e-markets may allow other companies to join the exchange, providing the CTX with an expanding number of members.

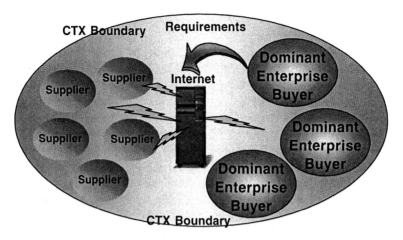

FIGURE 3.7 Consortium Trading Exchange Model.

There are a number of significant drawbacks to establishing a CTX. To begin with, the ability to weld a number of competing super-enterprises and their supply chains into a single consortium is fraught with difficulties. Competitive pressures, technology selection, software selection and integration issues, and possible anti-trust interference from the government all militate against successful CTX formation.

Of these drawbacks, a major one is the Internet architecture of a CTX requiring consortia members to standardize processes and utilize a common e-business language. The need to establish a common platform can be a sticky negotiating point. In addition, although Internet companies such as *Commerce-One* and *RossettaNet* provide packaged solutions, the establishment of a CTX is an expensive affair and, regardless of the software vendors selected, must often be built from the ground up or heavily customized.

A number of consortia have grown to importance. For example, more than 50 major CPG companies have invested over $250 million in the creation of a CTX called *Transora*. The exchange handles everything from raw materials acquisition to finished goods distribution targeted at supermarkets and top mass retailers such as K Mart, Target, and Wal-Mart. Another CTX of note is the *Global Rail Exchange,* an offshoot of General Electric's *Global eXchange Services* (GXS). The exchange is focused on the domestic and international rail industry and offers a number of services, including the disposition of excess inventory, quick access to rail community expertise, electronic RFQ and reverse bidding, and a wide range of routing and adjudication issues.

Perhaps the most talked about consortium today is *Covisint*. Hoping to drastically reduce an estimated $100 billion in excess inventories from the automotive supply chain and increase time-to-market, DaimlerChrysler, Ford, and GM launched their own CTX in February of 2000. Shortly after the launch, two other automakers, Renault and Nissan joined the consortium. Ultimately, the goal of the exchange is to become the paramount supply chain management tool for the automotive industry, welding together some 90,000 automotive suppliers into a single supply network. To realize this objective, Covisint sees itself as offering three significant e-business tools: procurement management, collaborative supply chain development, and collaborative product development. The first tool, procurement, ranges from MRO to component parts acquisition. Key functions supported are auctions for new parts, sale of older equipment, issuance of RFPs, and design sharing. According to Covisint spokesman Dan Jankowski, as the CTX matures, it is expected that upwards of $1 trillion will be transacted annually between exchange partners. While the collaborative aspects of Covisint are still in development, they are of the greatest interest and indicate the power of a CTX. Because all members of the exchange are linked together, Covisint will have the ability to broadcast any volume changes directly to all supply tiers simultaneously, thereby cutting time and excess inventory costs from the supply chain. Similarly, engineers and designers will be able to use Covisint like an on-line meeting room. Collaborative planning and design would remove the barriers of time and distance, while shrinking costs.

While CTXs like Covisint hold out the promise for decreasing costs, speeding time-to-market, and fostering collaboration, there are many hurdles to climb. Internally, CTXs are grappling with technology issues such as standardization, integration, and deploying collaborative technologies. Externally, there is the daunting task of signing up members. Without liquidity, even the best-conceived CTX is doomed. Part of the problem is getting members up to speed technologically to participate in the exchange. Perhaps of greater importance is convincing suppliers that participation would be worth their efforts. Establishing a site governing body that is also seen as impartial, fears that CTXs will simply serve as an arena where the lowest price will win regardless of quality, and apprehension about data security all are critical issues that must be solved before a consortium can truly realize its potential.[15]

4. e-Collaboration Marketplaces

The power of e-business marketplaces to increase demand visibility, operational efficiencies, and customer segmentation, while simultaneously decreasing procurement costs, replenishment time, and geographical barriers has dramatically changed the nature of supply chain management. But, while all types of businesses in all types of industries have been able to utilize e-business technologies to gain significant benefits, it is evident that B2B e-marketplaces are actually in their infancy rather than mature tools for the kind of value chain management they will be capable of in the near future. As they evolve from transaction based to e-supply chain collaborative and synchronized systems, a variety of business management and technology changes must occur.

To date, the attempts companies have made to leverage B2B e-marketplace technologies have been largely focused on improving business with the channel partner found on the next network tier. These one-to-one relationships, as illustrated in Figure 3.8, consist of linear handoffs of goods and information from a company to the immediate supply partner, such as supplier-manufacturer or distributor-retailer. The chained pairs of relationships model, while facilitated by the power of the Internet, nevertheless, is incapable of responding to the value chain needs of groups or tiers of business relationships, because their interfaces limit interoperability, and their rigid architectures inhibit the synchronization of data from multiple sources.

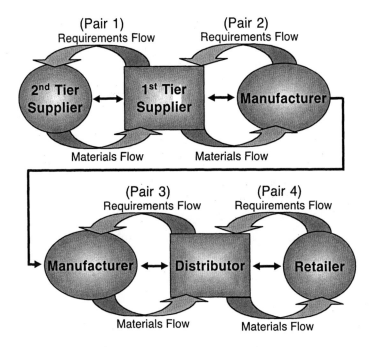

FIGURE 3.8 Supply chain trading pairs.

In the previous chapter, it was stated that the capabilities of the Internet have made real-time collaboration between supply chain partners possible. Termed *collaborative commerce* (c-commerce), the concept seeks to extend the enabling power of business relationships beyond transaction management to true collaboration across a network of channel allies. The goal of c-commerce is to extend the capabilities of the Internet to enable tools that provide for greater supply chain visibility and connectivity. As illustrated in Figure 3.9, these tools can be divided into three regions. The first, *Basic B2B Commerce,* consists of application tools that provide marketing information and transaction functions via the Web. While enabling companies to tap into the power of Internet-based commerce, these applications tools provide firms with tactical competitive advantage.

The second region, *Supply Chain Management,* seeks to develop the collaborative aspects of Internet technologies to better manage networked customers and inventories. Briefly, applications at this level can be described as follows:

- *Collaborative Channel Management.* These tools focus on two e-market objectives: to move beyond a marketing strategy that focuses purely on customer segmentation to one that can provide appropriate levels of services to customers with different value, and to construct Internet empowered logistics systems that link supplier selection and transportation visibility with company customer service functions.
- *Collaborative Inventory Management.* The ability to provide inventory visibility beyond chained network pairs is critical to removing the impediments

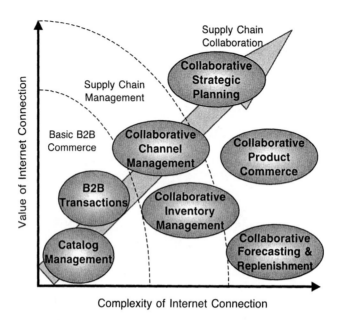

FIGURE 3.9 Regions of the B2B collaborative e-marketplace.

blocking effective channel inventory management. As changes occur either upstream or downstream in the supply chain, dynamic collaboration will enable network partners to react immediately to ensure customer service while guarding against excess inventories.

The final and most sophisticated of the c-commerce regions is *Supply Chain Collaboration*. Applications in this area seek to leverage the full value of real-time collaborative solutions. These tools can be described as:

- *Collaborative Forecasting and Replenishment.* Broadcasting demand requirements in real time across the channel network is one of the fundamental objectives of B2B e-marketplaces. Collaborative demand planning enables companies to escape from the restrictions of chains of paired channel relationships that conceal real network requirements and capability-to-promise.
- *Collaborative Product Commerce* (CPC). The needs of product outsourcing, shrinking time-to-market product development cycles, and requirements for increasingly agile manufacturing functions have necessitated that product design and engineering utilize a collaborative approach. CPC is defined as the deployment of cross-channel teams of developers and engineers who are responsible for parts of the overall design. Utilizing Internet tools to provide for information sharing and transactions, the goal is to collectively manage product content, sourcing, and communications between product OEMs, suppliers, and customers to eliminate redundancy, costs, and time from the product development process.

- *Collaborative Strategic Planning*. Perhaps the prime objective of c-commerce is the establishment of collaborative e-marketplaces, not only to redesign business and support processes that cross company boundaries, but also provide for a new vision of the strategic role of the supply value chain. Companies engaged in a c-commerce marketplace will be able to harness Internet technologies to create virtual corporations, brought about by any-to-any connections of value-added processes from anywhere in the supply chain system, capable of creating immense repositories of competitive advantage.

The *value web* produced by B2B collaborative marketplaces represents a dramatic departure from current views of the supply chain. The goal is to deconstruct the chains of network pairs and reassemble the disconnected amalgam of network business processes into webs of customer-focused suppliers, manufacturers, and distributors. Traditional supply chains are linear where monolithic systems, like EDI, govern sets of complex business processes. Such systems are difficult to build and expensive to maintain. Furthermore, they do not provide connectivity to capabilities and competencies beyond the members hard-linked into the network.

In contrast, Internet collaborative marketplace process webs provide any-to-any connections that can drive procurement webs, manufacturing webs, and even linked business strategies. Systems must be robust enough to service a single trading partner and agile enough to evoke worm-holes in the fabric of the possible supply universe in the search of any-to-any virtual supply sources capable of linking and unlinking resources in support of critical business processes. A possible model of collaborative e-marketplaces can be seen in Figure 3.10.

The capacity to access possible resource worm-holes and manage and optimize business process webs requires increased technical capabilities. The ability to process transactions and information is only one of the basics of what the Internet can offer to supply chains. Ultimately, the objective is for companies to share their planning systems and core competencies directly wherever they are on the globe. According to Smeltzer,[16] the technology tools and vision are in the process of happening and can be described as:

- New XML-based solutions, which will allow transaction documents to be quickly generated, while enabling sophisticated business rules to be built and modified faster and operated in real time.
- Business intelligence tools capable of supporting, extracting, and validating data in and out of a multiple, heterogeneous systems.
- Electronic catalogs with multimedia elements capable of synchronized product update and dynamic market-based pricing.
- Operational and supply chain applications capable of enabling coming real-time collaborative planning, forecasting, and replenishment systems.
- Technology application providers offering integration/collaboration application services that enable trading partners to limit investment in developing, maintaining, and supporting complex environments required to work with numerous companies across various networks.

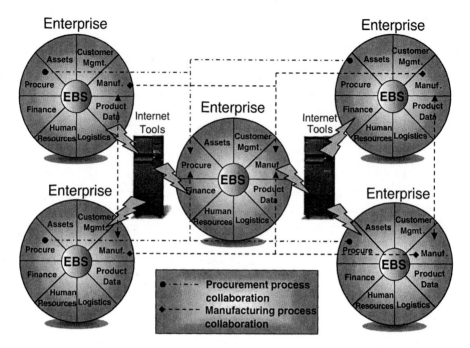

FIGURE 3.10 B2B e-collaborative marketplaces — procurement and manufacturing collaboration example.

While discussion about worm-holes in the customer/supplier universe enabling access and integration with remote trading partner competencies seems a little futuristic at this point, some of today's most advanced e-marketplaces are setting the stage for just such functionality. Hewlett Packard, for example, is supporting collaboration between 1,000 suppliers and its product divisions to manufacture nameplates for HP's various hardware offerings. Wal-Mart's *Retail Link* allows more than 10,000 suppliers to view sales on individual items at the group and store level for up to two years prior, thereby enhancing the marketplace's ability to collaborate on forecasts, production schedules, inventory levels, and real-time sales activity.

Covisint's efforts at e-marketplace collaboration are perhaps the most aggressive. Predecessor e-business efforts at GM and Ford were exclusively about buying and selling. Covisint, on the other hand, projects that its collaboration tools will be the greatest benefit offered by the exchange. In terms of collaborative demand planning, the CTX will permit automakers to escape from the existent linear supply network. For example, if an auto manufacturer changed the volume of production, the components requirements would proceed serially down through each supply tier, often taking weeks, obscuring the actual state of demand, and resulting in safety inventories at each channel tier. With Covisint, changes in demand can be broadcast to all members of the supply chain simultaneously, providing the demand visibility and synchronization that will increase serviceability and cut "just-in-case" inventories.

Even more critical to automakers is the potential for collaborative design. The goal is to bring design engineers together by connecting over the Web, in real time, tools such as CAD, to design parts, pass plans back and forth, update them, get quotes generated and components ordered, and follow the timetable to their deliverability. For example, designs for shock absorbers, seats, and instrument panels have already been put through Covisint's portal. In another example, Dana Corp, a tier one supplier, has been using the Covisint collaborative applications to reach out to design centers in Europe and Japan in an effort to reduce design cycle time. Previously, Dana spent up to six to ten weeks working with a sub-tier supplier. Utilizing Covisint's collaborative functions, this cycle time has been reduced to just a few days.

5. Today's e-Business Marketplaces — Summary

While the recession and tragic events of September 11 dramatically slowed down the implementation of c-commerce and e-SCM application suites in 2001, these tools continue to be seen as tomorrow's sources of competitive advantage. According to a survey reported by *Information Week* for 11 June 2001, efforts at e-business had been marked by significant success. Customer, partner, and supplier collaboration were ranked as somewhat or highly positive among 72%, 70%, and 65% of the respondents, respectively. Only four percent reported a highly or somewhat negative experience.[17]

While it is true that there was a lot of hype, a lot of promises that could not be fulfilled, a lot of misunderstanding about costs and the level of commitment involved, and a lot of confusion about how to effectively use the range of e-market tools available, there was also evident a lot of benefits that companies were taking to the bottom line. According to Accenture,[18] the range of benefits extends from:

- *Increased market supply and demand visibility:* enabling more customer choice, potentially better fit of products to buyers, and a larger market for sellers.
- *Price benefits from increased competition:* auctions and e-markets can be used to increase price competition and lead to dramatically lower procurement costs for buyers.
- *Increased operational efficiencies:* through improved procurement, order processing, and selling processes. Efficiencies can also include faster order cycle times.
- *Improved partner and customer segmentation:* e-market platforms can be used to transform customer segmentation and provide appropriate levels of services to customers with different value.
- *Improved supply chain collaboration:* e-market platforms will enable buyers and sellers to work together collaboratively for product design, planning, introduction, marketing campaigns, and life-cycle management programs.
- *Synchronized supply chains:* where visibility into operating information across the value chain allows companies to drive efficiencies across the entire value chain. These include increased inventory turnover, fast new product introductions, lower WIP inventories, and others.

Without a doubt, the requirements for cost management and work flow efficiencies on the tactical and collaborative functions on the strategic side will continue to propel the development of various forms of e-business markets. While the technical capabilities of e-marketplaces today limit the range of strategic collaboration, expect future e-markets to possess broader functionality. Not all will have the same capabilities. Expect ITXs to continue to move toward product and service niches. The power of CTXs can expect to grow as standardization and e-business tools become cheaper to acquire and integrate together. Likewise, PTXs can also be expected to increase their focus on direct material procurement and deep collaboration with trading partners and will most likely have the most sophisticated systems. Finally, it is expected that tomorrow's enterprise will participate in a portfolio of trading exchanges, selecting e-market exchanges that possess market dominance or unique capabilities that service a particular business requirement.

III. e-BUSINESS SYSTEM ARCHITECTURE

Internet-driven *supply chain management* (e-SCM) is the collaborative use of technology to merge the efficiencies and integration of internal EBS with the capabilities of business-to-business processes in order to improve marketplace speed, agility, real-time control, and customer satisfaction. To achieve these goals, today's enterprise is required to employ a variety of technology methods designed to construct a business architecture that is effective, efficient, purposeful, integrative, and collaborative. The resulting systems edifice must be capable of assembling into a single framework a mixture of often-disparate internal EBS applications, business processes, *business-to-business* (B2B) point solutions, and legacy systems.

The merger of information technologies as a business enabler is not a new idea. Historically, even in the days of silo-based organizations, the perpetual systems challenge always centered on integration and collaboration issues. The advent of e-business simply only heightened the gaps separating the "closed" environment of localized ERP and legacy systems and the requirement for "open" or networked operating systems, databases, and hardware platforms. According to Ulrich,[19] effectively meeting this challenge requires businesses to develop architectures and frameworks that permit enterprises to synthesize available integration software and existing solutions to address the ever-evolving structure of e-SCM business systems. Today's e-business enterprise system is much more than just moving information back and forth: it is also about integrating into whole business processes the capabilities of enterprises that span the supply chain universe.

A. e-SCM BUSINESS SYSTEM MODEL

At first sight, today's enterprise systems appear to be a maze of software products. ERP, CRM, SCM, EDI, EAI, and other technology acronyms litter current business literature and impart an impression of incoherency, comprehendible only to a select club of industry analysts and "techies." Even software analyst firms cannot make up their mind. AMR calls the configuration of EBS and e-applications *Enterprise Commerce Management*. The Gartner Group has termed it *ERPII*. Forrester Research uses the term *eXtended relationship management*. Old ERP companies have abandoned ERP and coined new terms, such as *e-Collaborative Applications* or *One-World,* to describe their business suites.

Figure 3.11 is an attempt to assemble the possible components of today's e-SCM business system into a coherent model. As can be seen, the model is divided into four distinct regions of software products: basic EBS, EDI, Middleware, and Web-based applications. Each of the regions can be briefly explained as follows:

1. *EBS:* The EBS still stands at the center of today's e-business solution. As described in detail at the beginning of this chapter, an EBS acts as the hub or "backbone" of an enterprise's transaction and information management functions. Based on the monolithic ERP software applications of the past, today's EBSs have been gradually converging with Web-based applications to form groupings of business software functions. For example, *supply chain planning* (SCP) and *advanced planning systems* (APS) are replacing most of the *Material Requirements Planning* (MRP) functions. e-Procurement is encroaching on traditional purchasing functions, while CRM has all but rendered obsolete ERP's one-dimensional customer service functions. Also, the trend to outsource select business softwares to third parties, such as *application service providers* (ASP), is moving tomorrow's EBS toward being a mixture of proprietary backbone applications, outsourced services, and trading exchanges.[20]

2. *EDI:* Despite the glamour of today's e-business applications, EDI is still a critical part of e-SCM. In many supply chain networks, EDI functions are still "mission critical." According to an AMR report,[21] a survey showed that 80% of electronic business transactions occurring in 2001 were driven in about equal halves by *value-added network* (VAN) and Internet-based EDI. Yet, despite EDI's preponderance, analysts are predicting that *extensible mark-up language* (XML), which accounts for the remaining 20% of transactions, will gain parity by 2003. The benefits and disadvantages of EDI were discussed earlier in the chapter.

3. *Web-Based Applications.* The third major area of today's e-SCM business system is composed of a variety of customer- and supplier-side software applications that are Web-enabled and directly integrated with EBS backbone applications. When they were first introduced, these applications were simply "bolted onto" supporting EBS applications. Today, the former monolithic structure of ERP is being decoupled and merged with these supporting e-business tools. For example, as Figure 3.12 illustrates, *advanced planning systems* (APS) that provide manufacturing functionality, such as finite loading, optimization, and production synchronization, have been integrated with traditional MRP to provide planning and control capabilities not possible with ERP architecture. This merging and fracturing of traditional ERP and specialized applications is expected to accelerate, and by 2005 ERP, as we know it today, will be completely transformed.

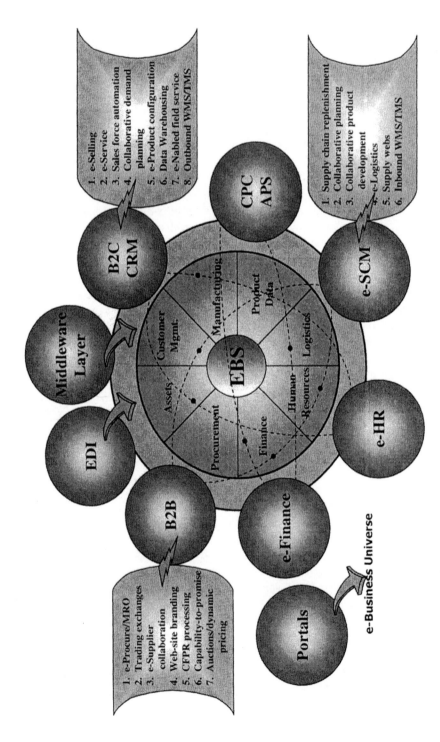

FIGURE 3.11 e-Business universe.

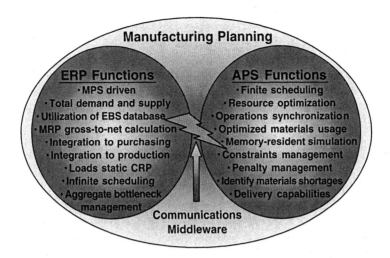

FIGURE 3.12 Merger of ERP and APS functions.

A brief review of the applications illustrated in Figure 3.11 are as follows:

- *B2C/CRM*: These e-business tools are perhaps today's most popular business applications. According to an *InformationWeek* survey conducted at the end of 2001, 98% of respondents consider CRM to be mission critical at their companies. 61% say that CRM tools have been implemented, while 39% are in the planning phase.[22] CRM is so important because it provides a number of critical customer-facing tools: Internet-driven order management, sales force automation, promotions and event management, customer information storage, analytics for marketing research, and e-customer service. The CRM body of knowledge is the subject matter of Chapter 5.
- *CPC*: *Collaborative product commerce* can be simply defined as the enablement, through Web-based tools, of virtual communities of manufacturing and product designers focused on new product development. Because it is Internet empowered, CPC permits companies to focus more intensely on their core capabilities, while leveraging external design partnerships to accelerate the time-to-market of product configuration. CPC will be discussed in much greater detail in Chapter 6.
- *SCM*: *Supply chain management* applications enable not just companies, but whole supply networks to be closely integrated. Internet-enabled SCM provides for the synchronization of the supply channel community, minimization of channel costs, optimization of network capabilities, real-time connectivity of channel supply and demand, and instantaneous visibility of the entire supply chain network. Through the use of optimization software, whole supply networks can make better decisions concerning priorities, demand, inventory, and asset utilization. e-SCM will be further reviewed in Chapter 4.

- *B2B/Procurement*: Much has already been discussed about the content of B2B Web-based applications in this chapter. Tools in this part of the e-SCM application suite are focused on deploying independent, private, and consortia exchanges to facilitate materials and finished goods acquisition, requisitioning, sourcing, contracting, ordering, and payment utilizing on-line catalogs, contracts, purchase orders, and shipping notices. This area will be discussed in much greater detail in Chapter 7.
- *e-Finance and Human Resources*: The utilization of Internet technologies to facilitate financial and human resource functions is a critical element in assisting companies to build competitive advantage in the Internet economy. e-Finance focuses on embedding core banking services, such as invoicing and payment, financing, and risk management, within logistics functions. A significant area is international commerce, where Web-applications will be used to settle transactions in real-time regardless of currency. In the area of human resources, companies are expected to make much greater use of on-line tools to help employees populate and access databases, such as human skills repositories, recruiting, hiring, compensation, payroll, and knowledge management solutions, housing the expertise and best practices of an entire corporate culture.
- *Portals*: Portal technologies are designed to provide company personnel and trading partners with secure, personalized access to data and self-service applications, enabling them to react to changes in production schedules, forecasts, and other information. Usually information is accessed through Web browsers. The data retrieved is normally static and there is no direct access to the stored data. Not to be confused with PTXs, which require extensive system-to-system, application-to-application integration at the process level, portals provide people-to-system coordination, where data from core functions such as ERP can be extracted, consolidated, and published on a portal for trading partners to see. Portals provide an effective medium to access information and knowledge across the supply network, while at the same time reducing the costs of distributing and sharing content and applications.

B. e-Business Integration Frameworks

The e-SCM application model suggested above implies that the range of EBS, resident-memory PC, and e-business applications are integrated together so that information and business processes flow freely from any one place in the networked supply chain to any other place. In greater detail, the model assumes that, *internally*, companies have accessible synchronized repositories of data about customers, processes, and products that transcend the boundaries of departments, divisions, and geographical units. The model likewise assumes that, *externally*, customers and suppliers have the ability to traverse supply channel silos to tap seamlessly into information or generate transactions. In reality, such a vision requires cross-functional integration linking applications and data across business units, operating systems, and hardware platforms. To meet this integration challenge, a number of critical issues need to be resolved:

- Integration standards must be available for document formats that enable the transfer of information between differing EBSs.
- Automated and standard transformation and routing tools must be available to convert and route data in varying formats and be compatible with existing investments in systems, transports, and business documents formats.
- A tool is needed to create and manage distributed business processes and the documents exchanged.
- Strong security allowing data transfer to be encrypted and digitally signed.
- The integration tools must leverage standard Internet transmission protocols as well as open data formats to facilitate data transfer between companies.
- The integration tools must be cost effective for small as well as large companies to enable mass market B2B transactions and trading.

In responding to such a formidable list of requirements, it is critical that companies develop an integration framework strategy. Such a strategy enables companies to implement scalable integration capabilities that provide system designers with the ability to partition the business process logic found across application programs (*components*) and arrange the collaborations needed to meet functional requirements.

At the heart of the integration architecture can be found a broad set of technology functions that has been termed *middleware*. The role of middleware is to coordinate and enable applications running on one computer to communicate with applications residing on another computer. Middleware provides an e-business structure to access legacy systems, EBSs, data structures, data warehouses, a repository containing a metamodel of the overall environment, and B2B interface points that constitute the range of network applications.[23] An illustration of an e-business integration structure can be seen in Figure 3.13.

Middleware provides the engine that enables internal and external business functions to pass data between each other. According to McWhirter[24], middleware can be said to fall into two categories:

- *Data-oriented middleware*: In this category, middleware facilitates the sharing of information between different applications, such as a CRM system and an EBS.
- *Process-oriented middleware*: This category of middleware enables the processing and integrity of transactions and insures system integrity.

Both categories can reside on a server embedded in one of many application layers. Functionally, when a transaction occurs in an application like e-procurement, the data passes through to the middleware layer, where it is translated into a common language by any one of a number of middleware tools, such as XML or Java. The

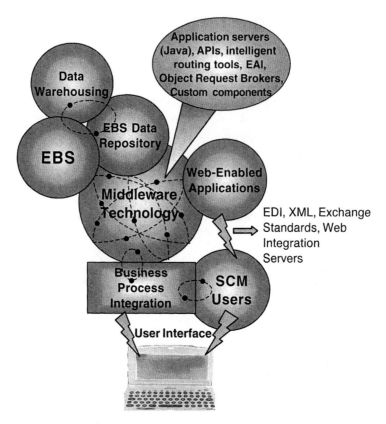

FIGURE 3.13 e-Business integration architecture.

data is then passed in a readable format into another application layer, say the purchasing application inside of an EBS.

As e-business collaborative commerce has expanded, the requirement for more complex connectivity tools, that can not only pass data but also facilitate process-oriented business workflows, has increased. Organized around the term *business process management* (BPM), this subset of middleware is focused on integrating business processes across business units, applications, and enterprises. The goal is simple: to let companies align business processes to deliver key information and key performance indicators, as opposed to just moving data back and forth. Through modeling tools that enable the creation of processes via a dynamic graphical environment, BPM provides visibility to business processes that span many types of computer systems and architectures to help managers monitor, measure, and resolve Web-enabled business processes throughout an e-business environment. BPM also provides tools that automate and integrate processes by generating graphical user interfaces to trigger event management across intercompany and networked supply chains. Finally, BPM activity output provides managers with metrics so that process integration can be further fine-tuned.[25]

IV. SUMMARY AND TRANSITION

The rise of SCM as perhaps today's most potent mechanism for competitive advantage has been enabled by the dramatic breakthroughs in information and communications technologies occurring over the past ten years. By its very nature SCM is a cross-enterprise management process requiring network partners to synchronize information transfer and business processes and provide close collaboration on everything from planning to transaction management. In the past, however, home-grown MRP II and ERP-type solutions looked inward. While such systems offered companies the possibility to continuously improve internal processes and performance, their architectures blocked them from connecting with trading partners outside the walls of the enterprise. Although tools like EDI provide electronic linkages, they are expensive and cumbersome, forcing companies to depend on manual data transmission and formal or implied contracts outside the enterprise system to manage the supply chain.

Sometime in the mid-1990s, companies began to harness the power of the Internet to overcome the limitations in their EBSs. By utilizing Web-based applications that could be made available to anyone, anywhere, at a very low threshold of cost and effort, the connectivity necessary to drive true SCM integration became possible for the first time. Web-enabled businesses could utilize four distinct, yet fully compatible regions of e-business to manage their supply chains. Through *I-Marketing*, companies could leverage the ubiquitous use of the Web to transcend the limitations of tradition marketing and reach out to any customer, anytime, anywhere on earth. Through *e-Commerce Storefronts*, companies could perform transactions and permit interactions between themselves and the customer over the Internet. e-Application categories, like consumer portals, bidding and auctioning, customer management, e-services, and electronic bill payment, not only pointed to radically new ways of doing business but seemed so revolutionary that they were seen as the drivers of a "new economy."

The third region, *e-Business Marketplaces*, seeks to apply the same tools of business-to-consumer to the business-to-business environment. There are three types of B2B marketplace exchanges: ITXs, which are open exchanges, normally presided over by an independent intermediary; PTXs, which are closed marketplaces controlled by a dominant player and its trading community; and CTXs, which normally are driven by an independent body composed of a few powerful companies and their trading communities. The last region, *e-Collaborative Marketplaces*, is by far the most advanced of the four e-business regions. Seeking to move beyond the linear supply chain dominated by the chained pairs of relationship model, this region extends Internet capabilities to foster the integration, synchronization, and collaboration of supply network partner channel strategies, inventories, forecast and replenishment functions, and product development life cycles.

Mapping out the application and integration architecture of today's e-SCM business system is a daunting task. Applications such as CRM, SCM, APS, e-procurement, and others have dramatically changed the configuration of yesterday's ERP. While EBSs still serve as the "backbone" of enterprise business management, the emerging functionality of workflow and process management middleware is slowly decoupling former monolithic ERP business software suites and merging them with e-business applications.

While the promise of the Internet seems to open up almost limitless possibilities, it is also fraught with grave dangers for the unprepared. As the dot-com crisis of 2000–2001 demonstrated, even the most technically advanced enterprise needs to painstakingly prepare an effective e-business strategy and then be capable of executing the plan. Developing the e-SCM strategy is the focus of Chapter 4.

ENDNOTES

1. For an interesting summary of early software systems see Davenport, Thomas H., *Mission Critical: Realizing the Promise of Enterprise Systems,* Harvard Business School Press, Boston, 2000, 1–54.
2. Norris, Grant, Hurley, James R., Hartley, Kenneth M., Dunleavy, John R., and Balls, John D., *E-Business and ERP: Transforming the Enterprise*, John Wiley & Sons, Inc., New York, 2000, 13.
3. Davenport, 23.
4. These points are taken from Ross, David F., *Competing Through Supply Chain Management,* Kluwer Academic, New York, 1998, 319.
5. Smeltzer, Larry R., "Integration Means Everybody – Big and Small," *Supply Chain Management Review*, 5, 5, 2001, 37.
6. *Economist*, May 10, 1997.
7. Hoque, Faisal, *e-Enterprise: Business Models, Architecture, and Components*, Cambridge University Press, Cambridge, UK, 2000, 57–87.
8. See the comments in Latham, Scott, "The New Internet Intermediary," *Supply Chain Management Review,* 4, 2, 2000, 25 and Starr, C. Edwin, Whitaker, Jonathan D., and Stephens, Jay A., "Which Independent Trading Exchanges Will Remain Standing?," *Supply Chain Management Review Global Supplement*, January/February 2001, 4–7.
9. Harbin, Joan, The 2001 AMR Research Survey: Top Trading Exchange Services for Industry Verticals, AMR Research, May 2001, 8.
10. Deedy, Steven, *2001 Consumer Goods Technology Trends Research Report,* Edgell Communications Inc., Randolph, NJ, 2001, 22–23.
11. Dik, Roger W. and Whitaker, Jonathan D., "The Power of Private Exchanges," *Supply Chain e-Business,* 2, 4, 2001, 44 and Whitaker, Jonathan D. Whitaker, Murphy, Matthew D., Haltzel, Andy H., and Dik, Roger W., "Private Exchanges: The Smart Path to Collaboration," *Supply Chain Management Review Global Supplement*, July/August, 2001, 8–11.
12. Parker, Bob, "Enterprise Commerce Management: The Blueprint for the Next Generation of Enterprise Systems," *AMR Research,* June, 2001, 14.
13. See the reference in Foster, Thomas A., "Plugging into Private Exchanges," *Supply Chain e-Business,* 2, 4, 2001, 16 and Buxbaum, Peter, "News from the Web-Enabled World," *Supply Chain Management Review*, 6, 5, 2001, 86.
14. This case study has been abstracted from an industry report by Aron, Laurie Joan, *Supply Chain Technology News*, 3, 7, 2001, 37–39.

15. Milligan, Brian, "What is Covisint?" *Purchasing*, 130, 5, 2001, 35–40; Schwartz, Beth, "Online Automotive Exchange: Big Change or Pipe Dream?," *Transportation and Distribution*, 41, 5, 2001, 4–6; Jankowski, Dan, "Enabling the Auto Industry: A Covisint Interview," in *Achieving Supply Chain Excellence Through Technology*, 3, Anderson, David, L., ed., Montgomery Research, San Francisco, 2001, 62.

16. Smeltzer, Larry R., "Integration Means Everybody – Big and Small," *Supply Chain Management Review*, 5, 5, 2001, 42.

17. Gonsalves, Antone, "Supply Chain Deployment Drops Off," *Information Week*, June 11, 2001, 87.

18. Starr, C. Edwin, Kambil, Ajit, Whitaker, Jonathan D., and Brooks, Jeffrey D., "One Size Does Not Fit All — The Need for an E-Marketplace Portfolio," in *Achieving Supply Chain Excellence Through Technology*, 3, Anderson, David, L., ed., Montgomery Research, San Francisco, 2001, 97.

19. Ulrich, William M., "E-Business Integration: A Framework for Success," *Software Magazine Supplement*, 21, 4, 2001, S3.

20. Reference the following two key reports from AMR Research regarding the future of ERP: *Enterprise Management Strategies: People, Process, and Profits*, AMR Research, January 2001 and Bermudez, John, "Enterprise Commerce Management: A New Era in Enterprise Systems," AMR Executive News Letter, March 2001.

21. Hedrick, Amy, *Reports of EDI's Death Were Premature,* AMR Research, July 2001.

22. Maselli, Jennifer, "CRM Shines on in a Cloudy Economy," *Information Week,* November 19, 2001, 88.

23. See the comments of Ulrich, S4.

24. McWhirter, Douglas, "Middleware: Directing Enterprise Traffic," *Customer Relationship Management,* 5, 8, 2001, 32.

25. For further information on BPM see Garrison, Sue, "Share Business Processes, Not Just Data," *Software Strategies*, 6, 9, 2001, 33–36 and Ulrich, S15.

4 Developing e-SCM Strategies: Creating the Game Plan for e-SCM Success

At the heart of the supply chain management concept can be found the continuous unfolding of a variety of dynamic organizational, technology, and business channel collaborative strategies. Unlike the corporate strategies of the past, which focused narrowly on internal budgets and detailed metrics regarding the performance of company-centric market segments, products, and processes, e-SCM requires enterprises to rethink the very nature of the way they do business, in light of the tremendous opportunities brought about by the merger of the competitive power of the supply chain network and Internet-based technologies. Progressive companies today seek to utilize the Web to drive new business models and attain levels of competitive advantage that consistently and continuously achieve order-of-magnitude breakthroughs in the creation of the products and services customers really want, by leveraging the capabilities found anywhere in the supply network to engineer seamless value chains capable of satisfying customers with any solution, at any time.

This chapter seeks to explore how companies can build effective market-winning business strategies by actualizing the opportunities to be found in SCM and the Internet. The discussion begins with an investigation of how today's dependence on supply chains has dramatically altered business strategy development. Structuring effective business strategies requires companies to closely integrate the physical capabilities, knowledge competencies, and technology connectivity of their supply chain networks alongside company-centric product, service, and infrastructure architectures. Building such a powerful e-SCM strategy requires that companies, first of all, energize and inform their organizations and their management staffs about the opportunities for competitive advantage available through the convergence of SCM enablers and Internet applications. As the chapter points out, strategists must be careful to craft a comprehensive business vision, assess the depth of current e-SCM trading partner connectivity, and identify and prioritize what initiatives must be undertaken to actualize new value chain partnerships. The chapter concludes with a detailed discussion of a proposed e-SCM strategy development model. The model consists of five critical steps, ranging from the architecting of purposeful supply chain value propositions to assembling performance metrics that can be used to ensure that the proposed e-SCM strategy is capable of achieving the desired marketplace advantage.

I. CHANGING VIEWS OF ENTERPRISE STRATEGY

The majority of companies today are restructuring their organizations, changing their productive processes, and retooling their technology capabilities in preparation to do business through the Internet. This may seem a rather over-optimistic statement in light of the implosion of the NASDAQ and the carnage of so many an upstart dot-com in 2001. In fact, the abrupt end of the dot-com era seemed to confirm to many what they had always surmised: there was no "new economy;" e-business did not really work; the often obscene capitalization accorded to all sorts of vague schemes associated with businesses whose strategies consisted solely of gathering customer databases and building Internet branding were indeed indecent and had little chance of success. The economic laws that had dominated for so long, which dictated that business be founded on products, assets, infrastructure, brand equity, and channels of long-standing customers, seemed to reassert themselves. Rightfully so, once maligned "bricks and mortar" companies took a deep breath and no longer worried about being "Amazon-ed" or "Enron-ed."

Still, while the new economic order had failed to materialize as promised, the revolution in business networking that had powered the would-be kings of the "new economy" had dramatically altered the playing field forever. For decades, companies had leveraged technology tools and management philosophies, such as MRP II, JIT, EDI, TQM, ERP, and BPR, to drain from enterprise processes stagnant pools of productivity, inefficiencies, waste, and lack of customer focus, while enabling bold innovation, the continuous generation of agile organizations positioned to deepen customer and supplier relationships, and the capability to leverage core competencies focused on creating new forms of customer value. With the application of the Internet in all of its various forms, enterprises were now poised to merge these inward-focused improvement tools with networking technologies capable of enabling unprecedented levels of productivity, market dominance, and customer responsiveness.

Utilizing the enabling power of the Internet, once maligned "old economy" companies were not only emerging from the dot-com crisis in good order but were actually threatening to turn entire industries upside down. Delphi Automotive Systems Corp., a $29 billion top-tier supplier of automotive components and systems, leverages a variety of e-business tools that provide the automotive supply giant with on-line RFQ, purchasing, inventory visibility, collaborative design, and supply chain integration capabilities to keep its suppliers and its biggest customer, GM, happy. Similar stories of e-business application have kept companies such as Proctor & Gamble, Cisco, IBM, Wal-Mart, and others in the position of industry market leaders.

The bottom line is that the Internet offers enterprises the potential to fundamentally transform themselves much like material requirements planning (MRP), just-in-time manufacturing and distribution (JIT), and total quality management (TQM) had provided companies with the capability to revolutionize business in the past. The difference is that the Internet enables companies to escape from old economy business models that view organizations as internally focused and distinctly separate from their customers and suppliers. The application of Web technologies is about firms exploring new value propositions on how to work with their customers. It is also about new methods of defining unexplored regions of collaboration and synchronization with their suppliers to define radically new infrastructures that will expand the dynamics of competition. Charting an effective e-business strategy is not merely a matter of buying and bolting-on Web-enabled software; it is about reinventing the corporation to become an e-business.

A. OVERVIEW

In the past, business schools taught and executives fashioned elegant corporate strategies designed to ensure that their businesses were able to gain and then sustain a competitive advantage in the marketplaces in which they competed. The object of strategic planning was straightforward: How should a company deploy the advantages it enjoyed in processes, products, services, assets, and brands to beat out the similar offerings of rival firms and capture a specific customer segment? Once market superiority was gained, market winners then strove to solidify their supremacy by continuously improving products and services, reducing process and overhead costs, and investing in new product development and productive processes to keep the engines of competitive advantage moving forward. Because neither markets nor products changed much over time, enterprises that gained initial superiority could leverage considerable resources and process knowledge, mature distribution channels, advertising and marketing clout, and the newest technologies to maintain that lead.

Today, it is evident not only that there is no such thing as *sustainable advantage,* but also that all advantage is *temporary.* As Fine in his concept of business "clockspeed" tells us, no core competency is unassailable, no lead is uncatchable, no kingdom is unbreachable.[1] In fact, the faster the marketing environment, the quicker the profits are amassed, and the more revolutionary the products and processes, the faster the clockspeed, the shorter the reign. And, clockspeeds are increasing in every industry, obsoleting products, processes, and infrastructures and abrogating power over markets.

What is causing this acceleration in the erosion of competitive advantage? In some cases, it can be traced to new technologies and the dramatic explosion in products and services and diminishing product life cycles that have been rapidly diminishing the longevity of corporate cash cows. In other cases, shocks to the business and economic environment, such as the recession of 2001–2002 and the terrorist attacks on September 11, 2001, can suddenly dry up capital investment, drive companies to focus inward, and result in mass unemployment and whispers of a deflating economy. Still more deadly is the sudden growth of new, unorthodox business models that have been quick to challenge long successful leaders for marketplace supremacy by leveraging special competencies, which permit them to violate market boundaries and raid targeted customer segments, once considered the exclusive preserve of more mature, established companies. Other threats can arise from upstarts utilizing radically new technologies or management styles that not only steal business away but also increasingly render obsolete the intellectual and physical assets of their more senior rivals. Such fast "clockspeed" businesses seem to be everywhere today: it took Amazon.com just two years to achieve the same total annual sales as it took Wal-Mart twelve years to achieve; in 1993, Dell computers had $2.9 billion in sales and $12.3 billion four years later.

B. THE PRIMACY OF VALUE CHAINS

The basis of every business enterprise rests upon two pillars: its core competencies and the capabilities of its channel trading partners. The sum total output of a business's core competencies can essentially be described as constituting its *value proposition*. The value proposition is comprised of the way a firm markets its products and services, the processes by which it acquires and manages its assets, and the organizational infrastructure that guides the overall direction of the business and ensures the continuous and effective tactical governance of the firm. The *function* of the enterprise can be summarized as its ability to continuously design, assemble, and deliver what can be said to constitute its *customer value proposition*. The *structure* of the enterprise is the particular configuration in time of its knowledge, capabilities, productive processes, and physical assets that enables fulfillment of the value proposition. And finally, the *business architecture* of the enterprise is the design of how the various parts of its structure are integrated and directed to realizing the goals of its function.

Historically, most of the literature regarding the development of business strategy has focused on designing the *business architecture* of the individual corporation. However, it is obvious that companies have never been self-sufficient entities and that their business architectures have always implied, even if in a passive manner, the inclusion of networks of business partners whose competencies and resources could be deployed to actualize the value proposition. In fact it can be argued that a truly comprehensive business architecture must not only focus on the core competencies *within* the boundaries of the enterprise but also on the competencies of the firm's *extended* organization. Recently, it has been often said that "*Companies no longer compete — supply chains do.*" While companies do indeed define the products and services they sell and how they will be managed, competitive differentiation today is determined by how fast, how cheaply, and how effectively whole supply networks deliver on customers' demands for those products and services.

Assembling an effective *supply chain business architecture* requires companies to move beyond viewing their trading partners purely as passive channel constituents. When supply chain relationships are static, suppliers and customers are perceived as separate, loosely linked business entities, whose separate strategic goals and operations capabilities stand outside, and sometimes, even in conflict with each other's value propositions. In contrast, today's market leaders differentiate themselves from their competitors by their ability to continually identify and invest in the rich array of supporting competencies to be found in their supply network partners. In fact, it may be said that a company's real competitive advantage consists in its ability to design and integrate the capabilities of its supply networks in the pursuit of marketplace advantage, albeit temporary, against the backdrop of accelerating

Supply Chain Business Architecture

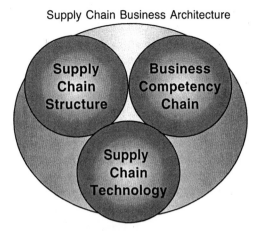

FIGURE 4.1 Supply chain strategic dimensions.

changes in markets and competitive forces. Success in tomorrow's marketplace will go to those enterprises that focus on the strategic capabilities of their entire value chain, rather than simply on the strength of company-centric products, services, and infrastructures.

Structuring a competitive *supply chain business architecture* requires strategic planners to view the supply chain from several perspectives. Dynamic channel architectures understand that trading partners provide a matrix of competitive advantages ranging from specialized competencies to collaborative relationships that provide the enterprise with a depth of customer satisfying values they could not possibly hope to assemble acting individually. Dynamic value chains consist of three interdependent dimensions as portrayed in Figure 4.1.

- *Supply Chain Structure.* This dimension details the *physical* composition and interconnecting links of the supply chain system. Understanding this dimension requires supply channel planners to, first of all, map out each network system that composes the entirety of the supply chain galaxy, beginning with the most remote supplier systems and concluding with the last customer to be found out on the rim of the channel network. The second activity of channel planners is to assess the importance of each network trading partner in relation to the value it contributes to the competitive advantage of the entire supply chain galaxy. These two exercises are directed at identifying trading partners that possess the greatest strategic importance and illuminating those regions that contain dramatically innovative network nodes that have the power to radically change and possibly destabilize the structure of the supply channel system.
- *Business Competency Chain.* Drafting a map of the physical structure of a value chain is a comparatively easy task in comparison to the second dimension, establishing a map of channel partner competencies. This process begins with a definition of the core capabilities existing within

the organization. Elements such as product design skills, marketing, logistics, and others are examples. Next, strategic planning teams need to understand what key capabilities each member physically constituting the supply chain system contributes to the firm's value proposition. Such an exercise should reveal the interrelationship of each trading node in the channel galaxy and provide answers to such questions as: Which are robust systems expanding at a stable rate that can be counted upon to steadily provide new ideas and new capacities? Which are old systems whose productivities are spent and will eventually darken and die? Which are brilliant novas that emit radically new competencies and challenge the prevailing architecture of the entire channel galaxy, but which have fast clockspeeds and are destined to die out after a brief and often unsettling life? The goal of the process is to identify the strengths and weaknesses of trading partners as a means to determine the level and volatility of value enablers from physical resources to innovation capabilities.

- *Supply Chain Technologies.* This final dimension of supply chain planning references the potential robustness of the connecting links integrating and synchronizing each node in the supply channel galaxy. The goal is to identify the technology tools that determine how databases and processes from each channel node can converge and support one another. Whether it be through the use of analog methods, *electronic data interchange* (EDI), or the Internet, it is critical that the technologies employed be reviewed to clarify how deep into the supply chain they provide for database and competency transfer. Some may be single pair connections that stop at the borders of the business relationship. Others may provide localized integration where isolated systems of suppliers and customers in some region of the network galaxy are closely synchronized. Still others may possess technologies that lie in far off regions, but are capable of opening wormholes in the fabric of the trading galaxy linking suppliers in the *nth* tier with customers far off on the rim of the supply chain system.

Being able to constantly generate the products and services necessary to win customers and drive home competitive advantage means that today's enterprise must be able to transcend the limits of company-centric products and process competencies by utilizing the capabilities of their supply chain partners. Viewing the supply chain galaxy from a three-dimensional perspective enables companies positioned within the network system to structure a host of collaborative and synchronized functions ranging from concurrent engineering, to forecasting, to customer database management, which can open immense opportunities to build and enhance market leadership. Focusing and energizing the supply chain business architecture requires that not just individual companies, but the entire supply chain system utilize integrative technologies to access databases and transmit process information in real time, unencumbered by traditional information silos. Thinking about the application of Internet-based forms of information and transaction management is the next step in the discussion before an e-SCM strategy can be detailed.

C. Barriers to e-SCM

In the early 1980s the concept of *just-in-time* (JIT) burst upon the scene as a revolutionary method of running the enterprise. At first it was thought that the dramatic breakthroughs in productivity being reported by Japanese companies could be duplicated by simply applying JIT to any production system. Papers and books were written detailing formulas and techniques. Executives went on plant tours. Current methods of traditional management, particularly *material requirements planning* (MRP), were deemed obsolete. Despite the hype, however, the results continued to be disappointing. Critics complained that the Japanese had unfair government support; they focused on commodity type products that easily fit the JIT model; their economic system of slow incremental growth did not fit the U.S. system of investor-driven high return. Even ignorant racial stereotypes about the homogeneity of Japanese society were offered as excuses for lack of success.

Slowly, it began to dawn on executives that the advantages of JIT could not be attained by simply "bolting-on" the *techniques* of JIT; companies also need to implement the *philosophy* of JIT. It simply did no good to design a shop floor *kanban* card system, if the demand side of the business did not also develop a comprehensive "pull system" so that customer orders, and not some form of *economic order quantity* (EOQ), drove production. Similarly, JIT required changes in purchasing, engineering, finance — well the entire infrastructure of the company! What is more, companies soon found that their JIT initiative did not really work if supply chain partners ran their businesses with methods that were out of synchronization with their JIT initiatives. It took a while for companies to understand that JIT was, in reality, both a technique *and* a philosophy for running not only individual enterprises but also entire supply chains in the pursuit of a common competitive advantage.

Today, as businesses struggle to find answers to what the Internet means to their businesses and supply chains and how they are going to integrate Web technologies with current business practices, companies are finding themselves facing the same kind of operational and philosophical conundrum characteristic of their past efforts to implement JIT. Utilizing the Web seems to be a relatively easy decision to make. The Internet offers companies a relatively low-cost technology that enables them to effectively connect with their customers and suppliers. However, once the Internet initiative begins, implementers are immediately faced with the same kind of problems facing JIT implementers. Unless the objective is to simply set up a static marketing site, a host of operational and strategic critical questions immediately becomes apparent. What impact will e-business have on business operations? How will Web tools work with current information technologies, and what will it take to integrate them? How will customers and suppliers react to the new technology? Can e-business open entirely new avenues of competitive advantage, and what kind of infrastructure must be in place to make such opportunities happen?

As Sawhney and Zabin point out,[2] e-business initiatives *always* result in one or more of the following possible sets of outcomes:

1. Cost reduction
2. Revenue expansion
3. Time reduction
4. Relationship enhancement

Deciding which of the above e-business values to implement is very similar to the choices that still confront executives embarking on JIT. e-Business functions that focus squarely on *cost reduction* are clearly the easiest to implement and can be seen directly on the firm's balance sheet. However, technology applications that are directed at simply automating cost out of processes constitute a purely tactical response to value generation, and their impact provides only temporary advantage. While a degree more difficult to achieve, e-business applications enabling *time reductions* are similarly focused on improving operating efficiencies and bottom-line results. For example, while an e-procurement portal may succeed in reducing MRO order processing and delivery times, the application simply is supercharging functions of the already existing purchasing process.

In contrast, e-business initiatives surrounding *revenue expansion* and *relationship enhancement* provide companies with *strategic* opportunities to generate not just bottom-line efficiencies but also radically new regions of competitive advantage. Similar to a JIT project that requires not only tactical but also strategic changes to the way a company relates to their supply chain trading partners, e-business tools enable companies to deconstruct and reassemble exciting new value chains or even reinvent whole industries. For example, when DuPont Performance Coatings, the $3.8 billion-a-year automotive paint arm of DuPont & Co., contemplated e-business tools, it was decided to implement a Web site where customers could place orders. However, the system was not fully integrated with their enterprise business system (EBS), with the result that orders had to be manually entered from the Web front-end to the EBS. Nine months after the implementation, management decided this tactical e-business initiative had to be completely reinvented. To begin with, the Web site was restructured to permit direct input of customer data into and out of the EBS. In addition, customers could now visit the Web site to access information on their accounts, place and change orders, and check order status. The Web site could also be customized so that customers using Web services would have a personalized experience. DuPont now is looking to extend the strategic reach of its e-business architecture by tightening relationships with its customers' customers — the body shops that actually buy and use the paints.[3]

Viewing e-business, as DuPont initially did, as simply a piece of automation software misses the real potential of Internet commerce. JIT cannot realize the opportunities it holds for both cost reduction and radical competitive enhancement until executives finally understand that JIT is a management philosophy guiding not just individual companies but entire supply chains. In a similar fashion, e-business strategies must be seen not merely as a component of a company's technology suite, but rather as a new business chain model that requires entire supply channels to be transformed into *value networks*. What are the characteristics of these *value networks*? They seek to utilize e-business architectures to achieve superior customer satisfaction as well as company profitability. They provide collaborative links matching customer demand with flexible, agile manufacturing product design and delivery. They provide for the real-time transfer and synchronization of plans and information enabling channels to bypass costly distribution intermediaries. They leverage digital technology to provide a seamless channel structure with network suppliers. They permit entire supply chain systems to adapt quickly to constant change.

As a prelude to discussing, in the next section, how to effectively create an e-SCM *value network* strategy, it might be valuable to conclude with a definition of what e-business is *not*.[4]

- *e-Business is not synonymous with the "new economy."* In the early days of the dot-com revolution it was said that the Internet was such a potent new force for business that it marked the end of the old "industrial economy" and inaugurated a new "digital economy." In retrospect, such claims were obviously over-inflated. While it is true that e-business does provide today's enterprise with radically new tools for data transfer, information analysis, transaction management, value delivery, and collaboration, just using Web technologies does not automatically make an enterprise a "new economy company." In fact, the collapse of the dot-com bubble and the recession of 2001–2002 proved that even the best Internet-enabled companies still had to pay due diligence to basic "old economy" principles such as profitability, asset management, and viable operations and strategic planning if they were to survive in a climate of constant change. Similar to the JIT revolution that shook the economic environment during the last decades of the twentieth century, e-business has changed the nature of product and service development and delivery, enabled the pursuit of often radically new competitive values, engendered new business infrastructures, and in some sectors, whole new businesses.
  In today's post-dot-com era, it is becoming abundantly clear that there is no real separation between "old" and "new economy" companies. Almost every business today has implemented some facet of Web-enabled tools, and many executives, whether consciously or not, are moving their enterprises incrementally toward the use of e-business to link their core competencies closer to customers and suppliers. In fact, look in the next several years for the ubiquitous "*e*," that now precedes just about all business functions, to disappear. Just as we do not speak of *JIT-business*, we will no longer use the artificial term *e-business*. It will be just "business," just as JIT-enabled business is today just "business."
- *e-Business is not just about technology.* As companies began to implement Internet applications, managers first considered Web-enabling tools purely as discrete software components that could be "bolted onto" the business architecture, in much the same fashion as EDI. Now, companies have become aware that the more e-business applications are used, the more the lines separating the technology from existing infrastructure, operations, and strategic functions are proportionately blurred. As has been pointed out, as Internet tools migrate from tactical to strategic, companies also find that their internal organizations, as well as their relations with

customers, suppliers, and business partners, have been transformed from being businesses to becoming e-businesses.

Such a metamorphosis requires that enterprises constantly re-evaluate their strategies, their infrastructures, and their supply chains. Similar to the adoption of the JIT concept, firms implementing Internet applications are beginning to understand that it is not the technology, but the opportunity to deconstruct rigidly held principles and management silos, and then to reassemble the components into whole new environments, organizational behaviors, cultures, and competitive values capable of leveraging radically new ways of working with the value chain, that constitutes the real importance of e-business. At bottom, e-business is more about changing infrastructure and channel management than it is about managing the technical aspects of Web applications.

- *e-Business management is not the responsibility of a company department.* Many companies have made the mistake of treating their e-business initiatives either as a computer project and, therefore, the responsibility of Information Services, or as the responsibility of an e-business department. Such operational decisions perceive much too narrowly the scope of e-business. Again, consider the example of JIT. It is virtually impossible to localize a JIT implementation or make a specific group responsible for the project: everyone in the company and in the supply chain, for that matter, must be in pursuit of JIT goals. e-Business, like JIT, cuts horizontally across the enterprise and its supply partners and requires buy in at all dimensions.

  Consider the implementation of a Web-based ordering system. Initially, the project is designed to provide customers with a real-time view of company products and services, facilitate the ordering process, reduce order inaccuracies, and accelerate deliveries. Pursuing all of these objectives, however, means that not only sales, but also just about every functional department will be impacted. Depending on how closely the order process is connected to business partners, the implementation could also reverberate throughout channel inventory replenishment, logistics, and outsourced functions as well. e-Business requires process architectures uninhibited by internal or external infrastructures that can constrain the flow of data and information necessary for full e-business functional application.

- *e-Business is not a close-ended project.* Earlier in this chapter it was said that all competitive advantage is *temporary*. This means that all management strategies, as well as product and service life cycles, have been continuously shrinking, and the prognosis is that the process will only accelerate in the years to come. To ensure that they are not caught behind the change management power curve, managers today have been countering the pressure by attempting to utilize e-business tools to remain competitive. In fact, much like in the heyday of ERP, companies are gradually moving into an e-business arms race era. Although the collapse of the dotcoms and the recession of 2001–2002 have dampened considerably the race, companies are aware that neither their legacy technology nor their past e-business investments guarantee them a source of marketplace differentiation tomorrow. Web enablers, such as on-line catalogues and the ability to build order management front-ends, that once produced so much wonder, are now commonplace for most companies. Considering the disruptive power of the Internet, a technology enhancement implemented by one business chain can have the power to destabilize the equilibrium and throw an entire industry into chaos.

In such a volatile environment, firms constantly need to be reviewing and planning how e-business technologies can be utilized in the continuous search for competitive advantage. Defining a purposeful e-business technology architecture is not simply a matter of checking off a list of software applications. Rather, it is about intelligently choosing e-business alternatives to migrate, say, from using the Web for information and performing trading partner transactions, to enabling full channel network collaboration. What can be said for sure is that very few companies that have begun the journey into e-business have decided to abandon the project as providing little or no competitive advantage. The goal for managers is to be vigilant in fashioning the business strategies that merge e-business enablers, core competencies, and supply partners capabilities with the continuous fracturing of what currently constitutes competitive marketplace value.

II. PRELIMINARY STEPS IN e-SCM STRATEGY DEVELOPMENT

The fundamental principle guiding SCM can be found in the capability of supply channel network partners to integrate and synchronize the flow of goods and information through the supply chain. SCM requires the establishment of business networks characterized by flexibility, agility, collaboration, and a focus on cross-enterprise processes. With the application of Internet technologies, the connectivity of SCM is greatly enhanced to permit instantaneous visibility to market conditions and to optimize process management. Whole supply chains are now freed from the tyranny of the *chain pairs of relationship model* and are capable of architecting networks where the impact of information, transactions, and collaborative productivities can be broadcast in real time to all trading partners, unencumbered by rigid channel tiers.

Assembling e-SCM value networks is also about dramatic shifts in the mindset of companies. While leveraging core competencies and pursuing brand and service leadership remain central, the e-SCM concept requires a migration of business strategies from the traditional focus on competition to collaboration, from considering information as proprietary to information as a shared resource, from company-centric data to the pursuit of open inter-enterprise and network thinking, where close trading partner coordination dominates. Pursuing the activation of e-SCM requires that executives possess the capability to continuously reinvent their businesses and the nature of their supply chain networks in light of the tremendous changes occurring in the marketplace and in e-business integrative technologies. In this section, the basics of fashioning an effective e-SCM value network strategy will be discussed.

A. OPENING ISSUES IN e-SCM STRATEGY DEVELOPMENT

"The Internet is a tool," says Intel chairman Andy Grove, "and the biggest impact of that tool is speed." For many of today's top companies it is *speed* that conveys the essence of their business strategies. Speed means the difference between satisfying customers and spiraling into extinction, between meeting marketplace demand and being stuck with unproductive assets, between success and failure. Speed, however, also means that companies must be constantly vigilant to ensure their businesses pursue optimal combinations of agility, visibility, intelligence, and technology to counter a marketplace characterized by increasing uncertainty, continued compression of business cycles, and expanding supply chain complexity. Responding to such a constantly mutating business environment requires that companies, more than ever, have a coherent e-SCM strategy in place. The good news is that companies capable of meeting the challenge of change management with effective e-business strategies can reap fabulous rewards; the bad news is that those that do not are destined to vanish as viable competitors.

As the toll of dot-com and "new economy" company disasters from Webvan to Enron piled up by the beginning of 2002, the ability to successfully traverse the e-business landscape has begun to appear to many companies as labyrinthine as ever. But what separates those companies who not only succeeded with their e-business initiatives, but succeed spectacularly, Dell Computer, Wal-Mart, e-Bay, Cisco Systems, and a host of others, is the ability of their management teams to architect an effective corporate strategy and then integrate a specific e-business model that supports that strategy. Many e-business failures occur when executives skip the infrastructure strategies necessary for customer fulfillment and concentrate solely on the elegance of the Web technology. On the other end of the spectrum, new failures are destined by established "bricks-and-mortar" companies who have taken a step into I-Marketing but are waiting too long to revamp their business strategies to include real Internet commerce initiatives.

Designing an effective e-SCM strategy can seem a daunting task. Immediately, a multitude of questions is before the management team. Should the company focus on B2C or B2B? How should working with ITXs or PTXs be determined? What will it take to rebuild the current corporate/divisional strategy around e-business functions? What is the ROI and is it feasible? Should the existing ERP system be upgraded, a "best-of-breed" approach be followed, or a customized solution undertaken? What impact will the new e-SCM strategy have on customers, suppliers, and the internal business infrastructure? Will the implementation of e-SCM transform the competitive landscape and the company's position in it? These and a host of other questions must be posed, prioritized, and integrated into the new business strategy.

Once such questions are sorted out, the crafted e-business decision may take several directions, depending on circumstances and the company's desired objectives. Some firms may start by building onto their initial I-Marketing initiatives, by implementing a *customer relationship management* (CRM) system that will provide customers with the ability to enter, revise, and track their orders. Another company, who may even be in the same industry, may start on the supply side by forming a

FIGURE 4.2 Initial e-SCM strategy steps.

PTX or joining a CTX. Still other enterprises might decide to embark upon a number of e-business initiatives simultaneously. Whatever the direction, the strategy must be designed to support both the firm's customer value proposition and supply chain effectiveness.

B. PRELIMINARY STEPS

The task of establishing a purposeful e-SCM strategy requires a number of preliminary steps. The goal of these first steps is to focus the enterprise on the impact of what e-business will mean to everyone, both within the organization and to trading partners out in the supply channel network. The critical starting point will be for the executive team to ensure that everyone involved, from employees to channel partners, understands that the creation of an e-SCM strategy will transform traditional roles for all involved. It is only through the detailed analysis of the current and anticipated interactions with customers and suppliers that a comprehensive e-business strategy, supporting a value proposition that provides for on-going competitive differentiation, can be created. Achieving this point in e-SCM strategy development involves a five-step approach (Figure 4.2).

Step 1: Energize the Organization

Preparing the organization for e-SCM is absolutely critical before a comprehensive business strategy can be articulated. Over the past decade executives have become aware that information technologies by themselves are rarely a source of sustainable competitive advantage. Successful technologies can be easily copied or supplied by software vendors, and Internet technologies are no exception. Rather, it is when technologies are utilized in support of business strategies by being focused on an individual firm's employees, customers, and suppliers, that a company can gain significant, and potentially sustainable, competitive advantage. Preparing the organization for e-SCM requires two major human resources initiatives: getting top management on board to spearhead the effort and energizing and integrating the company's people organization into e-SCM technologies. The following steps should be followed to inform and activate the top management team:

- *SCM and e-business education.* The executive team should be educated on the basics of SCM and e-business. In the past, CEOs could depend on fundamental principles in making decisions about products, markets, investments, and resources. Today, SCM and e-business have challenged virtually all of those assumptions. Executives will need to understand what e-SCM means, not just in theory, but how it can be used to respond to today's competitive environment.
- *Act as a sponsor.* Once education is complete, the executive team must act as champion or sponsor of the e-SCM effort. Such an effort is doomed without a major commitment and the involvement of senior management.
- *Develop a SCM strategy.* The development of an e-SCM strategy often means both redesigning the supply chain and integrating in e-business technologies. CEOs need to make sure their supply chain and e-business strategies are an integral part of the big picture. Business vision, e-commerce, supply chain, and customer management strategies all have to be aligned.
- *Develop the firm's human resources.* Designing infrastructure around cross-functional collaboration is a significant challenge for most companies. Many firms are still organized around the departmental silos of the past and have yet to be restructured around SCM thinking.
- *Invest in supply chain improvement.* Ongoing effectiveness of e-SCM strategies requires a supply chain improvement budget. Executives need to establish the means by which constant improvements in technology, external resources, and business processes can be continually funded.

The second initiative in preparing for e-SCM strategy development is energizing the company's people organization. According to Manheim,[5] there are 6 major "thrusts" that can be used to properly integrate e-SCM and people. The first "thrust" serves as the overarching theme of the business strategy; the next five are supportive "thrusts," each of which reinforces and amplifies the first "thrust."

Thrust 1: *Enhance the Ways in Which People Work.* The implementation of an e-SCM strategy will fundamentally alter the ways in which people, the organization, and supply chain partners work. Besides top management, the organization as a whole, and often trading partners, must be educated in e-business technologies and SCM philosophies. Similar to initiatives such as ERP or JIT, unless the people who will run the daily business buy into the technology fully, the strategy will achieve only a fraction of its potential.

Thrust 2: *Build Powerful Multi-Enterprise Processes with Appropriate IT Support.* A critical opening step is identifying across the supply chain critical business processes and designing or reconstructing them. Besides rendering processes more efficient and productive, this thrust also requires network partners to implement channel-integrating technologies that permit the management of processes within the enterprise and between enterprises in the supply chain.

Thrust 3: *Balance the Roles of People and Technology.* The adoption of an e-SCM strategy heightens the need for integration between people and technology. Three critical issues come to mind. To begin with, SCM-based business is about relationships. Trading partner perceptions, particularly Internet-based businesses, are heavily influenced by trust and the uniqueness of customer-supplier relationships. Second, the dynamic nature of today's business environment requires that companies be prepared to reinvent e-SCM models in response to changing competitive conditions, customer preferences, financial conditions, and supplier offerings. Finally, companies pursuing e-SCM must be adept at quickly turning channel data into knowledge useful for effective management decision-making.

Thrust 4: *Manage Multi-Enterprise Processes Flexibly and Dynamically.* The growth of Web-based applications and protocols has made it possible to tightly integrate the critical workflows occurring between network partners. The ability to perform transactions, store and retrieve documents, and pass information across different organizational units and supply chain partners must be determined before an e-SCM strategy can be deployed.

Thrust 5: *Manage Knowledge Strategically.* The effectiveness of e-SCM is based on the concept of gaining competitive advantage through people, enhanced by Internet technologies. Being able to standardize the enormous amount of human knowledge, work patterns, checklists, process rules, and best practices of the workforces to be found in individual companies and supply network systems is essential in managing and directing intellectual capital to continuously enrich e-SCM strategy development.

Thrust 6: *Enhance Individual Effectiveness.* The ability to increase the effectiveness of individuals at any node in the supply chain is a key element of e-SCM strategy. The philosophies and technologies associated with e-SCM can provide powerful enhancements to the way people think and act. SCM concepts enable people to deepen their relationships with channel partners, while computerized tools permit them to more effectively transfer and store data and communicate with their work partners and to facilitate change and decision management.

Step 2: Enterprise Vision

Visioning the competitive power of the business is the next step on the journey to building an effective e-SCM strategy. This step is about defining the nature of the competitive competencies possessed within the current infrastructure and outside in the supply chain network. In defining the enterprise vision executive teams need to think about such factors as:

- What is the historical nature of the firm?
- How has it traditionally approached the marketplace?
- What processes add the most value to customers?
- How have relationships with suppliers grown through time?
- What is the nature of the internal organization?

- What are the strengths and weaknesses of business partners?
- What capabilities are the most important in creating and sustaining competitive advantage?

The goal of this process is to ensure a deep degree of awareness, on the part of executives, concerning just what e-business means to the company, the steps necessary to build an effective e-SCM model and strategy, and how a new Internet-driven value proposition would translate into specific processes. This is not to say that other factors should be excluded from the visioning process. Current market conditions, existing channels of supply, product characteristics, competitive pressures, and legacy technology infrastructure should also be included to broaden the proposed competitive vision.

For example, Fresenius Medical Care, a manufacturer of dialysis equipment, has visioned itself in the position of a value network integrator in its industry. The company is successfully developing a total therapy concept based on its chain of over 1,100 clinics. These clinics are arranged into a network of therapy centers, providing a uniquely integrated value proposition linking equipment development and service to fit patient needs. To realize this strategic vision, the management system will use the Internet to link patients, nurses, physicians, researchers, pharmaceutical companies, and health insurance companies into a comprehensive treatment, therapy, and development process monitored and administered over the Web.[6]

Step 3: Supply Chain Value Assessment

The decision to implement Internet applications must be driven by a thorough understanding of which critical business processes should be moved to e-business. Not every company process needs to be converted to an e-business process. The processes to focus on should be those closely linked to the enterprise visioning activity detailed in *Step 2* above. Basically, companies should seek to convert to e-business those processes that deliver the most competitive advantage. Non-crucial processes should be left untouched, except in cases where they are impacted by an associated e-business initiative.

Perhaps the most effective method to begin matching Internet initiatives, business processes, and strategic visioning is to perform a *supply chain value assessment* (SCVA). The object of this activity is to identify and then prioritize which e-business initiatives should be undertaken that would provide the greatest enterprise and trading partner benefit. Far from being an isolated activity, an effective SCVA requires a collaborative effort, where internal value assessment teams are closely integrated with analogous teams appointed by supply chain partners. The ultimate objective is to determine whether the e-business vision and the impact it will have on the supply chain will be *evolutionary* or *revolutionary.*[7]

e-Business initiatives that are *evolutionary* are normally focused on improving core business functions and sustaining the competitive advantages they drive. Typically, these initiatives tend to center on process automation, are usually low risk and low return, tend to be inward-oriented, and focus on short-term bottom-line return. Examples would include selling products on-line, through a catalog with standard prices, or automating information on shipments and inventories. In contrast, *revolutionary* e-business initiatives attempt to create radically new supply chain network architectures that can actually transform internal core processes as well as those possessed by trading partners. Typically, these initiatives seek to create new value propositions, customers, and revenue streams and are, by their very nature, high risk and long-term, supply channel oriented, and focused on capital investment. An example would be a multi-channel customer cross-selling process that enables the configuration of complex products that combine trading partners' products and services.

Determining whether the e-business vision is evolutionary or revolutionary is the central outcome of the SCVA process. Unfortunately, popular assumptions are that all e-business initiatives are revolutionary and, likewise, that all revolutionary initiatives can be implemented through the same efforts as evolutionary initiatives. Obviously there is a qualitative gap between the two. Companies seeking revolutionary e-business will soon find that the approach requires a massive transformation in infrastructure, culture, competencies, learning capabilities, funding, people motivation, and, of course, technology. It will also normally destabilize existing channel configurations, time-proven business conventions, and long-standing partner relations.

Performing an effective SCVA can be distilled into three fundamental steps.

1. A collaborative team consisting of company and supply chain partners is formed. The operating basis of the team is to integrate supply chain, business process, and e-business knowledge. It is the responsibility of the team to identify company and supply chain business issues, prepare an as-is model of competitive processes, and begin detailing the implications of evolutionary versus revolutionary approaches to utilizing e-business for competitive advantage.
2. In the second step, the SCVA team breaks their findings down into *critical performance indicators* (KPIs) and supply network opportunities. As the broad outlines of possible e-business solutions become apparent, the team begins to investigate and detail solution approaches and concerns, obstacles and risks, and benchmarks to validate future performance.
3. In the third step, the SCVA team begins to match KPIs with proposed Internet applications to determine such decision points as objective of the initiative, risk/return profile, major risk factors, outcome metrics, value-adding processes impacted, competencies required, and overall impact on the organization and the supply chain. When the exercise is completed, both the firm and its supporting supply chain partners should be left with a detailed compendium of possible e-business alternatives to select from. It is this list that will then be used in the prioritization process to come.

Step 4: Opportunity Identification

The SCVA exercise should provide the collaborative e-business team with a map of possible choices for the application of Internet strategies. Perhaps the first activity

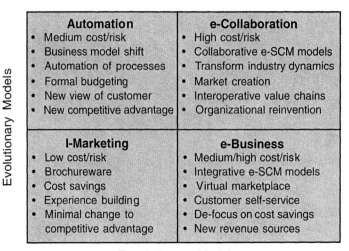

FIGURE 4.3 SCVA map of e-business opportunities.

in this step is to prioritize the possible e-business alternatives. Accomplishing this task will require the SCVA team to divide initiatives into those that are *evolutionary* and those that are *revolutionary* in nature (see Figure 4.3). This map will then enable the firm to begin the process of determining just what kind of e-SCM implementation they wish to embark on, the range of competitive opportunities made available, and the approximate costs both to the enterprise and to supply chain partners.

As SCVA teams begin detailing and prioritizing possible e-business solutions, several issues need to be kept to the forefront. To begin with, teams must understand what e-business technology does and does not do. During the dot-com craze, some technologists proclaimed that the Web signified the end of business as we know it. In reality, as Sawhney and Zabin point out,[8] "New technology does not introduce new business processes any more than product innovations create new customer needs. Instead, the Net creates new degrees of efficiency and effectiveness around business processes that have existed since time immemorial." Until a futuristic time when some fabulous machine can instantly transform thoughts into products, economies will have to contend with solving the age-old problems of production, demand, and distribution, regardless of how automated the process may become.

Another critical dimension of prioritizing the results of the SCVA revolves around executives understanding the expanding degree of involvement required of supply chain partners as the e-business initiative moves from evolutionary to revolutionary. The true value of network technology is that it enables companies to move beyond viewing the marketplace purely from *inside* the business. Even small-impact Internet automation projects soon force companies to shift their attention from managing internal to architecting interbusiness processes that are synchronized and intermeshed. Such *systemic* thinking will prevent e-SCM initiatives from failing prey to the deficiencies that plagued dot-com strategies, which simply forgot to integrate with the technology just how products and services were to be acquired, stored, and finally delivered to the customer. Business, in reality, has always been about the

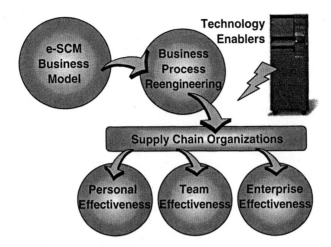

FIGURE 4.4 e-SCM organizational reengineering.

interconnections that exist between supply chain partners; it has only been with the rise of networking technologies, however, that those linkages have become visible and have enabled chains of companies to build radically new mechanisms of delivering value to the customer.

Finally, SCVA teams must be aware that, as the level of networking in the supply chain increases, the pressures on traditionally structured organizations will grow incrementally. In fact, the growing requirements for collaboration and the cross-functional nature of the Web tend to undermine hierarchical organizations. No matter in which of the four quadrants (see Figure 4.3) a company may wish to begin, business processes must be engineered to support the channel network model (Figure 4.4). For example, a B2B initiative would require changes to purchasing, planning, sourcing and negotiations, supplier relationships, delivery and receiving functions, and accounts payable. One e-business expert feels that e-SCM organizations will be characterized by growing flexibility and will find themselves being reorganized every six months or so, to accommodate changes to network models and to leverage new management skills.[9]

Step 5: Strategy Decision

Once the e-SCM opportunity map has been completed, company executives can then begin the process of planning a networked initiative or group of supporting initiatives. Regardless of whether the proposed solution involves a cautious evolutionary tactic or a dramatic Web-based strategy, the decision should focus on expected advantages. Whether the e-SCM initiative is focused on automating and integrating processes, reducing costs and increasing the flow of information through the supply chain, or engendering whole new businesses and forms of customer value is not important. What is critical is the understanding by the executive team that, by itself, the technology accomplishes nothing, and that the real objective of the e-SCM initiative is to utilize the power of trading partners to amplify existing marketplace advantages or realize radically new ways of providing value to the customer.

At this point, the preliminary steps necessary for e-SCM value network strategy formulation have been completed. In the next section, executive planners turn their attention to selecting the corporate e-SCM strategy and set in train the mechanisms for continuous strategy review.

III. DEVELOPING THE e-SCM STRATEGY

Earlier in this chapter, it was stated that the sum total output of a company and the way its infrastructure and value-enhancing resources are organized to meet its marketplace demand constitutes the firm's *business architecture*. To stay competitive, today's companies are being required to seriously reconstruct and, in some cases, reinvent their business architectures by including Internet capabilities. Undertaking such a task of enterprise deconstruction and rebirth can be a serious project, especially as firms move toward more *revolutionary* e-SCM models. In any case, once the preliminary analysis of what e-business technologies are available to the company has been completed, strategic planners must begin the task of transforming the enterprise, and often its supply chains, to realize the decided-upon e-SCM value network strategy.

To assist planning executives create business architectures that enable them to successfully leverage the Internet-driven models they would like to pursue, the following strategy design framework diagram has been created and is illustrated in Figure 4.5. While it is impossible to design a strategic planning model that would be applicable to all businesses in all industries, the following planning framework can offer at least a broad-brush landscape to assist planners to effectively begin their e-SCM plans. As can be seen, the diagram, first of all, is portrayed as a never-ending cycle, where enterprise e-SCM architectures and marketplace objectives are constructed, operated, reviewed for performance, and then reconstructed as business and technologies change through time. Also, the diagram shows that the design framework consists of two interconnected flows, one focused on continuously driving innovative strategic thinking, and the other focused on operational execution. To be effective, an e-SCM value network must be constructed utilizing each segment of the framework. Examining each of these segments is the subject of the remainder of this section.

A. CONSTRUCTING THE BUSINESS VALUE PROPOSITION

The purpose of performing the preliminary steps to e-SCM strategy development discussed above is to have available a map of possible e-business solutions, what impact the application of any one of the solutions will have on business infrastructure and competitive positioning, and what changes will have to be made in supply chain arrangements. The process of actually selecting the Internet technology solution to be implemented is the focus of this first step in e-SCM strategy development.

At the very core of strategy selection is the *business value proposition*. Companies exist to satisfy a particular need or want of their customers. In the past, firms could be halfhearted in listening to the "voice of the customer." Today, in this age of "temporary advantage," companies must be ever vigilant in ensuring that their

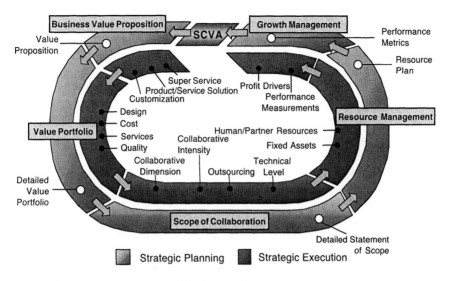

FIGURE 4.5 Structuring the e-SCM business architecture strategy.

organizations and their product and service offerings are synchronized to provide total value to the customer. Companies, however, must be careful to view a value proposition in its widest sense. While the end-customer has been the main focus, the term "customer" can be expanded to include suppliers, channel members, and partners.

In defining an e-SCM value proposition, planners are essentially concerned with the performance of two major activities. In the first, the customer segments to be served by an e-business initiative are identified. Here, the goal is to look for mismatches between the expected results of the Web technology to be implemented and the value of the targeted marketing segment. For example, in order for McKesson-HBOC, one of the world's largest providers of healthcare products, to be able to respond to catalog information, pricing, real-time ordering, and delivery tracking needs of a wide range of customer segments, from drug stores to mass merchandisers and hospitals, the company established a self-service Web site. When the site was launched, more than 6,000 customers immediately began to use it in their dealings with McKesson. While traditional customer services remain, this experiment in e-business helped the company fill the gaps in what had been a fragmented view of servicing a widely differentiated group of customer segments.

Once Web technologies are matched to intended customer segments, the next step is to ensure that the technologies to be implemented will fulfill the service expected by the customer. According to Bovet and Martha,[10] an effective value proposition must be ready to respond to three possible service values:

- *Super Service.* The ability to provide superior service enhances both the value of the product/services mix presented to the customer and the competitive differentiation of the provider. The two primary attributes constituting super service are *speed* and *reliable delivery.* Speed refers to the velocity of response desired and offered by the provider. Reliable delivery refers to the receipt by the customer of orders that meet expectations for capacity to absorb changes, accuracy, completeness, timeliness, fitness-for-use, and location.

- *Product/Service Solutions.* What constitutes "value" to the customer varies by the nature of the type of solution desired. Products and services that are commodity in nature have easily identifiable values, such as ownership, availability, low cost, convenience of acquisition, and a recognized level of quality. On the other hand, non-commodity-type products are surrounded by more complex customer values, such as possession, service performance completion, or unique product-information-service combinations that permit the customer to enrich their own competitive strategies. Dell Computer, for example, provides not just computers, but configurable information technology solutions designed to provide customers with value beyond mere possession of the product.

- *Customization.* As today's customers increasingly look toward *solutions* instead of just *products* and *services*, the capability for providers to offer configurable, customized choices that fit the precise need of the customer is growing as a prime attribute of a competitive strategy. Such a strategy can be realized by following an *assemble-to-order* (ATO), *make-to-order* (MTO), or through various forms of supply chain postponement.

The e-business value proposition is not a separate part of the over-all business strategy: it and other value initiatives *are* the *business value proposition*. Aligning a company's technology initiatives with its overall strategic framework sounds like basic advice, but for most firms this is the exception rather than the rule. Often, e-business initiatives do little to support a company's core marketing strategy or long-term customer satisfaction goals. In a study of 100 consumer goods companies conducted by Cap Gemini Ernst & Young in October 2001, only 12 percent felt their technology investments were "very effective" at supporting company strategy. Failure to view the business value proposition as an integrated part of the business strategy can not only endanger the e-SCM initiative, it can also endanger the firm's existence. In his analysis of the failure of Webvan, Mike Flamer, president of the Dorfman Group, cited these major failures in value proposition formulation:[11]

- Focus on the "commerce" and not just the "e." If the infrastructure is not there, even the best Web site design will fail.
- Do not absorb the cost of functions that consumers are willing to do for free, such as customers' overwhelming desire to shop for groceries.
- Do not offer consumers a new technology unless it solves their problems better than their current solution.
- Create e-tail strategies that match the lifestyle realities of market segments.
- Do not enter a mature, highly efficient industry with an inefficient strategy.
- Retailers should embrace the Internet for certain marketing and branding strategies, but never at the peril of ignoring how customers buy and use their products and services.

TABLE 4.1
Changes in Products and Services

Marketing Function	Past Market Values	e-SCM Market Values
Form Utility	Standardized product and services offerings	Configurable products providing customer choices
Time Utility	As available; customers willing to wait	When wanted; customers want immediate availability and delivery
Place Utility	Available where most sales occur	Available everywhere, physically and electronically
Quality Utility	Acceptable level of product quality	Total quality that exceeds customer expectations
Price Utility	Focus on offering the lowest standard price	Pricing based on value of the customer solution
Services Utility	Minimal service offerings	Complex packages of product and services
Information Utility	Product/service contains minimal to no information	Product/service contains rich information

B. DEFINING THE VALUE PORTFOLIO

Internet commerce has dramatically accelerated the changes occurring in the nature of product and service offerings. In the past, companies competed by selling relatively stable product lines consisting of standardized, mass-produced product/service offerings. Marketing concentrated on persuading customers to purchase products whose value was fixed in the form of standard pricing. The purchasing transaction was considered as the culmination of the sales process, after which neither seller nor buyer generally expected ongoing opportunities for increased value-added products or services. Today, as illustrated in Table 4.1, past views of product and service value have yielded to new marketplace requirements that stimulate the development of deep, sustainable relationships among producers, distributors, and customers. The central theme of the table is to illustrate the radical shift in the portfolio of what constitutes product and service value as it migrates from standardized to more customized offerings, always available, delivered instantaneously, and accessible through electronic mediums.

To leverage the enabling power of the Internet, companies need to closely align their e-SCM strategy with their operations capabilities to continuously provide the product/service wrap that satisfies the unique needs of the customer. The following process developments need to be structured to effectively support the *business value proposition*.

- *Design*. Products and services have been dramatically impacted by continuously shrinking life cycles and accelerating new product/service introduction. For example, the life cycle of any of Panasonic's line of consumer electronic products, such as CD players, TVs, and VCRs is just 90 days.

The market for personal computers is so volatile and dynamic that a product can be obsoleted while still in production. The ever-shrinking window of opportunity directly impacts accompanying service and delivery functions. Companies must continuously seek to uncover ever-new opportunities to wrap intelligent services around products and activate logistics functions to speed product movement through the distribution pipeline.

- *Cost.* Effective cost management requires companies not only to design product/service offerings with an eye toward continuous process improvement and cost reduction, but also be able to squeeze the time it takes from idea conception to sales. Achieving such objectives means that companies must leverage the capabilities of supply chain partners. Cook and Tyndall[12] relate a story about how Dell was able to steal time, cost, and leadership from a competitor. Because of its real-time demand management channel design process connectivities, when a sudden surge in two-gigabyte disk drives called for a switch from one-gigabyte drives, it quickly changed its ordering with its supplier. Because of a conventional six-week demand forecast, a Dell competitor missed the trend and continued to build the one-gigabyte PCs. By the time the competitor got the product to market nobody wanted one-gigabyte drives. As a result, the competitor lost market share and had to take a sizeable write-off.

- *Services.* Customers today, especially those utilizing Web technologies, expect their products to be accompanied with a matrix of value-added services. For many products, the associated service package is often more important to the customer than the product itself. For example, GE Capital IT Solutions (GECITS), created a special group to handle normally unavailable, out-of-warranty parts for electronic equipment. Customer calls for service are normally extremely urgent. Formerly, service reps had to perform a time-consuming search through catalogs and query dealers for parts availability. Service pressures eventually drove GECITS to adopt a Web-based solution that provides customers with the capability to perform their own catalog search, in addition to real-time pricing, credit management, even classroom and e-learning in IT systems. Recently the company completed a reverse auction pilot, where the company and the customer base could sell and request parts and upgrades. The results: a tripling of new customers and growing satisfaction with the availability of on-line processes.[13]

- *Quality.* Over the past years the concept of quality has moved from a concern with the standard dimensions of performance, reliability, conformance, etc., to the capability of *choosing* between a multiplicity of products and services, to today's Web-driven requirement for product and service *individualization*. Customers now expect suppliers to have the ability to assist them in selecting the right combination of product and/or service offerings, and then configure the purchase to meet unique requirements. For example, IBM's customer order system contains a sophisticated configurator translator that converts model and features decisions made by customers into a buildable product, and then hands the configuration to production. The entire process is designed to remove redundancies, reduce cycle times, and ensure the delivery of a quality product to the customer.

C. STRUCTURING THE SCOPE OF COLLABORATION

Once the *business value proposition* and the *value portfolio* have been formulated, strategic planners must then determine the scope of trading partner collaboration. In this step, companies need to decide what will be the scope of the firm's processes and activities and, correspondingly, what will be the level of collaboration with trading partners necessary to supply missing resources and competencies. Today, everyone accepts the idea that a company cannot and should not try to do everything, and that collaboration with supply network partners, suppliers, and customers is a necessity. But while the idea of collaboration is not new, drafting a collaboration agenda has become, in today's marketplace, a complex affair. Similar to other management concepts such as JIT and TQM, most of the ambiguity stems from the fact that collaboration is a multi-faceted philosophy of business that can be approached from several angles. Simple forms of collaboration occur when companies exchange information periodically. In contrast, collaboration can take the form of highly integrated, Web-enabled intermediaries, like Covisint, that are focused on the real-time transfer of information and complex multiyear product development and marketing projects. The following points will have to be reviewed in determining the *scope of collaboration* when architecting the e-SCM value network strategy.

- *Determining the Collaborative Dimension.* The supply chain enables companies to leverage the competencies and resources to be found in their trading partners to assist in the sourcing, creation, and delivery of determined value portfolios. According to Sawhney and Zabin,[14] strategists can view this collaboration as having a *vertical* and a *horizontal* dimension. The *vertical* dimension can be said to consist of the matrix of network partners that assist in sourcing a business's inputs (suppliers) and delivering its outputs (channel intermediaries). This network can be said to constitute the supply and demand chains, respectively, of a given business. In contrast, the *horizontal* collaborative dimension consists of channel partners that enhance or reinforce a firm's value portfolio and customer relationships. A vertical partner contributes resources and competencies directly to the value portfolio, while horizontal partners utilize a company's value portfolio to perform value-added enhancements. For example, the thousands of software packages that run on Microsoft's operating system have dramatically expanded the corporation's reach into the marketplace and protect its competitive advantage.

  Corporate strategists must be keenly aware of how dependent their value propositions are on the channel network. Often, a new value proposition that significantly expands the depth and breath of the demand channel, while requiring greater supply channel cooperation, will also require a new collaborative value network. To cut cost and expedite customer service, Owens & Minor Inc., a health-care products distributor, implemented a new Internet order-fulfillment system with the product catalog system of key supplier Kimberly-Clark. When a customer clicks for more information on a Kimberly-Clark product, there is a connection to Kimberly-Clark's own product information, such as safety data sheets, videos on proper usage, product substitution notices, and FDA announcements. The results are that Kimberly-Clark gets a direct link to the customer, Owens & Minor does not have to maintain an on-line catalog, and both are assured the information the customer is accessing is current.[15]

- *Collaborative Intensity.* Regardless of the dimension of collaboration needed, strategists must determine the intensity of the collaboration with trading partners necessary to realize the value proposition. As mentioned above, collaboration can be pursued on many levels. Low levels of collaboration, which focus on making information available to trading partners so they can be more efficient in their support, are relatively easy to achieve and require little in organizational change and technology expense. Conversely, high levels of collaboration, which require an increasing symbiosis of fundamental processes and shared goals, are complex and expensive to implement.

According to Prahalad and Ramaswamy,[16] there are four levels of collaboration intensity that can be pursued by strategic design teams.

1. *Arms-length relationships.* Normally this is the level of collaboration pursued by companies seeking to drive market-based transactions across network boundaries. Often such a strategy can effectively utilize a Web portal site but will not require any greater level of sophistication. The target value of the collaboration effort is to increase the number of participants in the system.

2. *Information sharing.* This level of collaboration is pursued by trading partners seeking to share a wide variety of information, ranging from sales and order data to forecasts and stocking levels. Such efforts will require systems that will network the transaction systems of supply chain members. The target value of the effort is to improve business processes through more real-time workflows. Accordingly, as the number of participants increases, the information becomes more effective for decision-making.

3. *Sharing and creating knowledge.* In this level of collaboration, strategists seek to utilize and integrate the competencies of network partners in value proposition and/or value portfolio development. Pursuit of this level will require systems that enable on-line collaboration networking and unified information access. The target value is the capability to leverage knowledge from anywhere in the network to import needed competencies as well as reduce functional redundancies.

4. *Sharing and creating new insights.* At the highest level of collaboration, networked trading partners feel that they share common business value

propositions and are willing to jointly leverage competencies and resources. Such a high level of collaboration requires common network information access, collaboration tools, and capacity for rapid knowledge creation and insight building. The value of this level of collaboration is to be found in the capability of companies across a network to devise and share a common vision regarding opportunities that reveal whole new competitive space and the capability of structuring the technical and social architectures necessary to achieve those visions.

As strategic planners begin the process of selecting the level of collaborative intensity, they will need to determine answers to a number of key questions. To begin, at what level of collaborative intensity is the company currently positioned? This will reveal the gap between the existing and expected level. It should also reveal the major hurdles. Second, the analysis should reveal what prerequisites need to be in place, the administrative costs, and the impact of existing cultures. Third, the viability of the existing information technology infrastructure to support the targeted level of collaboration should be made visible. Finally, strategists must access the real and hidden risks and costs of the collaboration initiative, both within the organization and with trading partners.

- *Technical Level.* One of the critical elements in establishing the targeted level of collaborative intensity is the information technology capabilities required of both individual companies and the network. From the start, however, it must be stated that not all collaborative efforts require an Internet technology solution. For decades, companies have established effective modes of collaboration with network partners utilizing EDI, fax, and even the phone. Simply being Web-enabled does not mean that a company has achieved a high level of business collaboration. Determining just what level of technical assistance is required is a matter of finding answers to three questions.
  - What is the level of collaborative intensity required?
  - Based on the level of intensity, do the competitive values available meet the requirements of the value proposition?
  - Based on the answers, what, then, should be the level of technology necessary to support the scope of collaboration?

A critical mistake that can be made is assuming that a single technology solution will be sufficient to meet the requirements of the scope of collaboration. In reality, the actual collaborative partnerships a company has may require quite different technology responses. Smaller trading partners who are working quite well with fax or phone connectivity will be resistant to high-tech solutions such as B2B sites. Strategic planners should be prepared to create a portfolio of technical solutions to meet the possible needs of their collaborative partners.

According to Treachy and Dobrin,[17] there are four possible technical responses to meet connectivity needs to support collaboration strategies.

1. *Non-Internet technologies.* Many companies utilize basic technology tools to connect to their trading partners. Devices such as EDI, fax,

and the telephone fall within this area. Normally, these tools are used by companies seeking to pass basic transactions and market information across the channel network. The benefit of this level of technical connectivity is its low cost and ease of operation.

2. *Visibility.* This technical strategy seeks to provide an open systems approach, whereby either information, such as schedules, forecasts, or orders, is broadcast to the channel network, or trading partners are provided with the capability to access system data. For the most part, basic Web-based tools are used to achieve this level of functionality. The benefit of this level of technical connectivity is an increase in the speed and accuracy of information and the ability of trading partners to more effectively coordinate channel business activities.

3. *Server-to-server.* This technical solution is used by trading partners requiring that data physically reside in the systems of trading partners to support the large-scale transmission of information. This solution utilizes concepts such as e-hubs and transmission standardization tools like RosettaNet and CPFR standards. The benefit of this level of technical connectivity is channel information scalability, permitting each trading partner to use their own systems without manual transformation.

4. *Process management.* This is the most challenging level of technical connectivity and is the focus of channel networks seeking to integrate intercompany processes at the applications level. The goal is to configure Web solutions that provide for real-time workflow sharing. The benefit of this level of technical connectivity is the capacity for channel partners to accommodate changes and support business-process management in the pursuit of radically new competitive space.

In developing an effective technology strategy, planners will need to determine answers to a number of key questions. To begin, what is the scope of collaboration, and what level of technology does the firm plan to use to tap into the network of trading partner relationships? Second, have clear business benefits been identified for each technical initiative? The goal here is to prioritize collaborative opportunities and devise simple, low-cost technology tools to achieve the necessary level of collaboration intensity. Third, have strategists designed a useable portfolio of technology-connective approaches? Fourth, do the technology solutions chosen represent the simplest and least costly methods, or are they characterized by over-elegance and complexity?

• *Outsourcing.* A critical part of the scope of collaboration is the decision to outsource functions currently performed by the firm. In the past, companies sought to control, through vertically integrated corporations, all aspects of supply and delivery. Today, businesses are increasingly moving toward outsourcing, contract manufacturing, and third-party logistics, as short product life cycles, spiraling operations costs, and global competition tighten profit margins. By divesting themselves of labor- and capital-intensive assets not central to their businesses, companies can focus on their core competencies to improve competitive positioning.

The rise in outsourcing of functions from manufacturing to human resources is supported by the figures. According to a study by Bear Stearns, the outsourcing of operations and facilities across industries rose 18 percent from 1999 to 2000 alone. The report also revealed that the average electronics OEM manufacturer would like to outsource 73 percent of its manufacturing, and 40 percent of all OEMs would like to outsource the manufacture of 90 percent or more of their final product.[18]

When formulating outsource initiatives, strategic planners must be careful to understand that outsourcing is not the strategy, but rather, a vehicle to strategy activation. According to Lynch,[19] there are a number of advantages to outsourcing business functions.

- *Return on assets.* By reducing costly assets like personnel, warehouses, non-core manufacturing, materials handling, transportation, information technology, and others, return on current assets and capital expenditure can be significantly enhanced.
- *Personnel productivity.* Non-core functions can be eliminated from company processes, thereby increasing employee productivity.
- *Flexibility.* Outsourcing permits companies to access new markets without initially shouldering the associated costs. As markets change and new products are developed, firms need to be as flexible as possible to manage service requirements, ordering methods, and competitive offerings.
- *Customer service.* Today's mantra of total customer satisfaction has greatly increased the importance of logistics. To assist in realizing this critical channel value, logistics providers have gradually been emerging into businesses that offer specialized services beyond the capability of most firms to achieve.
- *Information technology.* The increased demands for new information systems and resources can often be far more efficiently met through outsourcing. Whether leveraging logistics providers or contracting an *applications service provider* (ASP), firms can realize EBS, EDI, or Internet capabilities without the need to acquire or develop in-house resources.

In designing effective outsourcing approaches, strategists must keep several key principles in mind. To begin with, companies should never outsource core functions. The loss of core competencies results in a hollowing-out of a corporation that often sets off a downward spiraling effect that is difficult to reverse. Second, firms should never outsource functions their own personnel do not comprehend. This will result in trying to link the provider to performance metrics that have not been fully defined, communicated, or understood. Third, the channel value assessment team in charge of the initiative should be diligent in defining the precise objectives. Reasons should go beyond a simple focus on cost and consider network collaborative issues as well. Fourth, the exact nature of outsourced functions should be detailed. This step requires identifying expectations, productivity metrics, gain sharing incentives, service requirements, precise operations to be performed, level of electronic connectivity, and partnership boundaries. Finally, it is critical that the outsourcing project have the support of senior management and be integrated into the corporate plan.

As an example of drafting effective outsourcing strategies, General Motors decided that it needed a specialist to handle its warehousing and transportation functions. CNF, a $5.57 billion-a-year transportation company in Palo Alto, CA, agreed to set up a separate company, in partnership with GM, called Vector SCM. This company would serve as the automaker's day-to-day logistics operator. Although the outsourced collaboration effort is only in the first of a three-year implementation, it has already shaved by nearly one-third, to 10.5 days, the time it takes to ship finished vehicles in North America from factory to dealer. Such a trading partnership is critical for GM's attainment of its overall business value proposition.[20]

D. Ensuring Effective Resource Management

While the business value proposition will determine how the enterprise will approach the marketplace in terms of the products, services, and informational and delivery techniques it offers, the effective application of its assets and management of its internal and supply chain infrastructures are the drivers of growth and profits. Part of the role of plans in this segment of the e-SCM business strategy is to reengineer all business processes that are inefficient, and to rigorously eliminate all non-value-added activities. Cost containment and optimization, however, is only part of this step. Of far greater importance is the capacity to continuously reconfigure the resources found both within the organization and outside in the supply channel, in the pursuit of order-of-magnitude profit growth and competitive advantage. The ultimate goal is to construct business architectures that offer customers what they want: convenience in ordering, solutions to complex needs that often require "killer" services to be encapsulated with the product, speed of delivery, and ease of payment.

The content of an enterprise's resources consists of its assets and core competencies. In general, these resources can be divided into three major areas: the value that resides in human knowledge; the capital invested in physical assets; and the value to be found in the physical assets and human knowledge of customers, suppliers, and business partners.

- *Human knowledge.* In today's hyper-competitive environment, businesses have been migrating from a departmental focus on *Human Resources* to a far more strategic and expansive focus on *Human Capital Management* (HCM). HCM can be defined as the repository of human knowledge and skills found within an organization that result in the creation of products, technologies, systems, processes, and relationships. Human resources are intangible and tacit in nature, yet without them neither physical assets nor supply networking resources can be actualized and purposefully directed.

Today's best strategic planners continue to aggressively invest in management initiatives and knowledge expansion solutions that will enable their firms to leverage existing human capital. Key to HCM development has been a growing focus on technology to accelerate recruiting, optimize learning and skills development, measure and appraise performance, and more productively arrange the structure of infrastructure tasks. Benefits to effective HCM are as follows:[21]

1. *Stronger growth, productivity, performance, and profitability.* The acceleration in the level of human knowledge application will become more important as the complexity of networking methodologies and information technologies drive increased investment in performance management tools and corresponding opportunities for dynamic growth.

2. *Enhanced learning and development.* The tremendous growth in e-learning tools, from CBTs to on-line learning, promise to raise the productivity, quality, and personalization of knowledge transfer, while significantly cutting costs.

3. *Enhanced recruitment and retention.* Leading-edge recruitment functions that automate the workflow and communications associated with recruitment are enabling companies to save significant costs. Such tools are accelerating the time-to-hire, while improving the quality of hires.

4. *Personalizing employee relationships.* Increased personalization of human work and relationships encourages employee loyalty and motivates the kind of knowledge transfer, personal agility, and entrepreneurship necessary for today's competitive environment. It also allows managers to continuously match knowledge and skills to high-velocity projects.

- *Physical assets.* A business's *physical assets* are perhaps the easiest to understand and manipulate. Warehouses, offices, information systems, production and transportation equipment, patents, and inventories are examples of hard, tangible assets. Physical assets provide the mechanisms by which the firm transforms the value portfolio into competitive products and services.

The application of information technology to physical assets has a direct impact on cost and value producing attributes. In fact, there is a direct correlation of the level of information available about demand and supply and the level of capital investment in physical assets. Historically, disconnects in demand and supply information required businesses along the chain of supply to increase the level of physical assets to counter the infamous "bull-whip effect." Increases in unproductive assets to support a lack of knowledge regarding the actual impact of the demand pull through the supply network simply acts as a drain on cash and profits.

To counter this spiraling upward of channel costs and downward of competitive advantage, strategists need to determine which cost and process improvements can produce real advantage, which service enhancements customers will value, and how to utilize information technologies to integrate and synchronize internal operations with those of customers and suppliers. Networked channel leaders, such as Ford Motor Co., see beyond their own operations and linkages with tier-one suppliers, to a supply network or "ecosystem" in which the actions of each member have a direct bearing on every other member. Corporate planners should examine the entire supply chain, in detail, in an effort to achieve the following process values:

1. *Replacing physical assets with real-time information.* Information here refers to gathering accurate customer demand and enabling visibility to inventory and other assets as they exist at collection points in the supply chain.

2. *Reducing process complexity.* According to the Pareto principle, the vast majority of processes are employed to satisfy simple customer needs. Disproportionately, it is the complex processes that consume time and money. Eliminating complexity permits trading partners to remove excess assets that add very little value to the vast majority of customers.

3. *Reducing product complexity.* Product complexity also adds to assets. Solutions in this area can be found in greater use of ATO and MTO manufacturing or by closely examining the possibilities for pushing product differentiation down the supply chain as close to the end-customer as possible.

4. *Reducing partner supply variability.* The inability of suppliers to receive complete demand information and provide timely delivery also adds to the volume of capital assets in the supply network. Strategists can work on the creation of closer supplier relationships and the application of connectivity technologies to move as close as possible to real-time information transfer.

- *Business network resource management.* Network trading partners contribute competitive advantage by providing two critical resources: physical assets, such as plant and inventories, and core competencies, such as design or process skills. Partners can provide critical values simply by performing asset-intensive activities that enable partners to leverage their scale, experience, and financial resources. Increasingly, HCM is being expanded to encompass the networks of knowledge and skills that lie beyond the boundaries of the business. Developing effective e-SCM business strategies requires planners to explore ways to manage and capitalize not only on the hard assets but also on the competencies of contractors, suppliers, partners, customers, and even, in some cases, of competitors. Some of the critical dimensions involved in leveraging network trading partner resources are as follows:

1. *Synchronized delivery and production.* Tightly integrated connectivity between trading partners can dramatically enhance marketplace value surrounding capabilities that enhance speed, reliability, convenience, and efficiency. As the level of collaboration increases, network partners can change and better respond to market requirements as they ripple

through supply chain asset requirements, priorities, schedules, and optimization and substitution decisions.

2. *Outsourcing.* The capability to utilize the physical and knowledge assets of partners to achieve breakthroughs in competitive advantage is fundamental to an e-SCM strategy. Outsourcing permits opportunities for increased marketplace value, without often premature and massive expenditure, yet enables firms to hold tight the information, knowledge, and vision of the initiative.

3. *Creating collaborative solutions.* True collaboration occurs when everyone in the network arrangement receives agreed-upon value. Collaboration enables better product development, service design, inventory management, marketing, selling, ordering, and service. Internet tools that enable closer collaboration should be at the forefront of strategic planners' agenda.

E. PURSUING GROWTH MANAGEMENT

Perhaps one of the most important components of e-SCM business network strategy development is structuring a set of meaningful and focused performance measurements that will allow corporate planners to gauge the effectiveness of their supply chain solutions. Being able to determine the impact of a business strategy on profits and growth has always formed the only real cornerstone of competitive measurement, but with the advent of Internet technologies, the requirements for clear focus on supply chain direction and targeted metrics has never been more important. No company today would reject the principle that supply chain trading partners provide the potential for enormous competitive advantage and that exploring ways to gain greater connectivity and synchronization with the supply network is critical. However, determining just what the depth of partnership and the degree of integration should be requires a well-formulated plan and significant ongoing analysis. No strategist would disagree with AMR Research analyst Bob Ferrai when he says that "Applications such as supply-chain collaboration, demand planning and forecasting, and E-procurement support offer the most promising opportunities for bottom-line savings." The real issue is that not all companies will opt for sophisticated Internet solutions to run their supply chains and, even if they do, how should they be measured?

Clearly, one of the crucial problems in determining the level of supply chain collaboration is that it requires companies to rethink traditional measurements. In fact, it is being argued that a fundamental overhaul of measurement models has become imperative in the new economy. According to Forrester Research,[22] "E-business measurement as it exists today is broken," and requires the elimination or modification of traditional measurements, such as ROI, in favor of externally oriented statistics. The major problem is that Web-enabled techniques have often been blindly implemented, without any real method in place to detail what profit or growth values should be achieved for the time and cost. Similar to the chronic lament regarding the time and cost necessary to implement ERP, companies in the "post-dot-com age" have spent millions on Internet tools that are out of sync with their value propositions

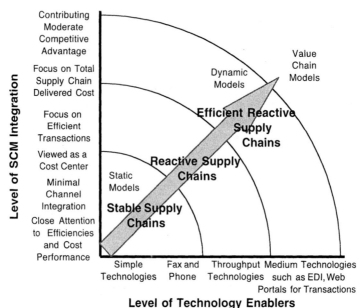

FIGURE 4.6 Supply chain cost models.

and value portfolios and have failed to architect the promised connectivity with network trading partners. In fleshing out the final component of the e-SCM value network strategic process, corporate strategists will have to consider the following three areas: supply chain cost, supply chain value, and detailing effective metrics.

1. Focus on Supply Chain Costs

For over two decades, executives have sought to increase corporate value by applying technologies and management methods such as ERP, JIT, TQM, and BRP in the pursuit of supply chain cost controls and improved operating performance. The impact of supply chain costs can be dramatic. In some industries, supply chain costs can equal 50 percent or more of a company's revenues. According to A.T. Kearney, supply inefficiencies can waste up to 25 percent of a firm's operating costs and, faced with razor-thin profit margins of three to four percent, even a small increase in supply chain efficiencies can double profitability.

Many companies have developed strategies that focus purely on the cost reduction opportunities to be found in their supply chains. According to Kavanaugh and Matthews,[23] cost-centered supply chain strategies can be considered as anchored on three models (see Figure 4.6).

- Basic Model — *Stable Supply Chains*. This model is the least strategic of the three and is normally applied to supply chains that have significant historical stability, such as table salt manufacturers, where demand and supply are in equilibrium. Because of long product life cycles, commodity-oriented processes that utilize scale production, and dedicated capital assets, supply chains using this method are heavily focused on execution, with close attention paid to efficiencies and cost performance. Connectivity technologies are normally very simple, with little need for sophisticated real-time enablers such as CPFR and complex collaborative synchronization.

- Model 2 — *Reactive Supply Chains*. Companies using this model still have minimal expectations of the value of their supply networks. Typically, supply chains in this model primarily act to fulfill demand by responding to and supporting trading partners' sales and marketing strategies. It is perceived by others and perceives itself as a cost center. Since network nodes are heavily focused on efficiency and cost management, minimal effort is spent on connectivity technologies or capital assets, except to support the latest sales and marketing needs. The mantra of a reactive supply chain is to ensure that throughput continues at any cost.
- Model 3 — *Efficient Reactive Supply Chains*. In this final model, the supply chain is still perceived as contributing minimal, or at best, moderate competitive positioning to trading partners. While still considered primarily as an operations function, the supply network assists competitive positioning by acting as an efficient, low cost, and integrated unit. Efficiencies and cost management transcends local departments or company focus and is centered on the total delivered cost of finished goods. Connectivity technology and new equipment dramatically increase in importance as channel partners search to automate functions, with a view to reduce labor costs and improve capacity and throughput. As an example, contract manufacturer Flash Electronics subscribes to a hosted Web-based system for managing RFQs. The system links the company to nearly all of its suppliers. The results to date have been a reduction of almost 50 percent in overall quote-process time and up to 65 percent in quote-processing costs, along with the ability to respond faster to its OEM customers.

The three above strategic performance models perceive the supply chain from a localized point of view as a cross-company cost center. The metrics utilized are based on traditional channel network performance models, which are centered on assessing the ROI of individual trading partners, and not on the potential for collaborative payback and joint strategic value. To leverage the competitive strength inherent in supply chains characterized by highly integrated and synchronized connectivity, network partners must begin the process of migrating from a *cost* focus to a *value* focus.

2. Focus on Supply Chain Value

An e-SCM strategy that focuses on cost management and optimizing channel functions will lead to less waste, higher productivity, greater market share and earnings, and greater competitive positioning. However, the benefits attained by just concentrating on process improvement are destined to be short-lived and will rapidly be neutralized as competitors copy processes and technologies. In order to create competitive advantage that is truly sustainable, strategic planners must look to developing e-SCM strategies that go beyond cost reduction and optimization and actually leverage the resources and competencies of trading partners to *support*, if not *facilitate*, the generation of value.

In today's environment of rapidly changing economic and technological changes that quickly destroy competitive advantage, strategies for maintaining sustainable profitability are increasingly factoring in the capabilities of supply chain partners as critical components driving marketplace advantage. While it is true that companies look to local decisions regarding customers and product/service offerings to produce growth, the level of participation and connectivity a business enjoys with its trading partners can dramatically assist in supporting current advantage, as well as generating radically new sources of competitive value. For example, McKessonHBOC's self-service Web site, established in January 2001, enables the company to more closely interact with distribution customers who can now perform real-time ordering, tracking, and managing of pharmaceutical and medical-surgical products. Although the Web site is barely over a year old, the company anticipates that eventually all of its customers — hospitals, health systems, retail pharmacies, physicians, long-term care facilities, and home healthcare agencies — will find the site of significant benefit. McKesson intends to enhance the customer-facing Web site by integrating in advanced tools and functionality that will combine it with the company's materials management systems. According to Graham King, president of McKesson's IT function, such systems will provide a dramatic growth engine "by integrating information technology and distribution services, providing seamless, end-to-end fulfillment."[24]

Creating e-SCM strategies that will leverage the supply network to generate *value* for the firm will require a dramatically higher level of commitment, collaboration, integration, and synchronization than what is characteristic of channel relationships focused purely on cost management. As Kavanaugh and Matthews point out,[25] there are two models of supply chain at this level.

- *Efficient Proactive Supply Chains.* The goal of proactive supply chains is to leverage total network partner resources to actively drive demand and supply requirements through the supply channel in order to support, if not expand, the profit and growth engines of the entire network ecosystem. Perhaps the most distinguishing characteristic of supply networks at this level is the dramatically increased integration of sales and marketing. In this strategic model, entire supply chains *proactively* pursue the management of total channel demand, not only to reduce costs, complexity, and efficiency, but also to drive the creation of new sources of value generation by suggesting product design or service changes. Efficient proactive supply chains invest in Internet technologies to integrate EBSs across the network and enable real-time visibility and synchronization regarding critical sales and marketing data as well as share ideas.
- *Revenue and Profit Driver Supply Chains.* At the highest level of supply chain performance, strategists perceive the supply network not only as a critical demand and supply integrator, but also as an active contributor in

the continuous generation of new forms of customer value. Through the application of advanced technology tools that provide real-time connectivity, network business nodes seek to explore the use of trading exchanges, collaborative product development and information sharing, and synchronization of resources and competencies that enable radically new opportunities for competitive advantage and profit growth. Forecasting, planning, and replenishment processes are fully integrated across the supply network; performance measurements focused on total supply chain revenue, cost, ROI, and profitability are developed.

The ability of today's enterprise to increase profitability and growth is, in some degree, dependent on their supply chain partners, whether they be OEMs, contract manufacturers, distributors, or suppliers. To use a biological term, supply chains are truly evolutionary "ecosystems," where the role of each participant is intertwined in a complex matrix of business strategies, trading networks, and levels of collaboration. Simply making the ecosystem more efficient does not guarantee its survival — interdependency enables the entire system to evolve to achieve levels of performance impossible to attain by companies working on their own. Similarly, as in the case of the high-tech industry, relationships between network partners must be inherently interdependent if the innovative products demanded by the marketplace are to be created. According to Rodin,[26] assembling supply chain systems that enable order-of-magnitude breakthroughs to profitability and growth are the results of finding answers to the following statements:

- Determine who the pivotal supply chain network partners are.
- Identify what collaborative supply chain strategies and technologies they have in place or are planning to implement.
- Find out what direct customers and customers of trading partners want the most from their supply chain providers.
- Identify the weak links in the supply chain process that have a direct impact on delivering customer value. If customers consider speed to be critical, determine what channel areas increase non-value added time to the fulfillment process and how they can be eliminated from the channel.
- Once the trouble points are identified, work with channel partners to determine what information could be shared among channel participants that would most improve the network's effectiveness in delivering value to the customer.
- Finally, map and integrate the value-enhancing steps into the e-SCM business and technology plan.

3. Design an Effective Performance Measurements Program

The ability to create effective performance measurements has always been a critical function of a successful enterprise. Performance measurements enable companies to determine the efficiency and effectiveness of business processes and provide overall metrics regarding profitability and growth. Over the past decade, companies have sought to extend the reach of their ability to manage costs, processes, and profitability by focusing on their supply chains. However, while much time and effort has been expended on the physical management of supply channels, there remains an immense gap in the ability of supply network partners to actually measure supply chain performance. While most executives realize that performance metrics are critical to achieve the type of intercompany collaboration necessary to satisfy customers, they are faced with a number of critical issues when it comes to the actual definition of SCM performance measurements.

Perhaps the fundamental problem is that SCM measurements transcend the performance of individual companies and seek to determine how well an allied group of businesses perform in regard to overall costs and profitability. According to Brewer and Speh,[27] SCM performance measurements require trading partners to transform traditional performance philosophies in three important ways. First, to provide meaningful information for decision-making, the performance measurements must be designed around true intercompany collaboration. Second, individual companies and their management and staffs must work in collaboration with channel partners. This means SCM metrics must be structured that provide incentives for collaborative behavior. Finally, each network business partner, no matter the position they occupy in the supply-chain constellation, must focus on performance that promotes the satisfaction and ultimate cost of servicing the customer from the perspective of the entire channel network.

Architecting a SCM infrastructure that promotes such channel-wide metrics is no easy task. Gaps in performance goals can easily occur when local measurements are pitted against global objectives. Even seemingly relevant measurements designed to provide short-term successes can have unintended consequences. Take, for instance, a company seeking to accelerate the speed of inventory through the supply pipeline. While the effort might provide initial cost reduction for one channel node, in the long run all that happens is that the channel system has to absorb additional inventories. In the end, the cost for holding this inventory comes back to the company in the form of higher prices.

One school of thinking holds that extending performance metrics to a supply chain is a massive task that borders almost on the impossible. One consultant feels that such an undertaking "is more of an idealistic concept because rarely do the interests of numerous trading partners align together. Most companies have a big enough challenge to meet performance measurements within their own four walls."[28] Such sentiments must be taken seriously. Companies can become easily discouraged just by trying to map out the hundreds of relationships that constitute their supply chains. Combined with the fact that each company has its own business systems and parochial measurements, the task of constructing a common set of performance metrics does indeed seem to contain almost insurmountable obstacles.

Still, no matter the degree of difficulty, there can be no doubt that there is inherent value in establishing some program of supply chain performance measurements. Since companies cannot escape the growing dependence they have on trading partners, it is critical that they develop forms of business performance statistics exchange, supported by analytical tools, which can be utilized from both an operational and strategic perspective. Lapide and others[29] have identified six possible measurement approaches that can be utilized by strategic planners. A short description of each model is as follows:

- *Cash Velocity.* The ability to cycle assets and cash to generate growth is directly dependent on how quickly value can be passed through the supply channel. Cash velocity in the supply chain is best considered as a component of value, rather than the value itself, and is affected by inventory turnover, transaction costs, current liabilities turnover, growth rate, net profit margin, and the tax rate. Where assets build at various points in the supply network, cash turns to cost. No better example can be seen than in the high-tech sector, where companies like Dell face short product life cycles that require rapid flow-through of assets from suppliers, to outsourced manufacturers, to the customer, measured in days. Optimizing cash velocity requires aligning supply network partner processes and resources with channel customers, products, and services to achieve the quickest return. Models to deploy to increase cash velocity include *optimal asset utilization* (OAU), *activity-based costing* (ABC), event-driven costing, and cash velocity levers, such as receivable and inventory turnover.
- *The Balanced Scorecard.* Originally developed by Kaplan and Norton,[30] this model, while not directly created for SCM, can be easily modified to generate an excellent method for managing supply chain performance. Briefly, the balanced scorecard refers to a performance strategy that seeks to achieve a balance between financial and non-financial performance across short-term and long-term time horizons. The model focuses on performance from four different perspectives: *financial results* (cash-to-cash cycle), the *customer* (viability of the value proposition), *business processes* (outputs measured in terms of quality, time, flexibility, and cost), and *innovation and learning* (capability of organizations to learn and grow). Figure 4.7 illustrates an example of applying the balanced scorecard to proposed SCM objectives and accompanying metrics.
- *SCOR Model.* Originally co-developed by Pittiglio Rabin Todd & McGrath and AMR Research, the *Supply Chain Operations Reference* model (SCOR) is a tool for translating strategy into supply chain performance goals. The SCOR model divides a supply chain into five distinct management processes: *Plan* (cycle time metrics associated with demand/supply planning and management), *Source* (cost metrics associated with sourcing, unit costs, lead times, and inventories), *Make* (asset metrics associated with production, quality, changeover, capacity utilization), *Deliver* (service metrics associated with on-time shipment, order fulfillment, warehousing, and transportation), and *Return* (returns and defective products). The goal of SCOR (Figure 4.8) is to decompose each of these processes into detailed metrics focused around the following performance attributes: reliability, responsiveness, flexibility, cost, and assets.[31]
- *The Logistics Scoreboard.* Developed by Logistics Resources International, a logistics consulting firm, this model recommends the use of an integrated group of performance measurements consisting of four general

	Strategic Theme	Strategic Objectives	Strategic Measures
Financial	Financial growth	Channel cost reduction Increased profit margins Revenue growth High return on assets	Cash flow Channel inventory costs Transportation costs Days of open AR & AP

Customer	Increased satisfaction
	Increased value
		Provide strategic solutions
		View customer as unique
		Alignment customer service
		  needs and priorities
		High velocity delivery
			Quality management
			Timeliness of delivery
			Flexibility and agility of
			  the supply channel
			Ability to deliver
			  customized solutions

Business Processes	Cost reduction
	Flexible response
	Closer collaboration
		Innovative products and
		  services
		Increased synchronization
		Increased communication
		More scalable supply chains
		Fast flow of inventories
		Real-time digitization of
		  internal and partner
		  processes and information
			Waste reduction
			Time compression
			Unit cost reduction
			Time-to-market reduction
			Order cycle time reduction
			Inventory acquisition costs
			Forecast accuracy
			Reduced communications
			  time

Innovation and Learning	Motivated and
	prepared supply
	channel workforce
		Product/process innovation
		Partnership management
		Increasing core competencies
		Motivating workers
		Skilling workers
		Staffing the e-business team
			Employee survey
			Personal balanced scorecard
			Total supply chain
			  competency available
			Total supply chain
			  information available

FIGURE 4.7 SCM balanced scorecard.

logistics performance categories: *financial* (e.g., costs and ROA), *productivity* (e.g., orders shipped per hour and number of deliveries made per day), *quality* (e.g., orders shipped without error and percent of damaged goods received), and *cycle time* (e.g., order fulfillment lead time and delivery lead time). To assist in tracking these logistics costs, Logistics Resources markets a spreadsheet-based tool — *The Logistics Scoreboard* — that firms can employ to measure supply chain performance metrics. The model and tool, however, have a shortcoming in that they are focused on logistics metrics and have limited usefulness in measuring total supply chain activities.

- *Activity-Based Costing* (ABC). ABC methods were originally developed to overcome the defects in tradition absorption-based cost models. The goal of the method is to ascertain the true cost of processes or products by breaking down the activities necessary to perform them into individual tasks or cost drivers, which could then be used to calculate the actual cost necessary to execute each task. These detail costs can then be rolled up to provide the total actual time or cost expended. ABC methods are extremely useful in the compilation of supply chain costs. For example,

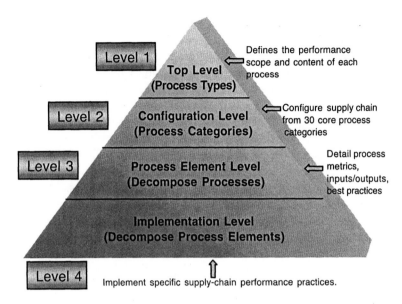

FIGURE 4.8 SCOR process detail levels.

the cost of transporting products through each node in the supply chain can be used as a driver to assist in the compilation of total supply chain logistics costs.

- *Economic Value-Added* (EVA). One of the criticisms of traditional accounting methods is that they tend to favor short-term profits and revenues, while neglecting the long-term economic well-being and potential profitability of the enterprise. To remedy this shortcoming, some financial planners advocate assessing a company's performance based on its return on capital or economic value-add. The EVA model attempts to quantify the value created by taking the after-tax operating profit of a company and subtracting the annual cost of all the capital the firm uses. Companies can also apply the model to measure their value-added contribution to total supply network profit. A defect of the model is that, while useful in assessing earnings above the cost of capital to be included in the executive portion of a balanced scorecard, it is less useful in structuring detailed supply chain metrics.

Supply chain networks strategists must perform a significant amount of work to be able to structure meaningful channel performance measurement programs. While the models outlined above provide excellent examples of where to begin, there is no one recommended approach or definitive set of supply chain measurements. However, such statements should not dissuade companies from taking up the challenge — there is just too much to be gained by harnessing the productive power of the various SCM initiatives that are today being implemented. Whether it is by beginning with a high-level executive performance scorecard or utilizing information technology to automate the capture of agreed upon metrics, it is critical that some plan be inaugurated.

Perhaps the first place to start is to form cross-enterprise performance design teams. To begin with, these teams will need to move beyond a concern with local function-based measurements, which tend to splinter the performance development effort, and focus on functional processes and accompanying metrics that will crystallize objectives designed to increase cross-network channel integration. The goal is not to eliminate function-based measurements, but rather, to broaden their effectiveness by integrating them with supply chain level metrics that will reveal how well each network business node is individually working toward goals that will improve not only their own performance but also the overall performance of the entire supply chain. In addition, teams must be strong enough to tackle several other critical problems inherent in determining supply chain metrics. The measures decided upon must be in synchronization with individual company and total supply chain strategies. The tendency to capture too many measurements must also be avoided. Participating companies must be encouraged to provide meaningful information on their performance. And finally, supply chain measurements can be beset by problems in defining basic terminology necessary to ensure common understanding of performance standards.

The following key steps should be taken when implementing a supply chain performance program.

- Begin by establishing a multi-business network performance measurement team. The role of this team is to prepare the program's overall strategy, detail current and future performance metric contents, set priorities, and ensure on-going progress.
- Ensure that the measurements detailed are in sync with individual company and overall supply chain strategies. Trading partner executives should articulate the supply chain vision and how the channel performance program will assist in strategic realization.
- The channel measurements defined must truly support customer satisfaction. The metrics must be focused on adding actual value to the customer and should not be abstract. If customers value receiving goods on the date requested, a metric focused on tracking on-time shipment will not result in a meaningful performance target.
- Once executive level metrics have been defined, they should be decomposed into tactical and operational measurements. The goal is to track whether actual performance at each business node in the supply network is in overall alignment with executive objectives.
- Focus only on key supply chain measurements. While literally hundreds of metrics could be applied, select the ones that best track the process measurements focused on the critical time, cost, and quality criteria most important to each channel partner.
- Use information technologies to gather, process, and analyze the information received. While disparities in data and computer architectures may make this task difficult, today's Internet-driven supply chain management systems, ERP software, and data warehousing tools will continue to make this effort easier in the future.

While these steps will be helpful in getting started, performance design teams must be ever vigilant in the pursuit of new technologies, greater performance collaboration, and the launch of new measurements programs.

IV. SUMMARY AND TRANSITION

The rise of new forms of supply chain connectivity caused by the application of the Internet has caused a virtual revolution in the development and implementation of business strategy. In the past, enterprises sought to create corporate marketing, product and service, cost management, and profitability plans that were inward focused. Over the past decade, however, the realization that the resources and competencies contributed by their supply chain trading partners were at least as critical to competitive survival as their own internal capabilities has driven companies to critically reexamine the place of SCM in the drafting of business strategy. Today, the tremendous integrative power of the Internet has elevated this concern with leveraging the supply channel network to a new level of awareness. All executives are keenly aware that success in tomorrow's marketplace will go to those enterprises that focus on the strategic capabilities of their entire value chain network, rather than on the temporary ascendancy of company-centric products, services, and infrastructures.

Structuring an effective *supply chain business architecture* requires strategic planners to view the supply chain as consisting of three interdependent dimensions. To begin with, planners must understand the supply chain from the *physical* point of view. This includes mapping out the terrain of the channel system and the level of value contributed by each channel business node. Second, planners must establish a map of trading partner competencies. The goal is to determine the key capabilities each member contributes to individual company and total supply chain value. The final dimension seeks to detail the type and robustness of the connecting links integrating each channel node. By identifying the technology tools in use in the supply chain, planners can determine how easily and effectively data and process information can traverse the channel network landscape. Viewing the supply chain from a three-dimensional perspective enables strategic planners to architect exciting and radical channel structures providing for a host of possible collaborative and synchronized opportunities to build and enhance market leadership.

Deciding on the proper blend of collaborative technologies and channel capabilities depends on how individual firms want to utilize their network relationships. Some companies may choose to implement simple analog methods to drive cost reduction and facilitate supply channel throughput. Still other companies will want to explore the application of e-business solutions that tightly link trading partners in the search for opportunities for revenue expansion and relationship enhancement. The more e-business connectivity strategies are employed, the more the supply chain model migrates from a method of simply moving goods at least cost to becoming a true *value network*, capable of generating collective competitive advantage far beyond the capacities of individual companies working on their own.

Structuring effective e-SCM strategic initiatives requires a two-step process. To begin with, corporate planners will need to ensure that certain preliminary steps have been completed. Individual businesses will need to be energized through education and training from the executive level down to all employees. A detailed vision of the business and the role of channel partners will have to be devised and broadcast. Channel strategic teams need to perform a value assessment (SCVA) that will identify which supply chain initiatives are *evolutionary* and which are *revolutionary*, and which channel processes need to be moved to e-business. Finally, the SCVA should provide strategists with a map of possible e-SCM choices that can then be prioritized in preparation for supply chain implementation.

The second part of e-SCM strategy development is the structuring of the actual supply chain strategy. The chapter suggests a possible five-stage planning process. The model begins by requiring planners to construct a *business value proposition*. Activities in this stage center on determining how customer value is going to be pursued with the opportunities provided by the technology alternatives identified in the preliminary step. In the second stage, companies will need to match the value proposition with the products and services constituting the *value portfolio*. Structuring the *scope of collaboration* is the subject of the third stage. Here, companies will decide what will be the content of the firm's processes and activities and, correspondingly, what will be the scope of trading partner collaboration. In stage four, firms will decide how internal and supply chain resources will be used in support of the e-SCM strategy. Basically, this stage seeks to determine how physical assets, human capital, and trading partner competencies can most effectively be utilized. Finally, before the e-SCM strategy can be considered as complete, planners must design a set of meaningful and focused performance measurements that will provide metrics detailing supply chain operational effectiveness and provide for continuous improvement and growth.

The ultimate benchmark charting the success of any strategic plan is winning the customer. As the failure of many an e-business during the dot-com craze can attest, focusing just on technology, no matter how much capital is invested, does not guarantee that the customer will come. In the next chapter the focus shifts to what today's enterprise must do to win customers and keep them coming back for more.

ENDNOTES

1. Fine, Charles H., *Clockspeed: Winning Industry Control in the Age of Temporary Advantage,* Perseus Books, Reading, Massachusetts, 1998, 11–23.
2. Sawhney, Mohan and Zabin, Jeff, *The Seven Steps to Nirvana: Strategic Insights into e-Business Transformation*, McGraw-Hill, New York, 2001, 25–26.
3. Colkin, Eileen, "DuPont Jumps Out of Dark Ages into E-Commerce," *Information Week,* December 10, 2001, 80.
4. Sawhney and Zabin, 26 – 34, have been most helpful in compiling this short section.
5. Manheim, Marvin, L., "Integrating People and Technology for Supply-Chain Advantage," in *Achieving Supply Chain Excellence Through Technology,* 1, Anderson, David L., ed., Montgomery Research, San Francisco, 1999, 304–313.
6. Lowe, Paul G. and Markham, William J., "Perspectives on Operations Excellence," *Supply Chain Management Review,* 5, 6, 2001, 60.
7. This critical distinction is made by Sawhney and Zabin, 68–70.

8. *Ibid., 56–57.*

9. Drapkin, Michael, *Three Clicks Away: Advice from the Trenches of E-Commerce,* John Wiley & Sons, New York, 2001.

10. Bovet, David and Martha, Joseph, *Value Nets: Breaking the Supply Chain to Unlock Hidden Profits,* John Wiley & Sons, New York, 2000, 37–53.

11. Flamer, Mike, "Why Webvan Went Bust...," *The Wall Street Journal, July 16, 2001.*

12. Cook, Miles and Tyndall, Rob, "Lessons from the Leaders," *Supply Chain Management Review,* 5, 6, 2001, 30.

13. Wreden, Nick, "Cover Story," *Beyond Computing,* 9, 7, 2001, 20–22.

14. Sawhney and Zabin, 100.

15. McGee, Marianne Kolbasuk and Murphy, Chis, "25 Innovators in Collaboration," *Information Week,* December 10, 2001.

16. Prahalad, C.K and Ramaswamy, Venkatram, "The Collaboration Continuum," *Optimize Magazine,* November, 2001, 31–39.

17. Treachy, Michael and Dobrin, Michael, "Make Progress in Small Steps," *Optimize Magazine,* December, 2001, 53–60.

18. Rodin, Rob, "Payback Time for Supply Chains," *Optimize Magazine,* December 2001, 33–34.

19. Lynch, Clifford F., "Understanding Outsourcing," *Inbound Logistics,* 21,1, 2001, 205–218.

20. Charbrow, Eric, "Collaboration Takes Different Roads," *Information Week,* December 10, 2001, 62.

21. These points have been summarized from Manasco, Britton, Hopkins, William S., and Perelman, Lewis J., "Human Capital Management Solution," *Software Business,* September 2001, 18–20.

22. "Measuring E-business Success," Forrester Research, Inc., December, 2000.

23. Kavanaugh, Kevin and Matthews, Paul, "Maximizing Supply Chain Value," in *Achieving Supply Chain Excellence Through Technology,* 1, Anderson, David L., ed., Montgomery Research, San Francisco, 1999, 278–281.

24. Davis, Kit, "McKessonHBOC's Rx for Healthy B2B Relationships," *Consumer Goods Technology,* 10, 8, 2001, 21–22.

25. Kavanaugh and Matthews, see note 23.

26. Rodin, see note 18.

27. Brewer, Peter C. and Speh, Thomas W., "Adapting the Balanced Scorecard to Supply Chain Management," *Supply Chain Management Review,* 5, 2, 2001, 48–56.

28. Dilger, Karen Abramic, "Say Good-bye to the Weakest Link with Supply Chain Metrics," *Global Logistics and Supply Chain Strategies,* 5, 6, 2001, 34–40.

29. Lapide, Larry, "What About Measuring Supply Chain Performance?," in *Achieving Supply Chain Excellence Through Technology,* 1, Anderson, David L., ed., Montgomery Research, San Francisco, 1999, 287–297; Grabski, John, "Valuation Methods for the New Supply Chain," in *Achieving Supply Chain Excellence Through Technology,* 3, Anderson, David L., ed., Montgomery Research, San Francisco, 2001, 254–255; and Bowman, Robert J., "From Cash to Cash: The Ultimate Supply Chain Measurement Tool," *Global Logistics and Supply Chain Strategies,* 5, 6, 2001, 42–48.

30. Kaplan, Robert S. and Norton, David, P., *The Balanced Scorecard,* Harvard Business School Press, Boston, Massachusetts, 1996 and *The Strategy Focused Organization,* Harvard Business Scholl Press, Boston, Massachusetts, 2001. See also the excellent article by Brewer and Speh cited above.

31. For a summary of the SCOR method see the white paper available from the Supply Chain Council titled "Supply-Chain Operations Reference-Model," SCOR version 5.0 found at www.supp-chain.org.

5 Customer and Service Management: Utilizing CRM to Drive Value to the Customer

The effective management of the customer has become the dominant objective for firms seeking to sustain leadership in their markets and industries. With their expectations set by world class companies and interactive technologies, today's customers are demanding to be treated as unique individuals and requiring their supply chains to consistently provide high-quality, configurable combinations of products, services, and information that are capable of evolving as their needs change. Companies know that, unless they can structure agile infrastructures and supply chains that can guarantee personalization, quick-response delivery, and the ability to provide unique sources of marketplace value, their customers will quickly migrate to alternative suppliers.

At the dawn of the twenty-first century, the growing power of the customer is being accelerated and amplified by the Internet revolution. The ubiquitous presence of the Web implies that whole supply chains are expected to provide all-around $7 \times 24 \times 365$ business coverage. Customers now assume they can view marketing materials, catalogs, and price lists, place orders as well as comparison shop, execute aggregate buys, participate in on-line auctions, receive a variety of information from correspondence to training, review delivery status, and check on financial information through the Internet. Responding to such a diverse array of requirements has forced most companies to explore radically new ways to reach and understand their customers. This movement has spawned a new science of customer management — *customer relationship management* (CRM) — and has simultaneously transformed and posed radically new challenges to how companies should be structured to execute the functions of marketing, sales, and service.

Defining the concepts and computerized toolsets available to manage effectively today's customer will be explored in this chapter. The chapter begins with an attempt to define CRM, detail its prominent characteristics, and outline its primary mission. Next, the discussion shifts to an attempt to paint a portrait of today's customer. The profile that emerges shows that customers are *value driven*, that they are looking for strong partnerships with their suppliers, and that they want to be treated as unique individuals. Retaining loyal customers and effectively searching for new ones is best achieved by a *customer-centric* organization. The steps for creating and nurturing such an organization are then outlined. The balance of the chapter is then focused on the CRM technology applications that companies can leverage in the pursuit of marketing, sales, and service initiatives. Among the technologies covered are Internet sales, sales force automation, service, partnership relationship management, electronic billing and payment, and CRM analytics.

I. CREATING THE CUSTOMER CENTRIC SUPPLY CHAIN

While technology tools have enabled customers to become more sophisticated, by providing them with a variety of choices and unprecedented access to information, they have also enabled customers to become more capricious in their buying habits and less inclined to remain faithful to past relationships. To counter these marketplace realities, many companies are in a life-and-death struggle to continuously develop business models that bring not only their organizations but also the entire supply chain closer to the customer in the search for the right mechanisms to attract and build sustainable customer loyalty. Achieving this goal requires that enterprises and their business networks focus on how they can become more "customer centric." It requires them to reengineer their strategic plans and measurements to ensure customer focus. Finally, it requires them to search for mechanisms to converge marketing, sales, and service functions to architect real-time, synchronized product and service fulfillment systems that add expanding value to the customer.

A. The Advent of Customer Relationship Management (CRM)

All businesses, whether product or services oriented, have a single, all-encompassing goal: *retaining loyal customers and utilizing whatever means possible to acquire new customers.* Realizing this goal in today's fiercely competitive marketplace is easier stated than done. Until very recently, most companies focused their energies on selling products and services, regardless of who was doing the buying. Nowadays, the tables have dramatically turned. The growing power of customers, facilitated by the Internet, to chose (and to change) who they buy from has required companies to shift their strategic focus from "what" they are selling to "who" they are selling to.

This dramatic transformation in the goals of marketing, sales, and service from a product- to a customer-centric focus has coalesced around the CRM concept. Far more than simply a methodology for improving sales and service effectiveness, the objective of CRM is to enable the continuous architecting of the value-generating productivities of enterprises and the supply chain networks in which they are participants, in the search to build profitable, sustainable relationships with customers. Such a statement about CRM is very broad indeed, and begs for a more detailed definition. However, while there is much debate about CRM, defining it in clear, universally accepted terms has yet to occur. While industry analysts, consultants, and practitioners alike are agreed that it is simply not just a technology, there is a wide divergence among those same professionals as to a precise definition of the full meaning of CRM. Some feel that it is a business strategy. Others think it is a methodology focused around a set of business processes. Still others consider it an integrated extension of the enterprise resource planning (ERP) philosophy.

In understanding the meaning of CRM it would perhaps be most fruitful to view some of the leading definitions. According to Greenberg,[1]

> CRM is a complete system that (1) provides a means and method to enhance the experience of the individual customers so that they will remain customers for life, (2) provides both technological and functional means of identifying, capturing, and retaining customers, and (3) provides a unified view of the customer across an enterprise.

Dyche feels that CRM can be defined as "The infrastructure that enables delineation of and increase in customer value, and the correct means by which to motivate valuable customers to remain loyal — indeed to buy again."[2] The final definition comes from Renner, Accenture's global CRM practice managing partner, who sees CRM as encompassing "all of the activities that go into identifying, attracting, and retaining customers, and focuses on aligning the whole organization to building profitable, lasting relationships with customers."[3]

Defining CRM means starting with the customer's point of view and working outward to the supply chains that service them. CRM can be characterized as follows:

1.   CRM Is a Strategic Tool

Much thinking today perceives CRM as a technology. In reality, no software tool can manage every aspect of customer relations. According to Michael Boyd, director of CRM at Eddie Bauer,

> Our experience tells us that CRM is in no way, shape, or form a software application. Fundamentally, it is a business strategy to try to optimize profitability, revenue, and satisfaction at an individual level. Everything in an organization — every single process, every single application — is a tool that can be used to serve the CRM goal.[4]

CRM is a comprehensive toolkit, encompassing marketing, sales, service, and supporting technologies, focused on forging customer relationships that provide mutual value, revenue, efficiency, and unique solutions to business problems.

2.   CRM Is Focused on Facilitating the Customer Service Process

Being more responsive to the customer requires that sales and service functions be able to make effective customer-management decisions based on their capability to identify what brings value to the customer. Often success requires the availability of metrics and analytical tools that provide a comprehensive, cohesive, and centralized portrait of the customer.

3.   CRM Is Focused on Optimizing the Customer's Experience

CRM is concerned with the goal of "owning the customer experience." CRM initiatives that continually win the customer can mean everything from providing a level of personalized service and customized products to utilizing advertising, ease in ordering a product, or ensuring a service callback that will positively influence a customer's perception of the buying experience. The end result is to make customers feel good and personally connected to their supplier.

4. CRM Provides a Window into the Customer

An effective CRM system ensures that everyone who can influence the customer experience is provided with critical information about the customer, what customers value the most, and how they can ensure the customer has a positive buying experience. Access to customer-winning attributes, such as buying habits, pricing and promotions, channel preferences, and historical contact information, must be all-pervasive, integrated, and insightful.

5. CRM Assists Suppliers to Measure Customer Profitability

Effective customer management requires that companies be able to determine which customers are profitable and which are not, what values drive profitability for each customer, and how firms can architect processes that consistently deliver to each customer the values they desire the most.

6. CRM Is About Partnership Management

Effective customer management is about knowing the needs, values, and visions of each customer. CRM is about nurturing mutually beneficial, long-term relationships intimate enough to provide improvement opportunities and tailored solutions to meet mutual needs beyond physical product and service delivery.

7. CRM Is a Major Facilitator of Supply Chain Collaboration

No customer transaction can be executed in a vacuum; each transaction is actually an instance in what is often a long chain of events, as products and information progress from one entity to the next in the supply chain. Firms that can create integrated, synchronized processes that satisfy the customer seamlessly across the supply channel network will be the ones that will have the most loyal customers, be the most attractive to new customers, have the most effective collaborative relationships, generate the highest revenues, and have sustainable competitive advantage.

B. MAPPING THE CLUSTER OF CRM COMPONENTS

To assist in better understanding the mission of CRM, it might be useful to sketch out a map of the functions associated with CRM found in the typical organization. As will be discussed, CRM is not concerned with a particular aspect of customer management, but actually encapsulates several related business processes and technologies and directs them to search for ways to optimize the customer experience. As detailed in Figure 5.1, the *customer* is the fulcrum of all CRM processes and acts as the centripetal force attracting the customer value-producing functions of the firm. Clustered around the customer are seven critical technology-driven processes.

FIGURE 5.1 CRM management sphere.

- *EBS.* The *enterprise business system* (EBS) provides the "backbone" for customer management. A firm's EBS consists of three critical components. The first, *transaction maintenance,* records the status of open orders and provides a repository of sales history. In the second component, *information,* the EBS provides visibility to such elements as pricing, promotions, and inventory balances. Finally, the EBS contains *financial detail* used for account balance information, collections, payment records, and financial analysis.
- *Web systems.* More and more of today's forward-looking companies provide their customers with easy-to-use Web sites. Effectively constructed Web sites enable customers to visit catalogs, enter orders, review pricing, configure orders, participate in auctions, and perform a host of self-service functions from order status review to on-line learning.
- *Marketing.* The ability to communicate product, brand, service, and company information is at the heart of customer management. Marketing's role is to identify the wants and needs of the customer, determine which target markets the business can best serve, decide on the appropriate mix of products, services, and programs to offer these markets, and generally motivate the organization to continuously focus on optimal customer service. In addition, marketing is concerned with identifying what each customer considers as value, what are the firm's selling, campaign, and pricing strategies, and how to generate profits by ensuring customer satisfaction.
- *External data.* The ability to sustain competitive leadership requires the continuous unfolding of collaborative relationships both within the organization and across resellers, suppliers, and channel support partners. Information from these internal and network nodes is critical in devising everything from promotional/product bundling, financing, and packaging design, to fulfillment, merchandising, and transportation.

- *CRM applications.* CRM technology can be separated into three segments. The first, *operations CRM*, consists of the traditional functions of customer service, ordering, invoicing/billing, and sales statistics found in the EBS backbone. This also includes *e-CRM* Internet-driven applications like portals and exchanges, e-mail, EDI, sales force automation, and wireless customer management. The second, *collaborative CRM,* focuses on channel-spanning functions such as forecasting and process design. The third segment, *analytical CRM,* consists of the capture, storage, extraction, reporting, and analysis of historical customer data.
- *Analytics.* Effective management of the customer requires a way to access accurate and timely business intelligence. Information can come from sales activities and can include databases containing customer prospecting, product lists, and payment data. It can also come from marketing and can include information such as sales revenues, customer segmentation, campaign responses, and promotions history. Finally, information used for analysis and reporting can come from service and can consist of customer contacts, support request incidents, and survey responses. *Business intelligence*, or as some say, *data warehousing*, however, is not the same thing as CRM. The difference, according to Dyche,[5] is that CRM *"integrates information with business action."* The goal of CRM analytics is to deploy the ability to *act* on the data and analysis mined from customer and marketing repositories to improve business processes so that they are more customer-centric.
- *Service.* The last component in the cluster of CRM functions is customer service. Being able to efficiently and effectively respond to the customer *after* the sale is critical in keeping current customers and acquiring new ones. Whether they are termed contact centers, customer interaction centers, or customer care centers, companies have increasingly been realizing that the strength of their support functions is instrumental in enriching their customer relationships. Recently, Internet and other technologies have been applied to the service function, in the form of automated contact centers, computer telephony integration, Web-based self-service, cyber-agents, and electronic service surveys.

The goal of CRM is to provide a 360-degree view of the customer. The cluster of CRM components attempts to provide companies with an understanding of who their customers really are, what they value in a business relationship, what solutions they wish to buy, and how they want to interact in the sales and service process. An accurate and intimate knowledge of each customer's behavior, preferences, and sales history will significantly assist businesses move their customers from being simply buyers of goods and services, to loyal partners who keep coming back for more, to value chain collaborators who see their suppliers as the primary contact node in an integrated, seamless channel focused on total customer satisfaction.

C. Understanding Today's Customer Dynamics

CRM is about providing companies with the ability to explore new ways of responding to the realities of the expanding power of today's customer. While, on the surface of things, much emphasis has been placed on customers' immediate concerns, such as personalization, super service, convenient solutions, and product and service customization, today's customer is, in actuality, being driven by two very powerful needs. To begin with, today's customer is *value driven*. While it is true that customers will continue to search for the best value when they make a purchasing decision, it does not mean that price will be the sole determining factor. It does mean, however, that customers, aided by the ubiquitous power of the Internet, will be factoring in more alternatives than ever before in matching available options against individual profiles of value. For the supplier, it is critical to move beyond just knowing past transactions to a position of understanding what are the personal needs, wants, and preferences that constitute value for each customer. Once such a "value profile" has been populated, a meaningful *value proposition* can then be drafted that will detail how each individual customer's perception of value can be consistently realized.

Second, despite all the hype about the fickleness of the consumer, today's customers are, more than ever, looking to build strong *relationships* with their suppliers. In the past, customers often focused their purchasing habits around product and service brands. While today's consumer will still bypass cheaper alternatives to buy Tide or Coca-Cola, increasingly brand loyalty is being transferred from products to the provider. Whether it is Amazon.com, Nordstrom's, or Federal Express, consumers are now looking to their suppliers as "brands" that they can consistently count on to provide expected value, regardless of the actual products or services purchased. This means that businesses must continuously reinvent their "brand-image" in often radically new ways that makes their customers feel as if they are always getting a level of expected value, that they are in control of their purchasing experience, that they have confidence in what they buy and who they are buying from. Customers want their suppliers to customize their offerings to fit their individual needs and to feel that their participation in the actual purchase process provides a sense of empowerment as well as partnership.

The risks of ignoring these critical customer expectations can be catastrophic. In the past, businesses atomized each customer transaction and considered them independent of those executed in the past, the ones to follow, or any other related transaction. Today, customers are very aware of the service, products, and personal experience they receive. A single failure may drive them to an easily accessible competitor, and they will normally tell their friends and associates about their decision. Unsatisfied customers can be a significant negative force in today's Internet-empowered business environment that can destroy trust and abruptly end what once had been a long-lived relationship. The opposite is also true. Companies that let their customers know, by attending to their individualized needs, that they not only want their customers' business but want to establish a trustworthy relationship, will be able to weather the storms of an uncertain economy and the encroachment of global competitors.

While the mission of CRM is to look for new ways to retain existing and woo new customers, from the outset it is critical to note that CRM has an accompanying object, and that, in the words of a recent Gartner Group Research Note Tutorial, "is the optimization of profitability. It begins with the premise that not all customers are created equal." In the past, companies treated their customers as if they were all the same. Each received the same level of service, each was charged the same for the products offered, regardless of whether they afforded the company a profit. In reality, a small percentage of a firm's customer base provides most of the profits. This means that anywhere from 70 to 80% of the customer base either provides little or no profit; as much as 40% actually will cost a company money. Today's best companies know who their profitable customers are and will focus their businesses on retaining them. At Dell Computer, for example,

> Not all customers at Dell are created equal, nor are they treated equally. Dell's data enable it to know the ultimate fact about its largest customers — exactly how profitable they are. The more money a customer brings in, the better treatment it gets; for instance, someone who buys servers and storage from Dell is more likely to get a special package that includes PCs and portables. Other industries... have also begun to offer better service and process to large accounts, but they don't like to say so. Dell is willing not only to admit it but also to say that some accounts may not be worth its time.[6]

Knowing which customers are profitable and which are not is as important as the ability of an enterprise to tailor its resources and capabilities to respond to the individual needs of each customer. As a yardstick, customer profitability enables companies to differentiate the levels of relationship and accompanying service to be rendered to each customer, so that their needs and the corresponding value to the business can both be realized. An interesting way to understand the relation between customer cost and profitability is the use of a metric called the *lifetime customer value* (LCV). The formula for the metric is as follows: the total sales revenue of a customer over the lifetime of their relationship, discounted by interest and inflation rates as appropriate.[7] Good customers will have high LCVs and can be segregated and targeted for much greater attention. For example, AMR Research, Boston, says that retailers have already begun to utilize CRM technology tools to retain high- and mid-value customers, while pushing away the bottom low-value ones. Higher value companies receive what AMR calls "personalized fulfillment." This model strives to customize the entire experience of the customer, ranging from customer profiles and order generation to fulfillment, logistics, and returns. Conversely, bottom-value customers will increasingly be charged for every service.[8] Cokins[9] feels that the application of activity-based costing profiles, which act like business electrocardiograms, can help identify not only which products, but also which customers are the most profitable. By generating metrics that provide a measure of the "cost-to-serve," a customer "profit and loss" statement can be constructed. Once this data has been attained, marketers then can construct strategies for each customer that result in (1) managing their "cost-to-serve" to a lower level, (2) reducing their services, or (3) raising prices or shifting the customers' buying to higher-margin products and service lines.

Extending utilization of CRM activities to the management of the customer out into the supply chain is potentially one of CRM's strongest functions. In its simplest form, sharing information about customer transactions can assist each channel business node manage the product and information flow along the demand and fulfillment network. For example, call-center or sales force order promising and management is much more effective when accurate information about product/service availability and delivery can be obtained based on visibility into trading partner capabilities. By combining the metrics and relationship-building capabilities of CRM and the electronic linkages provided by today's Internet technologies, the supply chain can become more responsive and facilitate continuous product and fulfillment planning. In a wider sense, the information gathered via sales force and marketing surveys, and electronically through billing, customer information systems, and call-center data, can provide channel partners with insights into the customer that can assist in product development and process design.

D. CREATING THE CUSTOMER-CENTRIC ORGANIZATION

In 1999 e-tailer Buy.com had been gripped in a downward spiral of unprofitability. The company's original strategy — sell products under cost and generate revenues through advertising — had proven, like it had for many a dot-com e-tailer, to be untenable. While Buy.com's low prices were attractive, the company was notorious for its almost non-existent service and support, which resulted in a poor track record of customer loyalty. In an effort to reverse this perception, company management embarked on a multifront strategy that included implementing new technology tools, building a dedicated call center, increasing information availability at customer contact points, and initiating various cost-cutting programs. The results were dramatic. By 2001, order processing cost had dramatically declined, service had skyrocketed (both Forrester Research and Gomez.com ranked Buy.com No. 1 for quality of support), its margins had risen to the point that it was ranked the second largest multicategory Internet retailer in the industry, and its CRM technologies had dramatically increased the quality of the experience customers enjoyed when they visited Buy.com's Web site. "The key to our success," recalled Tom Silvell, vice president of customer support,

> is that we built our programs and technologies around what customers wanted and needed instead of letting our programs and technologies drive their behavior. This tactic helped transition us from a price-sensitive shop to one focused on the customer experience, on offering value to clients, and on providing quality merchandise at reasonable prices.[10]

The dramatic change in Buy.com's fortunes has been the direct result of the implementation of an effective CRM strategy dedicated to the creation of a customer-centric organization. Achieving such a level of customer focus is not easy. According to Michael Maoz from Gartner Group, only five percent of companies today can say that they have implemented similar levels of customer service. Creating a customer-centric company capable of consistently delivering customer value while building customer loyalty is a multiphased process that involves reshaping the infrastructures of both individual organizations and accompanying supply chains as much as it does implementing computerized CRM functions. The following steps should be considered in architecting such individual companies and supply chains systems.

1. Establish a Customer-Centric Organization

Migrating the enterprise from a product- to a customer-centric focus will require changes in the way companies have managed everything from customer service to product design. Literally every customer touch point needs to be oriented around how each business function can continuously foster customer service. A new management position that organizations have been establishing to achieve customer-centric organizations is the *chief customer officer* (CCO). Basically, this position acts as a liaison between customers and the firm. Requiring strong operational, marketing, and financial skills, the CCO, according to Manring,[11] will identify customer touch points, define and enforce service standards, assist customers to navigate the organization, and search for methods to enrich the customer experience. Strategically, the CCO will be responsible for "integrating and leveraging customer information across the organization or owning and managing customer segments as units of optimization."

For example, Angie Kim of EqualFooting.com, a firm offering purchasing, financing, and shipping services from provider partners via its Web site, feels that her role "signals how much we value the customer, something we want investors, partners, and, of course, customers themselves to know." Reporting to the firm's CEO, her role consists of three operational functions: customer acquisition, corporate partnership, and operations and service. Kim considers her interpretation of customer-centricity to be a manifestation of her notion of customer advocacy, which she vigorously promotes among the 50 employees constituting the company's customer service group. Her belief is simple: treat the customer the way you would treat your boss. "That means," she explains, "recognizing your own interests align with those of your customer, treating the customer with respect, and treading cautiously when you believe a customer is mistaken."[12]

2. Determine Existing Customer Positioning

Understanding the customer is fundamental to a customer-centric focus. The goal is to unearth what each customer values and from these metrics to design the products, services, and communication infrastructure that will drive increasing customer loyalty. The process should begin by measuring the customer landscape. This can be accomplished by identifying the best customers with the greatest lifetime value (LTV). Their buying values should be detailed and contrasted with low LTV or lost customers. Next, qualitative research through surveys, face-to-face interviews, and other techniques should be conducted with each customer segment identified. The goal is to learn firsthand how customers view their relationship with your company and with the competition. Finally, quantitative research tools should be applied to reveal concrete metrics associated with the notions of needs, behaviors, motivations, and attitudes identified in the qualitative review. A critical problem is knowing what to do with this data. In this area a CCO could spearhead the analysis and devise action plans to turn the feedback into results or utilize it for strategic planning or resource allocation.

3. Devise a Map of Customer Segments

The qualitative and analytical data arising from the above step should provide a clear geography of the customer base and illuminate key drivers, such as convenience, price, reliability, etc., of loyalty, value, and satisfaction. The goal is to focus company service efforts around processes that support and encourage the buying behavior of the firm's top customers and how they can be applied to less profitable marketplace segments. By pinpointing what provides true customer differentiation, competitive advantage factors can be leveraged to consistently enhance customer value at every touch point across the internal and supply chain organization. In addition, the map should also reveal the effectiveness of current company product and service strategies and the core competencies of the organization. Businesses should be diligent in assuring there is not a mismatch between their offerings and what the customer base truly values.

4. Develop and Implement the Solution

An effective CRM program should be tireless in searching for opportunities for enhancing customer experiences. Transforming these programs into meaningful marketplace initiatives, promotions, and points of customer contact that improve company visibility, confirm customer value expectations, and cement loyalties is the next step in the process of generating a customer-centric organization. Unfortunately, there is no boilerplate methodology that companies can easily snap into place. Each company must painstakingly investigate its own customer-centricity strengths and weaknesses. In structuring these programs companies must be careful to ensure financial profitability by matching sound business scenarios with measurements such as return on investment (ROI) and *net present value* (NPV). Once these CRM initiatives have been verified, marketers can then begin the process of utilizing the CRM customer data warehouse to begin mining the data in an effort to locate the company's best customers and determine how retention and new customer acquisition programs can be best applied.

5. Monitor, Measure, and Refine

The elements of the previous step need to be performed iteratively. The driver of CRM project review is obviously the metrics arising out of the record of customer contact and exchange. Without such processes in place the quest will ultimately fail. Marketers must be careful to continuously research and document what is working and what is not, by utilizing the analytical tools available within most CRM applications. These tools should provide ongoing quantitative tracking of buying patterns, customer attitudes, and degrees of satisfaction for all market segments and points of contact. One analyst recommends conducting focus groups at least once a year with the best and the worst customers, as well as the internal service staff.[13] Such a procedure will enable effective monitoring of the qualitative input to assist in massaging the quantitative results of performance metrics.

The successful implementation of a customer-centric organization requires that everyone in the business be aware and prepared to execute the enterprise's CRM strategy. Driving the CRM strategy requires, in turn, the firm support and active participation of senior management who need to provide the vision and to focus the energies of the organization on communicating the CRM initiative to customers and partners as well as to the internal staff. Without such direction and sponsorship, most CRM programs will quickly decay and revert to previous "silo" operating methods.

II. APPLYING TECHNOLOGY TO CRM

CRM can be divided into three major functions: *marketing*, the activities associated with creating company branding, identifying the customer, selecting product/service offerings, and designing promotions, advertising, and pricing; *sales*, the actual selling and distribution of products and services; and *service*, activities encompassing customer support, call-center management, and customer communication. Together, the mission of these functions is to inform the organization of who its customers are, how to better understand what customers want and need, what is to be the product and service mix to be taken to the market, and how to provide the ongoing services and values that provide profitability and expand relationships. These functions also detail the technologies that will be used to market to the customer base, conduct transactions, respond to customer service issues, collect marketplace metrics, and format customer contact information for review and analysis. These functions also assist in the development of the strategies governing how the supply channel network is to be constructed and the nature of trading relationships. Finally, these functions should provide the entire organization with the information and motivation necessary to continuously reshape the enterprise's perception of customer service, reengineer vestiges of "silo" management styles, and architect infrastructures that foster customer collaboration.

In the past, the functions of marketing, sales, and service were, at best, loosely connected with each other and utilized varying levels of technology to transact business, collect information, and communicate with the customer. Even the software tools that had evolved, such as ERP, *sales force automation* (SFA), and call center applications, were developed in isolation or heavily focused on the transaction engine, while leaving the marketing and service component fairly underdeveloped. Marketing in the "Industrial Age" focused on direct contact with the customer and relied heavily on printed matter such as catalogs, direct marketing, and mass media advertising. Until the 1980s, sales had relatively little to do with technology and perceived their function as centered around salesmanship and leveraging personal relationships. Finally, customer service, while always open to adopting the latest technologies to communicate with the customer, was often separated from the product-producing and sales functions of the business. Up to just a few years ago, customer service consisted mainly in employing banks of service reps fielding customer inquiries by mail, phone, or fax.[14]

While it can be argued that many companies have, for years, utilized CRM methods to deal with their customers, the rise of Internet technologies has obsoleted many of the traditional concepts of CRM through the creation of new computerized toolsets that have significantly expanded existing CRM functions and capabilities. Today's e-business applications provide companies with radically new avenues to gain visibility to customer value, retain and attract new customers, enhance transaction and service capabilities, and generate integrated, customer-centric infrastructures that enable businesses to realize opportunities for profitability while providing the customer with a level of seamless end-to-end service impossible less than a decade ago. In fact, over the past several years CRM software has been one of the hottest segments in the business solutions marketplace. According to an *Information Week* survey (November 19, 2001), 98% of the business-technology professionals interviewed said that CRM is a strategic initiative at their company. Sixty-one percent stated that they have already deployed CRM software, while 39% are in the planning phase. The Gartner Group expects worldwide CRM license revenues for 2001 to total in excess of $5.6 billion, up from $4 billion in 2000, despite the economic challenges of a year that ended not a few software vendors.

The rest of this section is devoted to exploring the geography of what is rapidly coming to be known as *Internet-based* CRM or e-CRM. Figure 5.2 provides an illustration of the three major functions of CRM and associated Web-enabled applications.

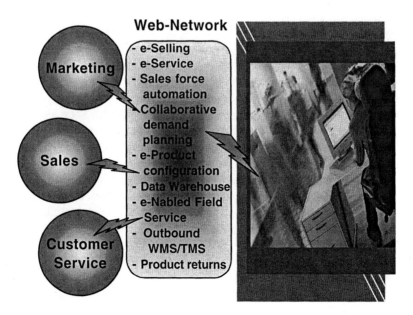

FIGURE 5.2 Range of e-CRM functions.

A. CRM AND INTERNET SALES

Until fairly recently, the sales process was pretty much an affair that had little to do with technology and everything to do with the ability of the individual salesperson to win deals by leveraging their personal sales savvy combined with their knowledge of products, the marketplace, pricing, and the competition. Today, Web-driven applications have opened radically different opportunities for technology-assisted selling. It is not that the salesperson has become obsolete. The salesperson role, in fact, has become more important than ever in developing circles of closely defined business and mutually supportive relationships between their companies and their customer base.

According to Poirier and Bauer,[15] the role of the sales force takes on added significance as an advocate for the customer:

- Providing information about company products and services.
- Coordinating company resources to ensure superlative response to customer needs, and linking channel resources with customer demand requirements;
- Acting as an initiator for the conveyance of information regarding process improvement changes from the company to the demand channel targeted at realizing mutual advantage.
- Providing a medium by which critical company resources in the form of marketing information, training, logistics opportunities, customer and supply channel diagnostics, and collaborative planning initiatives are made available to each customer.

Besides changing the role of the sales force, technology-assisted selling will broaden both selling and buying opportunities. Web applications enable companies to sell directly to the customer thereby bypassing costly channel intermediaries. Further, through the device of real-time technologies, companies will be able to improve effectiveness and better utilize resources. In addition, according to Sawhney and Zabin,[16] "technology-enabled selling will be used increasingly to synchronize and integrate all selling channels used by the enterprise, including telesales, the Net, resellers, and the direct sales force, through the use of a common customer relationship repository, a common applications infrastructure, and a shared business process."

For the customer, technology-enabled selling opens other doors for productivities. To begin with, Web-based search engines have significantly enabled customers to find new suppliers and easily view the range of their product and service offerings. Additionally, Internet applications have dramatically simplified the ordering process and streamlined open-order inquiry. Web-enabled communication tools have made it easy for customers and suppliers to engage in bidirectional communication, a feature that increases one-to-one personalization of the transaction experience. Finally, the Web offers customers options for a buying experience unattainable in the past. Attributes such as $24 \times 7 \times 365$ service, real-time information, on-line customer support, instantaneous availability of documentation, self-service, and Web-page personalization offer customers new ways of realizing the value propositions that meet their individual needs.

One of the primary Web-based tools offered by companies today is the customer *portal*. A portal is basically a Web-based application that aggregates information, third-party resources, and reference materials arranged in a specific Web content that can be customized and personalized to sell to and service prospects, a known customer, or customer segments across multiple channels. Beyond portals, customers can also directly access seller services through independent, private, and consortium exchanges. Some of the basic application functions available in on-line sales can be described as follows:[17]

- *On-line catalogs* that provide customers with the opportunity to research and compare the array of products, prices, and services offered by a supplier.
- *On-line order processing* is the most widely known form of e-CRM. It provides prospects and customers with on-line access to supplier product information, pricing, and fulfillment capabilities. Web-based shopping provides customers with tools to comparison shop, search for desired quality and service requirements, view product/service aggregations, participate in on-line auctions, and access related product/service mixes through on-screen portals. For suppliers, Web-enabled selling permits the development of what Tom Peters calls *microbrands* or customized Web sites that appeal to very narrow groups of customers. In addition, Internet selling enables companies to receive a detailed picture of their customers' buying habits and experiences that can be used for cross-selling, up-selling, and customer service.
- *On-line order configurability* enables customers to design their own products and services through special configuration capabilities.
- *Lead capture and profiling* provides detailed repositories of prospect inquiries, customer sales, and profile information that can be mined to provide information for Web-site personalization or marketing follow-up.
- *On-line surveys* enable marketers to quickly test the attitudes and possible behavior of prospects and customers critical for Web-site customization and market segmentation.
- *Literature fulfillment* provides customers with easy access to company and product/service information that can be downloaded or sent via e-mail to qualifying prospects and customers.
- *e-Mail marketing* enables companies to leverage captured prospect/customer information to establish customized marketing campaigns communicated to the marketplace via e-mail.

The Internet is critical in assisting companies to deliver tailored responses to their marketplaces by effectively sorting good customers (profitable/valuable) from the bad (unprofitable/nonvaluable). Once stratification of the customer base is completed, businesses can then architect an individualized response commensurate with the expected level of customer profitability potential. According to a survey performed by Deloitte Consulting, today's leading companies will continue to enhance their capability to *discern* the best customers and *differentiate* their response through the use of Internet capabilities to structure "digital loyal networks." Such networks focus on customer *loyalty* by managing a portfolio of customers and matching them profitably with capabilities to serve and retain them over the long term. It then works as a *network* that collects, manages, and shares information seamlessly across organizational boundaries with customers and suppliers. All of this is *digitally* enabled by the Internet and new technology platforms for supply chain and customer relationship management.

While the survey concluded that only about 15% of the 850-plus companies that responded could demonstrate the degree of both customer loyalty and supply chain collaboration necessary to utilize effectively loyalty networks, the firms that could "significantly outperformed their peers on dimensions ranging from supply chain performance to shareholder returns."[18]

B. SALES FORCE AUTOMATION (SFA)

The advent of SFA has been credited as being the foundation for today's e-CRM business model. Beginning in the early 1990s, SFA was conceived as an electronic method to collect and analyze customer information from marketing and contact center organizations that, in turn, could be used to advance opportunities for customer retention and acquisition as well as enhance marketplace relationships and revenues. In addition, the sales force needed automation tools that could assist them to more effectively manage their existing accounts, prospect for new customers, track the impact of pricing, promotions, campaigns, forecasts, and other sales efforts on their pipelines, generate meaningful analysis and statistics from their sales database, become more mobile, organize their contact lists, and have real-time customer information in an easily accessed presentation. According to Dyche,[19] the mission of SFA "was to put account information directly in the hands of field sales staff, making them responsible for it, and ultimately rendering them (and the rest of the company) more profitable."

Although early SFA applications were plagued by downtime due to cumbersome data downloading, less than timely information, and often the inability to send data back to backbone business systems, today's technologies drive powerful SFA systems capable of synchronizing data from unconnected sources, such as laptops, mobile devices, and desktops, and utilizing flexible and scaleable databases, such as Microsoft SQL or Oracle, and memory-resident PC applications equipped with scoreboards, and reporting functionality that can exploit powerful engines such as HTML and Java to drive real-time information sharing. While the SFA marketplace contains a number of software vendors and competing products, they all posses, to some degree, the following functionality:

- *Contact Management.* This application is one of the original components of today's SFA product suite. The basic function of the software is to enable the organization and management of prospect and customer data, such as name address, phone numbers, titles, etc., the creation and display of organizational charts, the ability to maintain marketing notes, identification of decision makers, and capability to link to supplementary databases. Today's packages also provide sales reps with enhanced contact lists and calendars and the functionality to merge them with customer contact efforts or automated workflow programs capable of assigning and routing appointments. According to Dyche,[20] "The real value of contact management CRM is in its capability to track not only where customers are but also *who* they are in terms of their influence and decision-making clout."

- *Account Management.* Often, individual sales reps and managers are responsible for large territories and tens or hundreds of customers. Account management applications are designed to provide detail information regarding account data and sales activity that can be accessed on-demand. In addition, these tools permit managers to effectively develop and assign field sales and marketing teams to match customer characteristics.

- *Sales Process/Activity Management.* Many SFA applications provide imbedded, customizable sales process methodologies designed to serve as a road map guiding sales activity management. Each of the steps comprises an aspect of the sales cycle and details a defined set of activities to be followed by each sales rep. In addition, SFA tools also can ensure that major sales events, such as product demos or proposal deadlines, trigger alarms as they become due and remind sales reps of closing dates. While such tools today lack sophistication and deep functionality, they do assist in promoting sales process standardization and, ultimately, greater productivity.

- *Opportunity Management.* Also known as *pipeline management,* this aspect of SFA is concerned with applications that assist in converting leads into sales. In general, these toolsets detail the specific opportunity, the company involved, the assigned sales team, the revenue credits, the status of the opportunity, and the proposed closing date. Some applications provide for the automated distribution of leads to sales teams, who the competition is and what are their advantages/disadvantages, product/service/pricing competitive matrices, and even the probability of successful closing. Still other tools provide performance metrics compiling for each person/team sales opportunities won and lost.

- *Quotation Management.* When not available from an EBS backbone, SFA systems can assist in the development of quotations for complex orders requiring product configuration and pricing. Some vendors provide applications that use graphical tools to map and calculate the quotation process. Once the order has been completed, the order can be transmitted via e-mail or the Internet for management authorization and inventory and process availability check and then quickly returned back to the sales rep for final review and signoff by the prospect.

- *Knowledge Management.* Much of the software composing today's suite of SFA products is oriented around standardizing and automating sales processes. However, effective sales management also requires access to resources that provide sources of information that reside in each company and are difficult to automate. Such information might include documentation such as policy handbooks, sales/marketing presentation materials, standardized forms and templates, such as contracts and estimating, historical sales and marketing reporting, and industry and competitor analysis. Often termed *knowledge management* systems, these applications can act as a repository of all forms of information that can be easily added to and referenced through on-line tools such as Lotus Notes or Web-based browsers.

C. e-CRM Marketing

Effective marketing is and will always be founded on a simple premise: customers are won by personalizing the communication between the seller and the buyer and customizing the product and service offerings so they directly appeal to the desires and needs of individual customers. In a preindustrial economy, selling is always a one-to-one affair and is characterized by personal contact, whereby the buyer examines physically the array of available goods and services, and the seller negotiates an individual contract to sell. In the Industrial Age, the concepts of *brand* and *mass marketing* replaced personal relationship and direct review of available goods and services. Mass marketing meant standardization of products and services, as well as pricing, and assumed uniformity of customer wants and needs. The prospect for marketplace success was focused on the availability and choice of the products/services companies offered. Although by the mid-1990s modifications to the mass marketing approach, such as *direct-marketing, target marketing,* and *relationship marketing,* began to point the way toward a return to one-to-one buyer-seller contact, marketers lacked the mechanism to initiate what could be termed *personal marketing*. This approach can be defined as the capability of companies to present their goods and services customized to fit the distinct personal interests and needs of the customer. A critical feature of this strategy is that the array of offerings is presented with the permission of the customer.

With the advent of the Internet, marketers were finally empowered with a mechanism to activate *personal marketing*. What had always been needed was a medium whereby the interactive, two-way dialogue between customer and supplier, so necessary for the establishment of true one-to-one relationships, could be established. According to Fingar, Kumar, and Sharma,[21]

> *Customization* is the byword of the 21st century marketing revolution. By interacting with customers electronically, their buying behavior can be evaluated and responses to their needs can be tailored. Customization provides value to customers, by allowing them to find solutions that better fit their needs, and saves them time in searching for their solutions.... Not only can a solution be pinpointed for a customer, but also as the relationship grows, a business knows more about individual buying behavior. As a result of the growing relationship, cross-selling opportunities will abound. With the Net, the savvy marketer can sense and respond to customer needs in real-time, one-to-one.... In the world of electronic consumer markets the success factor mantra is: relationship, relationship, and relationship.

When it is considered that the cost of gaining a new customer is five to eight times greater than marketing to an existing customer, companies who can leverage the power of *personal marketing* are infinite better positioned to keep their customer base intact.

Perhaps the importance of the Internet to marketing can be best seen in the concept of *brand management*. According to Taylor and Terhune,[22] brand can be defined as a complex set of elements "including awareness or recognition, customer loyalty, image or brand traits, name and logo design, personal benefits, positioning in relation to competitors, media presence, pricing relative to value, perceived quality, reported satisfaction via word of mouth, reputation, and perceived popularity." In the past, the concept of a brand was linked to the properties to be found in a company's products and services. Today, the Internet provides the power to deliver targeted brand messages, interactive experiences, and lifestyle appeals that make it possible not just to offer unique, personalized products, but also to define narrow groups of customers, or *microbrands*, that seek to create a one-to-one match between the needs/wants of the customer and the capabilities of a set of products and services. In the Internet Age, e-businesses have tried to establish their Web sites as brands. Dot-coms, such as Yahoo, Barnes&Noble.com, and Amazon.com, have become successful because they have been able to provide their customers with a unique experience and have generated an emotional loyalty. Such companies have created interactive experiences that provide customers with a quick and complete solution and, in the effort, established themselves in the psyche of the customer. "The bottom line," state Taylor and Terhune, "is that as we know more about who people are, we can use the power of the Internet to create thousands of combinations of product, service, and packaging characteristics. To craft a message that is as flexible and multifaceted as the human experience itself."[23]

The explosion of Amazon.com on the scene was the harbinger of change to the concept of brand. Many analysts have credited Jeff Bezos as being the first to understand that customer relationships could escape from being physical to being virtual. Bezos had been the first to understand that he could win the customer by providing them with individual attention and a killer marketing strategy. "First of all," states Voth,

> You could get stuff cheap. You could buy your *New York Times* bestseller at or below the price you would pay at Barnes and Noble's, and you could buy them tax-free. You had a seamless customer experience — so you didn't have to wait in line, you could always find what you wanted and you could easily send gifts to your friends and families. Amazon would take care of the wrapping. Christmas and birthday shopping suddenly became much easier. Amazon was able to capitalize on the fact that shopping for books and music are a function of time. This changed the fundamentals.[24]

Such a strategy guides companies, such as Dell Computers and Cisco, which have come to understand that individualizing and enhancing customer relationships will cement marketplace loyalties and expand the lifetime value of their customers.

Automating the marketing function requires the use of software applications that enable companies to compile, search, and utilize customer databases to define who the customer is and then generate targeted marketing campaigns via e-mail, e-fax, the Web, the telephone, or other technology tools to reach the marketplace. The focus of what has come to be known as *enterprise marketing automation* (EMA) is *campaign management*. In the past, campaign management was a labor-intensive affair where customer databases were reviewed and a campaign based on a carpet-bombing strategy was launched to pulverize the marketplace. Analyzing the impact of the campaign often took months or even years. Today, EMA provides the capability to automate the entire campaign process. The suite of toolsets available include customer intelligence and data extraction, campaign definition, detailed campaign planning and program launch, scheduling of activities and continuous performance measurement, and response management. While many of the activities appear similar to traditional marketing campaign processes, the major difference is that EMA utilizes the Internet to capture, extract, and analyze campaign inputs. By tracking campaign results over time, marketers are then better equipped to construct future campaigns that can enhance one-to-one marketing relationships.

The major components of an EMA-driven marketing campaign can be described as follows:

- *Promotions*. EMA provides the ability to bring the promotional side of a campaign directly before a customer as never before. Whether it be give-aways, contests, or discounting, *opt in–opt out* capabilities on the Web page give an immediacy to customers' willingness to engage in the promotion impossible with paper-based or telemarketing-type methods. Once data is captured, it can be directly input into the marketing database and used for ongoing review and campaign modification.
- *Cross-Selling and Up-Selling*. Cross-selling is the practice of offering to the customer related products or services during the buying process. Up-selling is the practice of motivating customers to purchase more expensive (and more profitable) products. To be effective, Web-site and buying exchanges must be able to analyze the customer and prepare alterative offerings that will truly arouse their interest.
- *Marketing Events*. In the past, trade shows and exhibitions provided customers with opportunities to view new products and services. Today, marketers can broadcast the latest marketing information through on-line newsletters, Web-based seminars, and special Webcasts.
- *Customer Retention*. While companies spend lavishly to attract new customers (it is estimated that over $180 billion is spent each year in the US on advertising alone), it is with bitter resignation that marketers must accept the fact that, statistically, as high as 50% of their customers will be lost over a five-year period. Utilizing EMA toolsets can assist companies not only to isolate and rank customers most likely to leave but also to weigh the possible impact of promotional efforts on this class of customers. The goal is to mine the customer data and devise models that can assist in the prediction of customer behavior.
- *Response Management*. Once data from a marketing campaign begins to stream in, marketers need to be able to utilize the information to perform several crucial tasks. First, they must be able to gather, extract, and analyze

the data. Second, they must be able to determine the impact of the campaign by calculating actual customer profitability. A value model, such as a customer's LTV, can dramatically assist in the process of making sense of the deluge of data collected. And, finally, the marketing automation tools must be able to assist in refining and possibly altering the course of the campaign.

1. e-Marketing at Borders

Borders' e-CRM software has, in the words Gordon Eiland, VP of planning and analysis, initiated "the start of a more personal relationship with our customers." Borders' system enables the marketing staff to customize each campaign by utilizing its customer profiles. For example, the company can broadcast events to targeted customer groups, such as a jazz concert in one of its stores. By offering an in-store discount tracked through the e-CRM system, Borders will be able to calculate the success of the promotion and the likely success of similar events. To avoid alienating customers, Borders is careful to protect privacy by asking customers to subscribe to newsletters where they are, in addition, required to *opt in* to receive marketing-related e-mails.[25]

D. CUSTOMER SERVICE MANAGEMENT (CSM)

The ongoing management of the customer, once the sale has been completed, has traditionally been organized around the *customer service* function. The impact of *customer care* on the continuing success of a business has been widely known and is part of service folklore.

- "The average company loses half its customers over a five year period."
- "Reducing defections five percent can boost profits from 25% to 85%."
- "Yet companies typically spend five times more on customer acquisition than on retention."
- "65% to 85% of customers who defect say they were satisfied with their former supplier."
- "Totally satisfied customers are six times more likely to repurchase than satisfied customers."
- "A happy customer will tell five people about their experience, while each dissatisfied customer will tell nine."
- "U.S. on-line businesses lost more than $6.1 billion in potential sales in 1999 due to poor customer service at their Web sites."[26]

Regardless of the accuracy of these metrics, they do reveal an essential reality: total customer care is the cornerstone of the customer-centric organization. According to Fingar, Kumar, and Sharma,[27] the mission of customer care functions include the following:

- Improve customer service while reducing costs.
- Put the customer in control by providing self-service and solution-centered support.
- Segment customer behavior 1-to-1 to individualize goods and services.
- Earn customer loyalty to gain a lifetime of business.

Over the past 25 years the purpose, scope, and mission of CSM has changed dramatically. In the beginning, customer service consisted in receiving and answering personally correspondence with customers who had questions or problems about products or information. Next came the *help desk* where, instead of writing, customers could talk directly to a service rep about their issues. By the 1990s the purpose and function of CSM had evolved beyond just an 800 telephone number to encompass a wide field of customer care objectives and activities. Known as *contact centers* or *customer interaction centers* (CIC), service functions sought to deploy a range of multimedia tools to not only relate order and account status, but also to manage every component affecting the customer from product information to maintenance, warranties, and upgrades.

Today, the capabilities of CICs have been pushed to a new dimension with the advent of exciting new toolsets, such as the Internet, wireless communications, speech recognition, and video, to join older technologies such as phone, caller-ID, fax, e-mail, and EDI (Figure 5.3). Such applications provide customers with even more opportunities for control of service dimensions, while enabling companies to integrate all avenues of customer interaction on a central platform. Self-service opens a new dimension of customer service at less cost, while service databases improve knowledge of customer behavior that enable the delivery of customized sales and service one customer at a time.

FIGURE 5.3 Dell Computer's Internet service site.

Over the past few years, CIC has been transformed from a bank of service reps connected to customers by phone and fax to a highly automated communications center. The mission of these applications is to enable companies to activate open, productive dialogues with the customer that are *personalized*, in that they reflect each individual customer's needs; *self-activating*, in that they permit the customer to successfully self-service their questions; with *immediacy*, in that critical information can be conveyed in real-time; and *intimate*, in that the customer feels the supplier is sincerely concerned about their issues, and that the outcome will provide a basis for future sales and service interaction. The following seeks to detail the technologies currently in use.

- *Automatic call distribution* (ACD). This technology provides for routing incoming customer calls to the proper service resources based on defining characteristics. This toolset seeks to minimize customer waiting by monitoring the call queue, automatically switching calls to available resources, matching the call requirements to service reps with particular areas of expertise, and even prioritizing calls to favor high profile customers.
- *Interactive voice response* (IVR). These systems provide $24 \times 7 \times 365$ routing of service calls based on the customer's response typed on the telephone keypad. The objective of these applications is to provide information or to qualify and route a call without human interaction. A new and more sophisticated tool, automated speech recognition, provides callers with the ability to communicate their questions verbally without having to use the telephone keypad.
- *Computer telephony integration* (CTI). These applications provide the technologies necessary to integrate data with telephones. For example, it is CTI that enables a service phone call to be routed to a particular service rep or other resource.
- *Internet call management*. The use of Web-based self-service has enabled companies to escape from the frustrations associated with IVR-driven keypadding. The advantage of Web-activated service is that the customer is able to enjoy a significant level of self-driven interactivity. Information ranging from proactive notification of new products to trouble-shooting tools, support guides, and on-line forums has changed the scope of service management. CICs can also overcome customer frustrations with the service Web site by including a "Call me" button that provides for in-person contact. Land's End, for example, enables customers to chat on-line with a service rep.
- *Service cyberagents, bots, and avatars*. While in its infancy, the use of automated intelligent agents is expected to expand dramatically in the forthcoming years. The goal is to equip bots with specific expertise, instructability, simplified reasoning, and the ability to cooperate with other bots to guide cyberagents in solving problems for customers.
- *Call center analytics*. A critical part of effective customer service is being able to assemble a holistic view of the customer. Realizing such an objective will mean correlating massive amounts of Web data with information

in other databases. For example, the CRM system will contain the customer profile that, when combined with behavioral Web activity, will enable service reps to model the customer and architect the service criteria necessary to respond effectively to customer needs.
- *Performance measurement.* To be effective, CSM systems must contain tools for service performance monitoring. Applications must possess analytics gathering to record and evaluate customer service interactions as well as metrics to evaluate, measure, and manage service rep quality and productivity.

Being able to streamline today's explosion in service requirements is essential. Cisco, for example, has, over the past few years, moved aggressively to replace phone- and fax-driven service to a Web-based technical support site that, in the words of Sean Iverson, the company's Technical Assistance Center Manager, "has more than paid for itself in satisfaction and savings for the company." Similarly, Otis Elevator, Farmington, CT, is in the middle of a $20-million service overhaul focused on Internet and CRM technologies. Service records are now stored on an Otis Web site, easily accessible to customers checking on maintenance history or existing contracts. Otis also has available a "remote elevator monitoring system" that can automatically report impending faults to Otis's service center and trigger a service visit with the proper replacement part. In addition, the system has enabled the company to set a standard of four hours for turn-around on customer service inquiries[28].

The requirements of today's customer and advances in technology have transformed the scope and mission of customer service. A few years ago, companies considered their customer service functions as purely a cost center and a drain on profitability. In contrast, today's enterprise views customer service as a necessary investment in cementing customer loyalties and assuring maximum customer value. As evidence, the changing of the function's name from "help desk" to "customer integration center" confirms the central position it occupies in architecting the interconnectedness of the customer-centric organization. CICs, in the view of some companies, have actually become a vital link in the supply chain. According to Dave Csira, VP and GM of e-services for USCO Logistics, Naugatuck, CT, "we have made our call center responsible for forward planning so that, in essence, they are the forefront edge of the supply chain for us."

III. CRM AND THE SUPPLY CHAIN

While CRM functions are primarily turned inward, several applications are essential in facilitating the management of customer and channel network partners. Among these toolsets can be found the following.

A. PARTNER RELATIONSHIP MANAGEMENT (PRM)

During the 1990s many sectors of the economy had begun to explore ways to disintermediate wholesale/distribution partners in the search to streamline operations, cut costs, and increase revenues. Spurred by advances in information technology, the growth of warehouse clubs and mass merchants, excess capacities, and the emergence of competing channel formats, the wholesale/distribution industry had begun to seriously feel the competition. By the end of the decade the Internet seemed to portend the day when all forms of channel intermediary could be eliminated. In reality, when the business practices and the numbers were examined, it was obvious companies had actually become more and not less dependent on their channel partners. For example, according to AMR Research, by the end of 2001 dealers, agents, resellers, brokers, and other forms of indirect sales channels represented between 40% and 70% of many companies' revenues. Even in the high-tech sector, about 60% of sales was estimated to have come through indirect sales partners.

The reason for what has been termed the *reintermediation* of the supply channel is simple. No single company can hope to fill all of the needs of its customers. Channel partners solve this problem through their ability to personalize and customize the customer experience by providing products and services from many producers. Take for example Amazon.com and Yahoo! They are succeeding because they have the capability to offer unique value to the customer. Instead of bypassing channel intermediaries, companies have become acutely aware of the need to architect more closely structured partnerships with channel partners, dealers, and resellers. This growing movement to search for management methods and software technologies to expand partner relationships has coalesced around a subset of e-CRM termed *partnership relationship management* (PRM).

Simplistically, the mission of PRM can be defined as a business strategy and a set of application tools designed to increase the long-term value of a firm's channel network by assisting companies to select the right partners, supporting them by offering timely and accurate information and knowledge management resources to deal successfully with channel customers, collectively searching for ways to improve sales, productivity, and competitiveness, and ensuring that each trading partner contributes to customer satisfaction. It would be very wrong, however, to assume that PRM is merely prospecting and announcing promotions or, as Greenberg so aptly describes it, "PRM is not just sales force automation and a partner."[29] One of the key differences between sales and PRM is that in customer-facing activities, companies are dealing directly with the customer. In contrast, managing partners focuses on the indirect automation and optimization of layers of network trading partners. The sheer complexity of many supply chains makes allocation of resources, sourcing, lead generation and review, and sales productivity measurement difficult to track and will require companies to completely rethink their former channel strategies. PRM is fundamental in driving this new strategic viewpoint, by providing software toolsets designed to automate and enhance communications, processes, and transactions throughout the supply chain system.

The foundations of PRM are not unlike those of CRM itself. PRM started as a means to facilitate channel sales and gather metrics based on the marketing and sales efforts of network trading partners. Today, PRM functionality can be separated into five categories.

1. Partner Recruitment, Development, and Profiling

A critical component of PRM is the ability to assist in the recruitment and qualification of potential channel partners. Once the personal contact with new partner recruits has been completed, PRM tools can assist in ranking the partner database for ongoing marketing/sales assignments. The essential component of PRM software is the population of a *partner profile*. Such a database is critical in managing the capabilities of each partner, from contact information and infrastructure to past sales contribution and general performance. By enabling a method to standardize the partner channel, PRM can better enable companies to manage the life cycles of their partners by providing visibility to partnership risks and rewards, ongoing contract maintenance, forecast of planned revenues, and availability of metrics bearing on profitability and loss.

2. Marketing Development

This component of PRM is concerned with communicating marketplace opportunities to the partner network. Perhaps the most important function is *lead generation*. This tool enables parent companies to match customer leads with partners based on their capability profiles. Procedurally, marketers can use the system to analyze the lead, assign it to the most qualified partner, and then capture partner win/loss results. This area of PRM also includes functions to link channel partners to campaigns and promotions and to measure their results. Finally, it also provides for the allocation and budgeting of cooperative marketing funding, charts the productivity of marketing spending, and illuminates methods for improving accountability of partners and promotional campaigns.

3. Sales Management

This component of PRM consists of several functions that include team selling, catalog management, needs analysis, and order management. Other toolsets provide for quotation management and configuration capabilities that can activate interactive selling tools to customize partner and marketplace needs. Finally, PRM systems should provide partners a window into channel product availability, order status, and service requests and warranties.

4. Services Management

A rapidly growing requirement of PRM is the ability to provide for the ongoing training and certification of partners and activation of support capabilities. For example, a partner can get trained on a certain product line, become certified, and then the PRM system will route leads associated with that line to that partner. Also of importance is the ability to provide partners with interactive demos and presentation software that combine content and configurability capabilities that dramatically present product to prospects.

5. PRM Collaboration

In addition to basic functions, PRM systems should facilitate channel networks to codevelop marketing programs and joint business plans. Finally, effective collaboration will require the ability to transmit analytics and metrics of customer performance, channel sales forecasts, and general marketplace feedback.

Overall, the mission of PRM is to reduce channel costs and maximize total network revenues. For example, about 90% of the sales of Captaris, a provider of unified communications and mobile business solutions, comes through its 3,000 channel partners. To keep this channel focused, the company's PRM system permits it to establish a single contact point. Additionally, the system assists in managing the *value added reseller* (VAR) channel. When a new VAR registers, an e-mail is automatically sent to internal salespeople, who can instantly see the profile and then place a contact call, often within minutes. VARs, in turn, can retrieve basic data, such as price lists, directly with call center assistance. Partners can also update their own profiles, assist Captaris to pinpoint ones that need training or business help, or target qualified VARs for new product introduction. Of greatest importance is lead management. There can be as many as 5,000 open leads at a time. The PRM system guarantees that no leads are lost, by providing partners with the capability to update leads, so internal staff can document lead-to-closing metrics.[30]

B. Electronic Bill Presentment and Payment (EBPP)

The introduction of Internet-driven applications has produced a revolution in the way today's business is run, how customers are treated, how products are purchased and produced, and how logistics services are contracted. Unfortunately, despite the flourish of high-tech applications, the management of *financial* processes largely remains a paper-bound function, circumscribed by traditional methods of bill and payment transmission. According to the Gartner Group, today only about 17% of all business-to-business payments are handled electronically, most of it going through wire transfers, automated clearinghouses, EDI, and credit cards. Still other tools, such as purchasing cards (p-cards), debit cards, and e-mail billing, can be found on the fringe of EBPP. For the most part, invoicing is still a manual process that can take weeks. Costs for handling can mount quickly. According to industry research, the cost to the seller to manually generate an invoice averages about $3.45; it costs the payer about $0.60 to pay it manually.[31] While it has yet to become a major bottleneck to e-business, analysts are predicting that within the next few years electronic bill payment will emerge as a critical component of tomorrow's Internet-driven systems.

Clearly, companies will either need to acquire or contract electronic payment systems that enable trading partners to receive bills, authorize payments, match payments to purchase orders, and download the data into ERP and accounting systems in a digital format that will be cheaper than credit cards, EDI, or checks. Currently, resources offering electronic billing solutions can be broken down into the following four categories:[32]

- *Software Suppliers.* Software companies that have developed applications focusing specifically on EBPP functionality.
- *Financial Service Providers.* In this grouping can be found banks and credit unions. As some of the largest billers in business themselves, these institutions have always been keen to deliver their own billing and statements electronically as well as move payments from their client to electronic formats.
- *Consolidators.* These businesses seek to provide services directed at aggregating a customer's bills into a single payment instrument. Acting as a coordinator, these contracted institutions will centralize billing functions and assume the task of paying bills on-line.
- *Portals and Exchanges.* For the most part, companies in this group offer Internet consumers access to various bill presentment and payment toolsets. Companies such as Quicken.com and Yahoo! have built early leads in this area.

As e-billing capabilities grow, many companies have begun the process of integrating EBPP into their CRM toolsets. Forward-thinking executives have come to understand that the merger of EBPP and CRM provides them with radically new opportunities to develop customer relationships. To begin with, the merger enables companies to offer greater *convenience* when it comes to customers accessing their accounts and answering questions about financial issues. It also provides greater *personalization* that will enable the biller to customize financial transactions and draw the customer closer to the biller's Web site and other services. By utilizing electronic messaging, another channel for *marketing* and cross-selling can be opened, thereby increasing CRM value to the biller. CRM *customer service* functions will be enhanced by the addition of bill and statement information. And finally, customers will gain another avenue for *self-service* and personal management that provides them with the ability to manipulate and analyze financial data, thereby driving down biller services costs, increasing "mind-share," and informing customers in real-time about new policies and procedures.

C. CRM ANALYTICS

In today's business environment, companies are often suffering, not from a want of information about their markets and customers, but from a glut of too much data. Enterprise systems, marketing and customer service departments, and now the Internet are burying business analysts in a flood of information. The goal of CRM analytics is to provide companies with statistical, modeling, and optimization toolsets that empower organizations to analyze, combine, and stratify their data to better understand the state of their businesses and the status of their customers by group and individual needs. Ultimately, the goal is to provide an information conduit enabling decision makers to architect their organizations in an effort to continually identify and exploit opportunities wherever they may arise in the supply chain.

For the most part, CRM applications have been focused on *operational* functions, such as managing sales and service. While companies have long employed data warehousing and other intelligence toolsets to assist marketers, these applications were usually separate from their CRM program. Today, as analysts search to enhance the capability of their CRM systems, the incorporation of analytical functions that span marketing, sales and service (operational CRM), and partners and suppliers (collaborative CRM) have become the newest "killer apps." According to AMR Research,[33] investment in CRM analytics is expected to grow from $560M in 2000, or about eight percent of total CRM spending, to about double the rate of operational CRM systems. The market will expand to nearly $4.4B by 2005, which represents about 19% of the total CRM market by 2005.

What are the engines that drive CRM analytics? According to AMR Research,

> Analytical CRM uses On-line Analytical Processing (OLAP)/Relational On-line Analytical Processing (ROLAP), algorithms, and data mining techniques to provide insight and uncover trends in the data collected by its operational counterparts. The results of this analysis are then fed back into the operational applications to improve the next interaction.[34]

As illustrated in Figure 5.4, transactions, clickstream logs, and other customer data is entered through CRM and business system applications and driven into the company's data warehouse. Once the data is assembled, marketers can then apply OLAP, reporting, modeling, and data mining toolsets to identify relationships and patterns in the data that enable predictive analysis. Among the resulting output analysis can be found customer value measurement, risk scoring, campaign measurement, channel analysis, churn analysis and prediction, personalization and collaborative filtering, and revenue analysis. Finally, marketers can utilize the intelligence to drive the development of programs designed to pinpoint individual customer touch points. For example, interactive analytics enable marketers to slice and dice data to carryout what-if scenarios that could be used to create a promotions campaign.

While a significant tool to assist companies architect targeted marketing programs, industry analysts have been careful to point out what today's CRM analytics platforms can really do. According to AMR research, analytical CRM is being used to perform tasks such as profiling customers for focused communications and up-selling/cross-selling opportunities, predicting customer churn and profitability, executing real-time Internet personalization, and assembling the proper mixture of product, price, and channel that maximizes individual customer profitability. At the same time, AMR is careful to detail that analytical CRM is often not fully integrated with operational CRM and is not yet a fully automated set of business files flowing from one system to another.[35]

D. IMPLEMENTING CRM

While CRM provides companies with an array of application toolsets focused squarely on improving customer service and profitability, undertaking a CRM implementation is fraught with significant perils. In fact, by the beginning of 2002 the analysts and industry articles had switched their previously enthusiastic endorsement of CRM to one of caution. In a survey[36] published in January of 2002 regarding the level of CRM customer satisfaction, respondents awarded a composite score of

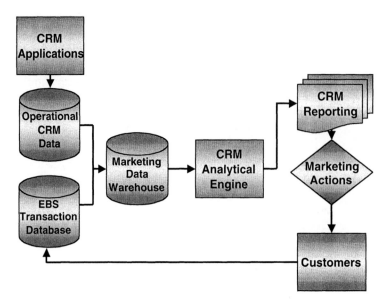

FIGURE 5.4 Analytical CRM architecture.

only 63.13 out of possible 100. Overall, these companies were displeased with the overall performance of CRM applications and the money they spent during the implementation.

Upon closer examination the survey also contained the clue as to why such a high dissatisfaction rate existed. Of the five negative factors identified as most important — functionality, price, ease of implementation, customer focus, and support — implementation ranked the highest. Similar to what happens in an ERP implementation, installing CRM must be seen as a multifaceted project that will impact the entire organization. As one analyst puts it,

> Too often we think of CRM as being a single concept. But it is not. It encompasses a variety of concepts: marketing automation, call center management, field sales support, product management, order processing, and customer support, to name a few. And within any of those concepts there are dozens of issues that impact the efficiency and effectiveness of our personnel.[37]

In addition, a company's relationship with its customers is complex. The services offered to customers can be almost infinite; approaches to collaborative activities, such as forecast and marketing data sharing, can be as numerous as the number of customers.

Ensuring an effective CRM system requires a comprehensive implementation plan. While the plan requires a detailed set of action steps to guide the implementation process, it also requires companies to clearly define a broader understanding of their CRM system as a business philosophy that extends beyond the software to encompass the entire organization, from executives to line workers, all customer-facing processes, and the content of the company's customer focus. The first step in the CRM implementation process is, therefore, to define the projected objectives and benefits of the project. Many companies fail to perform this step. CRM is often seen as a point solution, designed to automate tasks and improve efficiencies, and not as a clearly articulated strategy, complete with metrics to ensure maximum return on investment. Companies often spend large sums to achieve a single CRM function, utilized by just a single department, and wonder why the return does not have a company-wide affect. In contrast, an effective CRM plan starts with the project's ability to impact corporate strategy. According to Robb Eklund, vice president of CRM product marketing at PeopleSoft, "The Holy Grail of CRM is to move how it is being implemented — as a point solution, to manage sales or run call centers — to an enterprise solution, where CRM is integrated, and its business processes extended to other areas of a company where customer information may be."[38]

Once a comprehensive strategic plan and ROI objectives have been defined, companies can then begin the process of assembling the CRM suite of products. As discussed earlier in the chapter, a CRM system consists of three integrated functions: *operational* (such as transaction, event, and service management); *collaborative* (such as forecast, process, and information sharing); and *analytical* (such as churn analysis and prediction). Determining which sets of CRM applications to select for implementation should originate in the *requirements* specified in the project defini-tion. This element should clarify the business needs to be solved by the CRM tools. Next, implementers must be careful to match the CRM tool *functionality* to the required solution. Once the above steps have been completed, the specific CRM applications can then be selected. At the culmination of the process, the sum total functionality assembled should map back to the original requirements. Finally, as the project is implemented, CRM analysts must make sure that the proper perfor-mance metrics have been closely defined. While it is true CRM costs and lack of maturity of CRM technologies are part of the complaint about the lack of CRM projects showing real ROI, most lackluster efforts are more the direct result of concentrating heavily on the operational side of CRM, coupled with rather weakly defined ROI targets, such as customer satisfaction/retention rates, increased sales/revenues, and other metrics.

OSRAM SYLVANIA, a Danvers, MA–based manufacturer of lighting and other products in the automotive, computer, and aerospace markets, began their CRM implementation, according to company CIO Mehrdad Laghaeian, by determining a vision of what the company wanted to do with CRM that has kept the project focused on the critical business issues that were unearthed during the planning steps. "We've completed step one: the on-line catalog at the base of a triangle. Step two is building basic information (e.g., product availability, on-line pricing, order management) that customers need to let us know what they want us to do, leading to the ultimate goal: collaborative planning." While the company has developed metrics to measure the success of its CRM application through customer usage and feedback, it has also established ongoing hard measurements based on traditional business metrics. OSRAM SYLVANIA's CRM project has been a success because implementers had effectively architected a CRM strategy and then prioritized deployment of CRM toolsets based on the greatest needs/opportunities.[39]

IV. SUMMARY AND TRANSITION

Today's customers have at their disposal an array of technology tools that enable them to interact with their suppliers, view marketing materials, order products, check on delivery status, and pay for goods and services in real-time. This dramatic transformation in the way business is conducted has shifted companies from their traditional preoccupation with simply selling products to a focus on satisfying the needs of individual customers. Instead of a passive view of the customer, who makes decisions purely on branding and market leadership, marketers today are confronted with customers who can actively decide on which companies they wish to do business with. Building customer loyalty today requires businesses to abandon the "one size fits all" strategies of the past and be able to continuously architect organizations, systems, and supply chains agile enough to determine the exact needs of the customer and to propose customized solutions that resonate with the needs of individualized customers.

Establishing a *customer-centric* focus is a multiphased process that involves reshaping the infrastructures of both individual organizations and supply chain partners. To begin with, literally every customer touch point needs to be dismantled and rebuilt around customer service. Second, companies must understand what each customer values and from these metrics design products, services, and communications initiatives that will drive customer loyalty. Third, marketers must stratify their customer databases. Not all customers should be treated equally. By pinpointing what provides individual customer value, companies can define the proper mix of products, services, prices, and other factors to avoid mismatches between their offerings and what the customer truly values. Finally, enterprises must be vigilant in monitoring and measuring their own customer-centricity strengths and weaknesses.

To more effectively respond to the realities of today's marketplace, companies have increasingly turned their attention to *customer relationship management* (CRM) application toolsets. The mission of CRM is to assemble focused technologies, such as the Internet, *sales force automation* (SFA), CRM marketing functions, *customer service management* (CSM), *partner relationship management* (PRM), *electronic bill presentment and payment* (EBPP), and analytical CRM, to structure touch points that continuously enhance the buying experience of individual customers so that they will remain customers for life. CRM is about opening a window into the habits and needs of individual customers so that targeted marketing campaigns can be established, customer profitability can be measured, and mutually beneficial, long-term relationships can be nurtured. Finally, CRM serves as a key foundation in the structuring of integrated, synchronized supply chains that will provide for the seamless satisfaction of the customer across the supply channel network.

Once companies can assemble a view of what their customers value and how they should be managed, the process of architecting the business components that actually build, acquire, and offer the goods and services can effectively be undertaken. Chapter 6 focuses on how today's e-SCM has altered the way the manufacturing functions of the business are responding to the realities of e-business.

ENDNOTES

1. Greenberg, Paul, *CRM at The Speed of Light: Capturing and Keeping Customers in Internet Real Time,* McGraw-Hill, Berkley, CA, 2001, *xviii.* Greenberg also devotes 33 pages of his first chapter to detailing a variety of comprehensive definitions coming from a number of CEOs and COOs from companies such as PeopleSoft and Onyx Software.

2. Dyche, Jill, *The CRM Handbook: A Business Guide to Customer Relationship Management,* Addison-Wesley, Boston, MA, 2002, 4.

3. Renner, Dale H., "Closer to the Customer: Customer Relationship Management and the Supply Chain," in *Achieving Supply Chain Excellence Through Technology,* 1, Anderson, David L., ed., Montgomery Research, San Francisco, 1999, 108.

4. Hess, Ed, "The ABCs of CRM," *Integrated Solutions,* 5, 2, 2001, 41–48.

5. Dyche, 16.

6. Morris, Betsy, "Can Michael Dell Escape the Box?" *Fortune,* Oct 16, 2000.

7. An excellent discussion of the LCV metric can be found in Compton, Jason, "Tying the Knot," *Customer Relationship Management,* 5, 3, 2001, 44–48 and Greenberg, 343–349.

8. Murphy, Jean V., "Moving the Focus from Customers to Relationships," *Global Logistics and Supply Chain Strategies,* 5, 3, 2001, 56–59.

9. Cokins, Gary, "Are All of Your Trading Partners 'Worth It' to You?" in *Achieving Supply Chain Excellence Through Technology,* 1, Anderson, David, ed., L. Montgomery Research, San Francisco, 1999, 12.

10. The Buy.com story is related in Cooper, Ginger, "The Quest for Customer Centricity," *Customer Relationship Management,* 5, 9, 2001, 35.

11. Manring, Audrey, "Profiling the Chief Customer Officer," *Customer Relationship Management,* 4, 11, 2000, 84–95.

12. This story is found in *Ibid.*

13. Arnold-Ialongo, Donna, "Building Customer Loyalty," *Customer Relationship Management,* 5, 3, 2001, 25–26.

14. Sawhney, Mohan and Zabin, Jeff, *The Seven Steps to Nirvana: Strategic Insights into e-Business Transformation,* McGraw-Hill, New York, 2001, pp. 175–181 have been most helpful in writing the above two paragraphs.

15. Poirier, Charles C. and Bauer, Michael J., *E-Supply Chain: Using the Internet to Revolutionize Your Business,"* Berrett-Koehler Publishers, Inc., San Francisco, 2000, 154.

16. Sawhney and Zabin, 181.

17. These points have been adopted from Greenberg, 55–56.

18. Commentary from Deloitte Consulting concerning this survey conducted in early 2001 can be found in Sabath, Robert E. and Kumar, Himanshu, "The Advantage of Digital Loyalty Networks," *Supply Chain Management Review,* 5, 2, 2001, 66–74.

19. Dyche, 80.

20. *Ibid.,* 85.

21. Fingar, Peter, Kumar, Harsha, and Sharma, Tarun, *Enterprise E-Commerce: The Software Component Breakthrough for Business-to-Business Commerce,* Meghan-Kiffer Press, Tampa Florida, 2000, 89–90.

22. Taylor, David and Terhune, Alyse D., *Doing e-Business: Strategies for Thriving in an Electronic Marketplace,* John Wiley & Sons., New York, 2001, 61–62.

23. *Ibid.,* 79.

24. Voth, Danna, "Making Your Mark in the Information Age," *Customer Relationship Management,* 4, 6, 2000, 61–70.

25. Agnew, Marion, "CRM Plus Lots of Data Equals More Sales for Borders," *Information Week,* May 7, 2001, 114–118.

26. These metrics can be found in Giffler, Joe, "Capturing Customers For Life," *Decision Magazine,* May 1998 and Pechi, Tony, "Sublime Service," *Customer Relationship Magazine,*" 5, 8, 25–26.

27. Fingar, Kumar, and Sharma, 108.

28. The Otis service story is related in Compton, Jason, "Service... With a Smile," *Customer Relationship Management,* 5, 1, 2001, 34–40.

29. Greenberg, 151.

30. Compton, Jason, "Mission Critical: Encouraging Collaboration," *Customer Relationship Management,* 5, 10, 2001, 50–51.

31. Guerrisi, Joseph, "Making Money Move Faster," *Supply Chain Management Review,* 5, 1, 2001, 17–18.

32. See the discussion in Hill, Kimberly, "The Direction of the Industry," *e.bill,* 3, 5, 2001, 20–22.

33. Scott, Kevin, "Analytical Customer Relationship Management: Myth or Reality," *AMR Research Report,* March, 2001, 9.

34. *Ibid.,* 5.

35. *Ibid.* 6–7.

36. Lee, Dick, "Great Expectations, " *Customer Relationship Management,* 6,1, 2001, 50–54.

37. Dickie, Jim, "CRM — Is It True This Dog Don't Hunt?" *Customer Relationship Management,* 6, 1, 2002, 22–23.

38. Weil, Mary, "A Measure of Vision," *Software Strategies,* 6, 9, 2001, 38–41.

39. This case study can be found in *Ibid.,* 9.

6 Manufacturing and Supply Chain Planning: Linking Product Design, Manufacture, and Planning to Provide Value to Customers

e-SCM applies Internet-enabled application toolsets and the SCM business model to architect collaborative supply chain networks that closely integrate customers, suppliers, business partners, logistics providers, and other functions that have coalesced into various forms of channel configurations. The objective is to engineer the real-time transfer of information anywhere, any time, within the network and provide the connectivity necessary to coordinate and optimize the flow of materials, products, and services. One of the most critical components, which stands perhaps at the heart of this convergence of business functions, is manufacturing. In fact, it can truly be said that all channel value starts with the conversion of raw materials and components through the production process into products. Once goods have been produced, they then enter the supply channel, where various support functions and services, from sales and marketing to distribution and delivery, augment and complete the transfer to the end consumer.

Optimization of supply chain value can therefore be said to start with the ability of companies to optimize their productive resources in an effort to make and distribute their products as efficiently as possible. Managing productive processes means planning for and controlling the resources, such as product design, materials, labor, and overheads, expended during the process of product conversion. Underlying this management process is, first of all, a model of the plant itself, which describes characteristics such as capacity, cost, cycle times, and constraints. This model, in turn, enables the particular configuration by which the plant executes productive processes to achieve targeted objectives such as quality, order due date completion, quantity, and cost. Realizing plant process output, however, is not automatic. Effectively optimizing productive functions is a dynamic management process, and as the variables associated with product and process life cycles, quality, reliance on outside resources, and other factors increase, so does the complexity of the models and methods necessary to manage them. Without effective planning and control tools, even the best structured process can not efficiently work and will be poorly utilized, and without the necessary process output, the supply chain pipeline will slowly dry up and the profitability, indeed the very existence, of the entire channel network will be threatened.

Examining today's best business practices and technology toolsets to ensure the efficient and timely flow of information and materials from the manufacturer through the supply chain to the final customer is the subject of this chapter. The discussion begins by reviewing the role of manufacturing in the "age of e-business." What has become apparent is that the traditional objectives and methodologies of manufacturing have recently undergone tremendous change, in response to the migration of once large, vertical organizations to increased outsourcing, the dramatic shortening of product life cycles and growing requirements for rapid design and release of new products to market, and the creation of new performance metrics to replace dependencies on efficiencies and utilization as benchmarks of manufacturing productivity. Of particular importance is the almost bewildering array of technology tools available to manufacturing to assist in the management of almost every aspect of the business from transaction control to Internet-enabled B2B exchanges. The chapter discusses one of today's most important drivers of productivity — the ability of manufacturing firms to architect collaborative relationships with business partners to synchronize, through the Internet, all aspects of product design and time-to-market. Today, manufacturing firms are engaged in what can be called *design for the supply chain*, signifying that the ability to build and distribute products is the focus of not just individual firms but of whole supply networks. Finally, the chapter concludes with an analysis of today's advanced manufacturing planning functions that seek to apply the latest optimization and Web-based applications to interconnect and make visible the demand and replenishment needs of whole supply network systems in the pursuit of competitive advantage.

I. MANUFACTURING IN THE AGE OF e-BUSINESS

Manufacturing can be represented as residing at the center of the supply chain process. The manufacturing function has often been described as the "800-pound gorilla" of the channel network. As illustrated in Figure 6.1, manufacturing owns, interfaces, or is influenced by almost every function inside the organization and outside in the supply channel. According to Staid and Matthews from Accenture,[1]

> A single manufacturing location may represent hundreds of millions of dollars of investment, employ tens of thousands of suppliers, thousands of customers, and supply products that are sold for billions of dollars worth of revenue. As such, manufacturing operations typically represent the bulk of cost/value added within a company's supply chain. Achieving actual sellable output in the face of such complexity and interdependency represents a daily logistical triumph.

Because it is such a critical driver of the supply chain, any changes in manufacturing processes are bound to reverberate throughout the entire channel ecosystem.

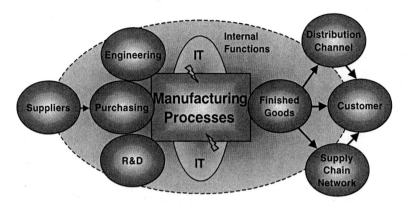

FIGURE 6.1 Role of manufacturing functions.

As manufacturing philosophies change to respond to new product requirements and cost and quality improvement efforts, evolve to leverage internal methods changes and technology breakthroughs, and adapt to meet the needs of suppliers and customers at either end of the channel system, supply chain strategists must continually rethink the role of manufacturing and how operational, technological, and management changes will impact the entire supply channel galaxy.

There can be little doubt that the operational and theoretical management of manufacturing has dramatically changed over the past decade. In the past, acquiring new productive resources and making capital improvements to expand capacities and lower costs differentiated manufacturers and defined industry leadership. Today, manufacturers have come under intense pressure to reduce investment in plant and equipment and reengineer the core processes that do exist to be as agile as possible. Part of this shift in the fundamentals of manufacturing strategy is the result of ensuring that companies meet return on investment (ROA) expectations. Value tied up in inflexible equipment and inventories that are peripheral to the business or have poor utilization act as an enormous rock that sinks ROA. Another factor is the declining shelf life of products. Obsolete products and the processes that make them simply add to the asset and not the income side of ROA.

Partly as a result of investment requirements, partly as a response to the demands of e-commerce and SCM, many manufacturers have seriously begun to rethink their mission and the architecture of their businesses. Many have begun in earnest the process of "de-verticalizing" their productive functions. Companies that once built their own assemblies, offered in-house services, and distributed goods are now outsourcing these functions to channel partners who have much stronger core competencies and efficiencies in these areas. The most radical example of this philosophy is the decision of some former manufacturers to completely outsource all manufacturing and logistics functions and become a "virtual enterprise," focused perhaps on strong internal competencies in brand management or engineering. An example of this trend to reduce assets and refocus on nonmanufacturing competencies is Sara Lee Corporation. By 2000 the company had sold or closed more than 100 facilities and entered into 30 outsourcing agreements. The goal of the strategy was to de-emphasize Sara Lee's role as a manufacturer and to reposition it as a brand management company. Similar strategies have begun to be heard at the big three automakers who have long sought to outsource as much manufacturing as possible and refocus efforts on brand management.

For most of us who have grown up in the belief that manufacturing *was* the core competency of any company, this change has been quite dramatic, if not bewildering. "Not all companies," writes Don Swann, "have pushed manufacturing to the point of being a contracted commodity service. But the trend is to view manufacturing as an asset-intensive necessary evil rather than the core competency that defines a company's personality, culture, and reputation."[2] What this means is that manufacturing is now faced with the necessity of redefining its role and meeting the new challenges brought about by today's marketplace realities. There can be little doubt that today's manufacturer faces a host of complex and interrelated challenges unparalleled in history. Everything is changing, and the pace of change is exponentially accelerating. The transformation of global markets and changes to product life cycles, competition, technology and communications, and popular culture are occurring explosively and simultaneously. The effective management of time, rather than of physical assets such as equipment and inventories, has become today's most critical business dimension. The ability to exploit human knowledge and diffuse information real-time has replaced past models based on hierarchical management and control principles.

Surviving and thriving in this brave new world requires manufacturers and distributors to continuously develop solutions to the following four themes. Collectively, these themes present a dramatic departure from past management modes, each requiring radically new solutions. Understanding today's customer is the first theme. The key to this theme for manufacturers is architecting customer-centric organizations capable of providing combinations of configurable products, services, and information that will provide the customer with unique value and a solution to their buying needs. The second theme, managing the impact of time and change, requires manufacturers to develop processes and infrastructures resilient enough to thrive in an era of global competition, while leveraging advances in materials, processes, and technologies. Successfully adapting company infrastructure to meet the realities of today's business environment comprises the third theme. Time, technology, and knowledge-based competition have required many companies to rethink their mission and how they are organized. Finally, changes to the importance of manufacturing to the firm have given rise to a new set of performance standards for manufacturing. In this fourth dynamic, some of the traditional manufacturing performance benchmarks, such as efficiencies and asset management, will be revisited.

A. DOMINANCE OF THE CUSTOMER

Through this book, the expanding power of the customer over the supply chain has been documented as perhaps the hallmark of the current age. Unfortunately, many of today's manufacturing companies are still not customer-centric. Most manufacturers continue to develop their marketplace strategies around their product lines or brands and service offerings. For example, at Frito-Lay there is a Doritos brand manager; at Proctor & Gamble there is a Tide brand manager. The focus of such a structure is on developing product and service mixes that correspond to the needs and desires of a majority of the firm's customers. The goal is to utilize lean manufacturing principles to develop processes that minimize the impact of product design changes, maintain or shrink production costs, permit the recycling of marketing and advertising, and utilize the existing distribution infrastructure.

Today, dependence on such a philosophy is an invitation to disaster. While a few commodity manufacturers can rest upon brand loyalty for their products — it would be hard to replace the physical and psychological expectation that a handful of M&M candies produces — most manufacturers are not so fortunate. Even Mars has experimented with different colors of M&Ms, and rumors about the properties of certain colors and promotional prizes have added to the fun. Instead of accepting standardized products, customers today demand customized goods and services that delight them and keep them coming back for more. In the process they want exceptional convenience, reliability, speed, and self-directed control. In addition, breakthroughs in product design concepts and technologies, communications, and global logistics have extended the reach of competitors presenting expected levels of quality, functionality, and service to anywhere in the world.

Changing manufacturing companies to respond to today's marketplace is not easy. Some firms will need to undergo structural changes. For example, instead of a focus around brands, a customer-centric business would be organized around its various customers. Mars product design and distribution would be organized around, perhaps, age groups (a "children's brand manager," a "teen brand manager") and not particular product lines. In addition to organizational structure, customer-centric manufacturers would also closely incorporate the customer in the firm's product research and development, manufacturing process design, and fulfillment strategies. Perhaps the cardinal principle impressed upon everyone who participates in business is the saying "The customer is always right." Assembling manufacturing functions that realize this principle, and not just producing products for someone else in the supply channel to sell, is, without a doubt, the foremost challenge before today's manufacturer.

B. THE CENTRIPETAL FORCES OF TIME AND CHANGE

There can be little doubt that change and the acceleration of change on a global basis have become one the foremost topics of the new century, and its vernacular dominates today's management literature and technological objectives. In the past, manufacturing companies could rest on their brand image without a significant threat from competitors. Products had long life cycles, production processes were honed by JIT and lean manufacturing to ensure lowest cost, and customers were willing to purchase standardized products at standardized prices. In contrast, today's manufacturing environment is characterized by order-of-magnitude, often discontinuous change. Changes to product life cycles, production materials, processing equipment, planning and manufacturing information technology, workforce attitudes and culture, foreign competition, and a host of other conditions are not only systemic, but also seem to be occurring in ever shortening waves that threaten to swamp previously stable plant environments. *Time* to react to these changes has correspondingly grown shorter, creating a sense of urgency for company and plant management, who must consistently execute quick, crisp decisions that leverage productive resources to optimize temporary marketplace advantage while reducing costs.

According to Jordan and Michel,[3] today's typical manufacturing company faces change from the following four directions.

- *Technological change* resulting from the application of the computer and communications toolsets to manufacturing has had an enormous impact on automation, cost and quality control, planning, processing, workforce skills, and output management. Technologies from barcode reading to wireless devices on the low end, to *advanced planning systems* (APS), *supply chain management system* (SCM), and ERP on the high end, have accelerated process control and enabled manufacturers to move to new levels of internal integration, supply partner collaboration, and overall productivity.
- *Structural change* to manufacturing and distribution has accompanied each shift in customer assertiveness and technology advancement. Organizations have undergone a train of organizational changes ranging from *business process reengineer* (BRP) to the virtual factory. Today's manufacturer/distributor is squarely focused on their core competencies and has actively sought to maintain focus by leveraging channel partners to perform peripheral functions.
- The two most commonly used *managerial change* methods are reward systems and labor/management cooperation. Ensuring change management often means rewarding employees to utilize new tasks and operating structures, while creating the environment for improving morale, solving production and work/technology problems, effective training programs, and other positive and constructive initiatives that will facilitate corporate and labor goals.
- Channeling *human change* is perhaps a company's most important challenge in managing change. Manufacturers and distributors have more than ever come to realize the importance of human capital in constructing today's competitive enterprise. Managing change in this area consists in structuring organizations that develop individual, group, and even supply chain processes and practices with the mission of improving employee climate, values, health, productivity, and well-being.

C. MANUFACTURING/SUPPLY CHAIN INFRASTRUCTURE CHANGE

The growing power of the customer and the enabling capabilities of the Internet have changed the role of the manufacturer and the supply chain from stagnant to dynamic, high-performance organizations. Traditional functions focused on making standardized, "one size fits all" products pushed sequentially from one network node to another. In contrast, serving today's customer requires organizations capable of responding rapidly and efficiently to the demand for customer self-designed products with flexible and cost-effective manufacturing and with interactive channel pull

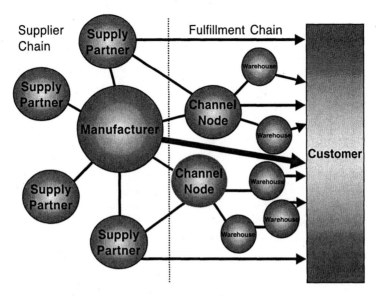

FIGURE 6.2 Today's manufacturing/fulfillment network.

systems capable of delivering the necessary product or service to the customer from even the remotest network node. As illustrated in Figure 6.2, the role of the manufacturer and the supply chain are drastically changed in this arrangement. The manufacturer serves as the prime contact with the customer and is responsible for relationship development, product design, marketing, etc. The channel partners that ring the manufacturer are responsible for a wide range of functions ranging from sourcing, outsourced manufacturing, delivery, and marketing information feedback from the customer. Often these partners may be connected to the customer and may supply products and services direct, bypassing traditional channel levels.

Architecting such a responsive supply chain constellation will require manufacturers and distributors to constantly focus on building organizations that have the following characteristics:

- *Customer-centric.* The ability of the customer to self-configure their own products and services, rather than offerings activated by channel push-logic triggers, such as forecasting, will drive the cycle of sourcing, manufacture, and fulfillment. Effectively responding to pull-signals will require that all channel nodes be uniquely aligned and networked with the customer.
- *Collaborative networking.* Even the largest of manufacturers cannot possibly assemble the entire suite of core competencies necessary to serve today's customer. In order to meet the timing and special needs of each customer, producers and distributors of products and services will be increasingly forced to utilize their channel partners to execute specialized productive functions.
- *Agile and scalable.* Responding to shortening product life cycles and increasingly configurable products will require incredibly agile product

design, manufacturing, distribution, and information-enabled supply chains. As delivery times continue to shrink, manufacturers will be faced not only with the task of engineering flexible productive capabilities but also with declining order-to-deliver cycles. In place of the traditional supply channel hierarchy, whole supply networks will have to be as scalable as possible, phasing-in and phasing-out functions and delivery/communications points as necessary.

- *e-Business enablers.* The traditional serial transfer of goods and information from channel node to channel node will not provide today's supply chain with the high-velocity information necessary to meet the needs of today's customer or counter the moves of competitors. With the advent of the Internet, winning manufacturers can truly link their productive capabilities with their network supply partners and their customers. Real-time data provides the fuel for powerful analytical engines enabling event-driven decision-making to optimize resources to respond to any opportunity.

In the past, manufacturers and distributors viewed the possession of physical assets, broad product lines of predefined, inventoried products, long production runs, and large R&D investment as providing organizations with health and stability. And now, investors and managers see assets as a severe impediment to ROA and flexibility that can threaten the capability of businesses to deploy capital and resources and leverage the core competencies of channel partners to meet today's rapidly changing business environment.

D. CHANGING PERFORMANCE TARGETS

A critical component of responding to the new roles and challenges manufacturers face is revamping the traditional benchmarks that measure the level of manufacturing process success. Past metrics that measured return on investment, asset optimization, and process performance clearly need to be modified and, in some cases, abandoned altogether. Today's manufacturing dynamics have definitely complicated matters. According to Olin Thompson,

> Some plants will face competition with outside resources to satisfy the demands of their own enterprises. New products may be sourced from outside the enterprise. Products with highly varying demand may be outsourced in part or in their entirety to provide more elasticity on the supply side. If a lower-cost producer is found for a product, the enterprise may go to that external source.[4]

To be able to compete in such an environment, manufacturers will have to shift the standards of performance from traditional concerns with efficiencies and utilization to flexibility and information collaboration with channel partners. Many components of plant management will not change: products will still have to be made at optimum quality, costs kept to a minimum, continuous improvement of processes pursued, and integration with engineering, customer, and logistics functions deepened. What will be different is the construction of agile, flexible processes that can tightly integrate a variety of information drivers originating from multiple regions in the supply chain. In fact, the ability to receive and transmit information rather than products will become the central competitive weapon for manufacturers, permitting them to deploy productive resources to meet differing demands from different channel networks and virtual companies.

Manufacturing performance centered on agility and flexibility will require significant alteration of traditional ROA and asset utilization metrics. To begin with, manufacturers will have to compress the time normally allocated for ROA. Investments in plant and equipment that exceed 18 months should be examined closely. Risk here involves the possibility of product and process obsolescence, excess capacity, and opportunity to utilize more cost-effective outsourcing alternatives. Another critical area is designing manufacturing processes that are truly customer driven. The goal is to construct productive capabilities that enable companies to make-to-final customer order by synchronizing their networked supply channels to meet order delivery dates, while recognizing material, manufacturing, assembly, and logistics constraints. Now known as "the direct model" or the "Dell model," the mechanics of the system seek direct connectivity of the customer with the manufacturer's supply chain that, together, fulfill the customer's demand. Here, the manufacturer retains the ownership of product design and targeted assembly, while linking in real time the total production requirement with outsourcing partners who, in turn, have the capability to pool inventories and leverage core manufacturing processes to supply some or all of the required end-product. A simple way to begin moving manufacturing to this model is to refocus traditional efficiencies from just making products, to realizing benchmark utilizations, to only making products to the demand schedule. In this scheme process efficiency is credited only when orders are built on time and then shipped to meet the customer delivery date.

While efficiency measurements must change, so must traditional views of plant utilization. Historically, plant managers have been rewarded on high utilizations, to ensure products are being made at high efficiency and low cost. Today, the measurement of utilization must revolve around how well productive processes produce to customer demand. While there may be an objection that high-volume process manufacturing will have a hard time moving to a customer-centric philosophy, nevertheless, managers even in these industries must migrate their planning and control systems to a philosophy that puts the customer at the center of all production decisions. Achieving such a strategy will mean that all aspects of the manufacturing process — product and process design, supporting planning systems, customer management systems, production management, and total plant performance — must continuously move toward greater integration with supply partners and customer-centricity.

II. IMPACT OF TECHNOLOGY
ON MANUFACTURING

Besides the growing power of the customer, the explosion in technology has had an enormous impact on today's manufacturer. Because of the scale, scope, and complexity of manufacturing, companies have for decades sought to utilize the processing power of computer systems, such as *material requirements planning* (MRP II) and *enterprise resource planning* (ERP), to calculate material planning, plan and control manufacturing activity, and integrate the various functions of the business. As was discussed in Chapter 3, the purpose of these *enterprise business systems* (EBS) is to provide for the organization and standardization of all of the data of a manufacturing company and to enable the integration and optimization of an enterprise's *internal* value chain for purchasing and inventory management through sales, production, and financial accounting.

Today, companies and software developers alike have begun the process of integrating into their EBSs manufacturing support applications that enhance tried-and-true MRP functionality for faster and more accurate planning and shop floor execution. In addition, savvy manufacturers have been quick to utilize the integrative and collaborative capabilities of the Internet. Advanced Web applications enable manufacturers to collaborate and be competitive in ways impossible just a few years ago. These toolsets provide the means to plan, control, and optimize operations by synchronizing production processes, not only with other company processes, but also through SCM systems, with supporting partners out in the supply chain.

Overall, businesses can expect breakthroughs in and novel applications of technology to continue to impact the theory and practice of manufacturing. In addition to enhancing operating and integrative efficiencies, technology will both drive and enable the development and deployment of new applications that will more closely synchronize supply chain demand with productive capabilities. Finally, technology will assist manufacturing functions to accelerate the move out of their historically reactive mode to the influx of new product and process changes and customer requirements to a proactive, strategic role in determining the competitive strength of their companies.

A. SHORT HISTORY OF MANUFACTURING PLANNING AND CONTROL SYSTEMS

Because of the sheer size, scope, complexity, and volume of manufacturing data and diversity of management methods, manufacturing has always been considered a prime area for computerization. As is illustrated in Figure 6.3, over the past 40 years manufacturers have sought to apply the newest hardware and software applications to solve the problem of collecting, calculating, reporting, and utilizing manufacturing information to assist them in making the best decisions for inventory planning, controlling the shop floor, and building products to meet customer demand. During the 1950s and 1960s, the first uses of the computer were in the inventory management area. In this era, companies sought to move critical inventory management functions, such as perpetual inventory control, calculation of requirements based on reorder points, and finally, time phased or MRP *bill of material* (BOM) explosion, from manual maintenance to the computer.

By the 1970s, advances in computer hardware and manufacturing theory assisted basic MRP to evolve from being purely an ordering system to a set of applications used to integrate company demand with the material plan calculation. Perhaps the most important aspect of what became known as *closed-loop MRP* (MRP I) was the

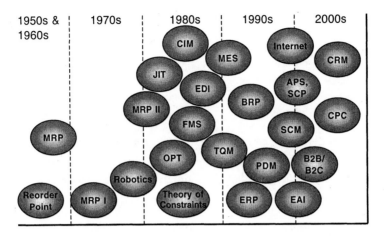

FIGURE 6.3 Chronology of major computerized manufacturing applications.

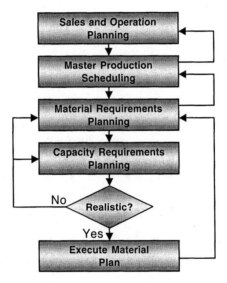

FIGURE 6.4 Closed-loop MRP.

inclusion of sales and operations planning and master scheduling into the system loop, to drive the MRP calculation and then to connect the output to shop floor and purchasing release and scheduling (Figure 6.4). As the 1970s closed, manufacturing theory was again changed with the rise of MRP II, which enclosed the function of business planning into the closed-loop system, and the appearance of a radical new manufacturing philosophy from Japan — *just-in-time* (JIT).

The 1980s witnessed a virtual explosion in new computerized tools and management philosophies. Manufacturers now had the opportunity to supplement weaknesses in the MRP II application suite with the addition of shop floor programmable controllers, *manufacturing execution systems* (MES) enabling tools, such as bar coding, to assist in shop floor data collection and scheduling, EDI systems enabling the first computer-to-computer linkages, *computer integrated manufacturing* (CIM) enabling the use of CAD/CAM applications for product design, and new production theories surrounding total quality management, constraints management, and high-powered tools for shop floor optimization and finite loading. These application toolsets were joined in the 1990s by enhancements to MRP II, which became *enterprise resource planning* (ERP), and *product data management* (PDM). This decade also was marked by the addition of powerful non-computerized philosophies, such as *business process reengineering* (BRP) and SCM, which changed forever the traditional structure and objectives of the enterprise. Today, as will be detailed below, the application of Internet tools has again dramatically changed the nature of manufacturing technologies and moved management from a concern with planning and controlling *internal* productive functions to the opportunity to synchronize plans and pursue collaborative relationships with supply network trading partners.

B. GEOGRAPHY OF TODAY'S MANUFACTURING SYSTEMS

The computer toolsets available to today's manufacturer have evolved and been architected to respond to the special needs of effectively and efficiently operating twenty-first century manufacturing. As illustrated in Figure 6.5, these applications can be essentially divided into manufacturing planning, production and process management, product design and engineering, plant and quality management, and product life cycle management. Each will be considered in detail.

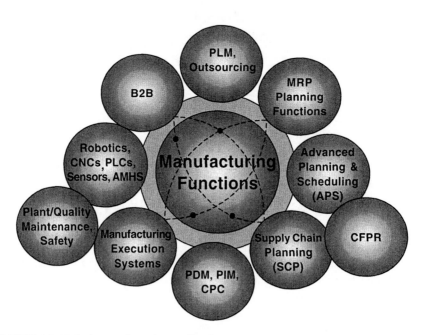

FIGURE 6.5 Today's manufacturing applications.

1. Manufacturing Planning

The ability to effectively plan, schedule, communicate, and manage the interaction between departments necessary to execute the timely acquisition of production inventories and finished goods through MRP is perhaps the most mature and recognizable component of today's suite of manufacturing applications. Classically, MRP can be broken down into three separate but integrated functions.

- *Material requirements planning* (MRP). This function utilizes item planning data to calculate and provide suggested inventory replenishment action to meet current demand. MRP's primary mission is to ensure *priority control*: the timely release and ongoing maintenance of open orders to ensure accurate due date completion.
- *Capacity requirements planning* (CRP). This function utilizes the MRP requirements output, converts it into load, and then matches it to available capacity. By balancing load and capacity, planners can ensure the feasibility of priority plans arising from MRP.
- *Shop floor control*. After priority and capacity plans have been validated, shop orders can then be released to manufacturing. Once on the floor, MRP utilizes tools, such as order dispatching and input-output control, to ensure jobs are being completed on time.

Despite the tremendous degree of planning and control afforded by MRP, today's requirements for often minute-by-minute update of data and reformulation of plans have rendered the labor-intensive planning and recalculation processes of MRP too cumbersome for real-time shop floor information and execution. Recently, these deficiencies in MRP have been answered with the rise of *advanced production planning* (APS) and *supply chain management* (SCM) systems. These applications, normally run on PCs and integrated with the MRP backbone, are designed to quickly recalculate shop priorities, level load and optimize resources, provide for inputs into purchasing, and enable planners a window into the material and capacity resources of supply chain partners. Today, these toolsets have been able to tap into the enabling power of the Internet to create real-time linkages with suppliers. Termed *collaborative planning, forecasting, and replenishment* (CPFR), this collection of business practices is designed to utilize Internet and existing technologies to link the demand and supply capabilities of manufacturers, distributors, retailers, and suppliers in order to integrate channel demand with total network resources, reduce channel inventories, and improve productivities.

2. Production and Process Management

The continuous search for more productive philosophies and methods to automate shop floor control and optimize scheduling and integrate it more closely with demand planning has been at the core of today's systems approach to manufacturing. Beginning first with the MRP crusade of the 1970s, shop floor management has been involved in a continuous process of innovation, resulting in a wide range of applications, from scheduling systems and collection devices to machine *programmable logic controllers* (PLCs) and *automated material handling systems* (AMHS). The collective objective of these applications has become mission critical for today's enterprise: how to simultaneously optimize factory productivities, keep costs to a minimum, reduce inventories and cycle times, effectively plan and utilize capacities, and be agile and responsive to the customer.

Fundamental to achieving shop floor management goals is the ability to track production in real time. For over a decade, *manufacturing execution systems* (MES) have attempted to fill in this gap in shop floor management. According to MESA International, a trade association of MES vendors, MES can be defined as a group of applications encompassing order dispatching, operations and detailed scheduling, work-in-process (WIP) tracking, labor/machine positing, maintenance, quality management, and document control. The prime function of MES is the control and coordination of work cell and equipment controllers to optimize plant efficiency. Unfortunately, the implementation of MES systems and their integration with EBS backbones and shop devices such as PLCs has been slow in coming. Much of the problem resides in the dynamic nature of MES systems, which makes it difficult to integrate them into MRP and supply chain systems as part of a comprehensive manufacturing model. In a survey conducted in December of 2001 by *Managing Automation* magazine, only 27% of respondents reported having a MES system installed. Although 41% felt that their companies had plans to implement MES, 59% reported that their companies had no plans for MES.[5] Still, forward-looking enterprises, such as GE Fanuc, have considered their MES system as the foundation for the inclusion of Web-based functions that provide visibility to real-time data from manufacturing and repair operations to their supply chain.

3. Product Design and Engineering

The explosion in technology over the past decade has provided for the creation of new computerized tools to assist in the design, development, and rollout of new products. The objective of all these applications is to reduce the cost of development and shrink the time from design to product availability. Some of these tools, such as *computer aided design* (CAD) and *computer aided manufacturing* (CAM) have been available since the 1980s. These tools provide design engineers with automated tools that facilitate product design and negotiate the smooth transition of the product structure into BOMs and process routings the MRP system can use for planning and production scheduling. These tools have become particularly important to support the trend toward make-to-order manufacturing. By enabling the quick custom design of modular components into customer-configured products that can be easily transferred to the MRP backbone, CAD/CAM applications can shorten the entire life cycle of design and manufacture.

As product innovation requirements accelerate, time to delivery shrinks, and companies increasingly turn to outside processing, manufacturers have been pursuing alternatives to the traditional departmental, sequential process of product design to one that is cross-company and concurrent. To meet these new challenges, the concept of *collaborative product commerce* (CPC) has arisen with the availability of Web-based technologies. Essentially, CPC can be described as a group of applications that attempt to foster communication and cooperation among the various functions, both within the enterprise and outside located in supply partners, who collectively are responsible for new product and process design and finished goods rollout. In effect, CPC enables manufacturers to create virtual communities consisting of component suppliers, contract manufacturers, third-party design partners, and customers that can generate new product ideas, designs, and accompanying processes quicker, faster, and cheaper.

4. Plant Maintenance and Quality Management

One of the most important benefits of an integrated factory system is the increased capacity for plant maintenance, quality, and safety. Manufacturing process controllers provide the real-time data necessary for the factory management system to effectively determine the status of equipment and process quality.

- *Plant Maintenance.* Whether a module in the plant's ERP system or a stand-alone application, the purpose of a *computerized maintenance management system* (CMMS) is to reduce equipment downtime and maximize production output. Effective plant maintenance, however, extends beyond the maintenance department. A poor maintenance program can be immediately seen in the form of lost production, poor product quality, increased scrap in WIP, missed deliveries, decreased market share, compromised safety on site, and shortened lifetimes of capital equipment. In today's highly competitive environment, integrating production and maintenance makes good business sense. Production wants to reduce downtime and prefers to have equipment maintenance scheduled in a way that maximizes production. Similarly, the maintenance department wishes to reduce downtime through the rapid diagnosis of impending problems by using real-time data to be able to predict the probability of failure. The solution is to engineer a CMMS that permits an accurate estimate of equipment failure in sufficient time to assemble the necessary resources from parts/spares control, purchasing, fixed asset management, and maintenance resources, and then to schedule production and maintenance together, slotting maintenance work into intermittent periods when production has planned stoppages.

  A critical part of any CMMS is the equipment database. Such a database should provide engineers with a detailed catalog of each piece of equipment and its place within the plant. Key data would consist of not only equipment process standards, but also recurring problems, equipment idiosyncrasies, and output quality that, linked together with regularly scheduled inspection and preventive maintenance, can provide an effective trigger, alerting maintenance of impending problems. Other technology tools, such as equipment sensors to detect impending violations of tolerances, GUI-type maintenance screens to facilitate estimating, planning, and scheduling of maintenance, powerful analysis tools that can generate visual representations from the EBS database, and futuristic modeling that

will automatically reroute production in anticipation of equipment shut-
down, assist CMMS to ensure effective maintenance does not significantly
impact production.

- *Quality Management.* For today's manufacturer, unbeatable quality is no
  longer considered a competitive advantage: it is merely the price of admission to the marketplace. Customers expect that products will either meet
  or exceed their expectations, not most of the time, but all of the time, or
  they simply will migrate to a competitor who can provide it. Most ERP
  systems, coupled with specialized equipment, can be leveraged to design
  a variety of quality strategies. These systems can utilize a number of
  methods ranging from periodic product sampling, to sophisticated *statistical process control* (SPC) tools such as a range of process control charts
  for plotting process errors, to databases that can be utilized to eliminate
  assignable and continuously reduce *random* causes of process error.
  The utilization of software quality management tools can assist a company
  define the strategic level of quality desired. The primary level of quality
  management is *inspection.* The purpose of this basic level of quality is to
  inspect process output for the purpose of plotting the instance of error.
  However, this method accepts that a certain percentage of output will
  always have some level of defect and clearly will not assist a company
  reduce quality error. The next level of quality, *process measurement and
  improvement*, enables quality management to turn its attention to uncovering and fixing the root causes of error with progress monitored through
  statistical measurements. The third level of quality management, *process
  control,* utilizes SPC control chart plotting to monitor processes to keep
  them under control by continuously eliminating all assignable causes of
  error and ensuring random causes of error are within proscribed tolerances. The final level of quality management, *design for quality,* requires
  the utilization of reliability engineering, cooperative design, value engineering, design for manufacturability, and *quality functional deployment*
  (QFD) toolsets to engineer into the product design characteristics that will
  maximally fulfill customer requirements and create quality characteristics,
  such as durability, performance, reliability, features, and serviceability,
  unmatched by the competition.

5. Product Life Cycle Management (PLM)

As the centripetal forces of time and change increase, manufacturers are more than
ever faced with the need to deploy technology tools and leverage their supply chain
partners in the quest for shorter product development cycle, agile production processing, and quick delivery-to-market capabilities. Although still in its infancy, PLM
holds out the promise of integrating supply chain partners and the product development life cycle. PLM can be defined as the quick, concurrent, coordinated, and
highly interactive development of the product and associated processes through the
collaboration of design teams from the manufacturer, the supplier base, and customers. Because of the complexity of the product development cycle, PLM should be

integrated, not only across company functions, but also across company boundaries. An effective PLM program consists of four simultaneously functioning components that can be described as follows:[6]

- *Structured processes.* PLM is a methodology that seeks to leverage modeling and simulation tools along with cross-functional communication, decision-making, and purposeful action, to continuously shrink the design and process times necessary to successfully bring new products to market. PLM is a vehicle to develop a repeatable, structured process that centers on toolsets, such as *quality functional deployment* (QFD), to unearth and validate customer requirements and relevant technologies that ensure built-in quality assurance and continuously shrinking product life cycle management efforts.
- *Process development tools.* Evolving PLM requires the application of a wide range of technology tools ranging from PDM and CAD through Web-enabled design tools and project management software for billing and reporting tasks. Included in this area are the ongoing deployment of responsive, flexible, modular, and in-line cellular processes and equipment that enable easy reconfigurability and versatility while meeting standards for quality and continuous product/process cost reduction. PLM in this area also seeks to effectively utilize computer modeling and simulation for rapid prototyping of products, processes, and systems and the application of programmable processes and equipment that, together, shrink risk and accentuate systems validation and assurance testing.
- *Supply chain partners.* Executing world-class PLM requires companies to expand their access to both internal skilled, multidisciplinary design teams and the physical capacities of supply chain. The shift to utilizing outsourced functions has been increasing as companies seek to leverage the core competencies and manufacturing capabilities of their supply networks. Cisco, for example, relies on its contract manufacturers to produce all of its printed circuit boards and to assemble 55% of its finished products. In the electronics industry alone, contract manufacturing is expected to grow from $118 billion in 2001 to $288 billion in 2005. The advantages to contract manufacturing are important: OEMs can stay centered on core strengths and outsource marginal functions to companies with specialized expertise; access to new technologies can be easily deployed without the capital expenditure; spikes in demand can be solved without increasing productive assets; and utilizing a partner with global operations can assist OEMs rapidly ramp-up a worldwide market presence.
- *Technology backbone.* Providing connectivity to PLM requires the architecting of enterprise and inter-enterprisewide computing environments that enable integrated, interoperable, and transparent design, manufacturing, quality, and maintenance systems. These systems include the following: CAD and *computer-aided engineering* (CAE) systems for design and development; PDM applications providing for product

definition, manufacturing process, change control, and documentation management; APS systems that optimize both local factory operations and trading partner supply chains; MES that monitor and control operations at the factory level; SCM systems that apply planning algorithms to activate real-time demand and supply information up and down the channel network; and ERP systems that provide the backbone for transaction posting, performance monitoring, and data repositories for reporting and analysis.

The capability to integrate all these possible manufacturing technologies has become critical for today's manufacturer. Although the concept of a seamlessly integrated manufacturing environment has been propounded for decades, the reality is that most companies, particularly smaller companies who lack the technology savvy, funding, and motivation to integrate their systems, remain far below the ideal. According to a survey conducted by *Managing Automation* in the October 2001 issue,[7] 53% of the participants said they had begun the work of linking their factory-floor PLCs, distributed control systems, and sensor devices to their ERP backbone. Nearly 20% indicated that 30% or more of their plant-floor systems and devices are now connected, and more than 40% say that 15% or more of the equipment is integrated.

The quest to continue the integration of manufacturing technologies, nevertheless, has been accentuated by the economic realities of the twenty-first century. The same *Managing Automation* survey revealed that 66% felt a strong urgency to complete the task of architecting an interconnected manufacturing environment within the next three years. The integration efforts can take several forms. "On a basic level," the survey states,

> A majority says that they want simple interfaces between factory-floor systems and business systems, with browser-based access to floor devices and systems a preferred approach. But when it comes to the hierarchy of their information architectures, the group is almost evenly split over whether factory-floor data will first pass to a manufacturing execution system (MES) and then on to an ERP system or whether those plant-level systems will feed data directly to the ERP backbone.[8]

Regardless of the path to integration chosen, an overwhelming 84% of the respondents to the survey felt that their fundamental goal is the ability to integrate and share information throughout the enterprise by providing a single information architecture. While 46% of the respondents felt that cost reduction was the sole driver of integration, the majority considered integration as the gateway to the creation of more customer-centric business models that prepared their organizations to seize any market opportunity.

C. IMPACT OF e-BUSINESS

An emerging component in manufacturing technologies today is the Internet. While the manufacturing technologies described above seem to be concerned with *internal* systems for product design and planning and running the shop floor, increasingly companies have become aware of the need for connectivity with their suppliers and outsourcing partners. As in other parts of the business, the utilization of e-business, however, means more than simply connecting the Web-based technologies to the shop floor. The application of thin clients, portal technologies, and Web-enabled devices means a fundamental change in the strategic mission of most manufacturers, which can be detailed as follows.

1. Manufacturing Process Synchronization

The application of Web-based toolsets has the capability of providing today's product design and manufacturing functions with the ability to receive real-time information from a variety of systems throughout the business and to develop action plans in conjunction with established performance metrics. These applications provide browser-based graphical representations of aggregated shop-floor data from multiple sources that facilitate real-time monitoring of productive processes. The goal of Internet integration, however, is more than simply enabling the planning and monitoring of production: real-time linkage of information will enable companies to be more proactive to impending changes in demand and supply by permitting them to more effectively synchronize and optimize resources. An example of such efforts is GE Fanuc Automation North America, Inc. (Charlottesville, VA), that coupled its suite of factory automation applications with a Web-based application that provides visibility to real-time data from manufacturing and repair operations throughout the supply chain. Similarly, other companies, such as USDATA Corp. (Richardson, TX), Intercim, Inc. (Burnsville, MN), Teradyne, and Camstar, Inc. (Campbell, CA), are using the Web to push traditional MES capabilities out into the supply chain.[9]

2. B2B Supplier Management

Although manufacturing, as an industry, has been slow to adopt B2B technologies for supplier management, marketplace exchanges have been growing in importance for manufacturers. Already, many firms have found the use of the Internet to facilitate product search, order status/tracking, product catalogs, vendor search capability, and supplier/buyer back-end integration to be particularly important. But of greater importance is the use of the Internet to increase collaboration with suppliers. Conventional methods for linking with suppliers, like EDI, are today too cumbersome and slow and focus solely on tactical benefits. Web-based connectivity tools, on the other hand, permit companies to dramatically increase acquisition functions beyond MRO-type purchasing. For example, in the automotive industry 66% of total procurement centers on direct-engineered components. Internet-enabled tools activate real-time design chains that facilitate custom design through a collaborative-design-chain process involving all elements of the supply network. In addition, B2B connectivity enables manufacturers to pursue business emerging in real time by permitting them to link information concerning productive capacity and WIP, both within the plant and outside in the supply channel. Such linkages are particularly important in JIT production systems that require tight production and financial integration between trading partners.

3. Internet-Driven Design Collaboration

As product life cycles plummet and new products proliferate geometrically, manufacturers have become aware that merely synchronizing their supply chain material flows is insufficient to remain competitive. Responding effectively to today's design environment requires firms to also execute flawlessly *product content synchronization*. Product content can be defined as all the data, such as BOMs, drawings, process execution information including operations and testing, and quality certification, needed to make a product to the correct specification. Accuracy of the product data is absolutely necessary if procurement is to acquire the right components and if manufacturing is to build the right product.

Product content synchronization has become even more important in today's manufacturing environment, as companies continue to outsource production. Outsourcing some or all of the design process has often resulted in out-of-sync product content information among supply chain members, who must struggle with conflicting drawings, CAD files, and design documents. Even simple issues such as *engineering change order* (ECO) changes are difficult to transmit, can cause confusion, and often result in component delivery delays. Finally, since channel partners rarely have compatible systems, synchronization of information is difficult and delays in the communication of critical data are common.

In the past, some of the world's largest enterprises, such as Hewlett-Packard and General Motors, developed their own computerized applications that would help coordinate the efforts of both internal and supply chain designers and manufacturers. These toolsets, however, floundered when applied to the proprietary systems often found within the corporation and outside in the supply chain. With the advent of the Internet, these early efforts at design and manufacturing synchronization and collaboration were significantly enhanced. By assembling all the components of a product's content for transmission through a single portal, designers and manufacturers can work with BOMs and process routings through a Web browser. Product ECO changes, documents, descriptive text, costs, all can be transmitted in real-time to associated engineers and production planners. In addition, this information could then be accessed in real-time by suppliers and business partners, who could also in real-time begin the synchronization of the flow of components with planned production. For example, 80% of the design of one of Volkswagen's models is executed in cooperation with company suppliers. This cooperative process led one vendor to conclude that the whole idea of using exchanges to interact with suppliers has more to do with the design process, rather than just refreshing inventory. Design, the most important function of a manufacturing company, now becomes a B2B fundamental.[10] Instead of an isolated group of designers, product development today is a responsibility of multitiered supply chains of design professionals driven by *peer-to-peer* (P2P) technologies that enable the construction of interoperable repositories of intellectual property. Instead of disconnected push systems that add time and cost to the product supply process, the Internet permits all participating supply chain partners to participate and collaborate in real time in the execution of product design and production processes.

D. CURRENT STATE OF e-BUSINESS AND MANUFACTURING

Despite the opportunities and the hype afforded by e-business applications to manufacturing, most manufacturing businesses lag behind other industries in e-business adoption. According to a survey performed by *Managing Automation* magazine at the beginning 2001, of the 200-plus respondents, more than 90% planned to do e-business, yet to date only 24% had acquired and implemented the necessary technologies. Of this group, only 36% had ERP software, 20% had CRM, 18% had licensed procurement applications, and just 16% had acquired SCM software. What is worse, after six years of e-business discussion and hype, over 30% of manufacturers responding felt that e-business activities would have little to no impact on their current business processes. Almost half felt that e-business would have no impact when it comes to the basic management philosophy used to run the company.[11]

There are several reasons for this state of affairs. The implosion of the dot-coms, the recession of 2001–2002, and the terrorist attacks of September 11 have undoubtedly had a very chilling affect on e-business adoption by the manufacturing community. Beyond economic and political events, a critical determinant is the fact that manufacturers have little expertise and even smaller pools of manpower to expend on Internet initiatives. Additionally, e-business requires a far more collaborative infrastructure than what is typically found in traditional, hierarchical manufacturing organizations. Another problem is getting top management, normally concerned first with engineering, processing, and sales issues, to climb on board the e-business bandwagon. Often e-business requirements are so radically different from existing core competencies that firms often choose, as did GM when it founded e-GM, to create independent business units to work with Internet-driven projects. According to a survey conducted by *Industry Week* magazine,[12] almost 29% of manufacturers cited integrating their e-business initiatives with their manufacturing operations as their foremost hurdle. Over 25% targeted integration with back-office systems as their second major obstacle, while 23% cited a lack of capital funding available to acquire e-business functions.

On the brighter side, four out of five manufacturers surveyed expect to establish e-procurement functions for the future. Similarly, roughly half of manufacturers responding reported moderate or extensive collaboration with suppliers and customers using the Internet. Still, the often proprietary nature of products and expanding philosophies for make-to-order manufacturing have negated for many manufacturers the value of on-line auctions or marketplaces to buy and sell products. The *Industry Week* survey concludes dismally with figures citing that over two-thirds of manufacturers do less than 5% of their sales electronically, and a whopping 78% with e-commerce strategies rated theirs a "somewhat effective" grade. In summary, while there remains a majority of manufacturers who have as yet to embrace e-business concepts, most recognize that, in whatever form, e-business holds out significant opportunities for the future.

III. COLLABORATIVE PRODUCT COMMERCE

Manufacturers have always known that the ability to converge cross-functional development teams, consisting of members spanning internal design, customers, suppliers, and business partners, added immense value to the product life cycle management process. Each "age" of business management has utilized available collaborative functions to facilitate the design, manufacture, and rollout of new products. During the 1960s and 1970s manufacturers sought to leverage business partners to achieve *design for cost* objectives. In the 1980s, *design for quality* became the mantra of product collaboration. By the 1990s, companies needed their channel partners not only to assist in controlling costs and maintaining the highest level of quality but also in executing *design for manufacturability* objectives as reengineering and JIT philosophies drove manufacturers to increase outsourcing of more of the functions of product management once performed internally. Today, manufacturing firms are engaged in *design for the supply chain* product management. This product management strategy requires businesses to execute product management processes in relation to how they will impact the production, planning, and distribution, in addition to the traditional cost, quality, and features, of products required by supply chain partners.

This increased focus on integrating and synchronizing the entire supply chain in the pursuit of faster product development, speed-to-market, and shortened time-to-profit is termed *collaborative product commerce* (CPC). CPC can mean several different things, depending on the context of the discussion. CPC can refer to a management philosophy used to leverage a company's supply chain to design and produce products. Then again, it can refer to a group of collaborative product life cycle management techniques. Finally, it can be identified with a group of growing computerized applications.

A. Defining CPC

The concept of *CPC* was first introduced by the Aberdeen Group, Boston, in 1999. While a definitive definition has yet to be formulated, CPC can be described as

> the convergence and rapid deployment of product life cycle management competencies and toolsets found anywhere in the supply chain linked by real-time computer applications focused on the collaborative execution of new products and manufacturing processes to meet the total requirements of the customer.

The difference between CPC and previous product design philosophies and toolsets is dramatic. In the past, all aspects of product design were considered a jealously guarded company secret. Only the most non-competitive processes were permitted to be discussed with business partners, and even these were communicated with the greatest of reluctance. Slowly, companies became aware that, by converging resources from all over the corporate development chain, new ideas could flourish, costs could be reduced, products marked by superlative quality and manufacturability increased, and time-to-market intervals shrunk. While some powerful technologies did emerge over time, such as *product data management* (PDM) and *product information management* (PIM), the scope of these design tools limited their use to the four walls of the enterprise.

Today, shrinking product life cycles, the growing predilection of customers for customizable, configurable products, and an increasing dependence on outside contracting have unequivocally moved manufacturers to a position of expanding interdependence with their supply chain partners. Instead of inward-focused product development functions, the critical need has shifted to *inter*-organizational collaboration, as companies search to increase their manufacturing and design responsibilities in order to more effectively focus on core capabilities. Guiding this new approach is CPC. With CPC, firms can escape the limitations of past philosophies of product development and utilize ideas, capabilities, processes, and technologies regardless of time or place. "As a result," states Richard Turner of Accenture,

> Innovative products come together faster and cheaper, and the core capabilities of multiple organizations are leveraged across the extended enterprise. The net effect is that companies that could not respond quickly to new market opportunities in previous eras can do so now.[13]

The object of CPC is simple: by enabling all stakeholders in the supply chain to have access to design information at any stage in the project, manufacturers feel that they can reduce communications costs, delays, and redundant re-engineering efforts while improving understanding of actual product performance requirements and characteristics in the early stages of design before significant cost and time have been expended. The following case study reveals how CPC basically works in a real life situation.

1. CPC at the Stephen Gould Company

Gould is a manufacturer of environmentally safe packaging solutions to Fortune 500 computer and automotive companies. Almost 99% of Gould's products are highly customizable and often require complex engineering to meet rigid customer specifications. Recently, Gould implemented a CPC system that enables the company to link together in real time engineers residing in different locations. According to Robert Sherman, the firm's GM, the system provides the ability for engineers to

> look at the same screen at the same time and communicate via (the system's) conferencing application or by telephone. One person at a time controls a pointer on the screen to show exactly where a suggested change needs to be made. The initial drawing is left undisturbed in the central repository while new versions with layered changes are date- and time-stamped and stored as well.

> When a drawing is finalized, Gould's customers can access it and communicate changes if the fit is not quite right. Everyone can sign off the prints in real-time.... Gould's design process continues with the toolmaker... (If a problem emerges), Gould can bring its engineers and customers back on-line to solve the problem right then and there, instead of going back and forth with the tool shop later during the production run.

Gould is also using their CPC system to facilitate the passage and approval of quality control documents. In addition, other functions, such as marketing engineering and production, can utilize the system to communicate necessary changes and concerns in a real-time workspace environment. Finally, the CPC system enables manufacturing to be integrated with possible ECO and BOM changes coming from the customer. Although the CPC system is in its early stages of implementation, Sherman has already found that it is saving Gould at least 20% of development time on some product designs.[14]

B. LINKING SUPPLY CHAIN DESIGN CAPABILITIES

The definition of CPC detailed above highlights the fact that the technique is primarily a knowledge management exercise focused on populating a common, interoperable repository of product design management data consisting of requirements specifications, design documentation, manufacturing process structures, and post-sales product support available in real-time to all concerned parties. Until just recently, however, collaborative manufacturing initiatives between channel network partners was cumbersome and required an enormous management effort to ensure that everything from product content, like BOMs and process routings, to demand forecasts was complete and accurate. As the requirement to satisfy what appears to be an unstoppable trend toward utilizing outsourcing, interoperable real-time access to design databases that provide information about product availability, supply plans, and product content changes from anywhere in the supply chain, CPC has become critical for effective decision-making. The supply chain focus of CPC should be applied to the following processes:[15]

- *Planning and Scheduling.* In conjunction with supply chain management applications and concepts, such as CPFR, CPC requires that channel network inventory be visible on a real-time basis, that effective forecasts and pull-systems accurately describe channel demand and supply requirements, and that network productive capacities are accurate and easily accessed.
- *Design.* While each channel node will possess certain core competencies in the design process, CPC toolsets should facilitate the creation of cross-enterprise design teams that are an integral part of all decisions from the point before specifications are finalized through to design for manufacturability.
- *Sourcing and Procurement.* Once product specifications have been completed, an effective CPC system should provide manufacturers with the ability to create intimate relationships with their supply chain. Visibility and collaboration efforts should facilitate vendor management, strategic sourcing, pricing, and linkages to vendor capacities.
- *New Product Introduction.* During the process of moving new products to production, the requirement for increased collaboration is intensified. CPC applications should provide for concurrent access to BOMs, design validation, prototyping, validation testing, and final transfer to volume production.

- *Product Content Management.* Once live production has begun, channel partners must be able to quickly respond to impending design and processing problems. CPC tools should drive product change generation, change impact assessment, change release, and change cut-over/phase-in.
- *Order Management.* Based on the product strategy, CPC applications should facilitate order management. Among the key components can be found order configuration functions, available to promise, order tracking, and exception management.

The paramount mission of CPC is to ensure the close integration and collaboration of supply chain partners by ensuring real-time communication and access to critical product databases. The rewards of CPC can be immense. According to CEO Kevin English, Covisint's CPC system is one of the major cornerstones of the giant automotive exchange's business strategy for "driving adoption of new technologies between suppliers and OEMs, reducing development times, resolving problems faster, improving quality, and getting product to market faster." When it is considered that each large OEM spends $50 to $60 billion annually on highly engineered parts and systems, if Covisint's CPC system could save just a tiny fraction "by getting everybody to participate in the solution, we're talking several hundred million dollars across the industry."[16]

C. DETAILING THE CONTENTS OF CPC

Today's CPC application suite represents a tremendous enhancement over previous product design software solutions. While many of the toolsets in CPC have their origins in CAD/CAM/PDM, there are several critical differences. The first is that CPC is Internet-driven. In fact, Web-based CPC is providing manufacturers the kind of efficiencies and creative benefits that the Internet had originally promised to deliver. Internet-enabled CPC is enabling manufacturers to leap over former barriers of geography and time by empowering product designers anywhere, anyplace on the globe, to exchange design data so they can collaborate on a project in real-time. "This is a unique time in the history of technology," says George Ashley, Ingersoll-Rand Co.'s manager of engineering business services.

> There has always been some technology limitation to real-time design collaboration, but now there is not. Design collaboration really works, and the challenge now is letting people learn how many ways they can think collaboratively.[17]

The goal of Ingersoll-Rand is to use their Web-based software to connect the $8 billion-a-year company, so that designers and factories anywhere in the world can work together on new products.

Besides the Internet, today's CPC is markedly different from yesterday's design applications. There are differences in architectures, implementation requirements, and the scope of business functions impacted by the computerized techniques. Compared to old PDM solutions, CPC toolsets require less data manipulation and are faster to implement. But most importantly, CPC applications help manufacturers

FIGURE 6.6 Today's collaborative product commerce environment.

realize the promise of today's new product development and design environments through the activation of virtual design teams that can utilize the Internet to leverage the core competencies of supply chain partners to achieve shorter design times and quicker product rollout to the marketplace.

While CPC solutions have had to battle the 2001–2002 recession and the general business disappointment in the Internet, sales of design collaboration and product development software is expected to explode in the next few years. A $720 million market in 2000, the Gartner Group estimates that the industry grew 40%, to more than $1 billion last year, and is expected to expand to around $1.6 billion by the end of 2002. When combined with implementation services, the Aberdeen Group estimated the total CPC marketplace at $18 billion in 2001, and feels that it will reach $22 billion in 2002.

Currently, there is no industry consensus on which software applications comprise the CPC suite of products. No one software company today provides a full range of technologies. Finally, exact definition of CPC terminology has yet to be formulated. Still, it may be useful to arrange, in a single diagram, the suite of toolsets normally associated with CPC. Figure 6.6 attempts such a definition and a brief review of each technology is as follows.

- *CAE/CAM.* Applications in this area contain some of the oldest product design toolsets. Among these applications are found computer-aided engineering, design, manufacturing, CAD, and other related development tools. The function of these applications is to assist product designers to utilize a single data repository to store requirements, specifications, BOMs, CAD drawings, approved suppliers, process descriptions, and other data. Data stored in these databases would be accessible only to internal design team members.

- *CRM.* Today's customer order management systems must provide configuration management functionality that feeds directly into the design engineering engines. The capability to manage these configured structures, so necessary for mass customization, can be found in supporting CAE, CAM, ERP, or PDM systems.
- *CSM/B2B. Component and supplier management* (CSM) systems work with design BOMs. These toolsets provide the logic to generate parts classification and sourcing as a prerequisite to the development of preferred parts lists and approved manufacturers' lists. The most advanced forms of CSM are Web-based portal solutions that enable suppliers to login and access designs and documentation to facilitate update of product changes.
- *DCS. Design collaboration software* (DCS) provides companies with the capability to define design teams that consist of members *outside* of the organization. These software products provide a medium for the synchronous and asynchronous peer-to-peer connection of a cross-company design organization. The best of these applications utilize the Internet to facilitate design data transmission and access, virtual manufacturing, life-cycle management, and interoperability.
- *ERP.* ERP backbones provide the foundations files for design and manufacturing management and product transactions. Many ERP vendors provide sophisticated product design tools or easily executed interfaces between their ERP systems and third-party CPC applications.
- *PDM/PLM.* Software in this area seeks to manage all forms of product design data. The mission of PDM/PLM is to drive requirements specifications, design documents, manufacturing process management, and post-release product support and evolution documents into a common data repository. Among the associated functionality in this area is electronic workflow, change notification, visualization applications that provide real-time synchronous modeling, CAD support such as versioning and red line markup, Web-based communication, automated e-mail event notification, and other visual tools such as project dashboards and integration to ERP, SCM, and CRM.
- *Security.* Database security is one of the critical components of an effective CPC system. Most manufacturing executives are uncomfortable with CPC security issues. CPC applications must provide companies with functionality to define access privileges, restrict some viewers to "read only" status, devise effective encryption solutions to Internet security, and limit designers' access, particularly from outside the company, to certain documents and CAD drawings.

While CPC can truly be said to be in its formative stages, the next several years should see its full definition and maturity alongside other timeworn manufacturing tools such as MRP. With new technologies enabling toolsets, such as peer-to-peer communications, and the trend toward outsourcing, driving the need for improved collaboration, the pressure for effective, comprehensive CPC solutions can only expect to grow.

IV. MANAGING MANUFACTURING PLANNING FUNCTIONS

Today's manufacturer is increasingly deploying computerized solutions that enable plants to be driven by actual channel demand that is synchronized with supply chain network resources and constraints. As is illustrated in Figure 6.7, the toolbox of possible applications includes ERP and MES, as well as new analytical tools, such as APS and SCM, that drive plant information systems and enable management methods, such as lean manufacturing, that combine planning and factory-level execution. According to Greg Gorbach from ARC Advisory Group, this computerization of plant operations

> must be seen in the context of the extended enterprise and supply chain. What we're talking about are systems for collaborative production management that focus on business processes, and on operating plants within the context of your whole supply chain.[18]

Perhaps the most exciting feature of this movement is the merger of tactical plant operations toolsets such as supervisory control, *human machine interface* (HMI) software, and laboratory information management with enterprise management tools, applications planning and scheduling analytics, and Web-based portals designed to keep the plant floor synchronized with the supply chain.

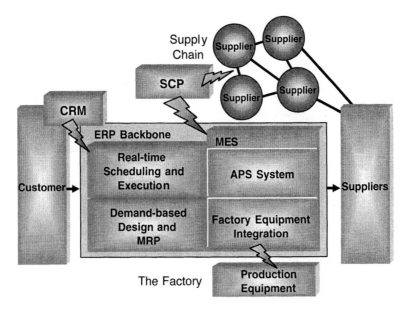

FIGURE 6.7 Manufacturing application suite.

In this section the applications associated with the capability of manufactures to merge plant intelligence coming from MES and industrial automation systems with the requirements necessary to effectively drive operational and business information into the supply chain will be explored. This area represents the forefront in plant management functions and is essential for today's focus on collaborative manufacturing and the pursuit of operational excellence through computerized analytical solutions.

A. ADVANCED PRODUCTION AND SCHEDULING SYSTEMS

Supply chain management is changing the face of business as it accelerates the flow of materials through manufacturing and distribution into the hands of the customer. The ability to execute mass customization and total serviceability while simultaneously reducing cost is possible only when the finite constraints and dependencies of each productive function found across the supply chain can be synchronized into a dynamic supply channel flow. The task of *advanced planning and scheduling* (APS) systems is to address plant-floor constraints and enable the optimization, synchronization, sequencing, and scheduling of plant demand with individual plant capacity and, ultimately, with total supply chain capacity. When integrated with MES, APS's computerized algorithms can be merged with real-time production-floor data to produced optimized schedules that enable effective planning of constraints, capacity, and demand due dates. When integrated with ERP, APS provides the short-term schedule that supports the longer-term resource management tools of ERP used to drive the commercial, financial, and foundation business applications of the enterprise and synchronization with the supply chain network.

The use of simulation and optimization technologies for advanced planning and scheduling solutions is not new and has been used in one form or another for the past 30 years. Early adopters of optimization technology tended to be quantitative analysts working in process industries such as chemical, paper, and steel. These early adopters used general-purpose optimization tools (linear programming packages) purchased from software suppliers to develop custom planning tools that typically ran in a batch mode. Few, if any, of the available software optimizers dealt with large portions of a company's total supply chain. Over the past few years, application suppliers have begun to offer more general-purpose optimization applications that enable linkage of problems — for example, blending with scheduling. Also important has been the growing power of software suppliers to embed optimization into their solutions more seamlessly and transparently.

Functionally, an APS system seeks to utilize all materials issued to and resources in a factory to calculate a simulation of the actual delivery capability and plant constraints. To make the APS system work, the following elements are necessary:

1. Accurate Data

The data coming from the plant floor is voluminous and dynamic. To effectively structure and filter this data requires that all data elements be as accurate as possible. The data will include such records as individual work center capacities, product structures, process dependencies, lead times, material availability, timely MRP/DRP generations, and accurate open order operational status information. APS data enables planners to realistically model a factory's manufacturing environment.

2. Planning Timeframe

APS provides for plant simulation over three planning time horizons. The first, *tactical*, utilizes APS simulation logic to make visible constraints over the short- to mid-term horizon to ensure the availability and synchronization of materials and capacities to meet due date commitments. In the second horizon, *operational*, the APS system should provide the capability to change the capacity loading on bottleneck resources and to simulate the effects. In the final horizon, *plant execution*, APS provides planners with tools for the concurrent, real-time management of capacity bottlenecks, adjusting operator shift patterns, balancing manpower allocation, modifying order priorities, and synchronizing materials and process capacities.

3. Planning Model

The overall mission of an APS system is to achieve an optimal balance between high throughput, minimum inventories, and low operating costs that results in optimum throughput of product to the customer. Synchronizing orders, operators, machines, and materials is the function of the planning model applied. Basically, there are three techniques available.

- *Mathematical models.* These models describe the plant environment mathematically and consist of a range of linear and mixed integer programming techniques. This model is best used in stable, repetitive environments.
- *Heuristics.* Models in this group are best used in configure-to-order and make-to-order environments, where plant data is not linear and is much too complex for mathematical models. Examples of techniques are *theory of constraints* (TOC) and process network-based systems that work from the top down — starting from the customer order and working down to the work center level
- *Simulation.* This model is characteristic of the earliest type of APS system that evolved into the finite capacity schedulers of the late 1980s. Based around some variation of the queuing theory, simulation models determine order priorities by a bottoms-up approach that proceeds from existing orders and demonstrate the optimal sequence of jobs based on the availability of capacity. This model is best applied in capital-intensive industries where the cost of idle machinery and equipment is prohibitive.

Modern APS applications often combine heuristics models with the sequencing functions found in simulation-based systems. The heuristics model assists planners to solve any synchronization issue while the sequencer helps to resolve local sequence conflicts.

4. Schedule Management

The goal of APS planners is to generate a common schedule of production that can be communicated to the entire factory and consists of the following elements:

- A schedule of optimized sequences for all orders and operations
- Realistic schedule of load priorities for each work center
- Sequenced start and finish times for all orders and resources
- Detailed dispatch list for each work center showing order sequence by operation

Today's APS systems are normally client/server based, utilize memory-resident technology so that the complex calculation engines do not have to write to disk, are linked to the ERP database, and provide users with interactive scoreboards and drill-down functions that provide drag-and-drop capabilities for working with schedule and material shortage management.

Although APS systems were heralded with great fanfare at the end of the 1990s, the hype has significantly decreased during the last couple of years. Several reasons have been cited to account for the fading interest. To begin with, many companies felt APS to contain more functionality than was required, and it often conflicted with the existing corporate culture. Second, interest in APS was lost during Y2K projects, and when the financial IT crunch struck in the new millennium, APS all too often was placed on hold. Also, many ERP vendors were including APS applications into their expanding suite of products. Because APS is driven by ERP planning data this seemed a logical outcome. Conversely, APS has often been by-passed because a large number of ERP vendors simply do not have it, and companies are unwilling to shoulder the cost and risk of implementing a third-party package. Another reason is the confusion between APS and SCM. While the two applications have a lot of similarities, they are focused on solving very different problems. However, many analysts agree that with the migration of APS to Web-based functions, such as browser-based interfaces, support for Internet-based B2B and B2C processes, and availability in an *application service provider* (ASP) model, the demand for APS can expect to expand in the mid-2000s.[19]

B. SUPPLY CHAIN OPTIMIZATION TOOLS

On September 11, 2001, supply chains all over the globe were put under an enormous strain. Focused more on efficiency than on flexibility, supply network capabilities immediately began to break down. Fortunately, while a few companies, such as Toyota, actually had to shut down, supply chains quickly returned to a semblance of normalcy. The lesson was obvious: glitches in the supply chain have not only been proven to torpedo shareholder value, they can also add dramatically to higher costs, lower efficiencies, and reduced flexibility.[20] Countering possible future crises means that today's manufacturer and distributor must search for alternate ways to construct redundancies in their supply chains through the use of powerful analytical and evaluation tools that allow them to switch channel network capacities on and off, similar to Internet technology where, while a node may be down, the entire network remains functional.

Over the past several years manufacturers and distributors have been using constraints-based optimization technologies resident in APS systems to assist in solving supply chain problems and collaborative planning. Today, these *supply chain planning* (SCP) systems have been expanded to include a variety of supply chain functions, including demand planning, supply planning, strategic network optimization, fulfillment scheduling, and *collaborative planning, forecasting, and replenishment* (CPFR). According to AMR Research, over $14.9 billion dollars of SCP software has been sold over the past three years, and is expected to grow by 20% in 2002 to around $7 billion.[21] The goal of supply chain optimization is to allow planners to generate a synergy across the supply chain that better physically positions manufacturing and distribution facilities to achieve the following objectives:

- Ability to network companies in a supply chain community in order to manage channel complexities by engineering enhanced planning and decision-making capabilities, starting with internal ERP systems and extending connectivity to Internet-linked channel trading partners.
- Ensuring that supply channel costs are minimized and that they represent, as much as possible, the most competitive across geographies and companies.
- Capturing the most profitable customers on a global basis by creating more compelling, value-based relationships than other supply chain networks.
- Securing access to the most value-added suppliers on a global basis by establishing superior Internet-enabled supply chains that offer B2B technology and trading partner relationships.
- Engineering flexible, agile organizations and supply networks that can leverage an array of Internet technologies, ranging from collaborative product commerce to multichannel e-information visibility, to capitalize on changes to customer demand and shifts in supply-side dynamics.

In many ways, applying optimization capabilities to supply channel management is little more than applying the toolsets and processes of APS. SCP requires first that the supply chain planning environment be described in terms of the actual channel network structure. The channel network structure illustrates the trading partner nodes that add value to the supply chain from raw materials through to finished goods. Similar to APS, SCP enables planning on three levels: *strategic* — concerned with questions relating to where company distribution centers should be located or what capacities are need from the supply channel; *tactical* — involves optimizing the flow of goods through a given supply chain configuration over a time horizon and executing sourcing, production, resource deployment, and distribution plans; and *operational* — largely involving scheduling, rescheduling, and execution of production and is usually equated with the function of APS.

To make a SCP system work the following components are necessary:

1. Accurate Data

SCP systems need to be seamlessly integrated with the company's ERP backbone and distribution, production, and demand planning requirements from all nodes in the supply chain galaxy. For the SCP optimization engines to function properly all data elements should be as accurate as possible. The data will include such records as

- *Supply chain structure.* The geography of the supply chain provides the structure for the determination of such elements as demand patterns, forecasts, replenishment, and transportation and their relationship to planning simulation.
- *Product data.* Data in this component includes demand for resources (production, transportation, warehouse space, etc.) and components and materials based on rough-cut routings capacities and item groupings.
- *Available capacity for all resources.* There are a wide variety of metrics that could be used including: for *purchasing,* capacity is measured in the number of item units that can be supplied per planning bucket; *transport* is measured in weight or volume units per planning bucket; *production* is based on capacity plans measured in hours per planning bucket; *receiving* is measured in weight or volume units; *dispatch* are the resources that represent equipment/personnel for shipping measured in weight or volume; and *stock area* is the volume or weight for each stock area resource.
- *Costs.* Total cost for purchasing, transportation, production, and inventory.
- *Penalties.* Penalties assist SCP tools to prioritize market demands when calculating capacity flows. There are two basic types: *Missed delivery penalties* (prioritization by penalty) and *bucket production penalties* (optimizing production by grouping production into fewer periods to produce in larger quantities).
- *Future demand for end products.* This can be expressed either in the form of a simulated demand schedule or sales forecasts for markets and customers.
- *Feedback to ERP/Server.* Time-phased sourcing rules and planning schedule developed during SCP simulation can be transferred to the ERP/Server on request.

2. Planning Timeframe

Similar to APS, SCP systems enable planning simulation over three planning time horizons: strategic, tactical, and operational.

3. Planning Model

The model chosen for the SCP optimization must be appropriate for the planning level. Planning can precede top down, by starting with data driven from the demand forecasting and order management system and then progressing through production and logistics aggregate optimization planning models and concluding with production and distribution scheduling optimization. Or, the process can precede bottom up by beginning with the MRP and DRP generation and then moving to detailed scheduling and, finally, aggregate planning.

4.   Optimization Techniques

SCP systems utilize the same optimization techniques as APS.

5.   Schedule Management

The goal of SCP planners is to generate a common schedule of demand priorities that can be communicated to the entire internal and external supply chain. The software optimization technique will permit planners to consolidate demand and capacity data from all points in the supply chain and then to map and manipulate through simulation various priority alternatives. It is possible to let the mathematical model decide that some demands should not be met because they would result in a loss. This decision is based on profitability (sales price − total costs = profitability). If all demands cannot be satisfied, a predefined prioritization helps to determine which demands to fulfill first. The objective is to meet demand results in the model by pulling product groups to the market while creating a cost-optimized, globally synchronized supply chain for end-items and materials. In the process, the model respects all finite capacity constraints and the supply chain network structure.

Planning the supply chain is a complex task, since constraints exist on all levels. To ensure that optimization applications provide reasonable, executable solutions several tool sets can be used.

- Most SCP systems today provide users with *graphical user interfaces* (GUIs) to facilitate manipulating data and modifying solutions. Typical tools include graphical drag-and-drop planning boards complete with drill down functions. Many graphical planning boards allow users to change a variable (e.g., date or order) and immediately see the impact on the costs, delivery due dates, possible penalties, and to assess new constraint violations. The planner can then make decisions about adjustments and priorities. These decisions automatically update the model's constraints and are sent to the optimizer, which will reoptimize everything based on the latest decisions. The different plans are then compared on the planning board.
- Users can also control the solution by allowing them to incorporate unique constraints or rules into the model. For example, a planning application might allow a user to specify that customer due dates can be relaxed by 1 or 2 days, or the user may approve the maximum level of overtime.
- Some software tools permit users to control the progress and performance of the solver method. This is usually accomplished by permitting the planner to set a time limit on the solver and then pause. This lets the planner evaluate the solution as it has been calculated to that point.
- Some software tools permit planners to define multiple objectives. For example, both customer service and costs can be optimized together —

despite the fact that two or more objectives cannot really be optimized because they are opposites. These tools provide the ability to strike a balance among competing objectives by a *priority sequence* or through the use of *weights*.[22]

- Today's cutting-edge SCP applications enable planners to use the Internet to receive and communicate demand and capacities in real time from all tiers in the supply chain and to use it in optimization calculations. Termed by Forrester Research *extended relationship management* (XRM), the use of portal and Web-based technologies enable planners to achieve supply chain connectivity and visibility in a $7 \times 24 \times 365$ real-time operational mode. By utilizing *supply chain event management* (SCEM) alert-messaging functionality planners can see looming constraints in channel trading partners.

SCP optimization applications enable planners to concentrate on making decisions, while the optimizer does the complex and detailed number crunching. The optimizer evaluates all possible solutions and presents the "best" one to the planner. The "best" solution is the one with the lowest total cost for meeting forecasted demand and the one that follows the selected optimization strategy. The result of an effective SCP system is a feasible and optimized plan, which provides the framework for distribution and production planning. All changes and decisions made, such as capacity adjustments or changes to demand and time-phased sourcing rules, are respected by distribution and production planning. SCP optimization assists planners in making controlled decisions in many ways and at different levels of detail. They range from a simple modification of a production capacity in a single planning time bucket to redesigning the entire supply chain structure.

C. COLLABORATIVE PLANNING, FORECASTING, AND REPLENISHMENT (CPFR)

The complexity of today's supply chain requires manufacturers and distributors to search for new methods to reduce costs, increase efficiencies, reinvent channel models, engineer collaborative relationships, and span functional, cultural, and personal boundaries. While APS and SCP applications provide for the optimization of the supply chain, CPFR seeks to act as a key enabler for the realization of synchronized supply chain forecasting and replenishment. CPFR is the latest generation in a train of channel management philosophies focused on supply chain synchronization. As illustrated in Figure 6.8, CPFR is the maturation of efforts such as *quick response* (QR), *vendor managed inventory* (VMI), and *efficient customer response* (ECR), and can be thought of as the perfect joining of ERP, CRM, and SCP in an Internet-driven supply chain environment dedicated to the integration and synchronization of the entirety of channel demand while reducing total network inventories and costs.

What is CPFR? As the name implies, the mission of CPFR is for all partners in a supply channel network to develop collaborative planning processes based on the timely communication of forecasts and inventory replenishment data to support the

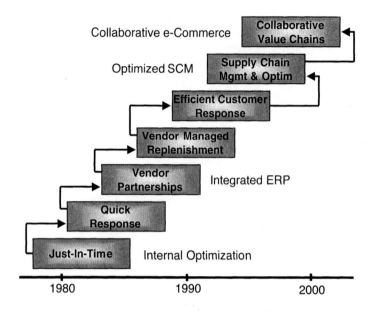

FIGURE 6.8 Stages of supply chain collaboration.

synchronization of activities necessary to effectively respond to total supply chain demand. CPFR begins with the development of an agreement between trading partners to develop a consensus forecast that begins at the retail level and makes it way all the way back to the manufacturer. This plan of supply chain demand and replenishment describes what will be sold and when, how it will be merchandized and promoted, in what marketplaces, and during what time period. CPFR interoperable technology permits this data to be freely transmitted up and down the supply channel, so that planners at any node in the network can see demand and adjust the plan, within certain limits, based on possible exception conditions, such as promotions, store openings, or capacity constraints that could impact delivery or sales performance anywhere in the channel. Trading partners would then collaborate to resolve any potential bottlenecks, adjust demand and replenishment plans, and then execute alternative courses of action. The final step in the process, channel replenishment, occurs after consensus on the final forecast.[23]

Based on the early experiences of companies such as Heineken USA, Eastman Chemical, Lucent Technologies, Sara Lee, Wal-Mart and others, the Voluntary Interindustry Commerce Standards Association (VICS) began the task of defining a CPFR standard governing business process, organizational, and technology recommendations in 1996. In June of 1998, VICS released a series of guidelines detailing CPFR industry standards. In the beginning, VICS standards focused on utilizing EDI as the medium for the transmission of collaborative information. Using EDI enabled companies to leverage existing technology investments to quickly launch CPFR initiatives. By the end of the 1990s however, the high cost of EDI technologies and the ubiquitous deployment of the Internet enabled even the smallest retailer and manufacturer to leverage the collaborative power of CPFR. In addition, Web-based applications allowed business partners to escape from the one-way transmission of data in favor of an interoperable toolset enabling open two-way conversation in real time supported by formal standards.

In the past, supply chain partners sought to utilize channel inventory management tools such as CRP, VMI, and QR to remove excess assets from the supply network and smooth out demand irregularities. While effective, these toolsets, however, lacked the ability to solve the twin problems at the core of channel replenishment management: forecast inaccuracies and the capability to utilize exception messaging to notify network partners of impending bumps in supply and demand. CPFR provides answers to these two issues by providing for the real-time sharing of sales promotions, *point-of-sale* (POS) transactions, and total channel inventory positioning that postpones inventory replenishment by linking each level in the supply network with the pull of actual demand. In addition, by systematizing the communication of critical demand and supply data among trading partners, CPFR makes visible all plans and planning variances, thereby assisting companies to improve their forecasting and replenishment decisions to yield the best results. For example, Kimberly-Clark's CPFR manager, Larry Roth, felt that the company's CPFR system has been instrumental in formalizing a structured replenishment approach with all of their suppliers. "Clearly," he says, "CPFR has been a catalyst for re-examining how our various supply chain systems work together and are affected by our customer's plans." There are new examples every month "where our internal plans are improved through both external and internal collaboration."[24]

V. SUMMARY AND TRANSITION

Perhaps the hallmark of the shift in today's economy from the "industrial age" to the "new economy" has been the dramatic changes that have occurred in manufacturing. A few decades ago, political economy was measured in industrial output of goods and services by global companies that considered their factories, business processes, equipment, and other assets as the very core of their competitiveness. Today, these same assets are considered as debilitating expenses that rob enterprises of flexibility, tie up capital, and blur the focus on core business competencies. Many companies are engaged in a life and death struggle to "de-verticalize" their productive functions, preferring to outsource noncritical processes to channel partners.

All of these dramatic sea changes have required manufacturing to radically redefine its role in order to meet the new challenges brought about by today's marketplace realities. The transformation of global markets and changes to product life cycles, competition, technology, and popular culture are occurring explosively and simultaneously. Responding to these changes requires manufacturers to develop solutions to four critical themes. The first is the absolute necessity of deconstructing past manufacturing management methods of dealing with the customer. The key to this theme is the architecting of customer-centric organizations capable of utilizing channel network partners to enable the delivery of combinations of configurable products, services, and information that provide unique value to the customer. Responding to the pressures of time and change constitute the second theme. The challenges in this area coalesce around today's ever-shortening life cycles in products, increased need for quick product development, time-to-market, and the opportunities offered by technology.

Parallel to the first two themes, manufacturers have had to make fundamental changes to infrastructure in their drive to germinate dynamic, high-performance organizations capable of responding rapidly and efficiently to demand for mass-customized products with flexible, cost-effective manufacturing and interactive channel pull systems capable of delivering the necessary product or service to the customer from anywhere in the supply chain. Today's most progressive infrastructures are customer-centric, collaborate with their supply partners, are agile and scalable, and are linked via Web-based architectures to their customers and supply channels. Finally, the concluding theme influencing today's manufacturer is the requirement for a complete revamping of traditional benchmarks of performance. Instead of viewing performance based on determining performance on ROI and asset optimization, companies need to refocus on agility, flexibility, information collaboration, and service to the customer.

For decades manufacturers have called upon computer systems, such as MRP and ERP, to assist in responding to the information management challenges before them. Today, companies have at their disposal an ever-expanding suite of computerized tools for manufacturing planning, production and process management, product design and engineering, plant maintenance and quality management, and product life cycle management. Of particular importance is the application of the Internet to the suite of manufacturing technologies. Past business systems, for the most part, consisted of applications used to run *internal* functions in product design, planning, and shop-floor scheduling. In contrast, the Internet enables manufacturers to expand design and planning capabilities outside the business to integrate and synchronize real-time demand and procurement data and plans with supply chain partners. While it is true that manufacturers have been slow to embrace Web-based components, the pressure to adopt Internet functions is expected to grow dramatically in the next few years.

Of the technology tools available to manufacturers, the most critical are collaborative product commerce and supply chain planning. CPC can be described as the convergence and rapid deployment of product life cycle management competencies and toolsets found anywhere in the supply chain to execute the design, manufacture, and release of new products and processes to the market. The mission of CPC is simple: the assembly of collaborative design teams from across the supply network utilizing product life cycle management tools linked by Web-based applications focused on understanding customer demand, designing, sourcing and procuring, prototyping and releasing new products to market, and ongoing maintenance. Once products have been designed and released to the marketplace, manufacturers have increasingly come to depend on optimization tools to assist in synchronizing supply chain network demand and individual plant and supply network resources and constraints. The task of APS systems is to address close-in plant-floor constraints and enable the optimization and synchronization of capacities and load. On the strategic and operations level SCP is employed to manage supply channel constraints, search for optimal costs, secure access to the most value-added suppliers, and assemble flexible, agile networks that can leverage the collaborative power of the

Internet to make visible in real-time the demand and resources available in the entire supply chain. Finally, manufacturers can apply CPFR functions to supply chain networks to execute the collaborative development of forecasts and synchronization of inventory replenishment. With the use of Internet-based applications, channel partners can freely pass planning information necessary to solve the twin problems of forecast inaccuracies and the capability to utilize exception messaging to notify channel members of possible bumps in supply and demand.

In order to make the wheels of manufacturing hum, the raw materials and finished components consumed in the manufacturing process must be on hand. As inventory and product life cycles continue to shrink and demand for immediate availability of finished products escalates, the pressure on manufacturing and distribution inventories has dramatically increased. In chapter 7, the function of purchasing and its impact on competitive advantage will be examined.

ENDNOTES

1. Staid, Paul J. and Matthews, Paul A., "The Role of Technology in Manufacturing," in *Achieving Supply Chain Excellence Through Technology,* 1, Anderson, David L., ed., Montgomery Research, San Francisco, 1999, 78–83.

2. Swann, Don, "It's Not Your Father's Manufacturing World," *APICS – The Performance Advantage,* 12, 1, 2002, 43–45.

3. Jordan, James A. and Michel, Frederick J., *Next Generation Manufacturing: Methods and Techniques,* John Wiley & Sons, New York, 2000, 267.

4. Thompson, Olin, "Plants in the Age of e-Commerce," *Midrange ERP,* 4, 7, 2001, 12–14.

5. Neil, Stephanie, "MES Meets the Supply Chain," *Managing Automation,* 16, 12, 2001, 18–22.

6. These comments have been adapted from Jordan and Michel, 85.

7. Brousell, David R., "The Integrated Enterprise Moves Closer to Reality," *Managing Automation,* 16, 10, 2001, 26–30.

8. Ibid.

9. These company stories can be found in Neil.

10. Teresko, John, "Catalyst for Collaboration," *Industry Week,* February 12, 2001, 23–28.

11. Callaway, Erin, "Building the Internet Infrastructure," *Managing Automation,* 16, 1, 2002, 28–33.

12. Bartholomew, Doug, "Getting E-Religion," *Industry Week,* March 19, 2001, 23–30.

13. Turner, Richard, "Leveraging 'Collaborative Product Commerce,'" in *Achieving Supply Chain Excellence Through Technology,* 3, Anderson, David, L., ed., Montgomery Research, San Francisco, 2001, 70–73.

14. This company story has been adapted from Wright, Christopher M., "They Don't Make 'Em Like They Used To," *APICS-The Performance Advantage,* 12, 3, 2001, 33–36.

15. These points have been selected from Cookson, Chris, "Linking Supply Chains to Support Collaborative Manufacturing," in *Achieving Supply Chain Excellence Through Technology,* 3, Anderson, David, L., ed., Montgomery Research, San Francisco, 2001, 56–58.

16. Murphy, Jean V., "New Product Collaboration: Getting It Right the First Time," *Global Logistics & Supply Chain Strategies,* 5, 11, 2001, 34–41.

17. Konicki, Steve, "Groupthink Gets Smart," *InformationWeek*, January 14, 2002, 40–46.
18. Michel, Roberto, "Plants Find a New Pace," *Manufacturing Systems,* 19, 12, 2001, 42–44.
19. For these comments see McCall, Jay, "Is APS Technology Obsolete?," *Integrated Solutions,* 5, 4, 2001, 72–76 and Krause, Jason, "ERP Opens the Door to Collaboration," *Supply Chain Systems*, 22, 2, 2002, 12–18.
20. Singhal, Vinod and Hendricks, Kevin B., "How Supply Chain Glitches Torpedo Shareholder Value," *Supply Chain Management Review,* 6, 1, 2002, 18–24.
21. O'Brien, David and McNerney, Gerald, *Supply Chain Software Yields ROI – But It Takes Time*, AMR Research, January, 2002.
22. Shepherd, Jim and Lapide, Larry, "Supply Chain Planning Optimization: Just the Facts," in *Achieving Supply Chain Excellence Through Technology,* 1, Anderson, David L., ed., Montgomery Research, San Francisco, 1999, 166–176 has been most helpful in preparing the above paragraphs.
23. An excellent methodology for implementing CPFR can be found in Lohse, Michelle and Ranch, Jeffrey, "Liking CPFR to SCOR," *Supply Chain Management Review,* 5, 4, 2001, 56–62.
24. Peck, Michael, "CPFR: It Takes 2," *Supply Chain Technology News,* 3, 2, 2001, 9–10.

7 Supplier Relationship Management: Integrating Suppliers into the e-Value Chain

The acquisition of the raw materials, components, and finished goods necessary to service channel network and end-customer demand resides at the very core of supply chain management. Whether manufacturer or distributor, the timely acquisition of inventory is fundamental to competitive advantage. Without sufficient inventories the wheels of manufacturing would slowly grind to a halt, and distribution pipelines would quickly run dry. Besides providing the goods necessary to meet customer demand, the procurement of inventories also directly affects company financial stability and profitability. Depending on the nature of the business, procurement and services costs can range from 40 to 80% of each sales dollar. To understand the impact of these costs, if, for instance, a five percent overall reduction in the procurement costs of a typical company could be achieved, it could represent as much as a 50% improvement to the bottom line. To achieve a similar impact, the same company would have to increase sales by 50%, cut overheads by almost 20%, or dramatically cut staff. From such figures it is easy to deduce that the effective management of procurement transcends the traditional mechanics of supplier sourcing, buying, and receiving: procurement is a strategic supply chain function that seeks to integrate and synchronize individual company inventory needs with total channel material flows, trading partner productive capacities, transportation, quality, marketing, finance, and global sources of supply.

The effective management of procurement is, however, more than just buying goods and services. For several decades companies have known that it is not the cost-effective purchasing of inventories, but rather the existing relationship between buyer and seller, that determines the real value-add component of procurement. As the demands of the customer and the capacities of the supplier are increasingly synchronized, the essential components of procurement are made more efficient, costs decline, the flow of channel inventories are accelerated, and cooperative alliances to improve planning and product information exchange are deepened. In addition, the more integrated the sharing of information becomes, the more supply chain partners can fashion truly collaborative relationships, where core competencies can be dynamically merged to generate a range of new products, processes, and technologies each partner acting on their own would be incapable of attaining.

In this chapter the functions of purchasing and *supplier relationship management* (SRM) will be explored. The chapter begins with a definition of the basic functions of purchasing. Following, a possible definition of SRM is attempted. Similar to the *customer relationship management* (CRM) concept, the strategic importance of SRM is to be found in the nurturing of continuously evolving, value-enriching business relationships, and this time focused on the buy rather than the sell-side. While collaborative sharing and merging of procurement competencies dominate the definition, the application of the Internet has opened an entirely new range of SRM toolsets, enabling companies to dramatically cut costs, automate functions such as sourcing, RFQ, and order generation and monitoring, and optimize supply chain partners to achieve the best products and the best prices from anywhere in the supply network. Following, the focus of the chapter then switches to a full discussion of the anatomy of today's e-SRM system, beginning with an outline of *enterprise business system* (EBS) backbone applications, progressing to e-SRM service functions, such as strategic sourcing and decision support tools, detailing e-SRM processing applications centered around catalog management, RFQ, PO generation, and logistics, and concluding with a short review of e-SRM technology services, such as Web processing, security, content management, and workflow. The chapter ends with an exploration of the e-SRM exchange environment, today's e-marketplace models, and the steps necessary to execute a successful e-SRM implementation.

I. DEFINING PURCHASING AND SUPPLIER RELATIONSHIP MANAGEMENT

The functions of purchasing and supplier management are indivisibly intertwined. Before an effective discussion can occur regarding the impact of the SCM concept on these twin functions, the elements of each must be closely defined.

A. DEFINING THE PURCHASING FUNCTION

The acquisition of MRO and indirect inventories and related services is a fundamental activity performed by all manufacturing, distribution, and retailing companies. According to the *Purchasing Handbook*,[1] purchasing can be defined as

> The body of integrated activities that focuses on the purchasing of materials, supplies, and services needed to reach organizational goals. In a narrow sense, purchasing describes the process of buying; in a broader context, purchasing involves determining the need; selecting the supplier; arriving at the appropriate price, terms, and conditions; issuing the contract or order; and following up to ensure delivery.

The purchasing function is normally responsible for the sourcing and acquisition of all products and services used by the enterprise. Broadly speaking, there are three types of purchasing: purchasing for consumption or conversion, purchasing for resale, and purchasing for goods and services consumed in maintenance, repair, and operations functions. Purchasing for *conversion or consumption* is the concern of

industrial buyers and covers a wide spectrum of activities beginning with a determination of what products the firm should produce or outsource, progressing to raw
materials and component sourcing, negotiation, purchase order generation and status
monitoring, and concluding with materials receipt. Goods purchased for *resale* are
the concern of distribution and retail buyers. In this area buyers determine what
goods their customers want, search and buy these goods based on targeted levels of
quality, delivery, quantity, and price, and sell them at a competitive level based on
price, quality, availability, and service. The final type of purchasing, *maintenance,
repair, and operating* (MRO) inventories, is concerned with the acquisition of the
supply and expensed items and services necessary for the efficient functioning of
the business.

The management, planning, and execution of purchasing functions are normally
the responsibility of a firm's purchasing department. Overall, the prime responsibility
of this function is to communicate the business's purchased inventory requirements
to the best suppliers and to ensure timely receipt of materials synchronized to meet
the needs of ongoing enterprise operations. The basic activities of purchasing have
been arranged below, commencing with functions of strategic importance, then
progressing to those performed on a daily basis.

- *Sourcing.* This high value-added activity is concerned with matching
  business purchasing requirements with sources of supply, ensuring continuity of supply, exploring alternative sources of supply, and validating
  the supplier compliance necessary to meet or exceed buyer criteria for
  quality, delivery, quantity, and price. For the past decade a critical component of sourcing has been reducing needless redundancies in the supplier base and increasing supplier collaborative partnering.
- *Value Analysis.* This set of functions is concerned with increasing the
  value-added elements of the purchasing process. Value analysis can consist of such components as price for quality received, financing, and
  delivery. An example would be identifying less expensive goods and
  services that could be substituted at comparable quality and value.
- *Supplier Development.* In today's environment, increasing collaboration
  with suppliers has become a requirement for doing business. Pursuing
  capabilities that promote supplier partnering require buyers to be knowledgeable of vendor capacities, resources, product lines, and delivery and
  information system capabilities. A key component in the strengthening of
  this partnership is the development of pricing, technology, and information-sharing agreements that link supplier and buyer together and provide
  for a continuous "win-win" environment.
- *Internal Integration.* Purchasing needs to be closely integrated with other
  enterprise business areas such as marketing, sales, inventory planning,
  transportation, and quality management. By providing key information
  and streamlining the acquisition process, the purchasing function can assist
  the enterprise to synchronize individual company replenishment requirements with the overall capacities of the supply network. Buyers must also
  be members of product market, research, and engineering development

teams if the proper inventory at the best quality, delivery, and cost is to be purchased.

- *Supplier Scheduling*. One of the keys to effective purchasing is the development of a valid schedule of inventory replenishment. By sharing the time-phased schedule of demand from *material requirements planning* (MRP), firms can provide detailed visibility to future requirements to supply chain partners, who, in turn, can plan the necessary material and capacity resources to support the schedule. In addition, the increased use of purchasing portals and B2B marketplaces has dramatically expanded buyers' ability to search anywhere in the world for sources to meet product and service replenishment needs.

- *Contracting*. Critical functions in this area consist of the development and analysis of *request for quotation* (RFQ) negotiation, when pricing, volume, length of contract time, or specific designs or specifications are significant issues, and supplier selection and monitoring of performance measurements.

- *Cost Management*. A critical function of purchasing is the continuous search for ways to reduce administrative costs, purchase prices, and inventory carrying costs while increasing value. The principle activities utilized to accomplish these objectives are purchase cost reduction programs, price change management programs, volume and "stockless" purchasing contracts, cash-flow forecasting, and strategic planning.

- *Purchasing and Receiving*. Activities in this component include order preparation, order entry, order transmission, status reporting, order receiving, quantity checking and stock put-away, invoice and discount review, and order closeout.

- *Performance Measurement*. Monitoring the quality and delivery performance of vendors over time is an integral part of supplier "benchmarking." The ability to measure performance is critical when evaluating the capabilities of competing suppliers and ensuring that costs, delivery, and collaborative targets are being attained.[2]

B. Defining SRM

Successful supplier management in the twenty-first century mandates that the relationship between buyer and supplier be increasingly conceived as a *collaborative partnership*. As lead times and product life cycles plummet, and pipeline flow velocities accelerate, supplier partnering in today's global business environment is no longer an option but has become a strategic requirement to maintain competitive advantage. Enhanced by Internet applications that draw buyers and suppliers together in real time, partnering can assume many forms based on the dynamics of the supply chain. Partnering can be found among allied industries or competitors and may exist for strategic or operational reasons. Whatever the formal arrangement, partnerships can be described as cooperative alliances formed to exponentially expand the capabilities involved in materials requisition, procurement operating procedures and efficiencies, and product information exchange.

TABLE 7.1
Traditional Purchasing vs. Collaborative Supplier Management

Traditional Approach	SRM Partnerships
Adversarial relationships	Collaborative partnerships
Many competing suppliers	Small core of supply partners
Contracts focused on price	Contracts focused on long term quality, mutual benefits
Proprietary product information	Collaborative sharing of information
Evaluation by bid	Evaluation by commitment to partnership
Supplier excluded from design process	Real-time communication of designs and specifications
Process improvements intermittent and unilateral	Close computer linkages for design and replenishment planning
Quality defects residue with the supplier	Mutual responsibility for total quality management
Clear boundaries of responsibility	"Virtual" organizations

The increasing focus on the development of synchronized, collaborative relationships between buyers and suppliers has evolved over time and is the product of several marketplace dynamics. As is illustrated in Table 7.1, supplier relationship management has undergone dramatic modification and is accented by today's requirement for ever-closer working business alliances. The adversarial nature of yesterday's purchasing arrangements have given way to the structuring of win-win relationships, a mutual commitment to sharing information and resources to achieve common objectives, and a long-term proposition meant to bind parties in good times and bad. Finally, collaborative partnership often means deconstructing traditional attitudes and practices concerning quality and reliability, delivery, price, responsiveness, trust, the sharing of research and development plans, and financial and business stability. Today's focus on supplier partnerships has grown as a response to the following marketplace realities:

- *Increasing requirements for supply chain collaboration.* No company in today's marketplace can hope to survive without strong supplier partnerships. As businesses continue to divest themselves of non-core competencies and increasingly turn toward outsourcing, a deepening of partnering agreements have been eagerly pursued in all industries as fundamental to continuous improvement strategies, total cost management, and competitive advantage.
- *Changing nature of the marketplace.* The dominance of the customer, shortening product life cycles, demands for configurable products, shrinking lead times, global competition, participative product design, and other issues discussed throughout this book have altered forever the nature of sourcing and purchasing and highlighted the importance of supply chain collaboration.

- *Changing business infrastructures.* It has been pointed out earlier in this book that today's enterprise must possess business architectures that are characterized by extreme agility and scalability and are customer-centric, collaborative, digital, and capable of reliable, convenient, and fast-flow delivery. While these attributes are normally focused on the sales side, they equally must apply to the supply side. The value chain can be compared to a coin: there is a customer-facing side and a supplier-facing side. The very existence of functions driving one side axiomatically requires the replication of the identical functions driving the other side.

- *Increased demand for cost control, quality, and innovation.* While SCM technologies have been receiving most of the attention, buyers are more than ever concerned about traditional purchasing values such as quality and reliability. Customers are no longer willing to do business with suppliers who not only cannot meet increasingly stringent product and delivery standards, but who also do not possess the capabilities to continuously unearth new product configurations and service management capabilities.

- *Increased demand for risk sharing.* True business partnerships mean that the need for trust and risk sharing must be a serious component in any collaborative relationship. As the cost of innovation and operations flexibility grows exponentially, and the level of profits shrink in the face of competition, partnership agreements that provide for the equal sharing of risk have become a critical method for the management of new product development and controlling spiraling operations costs.

- *Enabling power of Internet technologies.* The "age of e-business" has had a profound impact on many areas of purchasing, opening new and exciting doors that have provided supply chain partners with the ability to closely integrate demand and replenishment in ways impossible only a few years ago. Applications supporting such concepts as *supply chain planning* (SCP) and *collaborative planning, forecasting, and replenishment* (CPFR) enable whole supply networks to synchronize channel requirements, remove administrative costs, and cut costly lead times out of channel inventory management. In addition, Web-based tools have undercut the need for traditional purchasing functions such as lengthy negotiations, requisitions, and paper-based purchase orders.

- *Focus on continuous improvement.* At the core of SRM can be found a strong commitment to the joint pursuit of continuous improvement as a dynamic process rather than a static business principle. Whereas mutually profitable relations between trading partners might facilitate the achievement of common goals, only those companies pursuing closely integrated collaborative objectives can hope to continually streamline the development and guarantee the availability of superior products and services that consistently leapfrog the competition.

While the above marketplace realities are important in understanding the environment in which SRM resides, a detailed definition of SRM has yet to be formulated. For example, each SRM software vendor has its own interpretation and can run the gamut covering everything from supplier database analysis to product planning and outbound logistics, including e-procurement, strategic sourcing, auction management, and e-marketplaces. On the other hand, industry analysts feel that SRM is not software at all, but rather a set of business practices that involve the establishment and nurturing of closely intertwined relationships between buyers and suppliers. David Hope-Ross from Gartner research states that SRM "is a religion. A creed. A way of life." To complicate matters, the level of acceptance among industry groups is uneven and ranges from sophisticated adopters of e-business procurement models to those who are firmly committed to manual processes. In addition, SRM is not synonymous with the term B2B or e-business marketplaces. Today's most sophisticated applications of SRM will utilize the Internet to facilitate processes and architect new business models, but SRM is not simply a technology. Still, although SRM is in its embryonic stage, enough of the landscape has emerged to venture the following definition:

> SRM is the nurturing of continuously evolving, value-enriching relationships between supply chain buyers and seller that requires a firm commitment on the part of all trading parties to a mutually agreed upon set of goals and is manifested in the collaborative sharing and timely and cost-effective execution of sourcing and procurement competencies to facilitate the entire material replenishment lifecycle from concept to delivery.

C. COMPONENTS OF SRM

The mission of the purchasing function in today's environment can be summarized as the real-time synchronization of the firm's supply requirements with the capabilities of supply channel partners in order to support customers' demand for made-to-order, high quality, just-in-time goods and services while pursuing reductions in procurement costs and sustainable improvements in performance. According to Hirsch and Barbalho,[3] such an approach requires the combination of three critical components as illustrated in Figure 7.1 and detailed below.

FIGURE 7.1 Components of SRM.

1. Strategic Sourcing and Supply Management

Supplier partnerships require companies to look beyond the everyday purchase of materials to *strategic sourcing*. The goal of strategic sourcing is to find and cement close sourcing and procurement relationships with those trading partners that account for the majority of a company's purchasing dollars. While strategic sourcing will drive tactical decisions regarding the use of such technology toolsets as Web sites and portals to decide which products to purchase through the Internet and which through traditional mediums, the central focus is on selecting those suppliers who can support the customer-centric objectives of the company. While cost control is a critical element, strategic sourcing is a comprehensive supply management process that involves

> identifying the business requirements that cause you to purchase a good or service in the first place, conducting market analysis to determine typical cost for goods/services within a particular supply system, determining the universe of suppliers that best meet your requirements, determining an overall strategy to procure items in that category, and then selecting the strategic supplier(s).[4]

Depending on the category or type of purchasing to be sourced, other factors, such as the depth of supplier competencies, availability of required services, level of desired product quality, capacity for innovative thinking, and willingness to collaborate, can also be considered key strategic components. Take, for example, the capability of a supplier to support e-commerce functions. The procurement strategy may call for the best suppliers to have in place Web-based catalogue applications or interfaces to EBS backbone databases that enable pursuit of cost, quality, and continuous improvement targets.

2. Applying Technology to the Management of SRM

The effective management of procurement has always depended on the facilitating capabilities of communications technologies. Over the past 50 years, purchasing's ability to work with suppliers, communicate requirements, and negotiate quality, pricing, and delivery of goods and services has been driven by technology tools that either match or exceed the velocity of marketplace transactions. The first major technology employed was the telephone. Being able to transcend time and space through the telephone replaced the cumbersome processes of mail correspondence and the necessity of person-to-person contact. The arrival of the fax machine significantly accelerated the processes of negotiating contracts, sending orders, and checking on the status of open orders. *Electronic data interchange* (EDI) enabled trading partners to interface *enterprise resource planning* (ERP) systems, so that demand, order and shipment transmission, and electronic bill payment could be performed in a paperless environment. Today, with the application of the Internet to SRM, purchasers have been able to leverage new forms of procurement functions, such as on-line catalogs, interactive auction sites, radically new opportunities for sourcing and supplier management, and Web-based toolsets that provide for the real-time, simultaneous synchronization of demand and supply from anywhere, anytime in the supply chain network.

The application of e-business to the evolving SRM concept can be said to have spawned a new form of procurement management: *e-SRM*. While it is true that the dot-com mania has passed and companies are taking a hard look at the promises of the Internet, it is also true that business-to-business purchasing transactions continue to grow and are offering firms sustainable and meaningful procurement improvement opportunities from shorter sourcing and negotiation cycles, to reduced costs in ordering and more effective ways to ensure quality and delivery. As will be discussed later in this chapter, the concept of e-SRM has come to coalesce around two Internet-driven functions: *e-procurement*, the utilization of Web-toolsets to automate the activities associated with purchase order generation, order management, and procurement statistics, and *e-sourcing*, the utilization of the Web to develop long-term supplier relationships that will assist in the growth of collaborative approaches to joint product development, negotiation, contract management, and CPFR. While considerable debate still rages as to whether e-sourcing is simply an element of e-procurement or a separate function altogether, which precedes the other, and whether the terms can be used interchangeably, there is little doubt that companies are utilizing these functions to achieve dramatic breakthroughs in the management of direct and indirect procurement. For example, the National Association of Purchasing Management (NAPM) found in its *Report on e-Business* study (October 2001) that 49.5% of buying organizations use the Internet to collaborate with suppliers. Manufacturers' use of the Internet was even higher, standing at 52.4%. e-SRM can be defined as the utilization of e-business applications that facilitate the procurement of production and MRO inventories and services. e-SRM provides the mechanism for the structuring of formal and informal supply-side trading relationships that drive the functioning of dynamic value-chains.

3. SRM-Driven Infrastructures and Operations

SRM requires companies to constantly deconstruct and architect processes that can be rapidly deployed to meet the shifting of customer requirements while focusing on continuous improvement. Procurement functions unable to respond in a timely fashion to changes in the marketplace with complimentary organizational, technological, and performance management changes will consistently result in suboptimal customer performance. In a way that was virtually impossible in the past, Internet-based procurement toolsets have created an environment where best practices in purchasing can be automated and applied to the acquisition of just about any product and service. This standardization and optimization of the work of the procurement organization extends the expertise of a firm's best purchasing processes through the organization and out into the supply chain.

Finally, e-SRM requires the widening of traditional purchasing functions to include new players in the buy-side economy. As if purchasing professionals have not already been asked to integrate radically new *internal* procurement functions such as *private trading exchanges* (PTXs) and consortiums, they also have had to come to terms with new *external* trading entities. For example, procurement has had to expand its processes to include working with third-party organizations that run e-marketplaces. These *e-market-makers* utilize Internet technologies to connect multiple buyers with multiple suppliers, conduct e-commerce functions, and deploy various forms of Web services such as payment, logistics, credit, and shipping. How individual companies will react to these challenges to existing procurement practices depends greatly on the dynamics of their supply chain network systems. Each business has various types of customers and suppliers that must be served through traditional and e-business methods, along with internal systems that must be integrated.

II. THE INTERNET-DRIVEN SRM ENVIRONMENT

The term e-business in today's post-dot-com, post-9/11, post-Enron economic environment has lost most of the revolutionary fervor it had once inspired at the turn of the century. For example, many industry analysts had predicted in 2000 that there would be as many as 10,000 e-marketplaces by 2004. By the beginning of 2002, that prediction had been scaled back to less than 3,000 and most of those were to be found in the less risky private trading exchange (PTX) environment. According to industry observers, much of the reason for the failure of e-marketplaces to expand has been that suppliers have, as a whole, not bought into the e-market concept. Three reasons have been proposed. First, many suppliers feel that e-marketplaces have the affect of reducing their products and services to a commodity where a focus on price, and not quality or partnership, dominates the transaction. Second, many suppliers feel that e-business models force them to shoulder the cost of transaction fees, with buyers enjoying the benefit. This is compounded by the fact that an e-SRM system can cost more than a million dollars and that executives are increasingly concerned about ROI for such investments. Finally, many suppliers feel that e-markets are redundant in that they require suppliers to spend to acquire technology infrastructure in order to work with customers they already have.

However, despite the calls for "back to basics" and the reluctance on the part of suppliers to commitment to e-markets, using the Internet to generate better business processes, if not greater competitive advantage, continues to expand. The examples are dramatic and no more so than in the application of e-business to procurement. For example, in a very difficult period for the airline industry, Delta saved $65 million in the final three months of 2001 on its annual $9 billion in overall purchasing costs, thanks to a suite of e-SRM tools that went live in October. In the divisions where Proctor & Gamble had implemented e-SRM software, they were able to realize savings of up to 30% of the more than $8 billion in annual spending for indirect goods. Similar savings have been realized by smaller enterprises. ITT Industries, White Plaines, N.Y., has leveraged its new e-business tools to shave as much as five percent on contract items and thirteen percent on non-contract items from its more than $900 million dollar annual purchasing budget. DaimlerChrysler reports that its participation in Covisint continues to produce tangible benefits. During the past twelve months dating backward from March 2002, the automaker held 512 on-line bidding events, representing a purchasing volume of approximately ten billion euros, which amounts to about a third of the company's total procurement volume for the period.[5]

While the marketplace is still cautious about B2B adoption, and probably will be for the foreseeable future, Internet-enabled SRM is growing quietly behind the scenes. For example, the annual report on e-business (November 2001) released by NAPM and Forrester Research found that nearly 73% of organizations use the Internet for indirect purchasing, an increase from the 71% reported during the previous quarter. In addition, 54% of buyers reported using the Internet to purchase production materials, an increase from the 46% reported in the previous quarter. These on-line buyers reported ordering 9.8% of their total direct materials using Web-based applications. Finally, the survey revealed that the use of on-line auctions had expanded sharply. More than 20% of respondents purchased products or services via on-line auctions, up from 15% in the previous quarter. Aberdeen Research Inc. has found that e-SRM can reduce the price on goods and services by five to ten percent as compared to traditional methods. e-SRM initiatives also can cut purchase and fulfillment cycles to 2.3 from the previous 8.4-day standard, while reducing administrative costs to an average of $31 per requisition, down from the previous figure of $144. Finally, Aberdeen reports e-markets can reduce inventories by 25 to 50%.[6]

When all the facts, figures, and opinions are compiled, it is clear that the number of B2B e-marketplaces, whether private or independent, can only be expected to expand. To begin with, traditional buyer-supplier relationships will continue to be transformed into virtual enterprises and industry consortia. As the need for collaboration on all aspects of business accelerates, so will information and transaction management be transferred from manual to electronic. Second, as efforts to reduce costs and automate transaction processes are amplified, B2B e-marketplaces will increasingly be seen as critical to achieving operational objectives. Lastly, B2B provides companies that were once considered rivals to jointly participate in the creation of e-marketplaces where they can as a group leverage their collective purchasing power and, in the process, increase efficiency across the entire supply chain. The implementation of B2B e-marketplaces can be expected to achieve the following benefits:

- *Increased market supply and demand visibility.* B2B e-marketplaces provide customers with an ever-widening range of choices, an exchange point that enables the efficient matching of buyers and product/service mixes, and a larger market for suppliers.
- *Price benefits from increased competition.* On-line buying and use of auctions can be employed to increase price competition, thereby resulting in dramatically lower prices.
- *Increased operational efficiencies.* B2B applications have the capability to increase the automation and efficiency of procurement processes through decreased cycle times for supplier sourcing, order processing and management, and selling functions.
- *Enhanced customer management.* e-Marketplaces assist marketers to accumulate and utilize analytical tools that more sharply define customer

segmentation and develop new product/service value packages that deepen and make more visible customer sales campaigns.

- *Improved supply chain collaboration.* Today's B2B toolsets enable buyers and sellers to structure enhanced avenues for collaboration for product life cycle management, marketing campaigns, cross-channel demand and supply planning, and logistics support.
- *Synchronized supply chain networks.* The ability of e-markets to drive the real-time interoperability of functions anywhere in the supply network focused on merging information and providing for the execution of optimal choices provides supply partners with the capability to realize strategic and operation objectives. Among these can be included shorter cycle times for new product development and delivery, increased inventory turnover, lower WIP inventories, low-cost logistics, and others.[7]

A. e-SRM STRUCTURAL OVERVIEW

The growing evidence for the realization of the benefits outlined above produced by e-SRM have provoked significant changes in the procurement process and provided radically new toolsets. The challenge during this period has been to search for methods to accelerate the automation and optimization of sourcing and transactional processes through the use of the Internet, while at the same time deepening the strategic functions associated with supplier management. As a result of this movement on the part of software developers and procurement strategists, the traditional labor-intensive components of product/service sourcing, RFQ and supplier selection, order release, order receipt, and accounts payable have been greatly standardized and automated through the implementation of ERP systems and team-focused improvements. Today, the application of the Internet to the SRM management process has provided the purchasing organization with the opportunity to venture into unexplored regions of supply chain value using Web-based techniques.

Up until just a few years ago, the procurement process was executed through time-honored techniques. Business requirements were sourced, suppliers signed up, requirements communicated, and deals negotiated the old-fashioned way through personal meetings, phone calls, faxes, and mail delivery. While most companies did enjoy computerized order processing, order management, and supplier relationship functions through their ERP systems or even EDI, the automation of these back-end processes were inward-facing and did little to enhance the integration and collaborative relationships necessary to speed up the front-end processes that were outside resident in the supply chain. With the application of the Internet to SRM functionality, this gap in the automation of front-end procurement as well as full integration with EBS backbones is rapidly disappearing. Similar to what CRM has done for customer management, e-SRM is permitting today's cutting edge companies for the first time to assemble a complete picture of their supply relationships, apply Web technologies to dramatically cut cost and time out of sourcing and negotiating, and utilize real-time data to communicate requirements and make effective choices that result in real competitive breakthroughs.

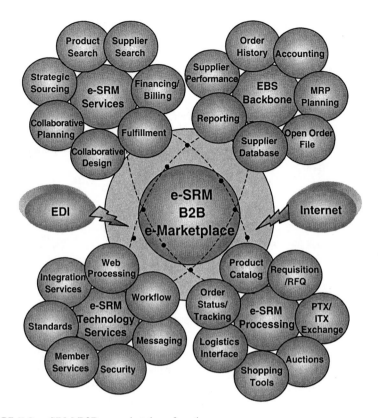

FIGURE 7.2 e-SRM B2B e-marketplace functions.

Figure 7.2 is an attempt to portray the components of today's e-SRM system. While, earlier in this chapter, e-SRM was described as consisting of two processes: *e-sourcing* and *e-procurement*, it is being proposed that, in order to facilitate under-standing, e-SRM should be viewed as being composed of four separate, but inte-grated areas. The first area, *EBS backbone*, is comprised of the traditional database and execution functions utilized by purchasing to generate orders, perform receiving and transfer to accounts payable, and record supplier statistics. The second area, *e-SRM services*, details the enhancement of traditional buyer functions, such as sourcing and supplier relationships, through the use of Web toolsets. The third area, *e-SRM processing,* lists the new functions provided by the Internet that facilitate the transaction process. The final area, *e-SRM technology services*, outlines the technical architecture that enables e-SRM front-end and backbone functions to be effectively applied to solve procurement strategies. A detailed description of each of these areas will be discussed below.

B. EBS BACKBONE FUNCTIONS

In this region can be found the procurement functions associated with traditional *enterprise resource planning* (ERP). The fundamental role of this area is to collect and provide a repository for internal database information to guide purchasing processes. The EBS backbone contains the following critical functions.

1. Procurement History

The collection of procurement information is fundamental to SRM. Data in this area ranges from static records, such as past transactions, to dynamic information, such as open PO status and active supplier and sourcing files. The accuracy and completeness of this information serves as the foundation for all internal and networked procurement activities.

2. Accounting

The completion of the purchase order process feeds directly into the firm's EBS backbone for order and price matching, invoice entry and payables, credit management, and any necessary financial reconciliation.

3. Purchasing Planning

Once total demand has been processed through the MRP processor, the schedule of planned purchase orders can be generated. Depending on the level of communication technologies and collaborative relationships, this statement of planned orders can be used to drive both MRO and indirect materials and production raw materials and component acquisition through the supply chain network.

4. Performance Measurement

As receiving and payables history is compiled, companies have the capability to generate meaningful reporting and performance measurements indicating the value of their supplier relationships and the degree of success of their continuous improvement initiatives.

The integration of e-SRM toolsets with the EBS backbone is absolutely essential for e-business success. Often overlooked during the frenzy of the dot-com revolution was the fact that e-markets cannot hope to deliver expected results unless they are connected to the databases resident in backbone business systems. According to AMR Research's Bob Parker, the crash of *independent trading exchanges* (ITXs) in 2001 was not the result of perceived risks, on the part of companies, of exposing mission-critical processes to competitors, but rather that ITXs "had to be integrated into their members' back-end systems, and very few companies were set up for that type of integration."[8] Deploying the technology architecture to connect local EBS backbones to the e-SRM applications is the first step in making e-SRM happen.

C. e-SRM Services Functions

The Internet provides purchasers with fresh new avenues to transform the services traditionally used to execute procurement processes. In the past, purchasers were required to perform laborious and time-consuming searches for sources of new products and services. In contrast, B2B marketplaces provide a level of service features, such as offering an on-line catalog of products, sales promotions and special pricing, payment processing facilities, and post-sales support, impossible in the past. Web-based technologies have made it possible for purchasing functions to significantly streamline this process by utilizing the following B2B marketplace service functions.

1. Supplier Search

Historically, the supplier search process has suffered from a high degree of fragmentation and discontinuous information flows. The normal process of locating suppliers, performing the mandatory round of RFQ negotiations, and securing contracts was slow moving and often adversarial. Virtual B2B marketplaces, on the other hand, offer large communities of buyers and sellers a completely new channel to reach out to each other in a two-way interactive mode that transcends barriers of time and space. Buyers can leverage Web-based technologies to deepen their existing relationship with preferred suppliers, while expanding their search for new suppliers on a global scale. In addition, buyers can explore new dynamic purchasing models, such as on-line auctions, for sourcing and spot buying.

2. Product Search

Instead of cumbersome paper-based catalogs, e-SRM services provide for the creation, aggregation, and Internet access to a wide range of on-line product and service catalogs that can significantly enhance the sourcing effort. B2B marketplaces host electronic product search for all types of goods and services, including MRO and indirect materials, production, administrative, and capital goods. According to Hoque,[9] catalog functionality "can range from a simple keyword search to complex product category classification, parametric search functionality, automatic comparison product offerings, bid-boards for collaborative buying, message boards for posting buyer testimonials, real-time chat for negotiating flexible pricing, and even bidding and auctioning." For example, Dow Chemical Company buys through a portfolio of B2B e-marketplaces. *Dow 1:1* provides for contractual fulfillment of strategic materials; *Dow e-Mart* is an internal buying tool equipped with a multivendor catalog of indirect goods and services; *Elernica* is a consortium e-market for contractual purchase of production materials; *Trade-Ranger* is a consortium e-market for sourcing, pricing, and contractual fulfillment of indirect goods; *ChemConnect* is an independent e-market through which Dow sources and negotiates purchase of raw materials; and *SciQuest* is an independent e-market for laboratory and scientific products and supplies.[10] Effective Web-based applications should enable e-marketplaces to centralize product and service content offerings, permit suppliers to host content on their own sites, and enable buyers to develop customized catalogs.

3. Strategic Sourcing

The challenge of e-SRM is to both automate and optimize procurement functions, while at the same time improving strategic procurement activities. The difference between the two is important. *e-Procurement* focuses on leveraging Web applications to reduce tactical costs and increase efficiencies and is primarily focused on non-strategic, indirect materials. In contrast, *e-sourcing* is focused on the more effective management of vendor sourcing, contract, and RFQ, and supplier management during the early stages of strategic, production materials life cycle management. According to AMR,[11] strategic sourcing can be defined as a systematic, cross-functional, and cross-enterprise process that seeks to optimize the performance of purchased goods and services through reductions in total cost, sourcing cycle time, and assets. It originates with product lifecycle management (PLM) and *asset life cycle management* (ALM) in the make/buy decision process and concludes with contracting and order generation.

The concept of supplier sourcing has been around for decades. However, for the most part it was an internalized, time-consuming, and laborious process centered on cross-functional management of spending categories, corporate aggregation of spending, supplier rationalization, and supplier partnership management. Using today's Web-based technologies, this past concept of strategic sourcing has been completely transformed. In fact, some analysts consider strategic sourcing as the "third generation" of e-procurement; the prior two stages were concerned with the automation of the purchase of standard, catalog-based products and the movement to trading exchanges. Termed now "e-sourcing," software companies, particularly those grounded in PLM technologies, have during the early 2000s developed applications that not only facilitate strategic sourcing but also provide for integration to SCP and ERP backbones. These applications can be divided into two categories:[12]

1. *Decision support tools* for creating an effective sourcing strategy that include:
   - *Spend analysis*: historical and forecasted spend by category, supplier, and organizational unit
   - *Item rationalization*: standardization and elimination of redundant items
   - *Contract management*: tools assisting in RFQ, bid analysis, negotiation, and contracting that result in lower opportunity, input, and quality costs and shorter product introduction time
   - *Supplier monitoring and improvement*: measurement of supplier transaction, quality, and collaborative performance
2. Negotiation automation tools that streamline:
   - *Supplier databases:* easily accessible databases that reveal supplier capabilities and performance levels to cut the supplier RFQ search effort
   - *e-RFP:* Web-applications that provide for electronic request for proposals that link with bid analysis tools
   - *e-Auctions:* Web-based tools that facilitate and fully document auction events

While the use of strategic sourcing technologies is still in its infancy, it is considered as the most important next wave in B2B e-marketplaces and is a critical component of the e-SRM suite. According to AMR Research, the e-sourcing software market is expected to grow from $275 million in 2000 to $3.5 billion in 2005. Even at this stage, businesses utilizing e-sourcing technologies have been able to report significant benefits: 5 to 25% reductions in negotiated unit prices; 25 to 35% reductions in sourcing cycle times; and 10 to 15% reductions in time to market.[13]

4. Value-Added Services

In addition to dramatically enhancing supplier and product search functions, e-SRM leverages the Web to pursue a variety of other critical value-added business services including:

- Financial and billing services such as the use of *payment cards,* or P-cards, credit approval, corporate check payment, clearinghouse functions, and direct electronic billing
- Comparison shopping functions
- Collaborative design and configuration management functions for complex, make-to-order production
- Advertising, promotions, and dynamic pricing models based on market demand and availability
- Transportation and logistics support to facilitate product fulfillment
- Synchronized supply chain procurement planning
- Establishment of marketplace performance benchmarks and key indicators

While such services are critical in the pursuit of short-term requirements for cost reduction, collaboration of supply chain competencies, and synchronization of channel network inventory plans, they also provide buyers and sellers with the capability to pursue strategic goals beyond pure transaction management that enable them to evolve into e-marketplaces communities.

D. e-SRM PROCESSING

The goal of e-SRM application toolsets is to streamline the procurement process for the goods and services necessary to produce products and run the enterprise. Up until just recently, the central focus of e-SRM Web-based applications has been on MRO and indirect inventories procurement. The reason for this is that these goods and services are extremely well suited to B2B e-markets. They are normally highly standardized commodities, purchased in large volumes, evaluated normally on price alone, require minimal negotiation, and often are acquired through frequent spot purchases. Transferring MRO procurement to the Web is also fairly easy to do, often amounting to little more than creating an on-line catalogue capable of being accessed through Internet-enabled order entry functions. In contrast, applying e-SRM tools to the purchase of production goods, such as raw materials, components, and production equipment, is much more difficult. Procurement in this area oftentimes is subject to highly detailed design constraints and mainly applies to specialized vertical industry suppliers who provide products without sufficient breadth and volume of market demand. What is more, because of the specialized nature of the product/service, actual procurement is often preceded by a complex negotiation process involving RFQ, competitive supplier bidding, long-term contracts, and continued involvement in relationship-specific investments between trading parties. e-SRM in this area is more about greasing the channel with trusted suppliers than opening up a free market bid/ask exchange.

e-SRM requires companies to merge Internet-driven MRO and production procurement under a common umbrella. By consolidating and automating enterprise buying processes, companies can capture procurement advantages through economies of scale, more effective negotiations resulting in better pricing, and a deepening of communications and coordination with channel suppliers that will translate into more efficient, collaborative buying. The detailed components constituting this area can be described as follows.

1. Product Catalog Management

The management of catalog content has been one of the most critical issues facing e-business from its very inception. The promise of "dynamic e-commerce," defined as the exchange of goods and services via electronic markets where buyers have access to virtual storefronts to search for any product/service mix at the lowest cost, depends on the availability of catalogs containing "dynamic content" that always provides the most current pricing, product information, and product specifications. Meeting this challenge requires content management functions capable of catalog normalization, rationalization, and scalability while providing for rapid supplier data extraction and cleaning, update, aggregation, end-to-end integration, and publishing. For example, Lincoln Electric, a Cleveland, OH manufacturer of welding products, implemented a dynamic catalog management process that enabled it to quickly broadcast product changes and introduce new items to customers. The goal is to engineer a catalog content management system for syndicating product information in formats that customers can receive and use without having to cleanse or reformat it. In addition, the system will allow the company to transmit product updates as changes rather than as a total catalog refresh.[14]

2. Requisitioning

e-SRM applications seek to facilitate the requisitioning process by integrating product/service catalogues hosted by exchange marketplaces, industry consortia, or third-party aggregators located across the Internet into a single "virtual" catalogue available through on-line interfaces. Creating such catalogues requires various levels of effort. Because MRO procurement usually involves highly standardized products and preferred vendors, integrating catalogs for indirect requisitioning is a fairly straightforward affair. On the other hand, developing similar sourcing references for production materials is much more complicated and requires the structuring of catalogs that present buyers with a range of possible suppliers and capabilities robust enough to permit them to perform the depth of value analysis and competitive comparison necessary to ensure alignment of purchasing decisions with strategic procurement targets.

In addition, e-SRM requisitioning applications must provide buyers with aggregate individual supplier statistics, such as specific contract pricing, service quality performance history, commitment to collaboration, and overall customer care rating. When requirements fail to isolate a preferred supplier, the e-SRM toolset must support such features as browsing, keyword/parametric searching, collaborative filtering, product configuration and other application functions. Finally, the e-SRM application must provide for on-line document interchange, supplier chat rooms, open requisition status, and access to the latest budgeting and inventory information for transfer to the firm's EBS backbone.[15]

3. RFQ

The use of manual forms of competitive pricing for procurement of goods and services normally involves a process that begins with the receipt of sealed bids from prospective suppliers, progresses through supplier selection, moves through negotiation of detailed terms, and ends with a specific contract. This process is usually a labor-intensive burden for both parties, may result in widely different terms from contract to contract, is dependent on the negotiation skills of both parties, and favors the use of existing suppliers with a disregard for past performance. By transferring this process to the Internet, buyers can significantly automate the RFQ process, thereby cutting costs and reducing cycle times. By opening up the bid to a form of real-time auction, buyers can greatly increase marketplace competition and solicit suppliers separated by geography and time to participate in the sourcing process.

For indirect and MRO bids, the RFQ can simply be passed to the PO–generation stage. For production materials or purchases subject to dynamic pricing, the buyer would initiate the RFQ process by either posting the RFQ in a public, on-line bulletin board for open bidding, or transmitting the RFQ to preferred suppliers by e-mail, fax, or private exchange. As Hoque points out,[16] this bid/ask RFQ process will increasingly occur in vertical industry exchanges specializing in specific market segments. In addition to simply hosting bid boards, these exchanges will enable companies to share buying experiences and exchange best-practice techniques.

4. Shopping Tools

While still in its infancy, the use of software shopping agents to perform the tasks of Internet browsing and initial gathering of and acting on basic information is expected to expand through time. Basically, shopping agents will augment the work of buyers by performing searches of possible B2B marketplace sites to identify and match targeted products, pricing, quality, delivery, or other desired procurement attributes and execute transactions on behalf of the buyer. In the future, sophisticated buying tools will be able to interact with each other to locate appropriate products or services on the Web and negotiate price, availability, and delivery with a minimum of human interaction. For example, a company's shopping agent would store information related to minimum inventory levels, which suppliers are used to replenish those items, what level of quality is required for each item, acceptable price ranges, and shipping instructions. The shopping agent would be able to interact with compatible software agents that reside in B2B exchanges, which track hundreds or even thousands of suppliers that have been screened relative to the company's buying criteria. Similar to the computer-to-computer interchange that occurs with EDI, these intelligent shopping agents would automate much of the drudgery of today's buyer.[17]

5. Auctions

The use of auctions is perhaps one of the most exciting options offered by Internet commerce. Used primarily as a means to buy and sell products whose value is difficult to determine, or those that are commodity-type items or are custom-designed, the ubiquitous presence and real-time capabilities provided by the Web have enabled this age-old method of purchase to expand beyond the domain of niche markets to reach potential bidders across geographic barriers and traditional industry lines. Almost any product, from airplane tickets to unique products, can be offered on an auction site. The use of auctions in e-SRM is, for the most part, confined to nonproduction-related inventories. The benefits can be significant. For example, Accenture hosted a reverse e-auction for stationery supplies using their own auctioning facility. In one hour, eight suppliers watched the contract bid drop from $1.29 million to $0.92 million. The winner of the contract tendered 10 bids during the auction with an average price drop of $46,000 per bid.[18]

According to Poirier and Bauer,[19] there are five types of e-auctions. The first type, *classical* or *forward auction,* consists of a single seller and multiple buyers who bid on a specific product or lot. The leading bid at the end of the allotted time wins the lot. This method is good for disposing of excess, aged, off-specification, or soon to be obsoleted inventories. The second type, *reverse auction,* is the classical auction in reverse in which one buyer and multiple sellers drive the auction. This method is an alternative to the traditional RFQ method by which buyers solicit bids from the marketplace for one-time, high-value purchases. *Dutch auction* is the third type. This auction is characterized by one seller and multiple buyers, but with multiple homogeneous lots available. The lowest successful bid sets the price for the entire collection. This method is applied to products subject to supply shortages or dramatic demand fluctuations. The fourth type, *demand management auction,* differs from the previous models in two ways: there are multiple buyers and sellers, and the market maker plays an active role as the intermediary. This model is used for products that are perishable, characterized by variable or unpredictable demand, and whose prices are marked by extreme elasticity. The final type, *stock market model,* is characterized by multiple sellers and buyers, homogeneity of commodity, and mutual indifference as to the supplier or buyer. This type of auction is limited to true commodities and is normally found in private markets.

6. Purchase Order Generation and Tracking

Once the order requisitioning or RFQ process has been approved, a purchase order is generated. POs can be created using EBS functionality and are then transmitted to the supplier through a paper order or electronically via fax, EDI, or the Internet. In addition to serving as the instrument communicating the contract to purchase, the PO can also provide valuable *internal* information. To begin with, the PO record provides purchasing management with information regarding outstanding order data, budgeting, and performance reporting. The progress of the PO can then be tracked and used to provide critical status information needed by manufacturing or distribution planners.

7. Logistics

Today's e-SRM order management functions can be significantly enhanced by the utilization of a variety of Web-based logistics services that can be integrated into the procurement process. Logistics partners have the capability to offer Internet enhanced services, such as inventory tracking, carrier selection, supplier management, shipment management, and freight bill management. In addition, logistics service providers can offer advanced functions, such as network planning, dynamic sourcing, and reverse logistics that integrate buyers with supplier e-fulfillment capabilities, dynamic strategies for cross-docking, in-transit merge hubs, postponed assembly, and commingling of loads to optimize shipments.

E. e-SRM TECHNOLOGY SERVICES

None of the components of e-SRM discussed above would be possible without the necessary supporting technology architecture. Over the past couple of years, interoperable protocols that enable computer systems to share information, such as *Transaction Control Protocol* (TCP/IP), *Hypertext Markup Language* (HTML), and *eXtensible Markup Language* (XML), have arisen as standards by which companies can conduct business on their own terms and yet be connected to their supply chain network. Also, industry action groups, such as the Uniform Code Council (UCC), have been established to offer companies leadership, influence, and collaboration in the development and deployment of e-business standards for transaction management, exchange protocols, and business processes. Unfortunately, while these toolsets have been growing in sophistication, they also often require a massive integration effort across e-commerce applications, legacy business systems, and "best-of-breed" models. Depending on the B2B application provider, different standards have been used, so that no one provider can be said to offer true end-to-end e-marketplace integration. In any case, e-SRM applications require the following technology support services.

1. Web Processing

The ability to drive e-SRM transactions requires a technology focus on data access and transactions as well as optimizing business processes. While the efficient processing of e-commerce transactions stands at the center of the B2B marketplace, the applications should provide for effective and timely decision-making prior to the point when the actual transaction is being made. In addition, the supporting technology should be scalable to handle maximum transaction and data communications volumes. Companies engaged in e-SRM should structure an IT structure equipped to perform load balancing across multiple servers to ensure adequate performance and high availability of Web-accessed applications.

2. Security

In today's post-9/11 business environment, security has risen to perhaps the key concern of companies engaged in e-market transactions. Security services include such components as information boundary definition, authentication, authorization, encryption, validation keys, and logging of attempted security breaches. The goal is to protect individual files so that confidential information cannot be accessed without validation. Many companies have elected not to participate in ITXs or Consortia because of a reluctance to share data for fear of compromising business data security. The predilection for private exchanges is often driven by the desire to severely restrict data interchange to only the most trusted of business partners.

3. Member Services

The quest to create Web sites that are characterized by extreme usability, personalization, and customization is perhaps the "holy grail" of e-business management. Winning Web exchanges require marketers to ensure that customers have, first of all, an effective *personal experience* — did each customer's visit validate their expectations and did they leave the Web site with what they wanted, and, second, an *emotional experience* — did each customer develop a positive perception of their interaction with the Web site, and do they wish to return for more in the future. Web-based toolsets can assist in developing detailed user profiles and analyzing user browser behavior and shopping preferences so that marketers can customize the customer's next visit to the site.

4. Content Search and Management

The essence of e-business is the capability of buyers and sellers to utilize knowledge bases, catalogs, text, graphics, embedded files, and applets to access and transact a broad range of products, services, and information over the Web. The ability to effectively search and pinpoint the desired object is, therefore, one of the most critical elements of e-SRM. Effective searching requires engines that provide access either by *content* (product description, type, business application, classification or category, etc.) or by *parameter* (how the content is organized using hierarchies that, for example, provide drill-down through a search tree or fuzzy logic.) In any case, once content is defined, it should possess the following baseline functionalities: (1) the ability to provide optimal content distribution and content organization to searchers, (2) the ability to transform potentially vast amounts of data resources into a useable format for the searcher, (3) the ability of content/application/system managers to define and organize criteria and rules regarding what may be customized and what potential combinations are valid, and (4) the ability of the content management component to integrate directly with the EBS backbone.[20]

5. Workflow

Effective e-SRM requires the delineation of the parameters determining the dependencies that exist between a series of procurement process steps. For example, what business rules govern the process a buyer must execute to move from requisition all the way through to actual purchase and payment? Workflow management provides the vehicle by which this path is detailed and optimized. According to Hoque,[21] an e-business workflow component must consist of the following three modules:

- *Workflow definition module.* The role of this module is to provide a visual model of the application workflow. An effective module should include several templates for basic processes that can be easily modified to match business-specific values and logic.
- *Business rules definition module.* The object of this module is to provide definition of the business rules that govern workflow decisions that are made during the e-business process. An example of a business rule would be determining that, if a certain dollar volume was accumulated on the order, the shipping would be free. This rule would be automatically incorporated into the workflow engine.
- *Workflow engine.* The workflow engine receives the user's request and determines the next sequence of screen displays that will match both the process and the business rules definition. As processes are dynamically updated during the course of continuous process engineering, the workflow engine must be capable of responding in real-time in order to transform models into actual working e-business sites.

III. ANATOMY OF THE e-SRM MARKETPLACE EXCHANGE ENVIRONMENT

The basic types of B2B e-marketplace exchanges were previously explored in Chapter 3. It was stated that they differ from B2C exchanges in several ways. To begin with, B2B marketplaces are concerned with the transaction of products and services between businesses. In addition, they closely resemble traditional purchasing in that the trading parties involved mostly depend on long-term, symbiotic, and relationship-based collaboration directed toward gain sharing. It was stated that currently B2B e-marketplaces could be described as belonging to three major types:

- *Independent Trading Exchanges* (ITX) described as many-to-many marketplaces composed of buyers and sellers networked through an independent intermediary. ITXs can further be divided into *vertical exchanges* focused on providing Internet trading functions to a particular industry and *horizontal exchanges* that facilitate e-business functions for products/services common across multiple industries.

- *Private Trading Exchanges* (PTX) described as a Web-based trading community hosted by a single company that recommends or requires trading partners participate in as a condition of doing business.
- *Consortia Trading Exchange* (CTX) described as a some-to-many network consisting of a few powerful companies organized into a consortium and their trading partners.

In this section e-marketplaces will be further discussed. This goal is to provide an anatomy of the B2B exchange environment and how it impacts e-SRM.

A. EMERGENCE OF TODAY'S B2B e-MARKETPLACE

The rise of Internet commerce over the past few years can be said to have ignited an explosion of strategies in just about every industry designed to utilize the Web as a vehicle for promoting and selling their products and services. Likewise, this rush for new business models has been propelled by a rising tide of corporate buyers who increasingly are turning to B2B exchanges that utilize electronic catalogs, product reviews, market research, and other information databases to access a wider marketplace and accelerate the evaluation and procurement of products and services. In fact, the rapid transition of many buyers from traditional to e-procurement models that promise low-cost, global marketplaces has in actuality generated an almost bewildering number of B2B buying sites driven by a proliferation of target markets, disparate standards, an expanding array of product offerings, and tangled technology tools ranging from homegrown code to off-the-shelf platforms from software vendors such as Commerce One and Ariba. The application of e-SRM technologies is almost limitless. On the simple side, for example, Hewlett-Packard established a Web-enabled extranet to connect all members of its supply chain, from contract manufacturers to component suppliers and plastic molders, in an effort to ensure the simultaneous communication of supply and demand requirements. In contrast, the giant automotive consortium, Covisint, provides an extremely sophisticated Web-enabled marketplace that will handle anything from on-line catalogs to electronic document exchange, on-line tracking of quality, product design, and auction sites.

The development of e-SRM can be said to have emerged over three distinct periods.[22] A short analysis of each period is as follows.

1. Foundations

The first period can be described as the establishment of the basic B2B model. In this era, e-business was confined to the use of independent portals centered on on-line catalog search, facilitating the RFQ process, and providing real-time order transaction and management. The goal of these sites was to sign up participants fast enough to satisfy capital investors. The first B2B trading sites sought to offer products and services through techniques, such as aggregation, performing buyer-seller matching, and hosting auctions. For the most part, these sites were focused on the buying and selling of MRO and nonproduction inventories. For buyers, ROI goals centered on automation and integrated point solutions. Overall, despite the immediate advantages, stage-one B2B procurement represented little more than moving catalog operations on-line and did not offer the marketplace a new business model.

2. Rise of Collaborative Commerce

The second period in the development of e-SRM materialized during the year 2000. The distinguishing characteristic separating phase-two e-marketplaces from their earlier predecessors was their focus on expanding the functions necessary to conduct collaborative procurement and address the issue of direct production materials. During this period, the field of trading exchanges became dramatically overpopulated; at least two exchanges could be found in almost every major industry category. Partly because of the ensuing confusion, but mostly as a way to gain control, companies began to by-pass the use of ITXs, preferring to establish private and industry consortia exchanges in an effort to ensure security and engineer the integration of buyer and supplier EBS backbone systems.

3. Development of Networked Exchanges

The third stage of e-SRM is expected to emerge after 2002. Perhaps the central characteristic of this stage is the transformation of the current field of independent and consortia marketplaces into fully networked exchanges featuring robust functions such as single-data models and joint order management, procurement, financial services, logistics, and network planning that facilitate multibuyer/multiseller interaction and collaboration. Some of these exchanges will focus on certain business processes, while others will focus on industry verticals. Interoperable technologies will enable full intercompany backbone integration and the seamless utilization of information fostering true marketplace-to-marketplace interaction. Marketmakers will finally abandon profitability models based on subscription and transaction fees in favor of fees matched to the value delivered to buyers and sellers. For buyers, the narrowing of the exchange marketplace and satisfactory fulfillment of targeted products and services will motivate them to gravitate to closer e-SRM partnerships.

B. DEFINING THE TRADING EXCHANGE

The effective application of e-SRM depends on decisions regarding procurement strategies and the choice of Internet applications that best service that strategy. Currently there are basically three models that companies can draw from: buyer-driven e-marketplaces, vertical e-marketplaces, and horizontal e-marketplaces.

- *Buyer-Driven e-Marketplaces:* This simple B2B model is designed to enable companies to facilitate internal procurement by linking through Internet tools divisions, partners, or companies in order to drive corporate purchasing processes and supplier relationships. These toolsets usually seek to facilitate RFQ and procurement functions by providing aggregate catalogues, either on their own systems or the Web sites of service providers, that can be used in turn by network trading partners. For example,

Chicago-based Quaker Oats' indirect purchasing function was originally comprised of 13 distinct, highly decentralized and paper-intensive processes spanning nine disparate systems handling more than 300,000 transactions with 30,000 suppliers. To solve the massive cost inefficiencies, Quaker established a centralized on-line catalog assembled from a number of MRO catalogs that could be accessed through a portal linked directly to supplier Web sites. The catalog reflects volume-based pricing and rule-based agreements negotiated with suppliers. Requisitions are automatically routed for approval and orders are placed and tracked through the Web portal. Finally, the portal handles paperless invoicing or automatic payment upon receipt.

- *Vertical e-Marketplaces:* These types of digital marketplaces act as hubs servicing a single industry. Normally this type of e-marketplace exists either because of severe inefficiencies in distribution, or sales or industry fragmentation due to the lack of dominant suppliers or buyers. By automating the exchange process through a combination of technology and deep experience in a particular industry, vertical e-marketplaces focus on reducing industry-specific problems, such as a lack of information flows, high inventory levels, requirements for joint forecasting and planning, or logistics sourcing and contracting. According to Raisch,[23] this type of e-marketplace can be divided into three groups:

  a. *Virtual distributors:* Participants in this group of vertical e-marketplaces seek to replace or improve a supply network by aggregating a variety of industry-specific product/service catalogues into a single Internet site. Instead of searching across a variety of sources, buyers can search on-line from a single venue, thereby reducing search and transaction costs while facilitating product and pricing information.

  b. *Exchanges:* This type of e-marketplace focuses on supply networks that are poorly or inefficiently constructed. The mission of exchanges is to facilitate information while reducing costs by permitting network members access to the distribution, price, and inventory information of participating companies. Buyers can freely bid and enter orders while viewing the offerings of marketplace sellers.

  c. *Enablers:* Often, excess capacities or materials exist in the marketplace. This type of e-marketplace attempts to leverage on-line tools that distributors or brokers can use to tap into this reservoir of productive resources and accelerate the matching of potential buyers and sellers. Collabria, for example, has created a market in the commercial printing industry in which they match idle print capacity as well as price and capabilities to meet buyer needs.

- *Horizontal e-Marketplaces:* B2B marketplaces in this area range from simple portals to sophisticated collaboration hubs. Perhaps the most important function of these marketplaces is the ability to enable multibuyer/multisupplier interaction and collaboration. By providing a sort of virtual trading "hub" where multiple buyers and sellers can be matched and conduct transactions, these Web sites enable manufacturers, distributors, buying groups, and service providers to develop shared marketplaces that deliver real-time, interactive commerce services through the Internet. Of equal importance is the ability to generate new forms of exchange, such as on-line sourcing, auctions, and negotiations. Finally, because of their role as a medium, these marketplaces enable trading communities to facilitate the exchange of common information and knowledge. Common horizontal marketplaces can be described as follows:

- *e-Business Portals* are perhaps the purest form of e-marketplace, portals are composed of third-party market-makers who provide on-line buying and selling services to small- and medium-size buyers to create an exchange. The portal offers buyers lower prices, gains in sales and service, and access to exchange members who can create, in turn, a trading community based on common interest. In exchange, the portal market-maker realizes a range of benefits, including an expanded branding awareness and widening exposure to potential customers. Portals include large financial institutions, utilities, telecommunications companies, IT service providers, and commerce service providers.[24]
- *One-to-Many Marketplaces* are typically PTXs that involve one buyer and multiple sellers. Companies hosting these marketplaces normally possess the buying power to force suppliers to participate in the exchange and dictate the terms for participation.
- *Aggregator Hubs* are third-party-led marketplaces that seek to combine the catalogs of several suppliers for display to potential buyers. The more sophisticated aggregator hubs provide contracts, authorizations, and other content.
- *Broker Hubs* normally consist of multiple buyers and sellers presided over by a broker. The central role of the broker is to match buyers and sellers based on product/service requirement and price. According to Hajibashi,[25] buyers send their requirements to the hub, which in turn consolidates them to facilitate volume buying and discounting. Sellers then respond to these aggregate requirements. Finally, transactions are typically handled by e-mail versus an automated bidding process, although real-time dynamic transactions are becoming more prevalent.
- *Collaboration Hubs* enable multiple buyers and sellers to correspond and share key procurement information. For example, buyers may share forecast information to facilitate supplier planning and shipment of products to correspond to required quantities, delivery, and service targets.
- *Translator Hubs* provide similar functions as collaboration hubs, but they facilitate trading functions by offering *enterprise application integration* (EAI) capabilities that provide true system/data integration between the business system environments of the trading partners. Among the technologies used are fax, EDI, e-mail, and XML.

C. Future of B2B e-Marketplaces

While the collapse of the dot-com revolution and the economic recession of 2001–2002 have temporarily relegated Internet-driven business initiatives to the background, Web-based sourcing, procurement, and SCM technologies have still managed to deliver considerable value to SRM functions. Despite the real advantages, B2B can best be described as being in its infancy. Several critical issues come to mind. To begin with, much of the focus of procurement applications using the Internet has centered on MRO/indirect materials purchasing to handle commodity, low-margin products and services purchased from numerous suppliers. While providing significant tools to automate procurement practices and cut costs, utilization of e-SRM functions for direct material procurement and planning has been, to date, very weak. In addition, deployment of these e-SRM technologies has been isolated and disconnected from larger SCM and EBS systems. According to the Aberdeen Group, e-SRM initiatives have been fragmented, with the result that potential productivities have been lost. For example, early adopters of e-sourcing saw initial cost savings squandered in inabilities to effectively communicate negotiated terms and insufficient integration between e-sourcing and order execution systems.

Technology issues have also hindered adoption. Broadly functional, highly scalable applications capable of being easily integrated and driven by a single standard have not happened. Companies that have not implemented e-SRM functions cite three critical issues: (1) implementing vanilla e-SRM solutions is difficult, and they often require a great deal of modification; (2) to be effective, e-SRM functions must be supported by data that is synchronized across the supply chain; and (3) often firms must change traditional business practices to gain practical advantage, including changing time-tested relationships with suppliers. Application-to-application B2B marketplace integration is an expensive affair, and the complexity of delivering such integration is expanding and will do so until EAI tools become more mature and have more available prebuilt options. Besides these technology points, companies have privacy fears about letting proprietary information flow into the marketplace and competitive worries regarding sharing internal processes that could negate a critical advantage and level the playing field. Finally, the expectations set by the analysts and software vendors of enormous cost savings have not been forthcoming. During 2000 and early 2001, executives spent heavily on B2B tools only to find, by 2002, that expected 20% or higher savings across the board were simply not going to happen.

Changing SRM from a preoccupation with the original trading exchange model (which emphasized MRO/indirect procurement) to the much more strategic e-SRM model of collaborative marketplace communities (which focuses on direct material procurement and planning) requires alteration to the way companies have thought about B2B marketplaces and the tools used to manage them. The starting point is to reexamine the very concept of SRM stated earlier in this chapter. SRM is about building and nurturing supplier relationships that foster the growth of collaboration and common destiny. Internet exchanges without the presence of a collaborative community of interest are merely transaction sites. Similar to the CRM model detailed in chapter 5, SRM provides an environment where a company plans to win with its suppliers by establishing a common value chain for the long-term sourcing and procurement of a buyer's critical production inventories rather than simply commodity transactions. According to Foster,[26] today's e-SRM functions seek to significantly expand the reach of collaborative supply communities and possess the following enablers:

- e-SRM expands the scope of procurement functions. Most e-SRM application solutions span the life cycle of several business processes, from product design through sourcing and manufacturing, and on to procurement execution and performance monitoring.
- e-SRM provides for deep integration of business processes. As technology enablers expand the integration between business processes, companies will be able to leverage higher levels of cooperation between functions, including engineering, purchasing, manufacturing, and supply-chain operations.
- e-SRM facilitates direct collaboration between manufacturers and their suppliers. Similar to CRM, the key word in SRM is *relationship*. While e-SRM will automate and standardize transaction information, such as RFQs and negotiations, it also will use relationship-building applications including CPFR planning data and information regarding product specifications, design, and quality.
- e-SRM enables increased speed and flexibility. Since the centerpiece of SRM is the tight linkage of trading partners, it can assist in shrinking product design and time-to-market life cycles, while facilitating the transmission of ECO changes across the entire supply chain.

These very real, immediately measurable advantages have also been accompanied by a change in the attitudes of once highly skeptical buyers. When the whole concept of B2B commerce appeared, many suppliers expected manufacturers to use the Web as a means to play suppliers off against each other in an effort to drive prices down. Now that e-SRM solutions have actually been implemented and have been driving procurement functions, suppliers' fears that B2B e-commerce would turn all products into commodities and destroy perhaps decades of buyer-seller relationships has been shown to be unfounded. If anything, e-SRM has provided buyers and suppliers the opportunity to enhance their relationships, and even the most anxious business executive is becoming more at ease with opportunities for information sharing and collaboration.

In summary, manufacturers and distributors can only expect the use of e-SRM applications to increase with time, as companies search for solutions that go far beyond simply automating procurement functions. In fact, while many other sectors of the technology software marketplace, such as ERP, SCP, and SCM, have not faired well during the recession of 2001–2002, e-SRM applications, because of the immediacy of their ROIs, have flourished. e-SRM is currently at a transition stage from its early buy-side focus on commodities sourcing to fully collaborative marketplace communities. Accomplishing this goal means that e-SRM must, first of all, respond to individual company e-SRM requirements, such as product, supplier, and catalog search capabilities, automated RFQ, Web-based order entry and order status tracking, integration with EBS backbone systems, collaborative planning, transportation management, and other exchange integration functions. Second, e-SRM must enable true collaboration across the supply chain. Such a goal requires the existence of enabling infrastructures and business strategies that streamline procurement functions to the point where buyer and seller application functionality, processes, systems, and organizations are merged.

IV. IMPLEMENTING e-SRM

While the potential benefits of e-SCM are indeed spectacular, achieving them requires a thoughtful and well-designed implementation process. Previously, several critical barriers to e-SRM were detailed. One of the most commonly stated problems is the investment necessary to achieve an e-SRM initiative. Another was the requirement that firms must first reengineer their businesses to align procurement processes with technology capabilities. Technology-wise, effective e-SRM requires companies to integrate their SRM applications with backbone and CRM systems. This also means that companies must have the e-business skills to not only successfully install the necessary software, but also to complete any integration requirements. In addition, e-SRM requires companies to take risks. Conducting business on the Internet, particularly open-bidding, requires revealing proprietary information to eyes other than those of the parties involved. Then there is the apprehension that open exchanges require price transparency. Open auctions on a global basis could lower profits to the point that companies would not be able to stay in business. Finally, there is the anxiety that engaging in e-business will hurt long-standing relationships with existing suppliers, permanently damaging years of patient negotiation and mutual efforts toward collaboration on specific issues such as product quality and delivery.

Responding effectively to these and other challenges requires a comprehensive e-SRM strategy. An e-SRM strategy must posses the flowing attributes: *comprehensive* (all critical opportunities have been reviewed and the impact on all stakeholders analyzed); *complete* (no area has been left out of the plan, and the results of the analysis are meaningful and have weight for the company); and *thoughtful* (the decisions about software, relationships with suppliers, and expected value added to the supply chain are well documented and capable of discursive analysis). The following critical drivers need to be carefully considered when designing an e-SRM strategy.

A. e-SRM VALUE DISCOVERY

Perhaps the first step that needs to be performed is the drafting of a statement of immediate economic benefits and long-term supply chain value to be achieved by an e-SRM implementation. The goal here is to formulate a compelling case that details and positions each of the organization's most critical procurement requirements (design, sourcing, plan, transact, move, and dispose) with the procurement technologies to be implemented to include ROI, total cost/benefit of ownership, and the risk of not engaging in an e-SRM solution. At the conclusion of the process, the matching of the procurement requirement with the e-marketplace solution should include metrics detailing potential *cost savings* through increased buying economies or improved leverage, enhanced *process efficiencies* attained through decreased time spent on procurement activities, *inventory optimization* achieved through better planning, vendor-managed inventories, or improved supply chain visibility, and *lower development costs* through collaborative design and increased standardization.[27] Finally, companies need to fully understand the magnitude of the project they are embarking on. An e-SRM project is simply not an IT project: it is a strategic enterprise supply chain management project that will impact the entire organization.

B. Infrastructure Analysis

The next step in the development of an effective e-SRM strategy is performing an assessment of current purchasing practices and organizational capabilities. The goals of the process are to determine the readiness of the organization to utilize Web-based toolsets and e-marketplaces and to decide which Internet-driven strategies possess the highest potential. According to Smeltzer and Carter,[28] this process requires the examination of four organizational characteristics. The first, *organizational structure,* seeks to determine the degree to which purchasing is centralized, the position of the purchasing function within the firm, and the level of communication existing between purchasing staff across the enterprise. The second characteristic, *information technology,* seeks to detail the sophistication of company use of technologies promoting purchasing automation, current use of e-markets and industry portals, and availability of decision support systems. The third characteristic, *employee capabilities,* seeks to determine the qualification of purchasing professionals to understand and work with e-SRM tools. And, finally, *current purchasing practices,* which reveal the level of procurement sophistication in regard to such practices as strategic sourcing, use of P-cards and supplier contracts, and application of supplier performance metrics.

C. Preparing for Organizational Change

Preparing the organization to pursue e-SRM opportunities requires a considerable degree of organizational readiness. A key task is developing an effective *change management* plan. Migrating to e-marketplace-based processes will require overt and subtle changes to the way people have traditionally worked. The change management plan must begin by evaluating existing procurement processes, mapping them out, designing new processes supported by the e-SRM technologies, and selecting methods to bridge current with new processes. Instrumental to managing this change is effective *education and training.* The mission here is to ensure that people know about the concepts and technologies necessary for them to understand and operate the system so they can execute necessary processes. The education should, finally, articulate the value proposition behind the e-SRM implementation and motivate people to search for new opportunities to leverage the system for cost reduction and collaborative enhancement.

D. Spend Analysis

Once internal organizational issues have been detailed, e-SRM implementers must conduct a thorough analysis of all the goods and services purchased across divisions and strategic business units to determine actual spend levels and degree of supplier fragmentation. The analysis should indicate how much is being spent on particular items as well as families of items. Finally, the analysis should identify how much is being purchased, by category, of goods and type of service from each supplier. The goal of the whole process is to unearth answers to such questions as what is being purchased, from whom, from where, and from what locations.

E. Item/Service Analysis

Once the initial spend analysis has been completed, the next step is to segment item/service purchases. A critical preliminary is the formulation of a standard for coding and indexing goods and services purchased across the enterprise. This process will further rationalize sourcing, reduce the number of suppliers, and facilitate aggregate demand planning and acquisition. Once completed, the next step is the categorization of purchased goods and services. In this process, planners must separate purchases according to their relative risk/exposure and cost/value to the firm. The mission of the segmentation strategy is to determine which purchases are truly commodities with low strategic impact on the organization, which are generic and marked by high dollar expenditures but pose low risk, which are critical and will bring high risk/exposure to the company, and which are strategic in that they provide a distinct competitive advantage. When finally selecting an e-SRM strategy, companies must be careful to architect a procurement system that possesses the capability to integrate applications that can simultaneously leverage automation tools for reducing costs on commodity items while ensuring that strong relations are established with suppliers providing strategic goods and services.

F. e-SRM Technology Choices

Segmentation of purchased items and services enables planners to more easily identify the required e-SRM applications that will have to be implemented to optimize various supply environments. The process starts by mapping each procurement segment to B2B application enablers, both e-sourcing tools, such as RFQ and catalog search, and e-procurement tools, such as Web-based transaction management. Results may indicate that a portfolio of e-SRM applications will be required for optimum results. Also, it is important to realize that, in selecting a technology solution today, companies often will have to merge e-sourcing platforms, e-procurement applications, contract management toolsets, supplier collaboration solutions, and content management solutions from several e-SRM software suppliers. The e-SRM choices available can be divided into several possible Web-based strategies. Some of these models have been considered extensively in this and other chapters and will be given only a light analysis here.

1. Hosted Supply Chain (HSC)

A possible strategy to assist in managing the cost of e-SRM technologies is to contract a *hosted supply chain* (HSC) service supplier. According to AMR Research,[29] an HSC can be defined as the use of a third-party software vendor who can provide an Internet-based platform in which multiple suppliers or trading partners can engage in cross-enterprise supply chain management processes that include extended supply chain visibility, workflow, event management, planning, process coordination, and replenishment. Often offering *application service provider* (ASP) platforms, HSC vendors provide companies with connectivity and capability to participate in trading exchanges and Web-based collaborative replenishment programs at a low cost. An HSC solution permits cash-strapped or reluctant companies to participate in Web-based technologies without committing to software licensing, extended implementations, and business process reengineering tasks.

2. Automation Applications

Much has already been said about the use of Web-based applications designed to automate the procurement process, enhance the productivity of the purchasing function, and facilitate e-sourcing and e-procurement processes. However, while a focus on cost reduction applications will produce short-term, tactical benefits, the biggest advantage will be found in the pursuit of technologies that enhance long-term buying strategies through standardization, aggregation, and leverage.

3. Portals

While portals have many applications and as many definitions, the function of Internet-based portals is to extract and aggregate data from multiple systems, apply certain rules and logic, and present relevant information in a personalized format. According to Poirier and Bauer[30], a procurement portal is a business entity, such as a software provider, a pooled purchasing group, an exchange, or an aggregator, that provides infrastructure and buying/selling services in support of procurement operations. The portal may be focused on a specific vertical industry, commodity-based (MRO supplies), or a hybrid. Portals provide a cost-effective, efficient way for companies to broadcast and link procurement information from EBS backbone systems to trading partners. Portals are relatively easy to implement in comparison to PTXs, largely because the requirement for deep system-to-system integration is minimal.

4. Exchanges and Auctions

Exchanges involve the use of a neutral third-party that operates the exchange, sets the conventions for trading activities, and charges buyers and sellers for its use. An auction site is also normally run by a third party who provides the functionality permitting buyers and sellers to bid on products and services.

5. PTXs and CTXs

A decision to participate in a PTX or CTX represents a considerable investment in time and money. These exchanges often require significant technical investment on the part of the host both to establish the exchange hub and to assist suppliers to "plug-into" the system. These private networks require trading partners to have a series of passcodes that enable them to enter the network and move to the exchange. Also, these exchanges are usually governed by specific agreements that determine the transaction services between partners. These types of e-SRM are strongly oriented around value chain partnering, led by a small group or a single powerful supply chain sponsor who has ownership of the exchange hub.

G. Performance Measurement

Ultimately, the success or failure of an e-SRM initiative can only be measured against the performance targets that were created at project inception. Dodds and Balchin from Accenture feel that there are essentially two clearly defined but closely related categories of *key performance indicators* (KPIs) at the foundation of an effective e-SRM strategy.[31] The first category, *implementation success KPIs,* measure the depth of the penetration of e-sourcing and e-procurement into the organization. The second category, *benefit KPIs,* provide the information necessary to determine the extent to which originally identified benefits have been realized. While each area requires different measurement tools and metrics, Dodds and Balchin are quick to point out that these two sets of KPIs must be considered as constituting a single overall measurement. Simply measuring, say the percentage of buying utilizing e-procurement tools, would be meaningless without other indirect metrics such as the proportion of procurement time freed up to focus on value-added strategic activities gained by using an on-line auctioning application.

Although it can be said that many of the KPIs that are being offered as measurements for e-SRM are essentially the same as those to be found in traditional purchasing management, today's balanced scorecard of e-SRM KPIs require companies to significantly increase the speed by which the data are collected, analyzed, and made available for decision-making. Some e-SRM consulting firms and application suppliers have been developing prepackaged, portal-based solutions and models to benchmark purchasing capabilities that can be plugged directly into the e-SRM project. Among these solutions can be found performance toolsets such as real-time alert notification, data mining and associated data presentation, flexible workflow-based business process definitions, flexible and user-defined KPI models, and exception-based management processes that are positioned on top of ERP or supply chain planning and execution business systems.

Today, these purchasing measurement systems are being merged with tools to manage performance across the entire supply chain. Termed *total cost management* (TCM), the Aberdeen Group describes the emerging framework of application and supporting infrastructure for performance measurement as providing for the development and coordination of new organizational and technology architectures that merge supply chain strategies and product and market intelligence with emerging sourcing, planning, procurement, monitoring, and analytics technologies. To effectively drive TCM, companies must build technology-based architectures that support the following:

- *Monitoring tools* that provide for the detailed measurement and enforcement of how closely the business complies with supplier contracts and how well suppliers execute negotiated trading agreements and anticipated performance targets.
- *Collaboration* of internal enterprise functions and supply network partners to promote the integration of all procurement and supply chain processes.
- *Process control* that utilizes all types of data communication, from EDI to XML, to engineer a central platform for the standardization and enforcement of common processes across individual companies and the entire supply chain.
- *Procurement intelligence* that provides a single source of intelligence for the entire supply chain for all procurement-related data and intelligence.[32]

V. SUMMARY AND TRANSITION

The demands of today's marketplace and the advent of Internet technologies have rendered traditional buy-side procurement solutions obsolete and marked the evolution of new procurement management concepts, principles, and computerized technologies that have come to coalesce around a new management term — *supplier relationship management* (SRM). Defining exactly what SRM means is currently, at best, a difficult task. Unlike its obvious counterpart (CRM) on the sell-side of the business, SRM is not an established management technique, nor does it come complete with a defined suite of software applications. In fact, the term SRM is being used to span a variety of procurement functions from supplier management, negotiation, and sourcing to automated order generation, order monitoring, payment, and performance measurement. In addition, SRM also encompasses strategic objectives associated with the integration of supplier collaboration into the mainstream of supply chain management thought and practice as well as the use of the Internet in the pursuit of tactical objectives such as purchasing activity automation and cost management. Despite the "fuzziness" of SRM elements at this point in time, the following definition of SRM was offered in the chapter:

SRM can be defined as the nurturing of continuously evolving, value-enriching relationships between supply chain buyers and sellers that requires a firm commitment on the part of all trading parties to a mutually agreed upon set of goals and is manifested in the collaborative sharing and timely and cost-effective execution of sourcing and procurement competencies to facilitate the entire material replenishment lifecycle from concept to delivery.

The application of the Internet to the evolving SRM concept can be said to have spawned a new form of procurement management: e-SRM. As was discussed in the chapter, the concept of e-SRM has come to coalesce around two Internet-driven functions: *e-procurement*, the utilization of Web-toolsets to automate the activities association with purchase order generation, order management, and procurement statistics, and *e-sourcing*, the utilization of the Web to develop long-term supplier relationships that will assist in the growth of collaborative approaches to joint product development, negotiation, contract management, and CPFR. While much discussion concerning the relationship and exact functioning of these two processes is still needed, the chapter proposed viewing e-SRM not as two, but rather as four separate processes. The first area, *EBS backbone*, is comprised of the traditional database and execution functions utilized by purchasing to generate orders, perform receiving and transfer to accounts payable, and record supplier statistics. The second area, *e-SRM services*, details the enhancement of traditional buyer functions, such as sourcing and supplier relationships, through the use of Web toolsets. The third area, *e-SRM processing,* lists the new functions provided by the Internet that automate and facilitate the transaction process. The final area, *e-SRM technology services*, outlines the technical architecture that enables e-SRM front-end and backbone functions to be effectively integrated to realize procurement strategies.

While e-SRM-driven processes have been undergoing evolution, so have the B2B marketplaces where the activities of buy-side and supplier management are carried out. In the first era of e-SRM, companies focused on Web-based applications to automate internal transaction processes and to use independent B2C portals for the acquisition of standardized MRO and indirect products. In the second era, companies began to migrate toward independent and consortia exchanges to address issues relating to security and control. In addition, these Internet solutions were seen as prerequisites for the kind of buyer-supplier collaboration required for the strategic sourcing and the purchase of direct or production inventories. The third stage of e-SRM marketplaces, which has only begun to emerge, can be characterized as the transformation of the current field of private and consortia exchanges into fully networked e-marketplaces. These future marketplaces will possess interoperable technologies that will enable true intercompany backbone integration and the seamless utilization of product design, sourcing, and contracting information fostering true marketplace-to-marketplace interaction.

Leveraging the tremendous advantages and benefits to be gained from an effective e-SRM solution requires companies to design an implementation plan that allows them to avoid the common pitfalls that are ready to entrap the unprepared. To begin with, companies must closely define what immediate economic benefits and long-term supply chain value is to be achieved by the e-SRM implementation. Metrics should include potential cost savings, process efficiencies, inventory optimization goals, and lower development costs as well as the types of supplier relationships they wish to build. Following, an assessment of current purchasing practices and organizational capabilities should be performed. The goal is to review the readiness of the organization, its technologies, its employees, and its procurement practices to pursue e-SRM. Critical to organizational readiness is an effective change management and education process. Next, a detailed spend analysis needs to be performed. This activity will define the product types, quantity, and cost of procurement across the entire enterprise. Once these preliminaries have been completed, implementers can choose the most applicable e-SRM strategy. Results may require the adoption of a portfolio of e-SRM applications, dictating the use of HSC solutions, the level of automation, and type of marketplace exchange. Finally, implementers must be careful to craft a range of meaningful implementation and expected benefit KPIs to monitor the ongoing success of the e-SRM effort.

The development of Web-based CRM and SRM tools to provide the marketplace with instantaneous access to products and services requires that the fulfillment side of e-SCM be equally as efficient and accessible. In Chapter 8, the application of Internet tools to logistics will be examined.

ENDNOTES

1. Williams, Alvin J. and Dukes, Kathleen A., "The Purchasing Function," in *The Purchasing Handbook,* 5th ed., McGraw-Hill, New York, 1993, 5.
2. These functions of purchasing have been summarized from Ross, David F., *Distribution: Planning and Control,* Chapman & Hall, New York, 1996, 443–445.
3. Hirsch, Chet and Barbalho, Marcos, "Toward World-Class Procurement," *Supply Chain Management Review,* 6, 5, 2001, 74–80.
4. *Ibid.*
5. These and other success stories can be found in Konicki, Steve, "E-Sourcing's Next Wave," *InformationWeek,* March 18, 2002, 57–62 and editors, "DaimlerChrysler Saves with E-Business Initiatives," *Global Logistics and Supply Strategies,* 6, 3, 2002, 30.
6. Dik, Roger W. and Whitaker, Jonathan D., "Suppliers: The Missing link," *Supply Chain e-Business,* 2, 5, 2001, 37–39.
7. Editors, "An e-Outlook," *Midrange Enterprise,* Oct./Nov., 2001, 5 and Burgert, Philip, "The Changing Face of B2B Commerce," *Electronic Commerce World,* 11, 8, 2001, 27–28.
8. These comments have been summarized from Starr, C. Edwin, Kambil, Ajit, Whitaker, Jonathan D., and Brooks, Jeffrey D., "One Size Does Not Fit All – The Need for an E-Marketplace Portfolio," in *Achieving Supply Chain Excellence Through Technology,* 3, Anderson, David, L., ed., Montgomery Research, San Francisco, 2001, 96–99 and Hill, Sidney, "Don't Speak," *Manufacturing Systems,* 20, 1, 2002, 34–38.
9. Hoque, Faisal, *e-Enterprise: Business Models, Architecture, and Components,* Cambridge University Press, 2000, 97.
10. Davenport, Thomas H., Brooks, Jeffrey D., and Cantrell, Susan, "E-Commerce Networks," Accenture Institute for Strategic Change.
11. Mitchell, Pierre, "Strategic Sourcing Gets an "E"," AMR Research Report, April, 2001.
12. Reference the analysis in Shea, Carrie, "The Evolution of Strategic Sourcing," B2B Retail and Consumer Goods Benchmarks Report, AT Kearney, September, 2001.
13. Hyland, Tricia, "Sourcing Drives Value in e-Procurement," *Transportation and Distribution,* 43, 1, 2002, 33–36.
14. Dilger, Karen Abramic, "Content Upkeep," *Manufacturing Systems,* 20, 4, 2002, 56–62.
15. See the analysis of B2B purchase requisitioning found in Hoque, 107–109.
16. *Ibid.,* 110.
17. For more discussion on shopping agents see Taylor, David and Terhune, Alyse D., *Doing E-Business: Strategies for Thriving in an Electronic Marketplace*, John Wiley & Sons, New York, 2001, 117–119.

18. Whitehouse, Rachel and Mangalindan, Yvette, "On-line Auctions: What is Your Bid?," in *Achieving Supply Chain Excellence Through Technology*, 3, Anderson, David, L., ed., Montgomery Research, San Francisco, 2001, 158–160.

19. Poirier, Charles C. and Bauer, Michael J., *E-Supply Chain*, Berrett-Koehler, San Francisco, 2000, 106–109.

20. See the discussion in Hoque, 215–219.

21. See *Ibid.,* 221–222.

22. These phases of B2B can be found in Hajibashi, Mohammed, "E-Marketplaces: The Shape of the New Economy," in *Achieving Supply Chain Excellence Through Technology*, 3, Anderson, David, L., ed., Montgomery Research, San Francisco, 2001, 162–166 and Temkin, Bruce, "Preparing for the Coming Shake-Out in On-line Markets," in *Achieving Supply Chain Excellence Through Technology*, 3, Anderson, David, L., ed., Montgomery Research, San Francisco, 2001, 102–107.

23. Raisch, Warren D., *The E-Marketplace: Strategies for Success in B2B Ecommerce*, McGraw-Hill, New York, 2001, 213–214.

24. Reference *Ibid.,* 51–52 and 214.

25. Hajibashi, Mohammed, "E-Marketplaces: The Shape of the New Economy," in *Achieving Supply Chain Excellence Through Technology*, 3, Anderson, David, L., ed., Montgomery Research, San Francisco, 2001, 162–166.

26. Foster, Thomas A., "With SRM, Everything is Relative," *Supply Chain e-Business,* 3, 2, 2002, 16–21.

27. See the excellent comments in Eichmann, Don A., "E-Marketplace Participation: Reaching the Bottom Line," in *Achieving Supply Chain Excellence Through Technology*, 3, Anderson, David, L., ed., Montgomery Research, San Francisco, 2001, 153–156.

28. Smeltzer, Larry R. and Carter, Joseph R., "How to Build an e-Procurement Strategy," *Supply Chain Management Review,* 5, 2, 2001, 76–83.

29. Ferrari, Robert, "The Hosted Supply Chain Emerges in B2B," *AMR Research Report,* April, 2001.

30. Poirier and Bauer, 101–102.

31. Dodds, Stuart and Balchin, John, "E-Procurement Measurement: It's Not Broken – But It Needs to Be Fixed," in *Achieving Supply Chain Excellence Through Technology*, 3, Anderson, David, L., ed., Montgomery Research, San Francisco, 2001, 148–151.

32. See the analysis of TCM found in Editor, "Capturing the Total Opportunity," *Supply Chain e-Business,* 2002, 6.

8 Logistics Resource Management: Utilizing the Internet to Enhance Logistics Competitive Advantage

Of the business functions of the modern enterprise, logistics has had perhaps the most visible impact on the economic condition of society. Historically, it has been the role of logistics to solve the problem of product distribution by providing for the efficient and speedy movement of goods from the point of manufacture to the point of consumption. Today, this basic role of logistics has been greatly accentuated by the continuous, downward spiraling of all facets of product cycle times, compounded by a relentless acceleration in marketplace demands for quick response, customizable services, and self-activating ordering systems. In addition, logistics functions must now be able to link customers with suppliers through both physical and now Internet-driven channels. In such an environment, the key to logistics competitiveness is to utilize the best service partners and technologies to ensure that the most timely information and efficient business systems can be leveraged in the pursuit of value-added processes driving the cycle of supply chain procurement, manufacturing, and delivery.

In fact, the tremendous challenges and strategic opportunities for logistics competitive advantage posed by today's global and Internet-driven environments requires redefinition of the logistics concept and the evolution of a new term — *logistics resource management* (LRM). Similar to the recent transformation of customer service and purchasing functions into CRM and SRM, the use of the term LRM is meant to convey a similar expansion of traditional logistics activities to encompass the multifaceted concept of supply chain management with its focus on trading partner collaboration, the removal of channel barriers causing excess costs and reduced cycle times, the espousal of Internet technologies that facilitate information and transaction data collection and flow through the supply pipeline, and the creation of agile, responsive organizations linked together in a single-minded pursuit of superior customer service.

In this chapter the elements of logistics management in the Internet Age will be examined. The discussion begins with a review of the function of logistics and its evolution to *logistics resource management* (LRM). After a detailed definition of the structure and key capabilities of LRM, the chapter proceeds to describe the different categories of LRM available today and the array of possible Web-based toolsets driving logistics performance measurement and warehouse and transportation management. Afterward, the use of third-party logistics services is reviewed. The different types of logistics service providers, the growth of Internet-enabled providers, and the challenges of choosing a logistics partner that matches, if not facilitates, overall company business strategies is explored in depth.

I. DEFINING LOGISTICS RESOURCE MANAGEMENT

Over the past quarter century, the science of logistics management has evolved from purely an operational function to a competitive weapon providing today's enterprise with the capability to leverage Internet technologies to closely link the farthest regions of the supply channel with market demand found anywhere in the globe. Originally, the mission of logistics was to provide efficient and cost-effective warehousing and transportation utilities that enabled companies to deliver products in support of internal marketing and financial objectives. In the age of e-business, modern logistics has become in itself a critical competitive resource, creating value by responding to ever-higher levels of customer expectation, engineering operations that integrate trading partners up and down the channel network while reducing costs and expanding the spectrum of value-added services necessary for electronic commerce.

The sheer size of the logistics function bears witness to its central position in business. According to Delaney,[1] the cost of logistics just in the U.S. for the year 2000 exceeded $1 trillion. This expenditure was equivalent of 10% of the U.S. gross domestic product measured in nominal dollars. The total included $377 billion of inventory carrying cost and $585 billion of transportation cost. Of total logistics costs, trucking accounted for nearly 82% of annual U.S. freight transportation expenditures.

While numerous definitions of logistics have been proposed, perhaps the most often quoted has been formulated by the Council of Logistics Management.

> Logistics is the process of planning, implementing, and controlling the efficient flow and storage of raw materials, in-process inventory, finished goods, services, and related information from point of origin to point of consumption (including inbound, outbound, internal, and external movements) for the purpose of conforming to customer requirements.

This and other definitions imply that LRM creates competitive value by ensuring the optimization of logistics operations costs and productivity, better capacity and resource utilization, inventory reduction, and closer integration with customers and suppliers. Beyond cost management, LRM also assists in the creation of marketplace leadership through customer service and timely product and service delivery. Furthermore, the overall success of these objectives depends upon the close collaboration and integration of all logistics partners that populate each node in the supply channel system and who are responsible for the efficient performance of logistics

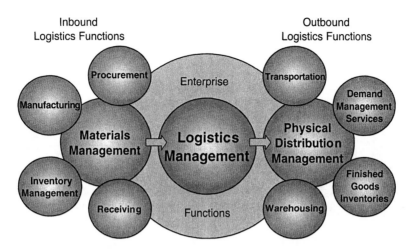

FIGURE 8.1 Logistics management functions.

processes. In addition to traditional operations functions, these processes include strategic decisions relating to channel design and structure, resource allocation, human capital, operations, and finance. LRM creates competitive advantage by flawlessly executing customer service objectives, achieving conformance to quality standards, and increasing marketplace value.[2]

Perhaps the best way to examine the contents of LRM is to divide it into two separate, yet closely integrated, sets of functions as illustrated if Figure 8.1. The first set of functions has classically been grouped under the term *materials management* and is identified with the management of the incoming flow of materials and services into the enterprise from the supply channel. Materials management can be further broken down into a subset of activities supporting the cycle of materials flow from the purchase, receipt, and control of inventory to manufacturing and delivery of finished goods to the supply channel system. The second set of functions can be termed *physical distribution*. This function is normally associated with the outbound flow of finished goods through the distribution channel to meet customer requirements. Detail activities can be described as including warehousing, transportation, finished goods management, customer order management services, product packaging, shipping, and returns goods management. While it can be argued that separating LRM into the above two regions is somewhat artificial and that processes, such as transportation and inventory management, overlap, the goal is not so much to delineate organizational identities as to facilitate understanding.

While the above definition attempts to view LRM from an organizational perspective, Accenture has developed a framework that seeks to describe LRM from a capability point of view.[3] As illustrated in Figure 8.2, LRM can be broken down into 19 strategic and tactical objectives distributed within a framework spanning three critical processes: *planning and collaboration, transaction,* and *execution.* In addition, the model contains a *technical infrastructure* component which will determine how information is exchanged, and an *infomediary* component which will detail the depth of knowledge and information required to support the capabilities, both

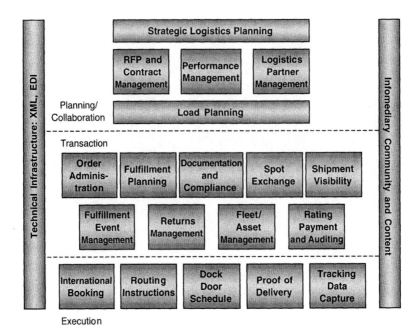

FIGURE 8.2 The logistics footprint. (Reprinted with permission of Accenture.)

internally and externally, to drive the logistics model. While it is critical to acknowledge that not all of the 19 processes will apply to all industries and companies, the LRM capability model does provide a structured approach to understanding the possible components involved in logistics and transportation. In addition, the model provides strategists with a framework for identifying strengths and weaknesses and for developing effective measurements to initiate continuous improvement.

While each of the 19 process capabilities are critical to effective LRM, five of these capabilities can be singled out as absolutely critical, regardless of industry.[4] Mastering these five capabilities provides companies with the most important drivers of logistics cost reduction, higher customer service, and higher ROI. In addition, these capabilities are the foundation upon which the remaining LRM capabilities can be improved. Developing these and the other capabilities will require strategists to closely define the objectives and processes of each capability and to architect enabling organizations and technologies. These capabilities can be described as follows.

A. LOGISTICS PERFORMANCE MANAGEMENT

Perhaps no other business area in the enterprise needs to be measured more closely than logistics. Such a judgment arises in part from the fact that the sheer size and complexity of LRM operations activities (inventory transactions, orders, shipments, and so on) touch so many facets, not only of individual businesses, but also of trading partners on a global scale. Furthermore, since LRM operations drive a significant share of overall enterprise costs, they must be carefully collected and monitored.

Accurate measurements assist managers to identify operating inefficiencies and reduce costs. In addition, effective LRM metrics enable strategists to detail how well the company is serving its customers, identify possible avenues for profit by uncovering new value-added services or by differentiating product/service delivery, and architect new channel strategies with suppliers that result in channel inventory reduction and overall improved efficiencies. Finally, as LRM evolves from a tactical to a strategic function, validating the capabilities of logistics has become a critical source of competitive advantage, not only for individual companies, but also for the entire supply chain.

LRM functions should conform to the level of performance expected by the customer. Essentially, logistics performance is composed of three key components. The first, *logistics productivity*, is demonstrated by the creation of measurements that can provide meaningful productivity standards, the ability to track and manage logistics costs, the integration of quality management processes, and the broadening of logistics service levels. The second component, *logistics service performance*, is concerned with tracking metrics associated with the ability of logistics functions to meet customer service goals, such as product availability, order cycle time, logistics system flexibility, depth of service information, utilization of technologies, and breadth of postsales service support. A critical issue in this component is ensuring logistics measures are in synch with company fulfillment strategies. For example, if a company's strategy is to be a low-cost provider of products, the logistics systems must be efficient and flexible enough to meet company goals while keeping fulfillment costs to a minimum.

The final LRM performance component, *logistics performance measurement systems*, focuses on what and how performance is to be tracked. Such a task is a difficult one and conceals several traps. Since there are literally hundreds of measurements possible, companies must be careful to select those that paint an accurate portrait of overall performance, such as the sourcing/procurement process, fulfillment process time, cost, quality, and planning, forecasting, and scheduling process accuracies. In addition, companies need to ensure that measurements are not subjective, thereby distorting reality. Finally, LRM information systems should be employed to gather, process, and analyze the tremendous volume of LRM performance activities. Often this means working closely with trading partners to ensure the proper data is being gathered from channel SCM systems, ERP systems, and data warehouses.

B. FULFILLMENT PLANNING AND EXECUTION

Whether traditional or e-commerce channel, one lesson has been made abundantly clear: without effective and timely product fulfillment, even the best marketing campaign or the cleverest Web site is destined for failure. In the past, buyer/seller exchange consisted of one-to-one paper-based systems. The fundamental problems revolving around data inaccuracies, lack of connectivity, and lack of information visibility that constrained the fulfillment process were masked by inflated cycle times and channel inventory buffers. In contrast, today's customers have the capability to view marketing materials and promotions and place orders and access shipment information almost instantaneously. Accordingly, customers have become increasingly impatient with the poorly synchronized, inflexible fulfillment processes of the past and require, in their place, integrated supply chains capable of compressing all aspects of fulfillment from order entry to delivery. In such an environment companies need LRM functions that place a premium on fulfillment speed, accuracy, visibility, personalization, and agility — attributes that require companies to deploy the right technologies in support of superbly engineered fulfillment processes that range from tightly synchronized trading partners to strategically located brick-and-mortar warehouses.

Architecting an effective LRM fulfillment plan requires close attention to both operational functionality and strategic capabilities. Operationally, fulfillment planning enables companies to convert customer demand into actual shipment schedules, optimize transportation management activities such as carrier selection and routing, and collect and provide fulfillment life cycle information. According to Poirier and Bauer,[5] the goal of the LRM process is the optimization of supply chain network fulfillment functions. These functions can be separated into the following five operations areas:

- *Freight cost and service management.* The main functions in this area consist of managing inbound/outbound freight, carrier management, total cost control, operations outsourcing decisions, and execution of administrative services. Effective fulfillment planning in this area requires the architecting of fulfillment functions that can optimize inbound materials and outbound product movement, warehousing, and administrative services that utilize the most cost-effective yet efficient transportation partners and carriers.
- *Fleet management.* This area is concerned with the effective utilization of physical transportation assets. Critical areas for fulfillment planning revolve around equipment utilization, equipment maintenance, and total cost. The goal is to determine the optimum use of transportation assets, whether internal or through a third-party supplier, without compromising service levels.
- *Load planning.* Utilizing transportation assets to achieve maximum fulfillment optimization requires detailed load planning. Critical functions in this area revolve around selection of the appropriate transportation mode, load building and consolidation, and possible third-party transfer point or cross-docking functions.
- *Routing and scheduling.* These functions are normally considered as the heart of transportation management. Areas to be considered are optimization of shipping capacity utilization, less-than-truckload (LTL) shipments, and postponement strategies that position actual product at the various nodes in the supply channel. An often-overlooked area is shipment documentation and compliance. Key points are concerned with ensuring accurate documentation regarding country quotas, tariffs, import/export regulations, product classification, and letters of credit.

- *Warehouse management.* The effective management of inventory in the supply chain requires efficient and well-managed warehousing techniques. Among the components of this area of traditional logistics management can be found order allocation and picking, packaging, receiving, putaway, returns management, and warehouse performance measurements.

Effectively managing each one of these logistics operations areas requires planners to constantly search for methods to automate functions through the use of computerized technologies. Whether through transaction devices, ERP, EDI, or the Internet, optimization requires planners to assemble technology toolsets that enable them to leverage channel information flows to make better decisions, thereby increasingly replacing inventory in the supply pipeline with information.

While effective LRM operations will assist in generating incremental improvements to supply chain fulfillment, order-of-magnitude acceleration of channel value will be achieved when whole channel networks leverage LRM to achieve strategic fulfillment objectives. The goal is to engineer highly integrated supply chain networks that are seamless to the customer, agile in their ability to change to meet marketplace needs, and electronically enabled to provide real-time connectivity. Effective LRM operations planning should provide fresh opportunities for the development of new fulfillment networks and relationships with logistics partners, reengineering of new organizational LRM roles and responsibilities, and the development and implementation of robust, flexible sourcing, warehousing, transportation, and delivery capabilities.

C. Logistics Partnership Management

Today's fast-paced, Internet-driven marketplace requires businesses to develop new models governing logistics relationships with third-party service providers. Often, achieving the level of operation optimization detailed above will require the use of a *third-party logistics* (3PL) firm or a lead logistics provider to support fulfillment objectives. According to Hintlian and Churchman,[6] today's LRM environment requires logistics service relationships characterized by:

- Increased collaboration between logistics services providers and their customers
- The establishment of contractual and operations arrangements that foster an environment of win-win between all parties
- A detailed and accurate catalog of core competencies possessed by logistics providers that can be outsourced
- The capability of logistics providers to design support systems that can be used to assist both individual companies and the supply chains to which they belong

LRM support partners have become more valuable as they utilize new technologies to integrate themselves into the supply chain system and create new forms of fulfillment support services. These new fulfillment functions can be divided into three technology-driven enablers. In one region can be found LRM providers who use the Internet to form logistics marketplaces that match buyers and sellers of logistics operational services. In another region can be found infomediaries who harness information technologies to support the synchronization of logistics operational, tactical, and strategic functions for a supply network. In the final region can be found flow management service providers that assist network partners to manage the movement of fulfillment transactions through the supply network.

D. Shipment Visibility

Shipment visibility today has become much greater than simply order "track and trace." While it is critical that current fulfillment functions provide the capability for customers to access real-time data regarding their shipments utilizing any one of a number of variables, ranging from SKU number to shipment origin, shipment visibility constitutes the very first layer in LRM. Of increasing importance to logistics managers is visibility to information about inventories and fulfillment capabilities found not just between immediate buyer and supplier, but also among trading partners constituting the entire supply chain. As cycle times and inventories shrink in the supply pipeline, substituting information for inventory has placed a premium on total supply network resource visibility. Assembling effective LRM capabilities has been made more difficult as the complexity of the supply chain has deepened, caused by the increase in contract manufacturing, raw material providers extending several levels upstream, and global sourcing efforts requiring overcoming geographic boarders and language barriers, and the establishment of often separate Internet sales functions increasingly renders just delivering the product to the customer a challenge. Inability to see shipments in the supply chain simply causes time delays, amplifying inventory reserves, and creating a bullwhip effect especially in complex supply channels with many depots where inventory tends to build. Supply chain visibility is about being able to access accurate information about inventory and shipments anywhere, anytime in the supply network, so planners can respond quickly and intelligently.

When coupled with event management functionality, the goal of visibility systems is to provide a real-time window into the life cycle of a product transaction, beginning with order placement, progressing through picking, packing, and shipment, and concluding with delivery, quality reporting, and performance statistics. Lanier, for example, used a third-party shipment solution to eliminate nearly 100,000 phone call inquiries about shipment status, when it provided dealers Web access to the status of their orders, from pick-and-pack all the way to delivery. Shipment visibility is also critical for inbound shipment management. Target, for example, receives thousands of inbound shipments each week into its 20 distribution centers. In the past, information was handled largely through faxes and phone calls between the company, suppliers, and carriers. Today, Target's supply channel visibility software enables the giant retailer to optimize shipments, consolidate LTL into full truckloads, and better plan the receiving process.[7]

As the value of information regarding delivering capability and shipment visibility grows, dependence on various levels of technology can be expected to correspondingly grow and will become a "must-have" for effective LRM. Inside the organization, companies can leverage ERP suites, *warehouse management systems* (WMS), and *transportation management systems* (TMS) to view shipment-order linkages and in-transit shipment information, track fill rates, ensure valid available-to-promise information, and control transportation costs. Externally, companies can now leverage supply chain planning, management, and execution applications that provide CPFR and *supply chain event management* (SCEM) solutions that provide LRM planners with visibility to the entire supply channel, enabling them to execute more effective strategic logistics solutions, and assist in architecting fulfillment processes that lead to a spiral of continuous improvement and superior service to the customer.

E. FULFILLMENT EVENT MANAGEMENT

Alongside logistics visibility, fulfillment event management (or its better known name — *supply chain event management* (SCEM)) has become one of today's most important buzzwords in supply chain management. According to one analyst, fulfillment event management is one of the most significant and far-reaching of today's software technologies that, when applied to warehouse, order, and transportation management, can assist to proactively reduce and eliminate common fulfillment errors, such as missed orders, late deliveries, and other shipment and service problems.[8] Such a view is shared by Steve Banker, director of supply chain solutions at ARC Advisory Group, who feels that event management systems can now feed data into performance management systems, so LRM planners can

> start to understand the root cause of why a truck didn't arrive when it should have. What we lacked before is visibility into the reasons why truck shipments have been delayed or why orders have been short. With more granular, extended supply-chain visibility we have the data to start to correct causes of these problems, which tightens up lead times and lets companies spit out better optimizations.[9]

Companies such as KBKids.com, a Denver-based division of Consolidated Stores Corp., the operator of 1,300 KB Toys stores nationwide, are using fulfillment event management applications to monitor and send alerts, create workflows, and set up escalation processes to enhance customer service, cut logistics costs, and improve supply chain efficiencies. Fulfillment data, such as when shipments are packed and shipped and which carriers are the most efficient and cost effective, are provided on their Web sites and e-mailed directly to the customer. AMR Research feels that such capabilities take fulfillment beyond mere track and trace: true SCEM applications should support business processes for:

- *Monitoring*: Providing real-time information about supply network events, such as the current status of channel inventory levels, open orders, production, and fulfillment.
- *Notifying*: Providing real-time exception management through alert messaging that will assist supply channel planners to make effective decisions as conditions change in the supply pipeline.

- *Simulating*: Providing tools that permit easy and fast supply channel modeling and "what-if" scenarios that recommend appropriate remedial action in response to an event or trend analysis.
- *Controlling*: Provides channel planners with capabilities to quickly and easily change a previous decision or condition, such as expediting an order or selecting less costly delivery opportunities.
- *Measuring:* Provides essential metrics and performance objectives or KPIs to assist supply chain strategists to assess the performance of existing channel relationships and to set realistic expectations for future performance.

ARC believes that fulfillment event management and performance management will eventually be integrated to provide what they term *supply-chain process management.*

SCEM can be described as an application integration layer that standardizes and transports fulfillment information as it flows between channel trading partners. SCEM is normally integrated with ERP and supply chain execution systems and has the potential to link to today's emerging forms of trading exchange. SCEM applications currently provide logistics planners with the following functions: order and shipment tracking, workflow, alert messaging/notification, escalation processes, and performance/compliance management. Basically, the system is engaged when an event, either planned or unplanned, occurs requiring planner intervention. Depending on the impact of the event, the system will trigger a signal, often using Boolean-type logic, to alert planners through a generic workflow process that an occurrence in the fulfillment pipeline has violated predetermined event boundaries. For example, Unilever Home & Personal Care uses their SCEM system to create close Internet links to their third-party manufacturers. This permits them to be aware of logistics events such as whether a product is produced, on hold, released, or available for pickup. It also has removed several days in the speed of cycle time fulfillment due to improved information flow through the supply channel.[10] However, while SCEM provides visibility to current events and permits planners to execute operational corrections, the real value in event management is to be found on the strategic level where predefined KPIs, performance scorecards, and dashboards can detail long-term spending and fulfillment performance on shipments and compare the data over a variety of carriers, time periods, and transportation modes to pinpoint critical variances.

Altogether, the benefits of applying the latest computerized techniques that seek to automate logistics functions and increase the accuracy of LRM decisions can produce enormous benefits not only for individual companies, but also for entire supply chains. Among the benefits are faster response times, so less expensive shipping is required, decreased manufacturing WIP, channel, and in-transit inventories, improved accuracy of order processing and tracking, increased velocity of order management, reduction of returns, and decreases in labor requirements. Additional hard benefits can be found in decreased inventory holding costs, increased inventory turns, and reductions in channel safety stocks.

F. DEALING WITH LOGISTICS UNCERTAINTIES

The recession of 2001–2002 and the events of 9/11 demonstrated the fragility of the concepts of JIT and SCM that had been guiding the conceptual and practical management of fulfillment functions for almost two decades. During the last few months of 2001, delays in transportation and at border crossings created too much stress on already lean inventory stocks and forced temporary shutdowns in automotive and electronics assembly plants. After years of JIT and demand-driven fulfillment, some analysts were declaring the end of JIT and fast-cycle procurement modes and the establishment of higher levels of safety stock. Manufacturers, retailers, and suppliers were being forced to reassess inventory management, sourcing, and transportation processes to guard against possible new supply chain disruptions. Apparent contradictions have only confused matters. According to Lewis Dibert, director of logistics at Red Gold Inc., "People are trying to cut inventories, but at the same time, they're trying to expand them. What is really happening is, while they're cutting inventory costs because sales are dropping, they're finding resupply is taking a lot longer."[11]

In addition to the economic and political challenges, cutbacks in technology spending, increased skepticism regarding B2B e-marketplaces, and the reluctance of most companies to automate supply chains have made many logistics managers hesitant about embarking on Internet technology initiatives. This disappointing result, according to one industry expert, has historically marked the entrance of other technologies into the logistics field. Twenty years after the rise of EDI, 72% of shippers and 38% of carriers have EDI capabilities. In the new world of Internet commerce (September 2001), only 8% of shippers and 4% of carriers are prepared for Web-based integration with their partners. Part of this reluctance can be traced to the learning curve for new integration technologies. Unfortunately, much of this reluctance can be attributed to unfounded fears about technology.[12]

While it is true that undertaking a supply chain integration project is difficult in itself without threats of trade disruptions and a soft economy, companies must be careful to avoid the following common misconceptions concerning the application of today's suite of LRM technologies.

1. *e-LRM is prohibitively expensive, must be debugged by a large in-house IS staff, and will take years before a satisfactory ROI can be achieved.* In reality, participating in e-LRM solutions requires little or no investment from trading partners. While customized private trading communities will require upfront expenses, most providers do not even charge a membership fee for participating in their trading communities. e-Logistics providers charge transaction fees when freight is tendered.

2. *e-LRM will require massive changes in the way the company has historically done business, thereby threatening operations during a period of uncertainty.* Leading-edge companies simply cannot wait. Most e-logistics providers possess technology infrastructures scalable enough to handle enormous transaction volumes, operating redundancies to respond to any emergency condition, and the agility and sophistication to manage even the most complex of supply chains.

3. *e-LRM will require massive changes to existing technology infrastructures.* In reality today's e-logistics providers can easily combine advanced technologies, such as the Internet, XML, and wireless communications, with legacy ERP and TMS solutions. Normally it is the responsibility of the logistics solution provider to provide the necessary connectivity for today's seamless supply chain.

4. *The use of nonproprietary information technologies risks a loss of control and security over sensitive company data.* Virtually all e-logistics marketplaces today are encrypted with sophisticated security technologies that provide safe transmission of sensitive data.

5. *e-Commerce requires a great deal of internal knowledge and it is hard to learn.* Any company with a computer will benefit from e-commerce. Most e-logistics suppliers provide complementary training and 24-hour help desks to support users, and even the most technology-challenged users can acquire sufficient skills to participate in an Internet-driven trading community.

6. *Using e-logistics trading communities will severely damage long-standing relationships with core logistics providers.* Logistics exchanges should be used to enhance, not replace, existing logistics relationships. Logistics managers might want to test the cost of services first on an exchange before turning to core providers. Internet-based logistics providers can also provide service to supply chain areas that have functioned independently of core carriers. Finally, e-logistics providers can add value to existing relationships by supplementing handling and automating financial settlements or special reporting functions that are beyond the competencies of existing logistics partners.

Removing these fears is going to be critical as more and more companies become more comfortable with technology. Many Web-based second-generation 3PLs are beginning to assemble a full range of Internet-enabled services that are flexible enough to meet a variety of customer systems. On-line marketplaces are also developing multiple response engines that are more sensitive to their customers' comfort with technology. Today's logistics marketplace is more and more focused on collaborative partnerships, where customer needs are identified, logistics process and readiness for e-commerce are mapped, and appropriate Web and EDI connections that accentuate logistics optimization, choice, and execution are discussed at the outset. Such an approach will go far in establishing the necessary trust and comfort and increase understanding of technology benefits.

In times of risk and uncertainty in the logistics channel, today's world-class companies turn to technology to maintain competitive momentum. For Sun Microsystems, managing logistics network risk is fundamental to survival. Components must be on hand to meet build requirements, but excess risks oversupply on parts that lose value daily. Sun's solution was to invest in a standardized, Web-based planning and procurement application that provides the ability to reduce risk and optimize the financial impact of a given demand. The system pinpoints critical shortages and possible surplus inventories, provides plans that seek profit optimization and product availability, and determines optimal supply plans that reduce risk and bring the greatest profits. The result has been an 11% reduction in buffer costs, a 14 to 18% reduction in exposure to excess supply costs, and an overall increase in the ability to cover demand and increase revenues.[13]

II. DEFINING LRM IN THE AGE OF e-BUSINESS

There can be little doubt that the advent of e-business has dramatically changed forever the nature and objectives of logistics. In the past, logistics was primarily a back-office function concerned with the day-to-day packing and shipment of products, rate calculations, transportation routing, and inventory chasing. Today, logistics has become a strategic advantage. As delivery times shrink from weeks to days or hours, fulfillment has become a hot topic and the path to survival in the growing e-business marketplace. As technology tools continue to mature, providing companies with logistics systems that can utilize positioning satellites to pinpoint truck, rail car, and shipments in transit, and accurately track transportation assets and the cargo they carry from origin to destination across the globe, competitive logistics depends on effective partnership management and real-time visibility to link all trading partners anywhere in the supply chain. Today's LRM application toolsets are providing better fill rates, lower levels of channel inventories, better on-time delivery, increased transportation asset utilization, and lower costs while improving customer demand for ever faster and cheaper order fulfillment.[14]

A. e-LRM FOUNDATIONS

The first applications of e-business to logistics were introduced in the mid-1990s. Despite the complexity of the array of possible logistics functions, the fact that logistics services were basically a commodity and could be easily adapted to the Internet made them an easy candidate for Web-based trading technologies. Although there was and continues to be much discussion over what is the proper function of e-logistics (should it provide an all-encompassing range of services, so that logistics relationships cover end-to-end management of fulfillment, or should it be focused on a cafeteria approach, where customers engage the discrete service they need), the application of the Internet to LRM has been eagerly adopted by all forms of carrier, shipper, and logistics services providers. Initially, logistics providers used the Web to detail information about the organization and company location, market their services and products, and respond to prospects regarding logistics capabilities. When the concept of exchanges arose, phase-two logistics providers focused on the buying and selling of logistics services, such as transportation. These early Internet-driven e-logistics offerings tended to be horizontal, public exchanges that provided buyers with the opportunity to post loads on a Web bulletin board; in turn logistics companies could then bid on those loads.[15]

When viewed in greater detail, these early efforts can be said to consist of two types of logistics exchange: auctions and spot markets.[16] A *logistics auction* features a single party who is soliciting logistics services from or selling logistics services to multiple parties through the Internet. Originally, it was assumed that reverse auctions, where shippers would be able to post requirements on the Web and then entertain bids from logistics providers, would provide fresh opportunity for cost reductions and increased services and dramatically change the nature of the logistics industry. The *spot market* concept seeks to broaden the number of players by increasing the auction to accommodate multiple buyers and sellers. The goal of the exchange is to match requirements and provider capabilities and possibly even to provide tools for managing the transaction or deepening the buyer-seller relationship.

Unfortunately, these first-generation public exchanges were gripped by the same centripetal forces that plagued the dot-com revolution. To begin with, many logistics providers avoided the exchanges in fear that spot market prices would be construed by buyers as constituting the base services price. Further, logistics services are not the same as commodity products. While the characteristics of commodities can be accurately determined, contracting logistics services requires more than attaining lowest price and must consider additional factors, such as transit, reliability, and availability of equipment. Also, the anonymity of the Web was quickly perceived as a detriment to historical relationships that existed between trading partners. Providers wanted to be assured that their customers would promptly pay for services and that there would be no frivolous claims. On their part, customers wanted to be assured that their providers were reputable and that their shipments would arrive on time without damage or pilferage. Finally, since so much business was already covered by logistics contracts (up to 85% of freight moved by truck and more than 90% of ocean shipments), most first-generation exchanges simply failed to generate critical mass and soon died. For companies that had already implemented EDI applications there was little incentive to migrate to the Web.

Today, e-logistics marketplaces have closely followed the experience of other areas of e-business as they migrate from independent to private exchanges and move their focus from cost economies and spot buys to developing collaborative communities. These private logistics exchanges are normally developed by a dominant or group of dominant players who have already established a clear e-LRM strategy and set of logistics partners. This existing relationship provides instant critical mass to the exchange, thereby forcing smaller trading partners in the channel to participate. But again, e-LRM PTX and CTX exchanges suffer from the same problems affecting other e-marketplaces. Numerous technical and standards issues must be worked out; while packages software exists, companies fear being trapped within the boundaries of a certain vendor; many companies are using 3PLs which have their own solutions, negating the use of independent and PTX/CTXs altogether.

By the early 2000s, the once frantic explosion in the e-logistics marketplace had dissipated, and survivors entered a period of shakeout and massive consolidation. Today, the lines separating companies competing in the e-logistics space have become blurred. Some providers offer on-line load/matching services, some e-logistics software, and others have expanded to include extensive logistics management and consulting services. According to Langley,[17] e-LRM solutions can be divided into the following five distinct categories:

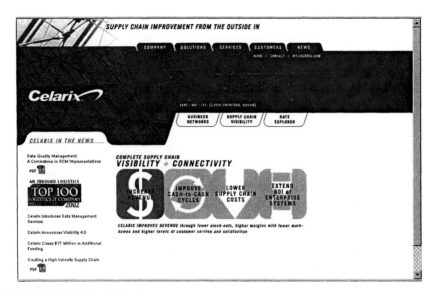

FIGURE 8.3 Celarix Web site.

- *Transportation exchanges.* This type of e-LRM provider acts as an e-marketplace where logistics providers can publicly post and match capacities with customer demands on a spot market basis. An example is NTE, which offers a variety of technology-based solutions, including ITX and PTX marketplaces, transportation management solutions, and other logistics value-added services.
- *Transportation network infrastructure.* This type of e-LRM provider offers logistics Web-based software applications and communications infrastructures for shippers, carriers, and 3PLs capable of automating global logistics transactions. For example, Celarix offers an EDI, XML, and Web-based suite of applications that address e-LRM requirements for data capture, data quality management, business process visibility, and event management (Figure 8.3).
- *Transportation management software* (TMS). This type of e-LRM provider offers server-based or Web-based software applications that enable companies to optimize bidding and load and route management, and assists in the management of contracts within the boundaries of the business. G-Log, for example, provides a fully Web-native logistics management solution that provides for global collaboration among trading partners by synchronizing physical shipment with total supply chain delivery capability, detail, real-time data capture about a shipment down to such records as line, SKU, and serial number, and real-time SCEM, which may be reviewed and acted upon in a cross-enterprise, collaborative fashion.
- *Third-party logistics provider.* This type of e-LRM provider acts as a third party offering transportation, warehousing services, shipment consolidation freight payables, reverse logistics, and other functions to clients.

Maersk Logistics, for example, offers a full array of document management, warehousing and distribution, ocean transport, air services, customs house brokerage, and miscellaneous services such as on-site management and consulting.

- *Collaborative logistics networks.* This final type of e-LRM provider enables any network member, including shippers and carriers, to connect to any other member in the selection and utilization of logistics functions. For example, Nistevo provides a modular network available to any member to respond to logistics needs. The Web site offers four modules: *connectivity,* which enables logistics service interoperability with any member regardless of data exchange standards; *event management* that provides visibility to any event occurring in the network, including off-contract purchasing, tendering, and in-transit delays, so logistics services can be managed by exception; *visibility* to logistics operations accessible by all supply chain participants; and *analysis* providing critical executive and management information containing KPIs across the entire supply chain.

While this breakdown can assist in segmenting the types of e-logistics markets, many of today's e-logistics companies have significantly expanded their services to the point that they bridge several of the above categories. Logistics.com has been increasing its footprint from its origins in Web-native, hosted solutions aimed at on-line transportation management, track and trace, and event management capabilities to encompass an integrated offering embracing complete transportation procurement, including the entire RFQ process, bid evaluation and optimization, and contract management. Once bids have been posted in its core module called *Network*, Logistics.com uses its optimization engine to package and organize lanes, and then to simulate possible scenarios for shippers and carriers. Another function, called *Lane*, enables customers to adjust existing contracts without complete renegotiation if their original logistics network needs change. When these functions are coupled with Logistics.com's TMS solution, called *OptiManage*, the company can offer critical transportation search, SCEM, and collaborative capabilities. The TMS consolidates orders into shipments, finds carriers based on an optimization guide, manages the shipments from origin to delivery, and dynamically monitors critical metrics, such as carrier compliance and events, so that proactive remedies can be taken when performance is below standard.[18]

B. ANATOMY OF e-LRM FUNCTIONS

Simply defined, e-LRM is the process whereby manufacturers, distributors, and suppliers move their products and services to their customers by utilizing the Internet. As was described above, early e-LRM providers utilized the Internet to provide basic services, such as selecting carriers, booking shipments, and tracking orders. These e-LRM functions, however, became so popular that they have, for the most part, become free value-added services from logistics providers and 3PL intermediaries. Like it has in so many areas, Web-based technologies in logistics have shifted from a focus on basic services to collaborative and supplier logistics management. The strategy is to utilize logistics functions not only to reduce costs and gain real-time visibility and control of inventory, but also to develop close-working partnerships with trading partners. For example, the Aberdeen Group sees e-LRM functions as acting in the role of a central clearinghouse of logistics data to meet a variety of other decision-making needs of the enterprise. "An LRM environment," Aberdeen says,

> "provides information on: cross-border regulatory compliance, total-landed costs that include duties, tariffs, and taxes; tracks goods movement and provides alert notification and management; supports carrier selection and negotiations; provides route and lane optimization; and full multimodal transport."[19]

In summary, e-LRM enables whole supply chains to make better decisions, trim costs and increase logistics efficiencies, and architect effective collaborative relations between all supply channel trading partners.

Despite the recent and dramatic downturn regarding all forms of e-business, Internet applications for procurement and logistics are expected to see a steady increase through at least mid-decade. The answer for the interest in Web-based tools in these areas is simple: when the Internet is applied to purchasing and logistics functions, companies can see positive, short-term gains in productivity, cost reduction, and ROI. For example, investment researcher Bear Stearns forecasts the e-LRM market to have been $42 billion in 2000, rising to $274 billion in 2004. Third-party outsourcing alone was $11 billion in 2000 and is expected to rise to $100 billion in 2004. Similar to what has occurred in the purchasing sphere, where early technology focused on short-term gains in MRO and indirect materials procurement, e-logistics functions are moving beyond a concern with the spot-buy market and are focusing on long-term logistics relations. The goal is be able to penetrate the contract logistics marketplace by offering automation and decision support tools to logistics planners.

e-LRM can be described as consisting of three major areas of Internet-assisted functions as depicted in Figure 8.4 and detailed as follows:

1. Enterprise Performance Measurement

Effective logistics management requires robust analytical solutions capable of providing planners with the capability to evaluate precisely the efficiencies and profitability of supply chain logistics processes. Critical performance metrics should enable analysis, measurement, and communication of the status of key business indicators at an operational and a strategic level. Operationally, Web-based support tools in this area should provide instant availability to information regarding the status of individual orders and shipments as well as the visibility to track individual products in real-time anywhere, at any time in the supply channel network. Strategically, all network trading partners should be provided with the ability to access in real-time the data they need to monitor the productivity of logistics functions, including an executive dashboard that tracks costs and revenues across the supply chain network.

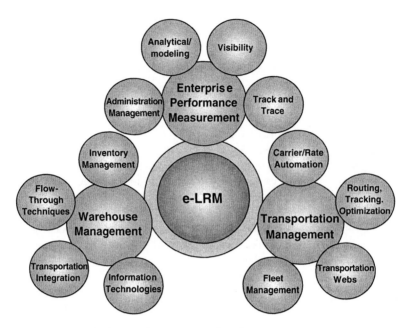

FIGURE 8.4 e-Logistics resource management functions.

Among the Web-based toolsets in this area can be found:

- *Analytical and modeling tools* providing mathematical algorithms and dynamic business modeling functions that can assist planners manage transit times, carrier selection, load matching, load optimization, routing, asset optimization and fleet management, and contract management.
- *Visibility tools* detailing inbound and outbound shipments to a company, its customers, and its trading partners. Included are windows into in-transit inventories, focused on customer service as well as sharpening the accuracy of replenishment cycles and reductions in channel-wide safety stocks. Visibility to channel resources can also assist companies in selecting the optimum location from which to fill an order based on delivery and inventory costs or other configurable business rules.
- *Track and trace tools* providing timely information regarding shipments at anytime, anywhere on the globe. Among the key functions found are:
  - Complete and real-time status and history on all shipments from booking to proof of delivery
  - Electronic transmission and access to bills of lading, shipping labels, waybills, SKU, and, other order details
  - Multimodal tracking for truck, air, ocean, or rail cartage
  - Costs and time requirements for international business
  - Web-access to shipments by pro number, bill of lading number, PO number, RMA, and other shipper reference numbers

- Availability of other shipment data such as on-line reports, document retrieval, claims status, and pickup requests.
- *Administration management tools* providing for the effective reporting and management of logistics financial functions. Among the events to view upon logistics transaction completion are proof of delivery, invoice generation, review and printing of bill of lading, freight bill review, total landed cost calculations, import/export documentation, and any necessary filing/status of loss and damage claims. By providing for Web-based applications that can assist in automating the execution of *bill of lading and delivery receipt* (POD), audit, and final payment, e-LRM provides shippers and carriers with the tools to manage fast closure of the order cycle and accelerate time to cash.

2. Warehouse Management

Warehouse management systems (WMS) provide today's logistics functions with exciting new tools to manage and optimize inventory in motion or at rest. The merger of WMSs, the Internet, and wireless technologies have permitted companies to push logistics inventory functions, such as merge in-transit, cross-docking, multicompany freight consolidation and deconsolidation, commingling of complimentary commodities, and other techniques, to the furthest limits of optimization to increase order-to-deliver cycles while decreasing overall logistics costs. With real-time visibility available through the Internet, trading partners anywhere in the supply chain possess feedback regarding live freight movement, warehouse status, and brokerage clearance information. Among today's WMS toolsets can be found *radio frequency* (RF) and bar coding, stock locator systems, integration with transportation, labor productivity and item velocity reporting, and value-added services such as packaging, kitting, and relabeling.

3. Transportation Management

The execution of world-class e-LRM functions requires flawless, accurate, and timely transportation systems that span the entire order cycle from bid to delivery. Today's Internet-integrated *transportation management systems* (TMS) provide a wide array of shipping solutions that automate and optimize provider selection, multicarrier compliance, rate quotation, routing, manifesting, tracking, cost analysis, and post-shipment analysis processes. As trading partners and logistics service providers become linked real-time into the logistics network web, companies can freely retrieve shipping, service, and contact information to identify carriers, transit times, and compliance issues such as Certificate of Origin, customs invoice, global settlement of freight payment and billing, allocating the true cost of transportation based on actual charges. They can also obtain electronic notice of consignment and statements of revised charges for change of destination of an in-transit shipment.

In addition, the inherent collaborative nature of e-LRM can serve as the foundation for the application of other shipment management applications that can be shared across logistics e-marketplaces. Among the new opportunities available for shippers and carriers is software for consolidating, cost optimizing, and collaborating on load planning. These applications can optimize orders into loads for tendering, matching loads across service providers, meeting hazmat requirements, optimizing available assets, and more effectively managing and measuring relationships and contracts. Finally, e-LRM assists carriers to optimize fleet management through interactive tools providing for dynamic routing, real-time dispatch, and wireless application integration.[20]

C. STUDIES IN e-LRM

After several years of flat growth, analysts are expecting the demand for logistics/SCM technologies to grow dramatically as the recession of 2001–2002 slowly disappears. According to AMR Research (April 2002), logistics/SCM software sales are expected to grow by 15 to 20%, and should approach the $7-billion mark. While software interest is growing, so is the rapidly expanding Web-enabled sector of transportation exchanges and private networks such as Nistevo, NTE, and LeanLogistics. The combination of internal logistics software implementation and the growing use of exchanges is producing real value for companies by reducing costs to the tune of 5 to 15%. In essence, companies have been utilizing these Web-based functions to optimize transportation operations and maximize usage of logistics assets. The following two examples illustrate the influence of today's e-LRM technologies and strategies.

1. e-LRM at Herman Miller

International office furniture giant Herman Miller has recently implemented a range of e-logistics functions in an effort to optimize its out-bound domestic shipments via private fleet and contract carriers. Part of the company's efforts is the utilization of LeanLogistics's Private Transportation Marketplace, which provides an array of hosted logistics services to its customers. Essentially, the e-marketplace enables companies to electronically tender shipments to its core carriers and provides planners with a view to carrier capacity at any time. The Web site provides the ability to make spot purchases to reduce costs while strengthening existing relationships with logistics partners. Herman Miller uses the spot marketplace as a segment of a three-pronged transportation strategy. Roundtrip cartage goes to the company's dedicated fleet. A percentage of shipment is reserved for partnership carriers. The remaining traffic is placed on LeanLogistic's private spot market, where anywhere from 10 to 25 bids, as a rule, are received. This approach has been reducing logistics costs from as much as 15% off the company's best contracted rates. In addition, Herman Miller is expecting to soon complete an interface between its internal logistics systems and its e-logistics marketplace. The goal is to eventually tender all loads, even to logistics partners, through the e-marketplace, where they will be rated. Carriers will be notified of the loads, and then will have the choice of declining or accepting. Once the load has been moved and the transaction completed, the freight bill will be paid electronically.[21]

2. NextJet.com: e-LRM in the Jet Stream

For some companies, competitive advantage requires delivery of products not during the same week or even next day, but *today*!! Established in 1999, Dallas-based NextJet Inc. brings airlines and ground transportation couriers together in a seamless process with the objective of guaranteeing same-day, door-to-door, small package delivery to any address in the U.S. Driving the business is a Web site that utilizes specially designed software that evaluates millions of potential shipment possibilities and automatically selects the most efficient routing option. The process works as follows: Shippers log onto NextJet.com and enter the zip codes of the origin and destination and packaging information such as weight, volume, contents, special shipping information, and pickup time. Within a matter of moments, the site software presents a list of rate quotations and shipping options. After an option is selected, an itinerary is generated. Next, a courier from the NextJet network will pick up the package, take it to the airport, and pass it on to the selected airlines. Once the package arrives, a courier will pick it up and deliver it to the final destination. In addition, NextJet provides proactive tracking and shipping, with the option of notification via e-mail or automated voicemail. Each time the shipment is scanned, everyone associated with the delivery is automatically notified of the progress of the delivery. Today, NextJet serves over 1,000 customers, mostly in the medical supplies, auto, electronics, and film industries. The Web site includes among its logistics partners a host of airlines, ground couriers, freight forwarders, and third-party logistics operators dedicated to using Internet tools to carve out a place in an exciting and new competitive space.[22]

III. UNDERSTANDING THE THIRD-PARTY LOGISTICS NETWORK

The requirements for logistics management in today's business environment have been dramatically accelerated by the pace of global competition and technology. Companies are currently locked in a struggle in which they must constantly search to improve their capabilities to respond to increasingly complex markets characterized by frequent new product introductions, the presence of new Internet-based sales channels, and information technologies that provide for real-time sales management, transaction control, and delivery visibility. Effectively responding to logistics challenges has driven many companies to look at outsourcing their logistics functions to logistics service companies termed *third-party logistics* (3PL) providers. Utilizing 3PLs enables firms to shrink dramatically physical logistics assets, such as delivery systems and computer technologies. Additionally, logistics outsourcing enables shippers to leverage 3PL investments in information, material handling, and operating equipment. Finally, the need to optimize the constantly shifting parameters of supply chain operations requires companies to possess a degree of agility that can only be found in logistics organizations that are totally dedicated to logistics management.

According to analysts, the use of 3PL services is increasing. In addition, while the base functions are expected to be enhanced, 3PL providers are expanding their offerings to encompass greater functionality in finance, inventory, technology, and data management. In the past, businesses often sought to utilize 3PLs to outsource noncore functions that were commoditized and could realize quick cost savings. In contrast, according to Roger Dik, a partner with Accenture, "if you look at some of the larger scale network reconfiguration taking place today, asset shifts, major organizational changes, new technologies, the creation of significantly more robust business processes around inventory visibility and reporting-outsourcing give companies the ability to very immediately transform major segments of supply-chain processes."[23] The fact of the matter is that the continuous squeeze on all elements of the supply cycle has simply pushed executives to explore 3PL services to realize added value. According to a study of 3PL value propositions, Mentzer[24] feels that companies today are looking to 3PLs to provide four key sources of logistics value.

- *Trust.* The goal of this value is to find a competent 3PL partner that can relieve the company of the task of managing the supply channel.
- *Information.* The objective of this value is to leverage the technology capabilities of 3PLs to provide logistics information accuracy, quality, and timeliness of the operations they deliver.
- *Capital Utilization.* The reduction of fixed assets in the form of physical plant and equipment is a major source of 3PL value. Less fixed expense can expect to be returned in the form of better working capital.
- *Expense Control.* The overall reduction of logistics channel costs is by far the primary objective of using a 3PL provider. Increase in customer service combined with lower logistics costs is seen by savvy CEOs as a critical path to survival.

A. ROLE OF THE 3PL

Outsourced logistics functions have always been part of the landscape of business. Continuously searching to reduce costs, improve inventory throughput, and realize competitive customer service, companies have traditionally used 3PLs to provide a wide variety of transportation and logistics functions beyond the immediate capability of the business. Among these core services can be found motor cartage, transportation leasing, warehouse operations, small package delivery, air freight, air freight forwarding, customs and export management, ocean freight, brokerage, and manufacturing. In addition to these core functions, the needs of the marketplace fueled by the explosion in technology tools, such as the Internet, have enabled today's top 3PLs to expand their offerings to embrace a variety of advanced services. These additional services include:[25]

- Direct transportation services
- Rotating on-site representatives
- Track and trace
- Warehouse management
- Shipment consolidation
- Rate negotiation/carrier selection
- Freight payables

- Relabling/repackaging
- Reverse logistics
- Order fulfillment
- Border control
- Compliance consulting
- Information technology

The addition of these and other services have driven many 3PLs to architect new strategies that are reshaping the type of markets they serve, the operation and technology skill sets required, the investments made, the ROI expected, and the types of partnerships established. While the number of possible permutations is large, today's *logistics service providers* (LSP) can be separated into two camps. On the one side can be found LSPs that are focused on offering a limited selection of cost-driven, standardized services through an owned network of transportation and warehouse functions. They provide value to their customers by leveraging their logistics assets to cut SCM costs, managing nonasset cost factors, and architecting process innovation. The overall goal is to attract customers by making their SCM network linkages global and their services ubiquitous. Because they face severe competition due to the commodity nature of their service offerings, these LSP normally are constantly on the lookout for opportunities to apply technologies and assets to enhance core service packages and seize upon new forms of business activities, such as B2B and wireless devices, as they reach critical mass.[26]

In the other camp stands a much more aggressive type of LSP that seek to manage their customers' logistics needs from end to end. Termed *fourth-party logistics* (4PL) or *lead logistics providers* (LLP), LSPs in this category can be defined as supply chain integrators whose strategy is to assemble and manage dynamic organizations composed of a wide range of resources, capabilities, and technologies, either within the organization or in partnership with complementary LSPs, to deliver a comprehensive, customized logistics solution to the customer through a central point of contact. The goal of the LLP is to manage all aspects of the logistics relationship, beginning with the *strategic definition* focused on applying technology and new management concepts to drive reinvention and transformation of the logistics effort, proceeding through *implementation* of business process realignment and systems integration, and concluding with the ongoing *execution* of operational functions associated with daily transportation and warehouse transactions.[27] In summary, an LLP provides a centralized point of contact for the customer with total responsibility for supply chain performance. Most 3PL arrangements fail to deliver benefits beyond one-time operating cost reductions and asset transfers: LLP's, on the other hand, are dedicated to long-term strategic logistics management and continuous growth in revenues and reductions in operating cost and fixed and working capital.

B. Internet-Driven LSPs

Today's LSP, whether a narrowly focused service provider or a full LLP, has been increasingly assuming the responsibilities for inventory ownership and carrying costs, transportation assets, financial functions, and even component testing and

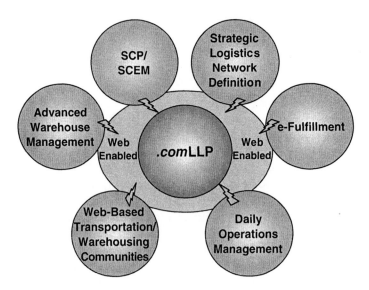

FIGURE 8.5 *.com*LLP functions.

inspection. As technology capabilities have grown, LSPs have also found themselves shouldering the cost for managing information capabilities. Many companies simply do not have the financial and people resources to hook up to today's fast-paced technology tools and are increasingly looking to their LSPs to provide the expertise to collect and scrub data and drive it directly into their backbone systems, perform e-commerce functions, provide proactive exception management, and enable participation in the Web-driven supply chain. APL Logistics, for example, provides not only core logistics services, but also advanced technology capabilities to its customers. APL, in fact, has an entire division devoted to developing and integrating the latest in proprietary and industry-standard supply chain technologies for product visibility, exception management, execution systems optimizing shipping and warehouse decisions, Web-based decision tools, and performance reporting. Customers have the capability to then turn up or phase down their use of these services, depending upon ongoing needs and level of internal expertise.

Earlier in this chapter, it was stated that a variety of LRM services, from inventory tracking and route optimization to carrier selection and freight bill management, were now Internet-driven. This growth in Web-based LRM services caused a couple of logistics experts to dub these LSPs *.com*LLPs.[28] The purpose of the description is to convey the critical competitive advantage available to customers from LLPs who have deep Internet capabilities (Figure 8.5). For example, Ryder Logistics utilizes a logistics exchange called Freight Matrix that offers shippers, carriers, and other LSPs a logistics solutions hub to buy and sell transportation, plan cargo requirements, and execute shipment delivery. On its part, the exchange enhances Ryder's ability to access global networked supply solutions, thereby enabling it to maintain its lead as the top LLP provider for Global 1000 companies.

In detail, dot-comLLPs have the ability to provide their customers the following additional information-based services:

- *Comprehensive solutions.* Without a doubt, perhaps the greatest advantage of a *.com*LLP is to use technology to reverse the increased propensity for logistics fragmentation as products make their way through the supply channel. *.com*LLPs possess the capability to offer customers a centralized, comprehensive logistics management point that can facilitate the merger of a community of functional logistics providers with the enabling power of a customized, client-optimized, uniform technology strategy. Such a technology-based solution has the capability of leveraging networking tools like the Internet to drive the synchronization of real-time logistics planning and execution across trading partners while increasing ever-widening collaborative cooperation.

- *Improved information flows.* The Internet provides LSPs with applications that enable real-time visibility to shipments anywhere, at anytime in the supply chain. In addition, Web-based workflow tools render the transfer of information, such as freight tenders and bookings, a simple process. Also, by significantly accelerating the flow of shipping information and providing electronic funds transfer capabilities, the payment cycle can be considerably shortened.

- *Enhanced fulfillment capabilities.* Even today's best companies are being faced with steep challenges when it comes to SCM fulfillment, and particularly fulfillment that is Internet driven. Historically, most companies have developed logistics practices and infrastructure geared to handle the bulk storage and movement of products through the supply network. Increasingly, customers are requiring order picking and fulfillment in smaller, more frequently delivered lot sizes and are turning to their LLPs for the answer. Responding to these fulfillment needs will require nimble LLPs, equipped with both the necessary infrastructure and access to Web-based logistics communities, that can make delivery of any order size at anytime a reality.

- *Supply chain inventory management.* Computerized SCM applications provide *.com*LLPs with a range of inventory throughput tools that seek to replace, when possible, information with inventories, enable nimble response to customer requirements, and reduce cycle times everywhere in the supply channel. Among these computerized functions can be found cross-docking, merge-in-transit, remote postponement, delayed allocation of orders to the latest possible moment before shipment, and the commingling of loads from multiple service providers in order to maximize shipment, provide pricing advantages to shippers, and remove waste from the fulfillment process.

C. Today's LSP Marketplace Challenges

The use of LSPs, like other business partnerships, has many challenges. On the one side, the need for outsourced logistics services has grown steeply over the years. According to Delaney,[29] during the past 20 years the U.S. market for LSP services has grown from $2 billion to $56 billion in 2001. It is expected that LSP providers will continue to grow yearly in the range of 15 to 20%. On the other hand, LSPs are subject to the same problems that plague other business partnerships. By its very nature, outsourcing requires two often very different organizations to find common ground on business terms, accounting information, operating philosophies, and technologies. While the goal is to construct a long-term relationship, often there are important changes in priorities, levels of urgency, and strategic direction. A lack of agreement on fundamentals, such as requirements and expectations, can serve to slowly erode even the best agreement. Finally, companies regularly cannot resist the opportunity to weigh the promise of exciting new technological, financial, and service enhancements of a new LSP against existing, less-capable LRM partnerships.

Dealing with these and other issues requires a special level of care in developing logistics outsourcing. Increasing use of logistics outsourcing requires that companies follow the following benchmarks before launching into a LSP relationship.[30]

- *Partnership flexibility.* The only thing known for sure about a logistics partnership is that the circumstances driving its inception will change through time. While a structured contract is essential for an effective outsourcing arrangement, logistics partners must provide for contract flexibility to account for service changes due to new technologies, remapping of the supply channel, new products, new competitors, change of management, and other issues. Open dialogue is critical in ensuring both parties have commonly accepted definitions and terms, detailed performance measurements, and a methodology to adjust logistics functions and expectations to meet current realities. Also, periodic review and affirmation of partnership objectives and measurements used to validate them must occur if the arrangement is to be evolutionary and not stagnant.
- *Defined cost of services.* In spite of the best-constructed contract, rarely are all the details governing cost and scope of services fully defined. Timeliness, accuracy, thoroughness, and level of service detail can often vary widely from agreed-upon contracted standards. Further, although the contract is designed to handle most of the services required, even small deviations and exceptions can stress a relationship. An effective method to cope with these issues is to plan for high, medium, and low costs in the contract. Consistently enforcing the low cost solution will unsettle even the best relationship.
- *Solving the human side of outsourcing.* The introduction of a LSP into the supply chain equation requires the effective education and concurrence of the people side of an organization. Outsourcing what were once internal functions to an outsider can cause friction and uneasiness among affected employees. Managers, supervisors, and staff should be an integral part of the review and transition process. Their feedback and support will enable them to be integrated into the new environment.
- *Realistic expectations.* Perhaps the most serious detriment to a relationship is the establishment of false expectations. Customers often overinflate expected savings and assumptions about the effectiveness of outsourced processes. On their part, LSPs can over promise benefits and services. In

reality, both parties must work closely together to establish realistic expectations and then structure a program to guide continuous improvement through time. From the beginning and throughout the life of the relationship, both parties must be prepared to work through practical examples, step-by-step, testing baseline and every possible type of exception process to remove false expectations and uncover measurable benefits.

- *Technology misunderstandings.* All too often customers and LSPs exaggerate their technologies capabilities and downplay what technology expertise is required of each other. Solving this problem requires both parties to come to the table with realistic technology statements of their capabilities. This analysis will then provide the relationship with a base from which to initiate technology improvements that enhance the partnership and drive new benefits.
- *Partnership commitment.* Before any negotiations can really begin, it is essential to secure the firm commitment of top and middle management to the proposed outsourced arrangement. The executive team must be apprised of their role as leaders and supporters in the ongoing management of the relationship, both from a change management and from an expanding collaborative partnership perspective.
- *Retain core skills.* Companies seeking outsourced logistics functions must be vigilant to ensure that critical skills and processes are not contracted away. A fine line must be preserved when outsourcing the expense, which retains the skill set to be able to reevaluate the arrangement, recapture the outsourced function, or rethink the entire outsourced strategy. Using a LSP service provider requires companies to thoroughly understand the process and to base their decisions on the cost of the investment and the likelihood of success.

IV. CHOOSING AND IMPLEMENTING AN LSP SOLUTION

There can be little doubt that the trend to outsource logistics functions will only continue to increase for the foreseeable future. In today's high-speed, integrated, and lean supply chains, companies are more than ever obliged to eliminate logistics bottlenecks that can bring even the best-run channel network to its knees and dramatically escalate costs. According to an A.T. Kearney study (April 2002), a sampling of 18 large companies revealed that LRM outsourcing could generate average cost savings of over 16%. Even more important than the direct cost reductions was the recognized performance improvements that could be realized when the management of logistics solution design and day-to-day logistics operations were turned over to world-class LSP partners.[31] When architecting an effective logistics outsourcing strategy, companies must be careful to align their overall business strategies with the logistics strategy it is designed to support. In this final section, the process of strategic logistics design will be discussed. The goal is to provide a broad roadmap to assist today's executive to execute a workable logistics outsourcing plan that not only meets today's competitive challenges but is capable of evolving to meet the needs of tomorrow's marketplace.

A. LSP Business Models

The trend toward outsourcing noncore competencies has become a widely accepted strategy for most industries today. The outsourcing of functions such as IT, human resources, warehousing, customer service, and others, has become commonplace as companies divest themselves of nonessential functions. Overall, such strategies realize two main goals. To begin with, outsourcing permits businesses to shed costly functions that are actually beyond the normal skill sets and traditional hard asset investments that are at the heart of the company. Secondly, by outsourcing these functions to third-party experts, firms can take advantage of world-class resources and processes without developing them in-house. However, while the idea of logistics outsourcing seems simple enough, companies need to perform their due diligence in deciding exactly what to outsource and with whom. To date, more than 100 Internet-based LSPs have failed, and many are facing consolidation in the short term ahead. But even traditional "hard asset" logistics firms are today becoming indistinguishable from the pure dot-coms: Schneider Logistics and Meno Logistics market their own ASP–based software solutions; UPS offers LLP–type consulting.

In tackling the construction of a logistics outsourcing strategy, it might be helpful to start by describing the array of possible LSP arrangements that are available. Possible strategies span a wide range of LRM operations models. A summary of each is as follows:

- *Traditional Logistics Model.* On the low end of the spectrum of LRM strategies can be found the traditional model, where internal company functions totally control logistics resources. Supply chain functions are determined solely by the company. If any LSP activities do occur, these would be for one-time spot buys to solve a temporary weakness in internal capabilities.
- *Classic 3PL Model.* The next outsourcing model seeks to develop a LSP partnership to service logistics functions that are on the periphery or are poorly performed by the internal logistics group. An example would be using an LSP to handle international distribution functions that are beyond the core competencies of the business. The use of spot buys for warehouse and transportations services dominate this model. For the most part, control of strategic logistics functions and design and execution of supply chain strategies is retained by the company.
- *Partial LLP Model.* In contrast to the first two models, which are focused strictly on operational objectives associated with cost and immediate performance, the LSP model at this level is characterized by a partial surrender of logistics control. While the shipper still acts in the role of logistics integrator and retains control of channel design, LLPs are given responsibility for managing entire portions of the supply chain. Normally, the shipper plays an active part in assisting the LLP to assemble the LSP

team, is responsible for enforcing LSP adherence to the channel strategy, and oversees operational logistics function execution.

- *Full LLP Model.* In the last LSP model, the shipper selects a LLP, who assumes full responsibility for logistics management. While the shipper is still an active partner in the architecting and maintenance of both the logistics strategy and the LRM community of providers, full responsibility for the total logistics solution is given to the LLP. The LLP assumes ownership for channel design, 3PL partner selection, and detail operations execution.

Whether a single or a portfolio-approach, logistics outsourcing, like any business decision, must take into consideration current and future needs. When beginning strategy formulation, companies must first step back and objectively understand the LSP environment, the role of technology, and their own supply chain logistics requirements. To begin with, companies must clearly articulate what types of opportunities can be realized by exploiting the merger of technology and operational excellence made possible by an LSP partnership. Among critical questions requiring answers can be found the following. What is the nature of the firm's current technical environment, asset and people-wise, to pursue targeted technologies? What types of logistics networks are envisioned, and how will they support competitive advantage? How customizable are LSP technology-driven services? Can the business take the lead in developing a collaborative logistics community, or is that task to be surrendered to a LLP?

Secondly, companies need to integrate new forms of relationships and services into their logistics solution. Today's Internet-based LRM solutions are taxing to the breaking point traditional logistics partnerships, calling upon companies to often architect dramatically new business relationships requiring fundamental process and cultural changes. The *relationship* portion of e-LRM means that logistics strategists must thoroughly understand what their core competencies are before an outsourcing strategy is executed. They must search for new dimensions of collaboration with their LSPs, ensure that contracts promote a win-win attitude, and construct an outsourcing strategy that promotes the productivity, not only of the company, but also of the entire supply chain. In the final analysis, it is not the technology, but rather the ability to create new forms of logistics relationship, that is the main driver of fulfillment competitive advantage.

Finally, companies must thoroughly understand the wide spectrum of LSP capabilities that are available when drafting a LRM strategy. In the past, 3PLs provided spot-buy services such as emergency shipping, freight forwarding, and small parcel delivery. Today's LSP provides a dramatically wider range of services to meet the needs of an Internet-driven fulfillment environment. Logistics planners can tap into e-marketplaces to search for services, settle a price, or match other buyers and sellers. Ivex Packaging Corp., Lincolnshire, Il, for example, launched a program to cut 15% from the company's $40 million logistics cost by using a collaborative logistics platform from Nistevo Corp. to partner with General Mills Inc. to fill trucks, share routes, and split the savings. Making these strategies work requires the type of real-time visibility, optimization, and planning that is only available through Web-enabled applications. In the last analysis, the choice of a LSP strategy again comes back to not only individual company fulfillment execution and scheduling, but also the optimization of these functions across extended, multipartner supply chains.

B. STEPS IN LRM STRATEGY DEVELOPMENT

Building a successful long-term LRM strategy requires considering the options available from two separate but interlinked perspectives. The process should begin first with the development of an effective internal analysis targeted at understanding the true logistics needs of the organization and gaining the support of company members. Once completed, the next step is to research the critical criteria necessary to guide logistics management in choosing the best LSP partners. Merging both sets of activities should provide a company with the right information to make and continue to make the right decisions concerning their LRM outsourcing strategy.

The internal aspects of a LRM project should consist of the following steps.

1. Logistics Analysis

Common to all outsourcing initiatives, the formulation of a logistics outsourcing strategy should begin with an analysis of the tradeoffs between using in-house logistics functions and the benefits of outsourcing them to a LSP. There are two parts to this analysis. To begin with, planners must determine how much of the day-to-day logistics functions should be outsourced and what methods are to be used in securing LSP services. Should traditional arrangements with LSPs be pursued, or should Internet solutions be employed as the basis for services selection? Secondly, firms must decide on how much of the logistics solution and supply chain design is to be surrendered to a LLP. This is a potentially dangerous area, where entrusting the total management of supply and fulfillment functions to the wrong LLP could spell disaster.

2. Support for the Customer Strategy

When performing the analysis of internal logistics strengths and weaknesses, companies must be careful to consider their marketplace cost and service strategies. The LRM strategy implemented must exploit the best combination of in-house and LSP logistics capabilities to realize competitive advantage targets. A number of critical questions come to mind: What new logistics functions will further cement customer loyalty and gain new customers? How deeply can the LRM strategy be integrated into the customer chain, and how extensive will be their collaboration?

3. Select a Technology Solution

Logistics technologies are evolving rapidly and are becoming increasingly more sophisticated. Companies can take advantage of these tools by either acquiring the expertise or by partnering with a provider who has built the capability. Today, there are many ERP, supply chain management, and B2B vendors who can provide companies with the ability to connect to Web-driven bulletin boards, portals, public exchanges, and auction sites or to implement their own private exchange or collaborative community. Whatever the path chosen, companies must be careful to select a technology solution that permits them to retain control of logistics information, while permitting them the freedom to switch applications and providers to leverage best-of-breed capabilities.

4. Gain Company Buy-In

Similar to any strategic project, logistics planners must be careful to gain the support of three critical groups. To begin with, a senior executive must sign on as the project's advocate on the top management team. This project champion should be a force in the organization, be a supporter of e-business tools, and be prepared to negate any internal resistance to change. The second group is the internal logistics team. Education and training for this group will be necessary to assist them to embrace the change positively as well as have the skills to run the new solution. The final group is the company's IT staff. It will be the responsibility of IT to assist in system integration and leveraging the LSP's technologies and capabilities. All must understand that the LRM outsourcing strategy is a path to improving existing infrastructure to be more competitive.

5. Start Small

Consultants and practitioners alike stress the need to build creditability by beginning the LRM outsourcing project by achieving some short-term wins. Achieving, for example, cost reductions by using the e-LRM functionality to manage an already successful transportation lane or for a particular division could help build company confidence. Once achieved, additional functionality can be phased in over time to tackle wider areas of operational efficiency or improved service qualities.

6. Performance Measurements

Finally, no logistics strategic effort should be undertaken without charting expected performance measurements. Metrics should enable strategists to determine what benefits are actually being achieved for the expenditure, how well technologies and LSPs are fueling advances in competitive advantage, and how closely results are matching customer expectations.

Searching for LSP partners constitutes the second part of LRM strategy development and are concerned with the following points:

7. Strength of the LSP

When searching for a logistics partner, companies should begin by investigating LSP financial strengths, availability of physical assets, investment in technology, capability of infrastructure, and historical commitment to providing logistics services. The goal of this step is to validate LSP partner long-term viability and capability to handle normal as well as increased volumes. During the exploration, the expertise and experience of the proposed LSP's management team should also be reviewed.

The advice is to shy away from virtual dot-com LSPs whose management staffs have weak logistics core competencies.

8. Select a Compatible Technology Solution

Logistics technologies are evolving rapidly and are becoming increasingly more sophisticated. Companies can take advantage of these tools by either acquiring the expertise or by partnering with a provider who has built the capability. Choosing the latter permits businesses to acquire the benefit of the technology investment without sacrificing their own capital assets. When selecting a partner, it is critical to confirm that perspective LSPs possess the necessary technology resources to continuously scale, develop, and implement Internet solutions, as strategies change, without endangering customer service.

9. Controlling Information

The LRM solution selected must enable companies to maintain control over critical logistics channel information flows. Without close control, a company's ability to respond effectively to change can limit its agility to respond to circumstances and the timely choice of alternative options that can result in increased costs and reduced responsiveness. The abundance of software choices and Internet-capable LSPs make it possible to architect a solution that will provide just the right amount of flexibility, automation, and collaboration.

10. Services and Capabilities

On the services side, LSP partners should be able to provide a competitive level of volume discounting. Choosing a provider with significant buying power in the logistics marketplace will enable them to provide the desired level of service at the lowest price. In addition to discounting, the LSP should provide other value-added services ranging from parcel carrier partnerships, automated materials handling and fleet management, and sorting and labeling to sophisticated e-fulfillment functions such as carrier analysis, network load building, and electronic payment, auditing, and claims management.

11. Customer Success

The best LSPs come to the table with a history of success. Proper due diligence requires a review of references and their success stories. Existing clients will provide valuable insight into actual provider capabilities, whether they are increasing services use, and the direction in which they see the LSP moving.

V. SUMMARY AND TRANSITION

The evolution of the concept of SCM and the application of the Internet to business has elevated logistics to a position of critical importance in today's marketplace. The mission of SCM is to activate the visioning and productive capabilities of extended communities of businesses to produce collaborative networks whereby products and services can be designed, produced, and distributed in as cost-effective and timely a manner as possible. Realizing the possibilities of strategic SCM requires the existence of logistics operations that are aligned and structured to meet the quick response needs of high-velocity supply chains. While it is the role of engineering, marketing, production, and sales to respond to the changes of business in the twenty-first century, it is logistics that will be responsible for building the channels where the cycle of innovation, design, production, distribution, and eventual obsolescence and return of materials will be played out.

Responding to the expansion of the role of logistics in today's Internet environment requires conceiving of it as more than just storing and moving products up and down the supply channel: logistics has become a strategic function. As such, the old term of logistics needs to give way to a new term — *logistics resource management* (LRM). Similar to the recent transformation of customer service and purchasing functions into CRM and SRM, the use of the term LRM is meant to convey a similar expansion of traditional logistics activities to encompass the multifaceted concept of supply chain management with its focus on trading partner collaboration, the removal of channel barriers causing excess costs and cycle times, the espousal of Internet technologies that facilitate information, transaction data collection, and flow through the supply pipeline, and the creation of agile, responsive organizations linked together in a single-minded pursuit of superior customer service. In detail, LRM provides channel management strategists with the following five key capabilities: logistics performance management, fulfillment and execution, logistics partnership management, shipment visibility, and event fulfillment management.

While the strategic side of LRM is propelling it into the mainstream of the current trends toward collaboration and Internet-based partnerships, the fact that logistics services are basically a commodity made it an early and easy candidate for Web-based trading technologies. From the beginning, LRM could be seen from two perspectives. Companies could utilize e-logistics to provide an all-encompassing range of services from carrier search, to rate negotiation, to emergency services selected by logistics managers based on a cafeteria approach. On the other hand, companies could utilize their service partners to provide an all-encompassing range of services where all aspects of the logistics channel, including strategy development, technology, and operations, would be handled by a lead logistics provider or LLP. In any case, the range of today's LRM solutions span the following five possible categories: independent *transportation exchanges* designed to match shippers and providers; *transportation network infrastructures* providing hosted Web-based applications to shippers and carriers; *transportation management software* vendors providing Web-enabled logistics software solutions; *3PLs* offering transportation and warehousing services to clients; and *collaborative logistics networks* using Web-based tools to enable communities of shippers and buyers to connect with each other and trade logistics functions.

As the importance of logistics has expanded in today's business climate, so has the propensity of businesses to outsource logistics functions. Historically, companies have always looked to third-party logistics partners to provide warehousing and transportation functions that were beyond internal capabilities. 3PLs enabled companies to spot buy services, shrink internal expenditures on company physical assets and technologies, and remain agile to meet changes in the logistics environment. The advent of e-commerce and acceleration in all aspects of business cycle times have engendered a new form of outsourcing partner: the lead logistics provider. The goal of the LLP is to manage all aspects of the logistics relationship, beginning with the *strategic definition* focused on applying technology and new management concepts to drive reinvention and transformation of the logistics effort, proceeding through *implementation* of business process realignment and systems integration, and concluding with the ongoing *execution* of operational functions associated with daily transportation and warehouse transactions.

Drafting a strategy to leverage the various categories of LRM and the various forms of service provider requires companies to take very seriously their search for effective logistics partners and type of technologies to be used. Companies can pursue LRM models than can span a variety of structures, ranging from the tradition model where internal functions manage all aspects of logistics, to models that are marked by a progressive surrender of control of operational functions, channel design, and, ultimately, logistics strategy development. Successful selection of the right strategy requires the creation of a continuous process of internal organizational preparation and strategic alignment and a ceaseless attention to the ever-changing capabilities of logistics service providers in the search for new avenues of competitive advantage.

The presence of enabling technologies not only stands as the basis for the dramatic changes impacting the field of logistics, but also has served as the central vehicle for the progress of today's business environment. Each chapter of this book has explored how information technology, and particularly the Internet, has reshaped almost every business function from sales and service, to new product development and procurement. In the final chapter in this book, the elements of today's technology environment will be explored.

ENDNOTES

1. Delaney, Robert V., "Third Party Logistics: Confessions and Observations," Cass Information Systems, November 14, 2001, 2.
2. See the comments in Ross, David F., *Competing Through Supply Chain Management: Creating Market-Winning Strategies Through Supply Chain Partnerships*, New York, Chapman & Hall, 1998, 24–25.
3. Hebert, Lisa, "The Logistics Footprint: Creating a Road Map to Excellence," in *Achieving Supply Chain Excellence Through Technology*, 4, Mulani, Narendra, ed., Montgomery Research, San Francisco, CA, 2002, 148–151.
4. These five capabilities of LRM have been identified in *Ibid.*
5. Poirier, Charles C. and Bauer, Michael J., *E-Supply Chain: Using the Internet to Revolutionize Your Business,* Berrett-Koehler, San Francisco, 2000, 135–136.
6. Hintlian, James T. and Churchman, Phil, "Integrated Fulfillment: Bring Together the Vision and the Reality," *Supply Chain Management Review Global Supplement,* 5, 1, 2001, 17–18.

7. The company examples were found in Murphy, Jean V., "Seeing Inventory in Real Time Lets You Have and Have Not," *Global Logistics and Supply Chain Strategies*, 6, 5, 2002, 34–40.

8. Dilger, Karen Abramic, "Warning Signals," *Manufacturing Systems*, 19, 1, 2001, 63–70.

9. Hoffman, Kurt C., "Performance Data Provides Key to Continuous Improvement," *Global Logistics and Supply Chain Strategies*, 6, 5, 2002, 48–53.

10. LePree, Joy, "Take the Right Path," *Manufacturing Systems*, 20, 1, 2002, 52–55.

11. Aichlmayr, Mary, "The Future of JIT — Time Will Tell," *Transportation and Distribution*, 42, 12, 2001, 18–23.

12. Davidson, James K., "Debunking the Myths of Electronic Supply-Chain Integration," *Global logistics and Supply Chain Strategies*, 5, 9, 2001, 59–60.

13. The Sun Microsystems story can be found in Aichlmayr.

14. For more on these opening thoughts on the importance of logistics in today's e-marketplace reference Poirier and Bauer, 136–138.

15. For a summary of the origins of e-LRM see Enslow, Beth, "The Virtual Logistics Department: Next Generation Logistics Exchanges," in *Achieving Supply Chain Excellence Through Technology*, 3, Anderson, David L., ed., Montgomery Research, San Francisco, CA, 2001, 278–281.

16. See the analysis in Prince, Theodore, "Transportation E-Commerce: Pressing Toward Portals," in *Achieving Supply Chain Excellence Through Technology*, 4, Mulani, Narendra, ed., Montgomery Research, San Francisco, CA, 2002, 184–187.

17. Langley, John C., "Analyzing Internet Logistics Markets," *Supply Chain e-Business*, 2, 5, 2001, 22–26.

18. Foster, Thomas A., "OptiBid 3.0 Offers Transportation Procurement and Collaboration," *Supply Chain e-Business*, 3, 3, 2002, 26–27. See also the Logistics.com Web site.

19. Editors, "New Logistics Solutions Focus on Data as Much as Freight," *Supply Chain e-Business*, 3, 1, 2002, 6.

20. Enslow, Beth and O'Reilly, Joseph, "Building the Perfect Load," *Inbound Logistics*, 22, 4, 2002, 46–50.

21. This story is found in Harps, Leslie Hansen, "Logistics IT: Turning Up the Heat," *Inbound Logistics*, 22, 4, 2002, 32–43.

22. Hyland, Tricia, "Same-day Shipping Company Takes Off," *Transportation and Distribution*, 42, 5, 2001, 2- 6. See also the details at NextJet.com.

23. Hoffman, Kurt C., "Clout of 3PLs Grows as Their Services Increase," *Global Logistics and Supply Chain Strategies*, 6, 4, 2002, 54–59.

24. Found in Sutherland, Joel and Speh, Thomas W., "Using 3PL Service Providers to Create and Deliver Significant Supply Chain Value," in *Achieving Supply Chain Excellence Through Technology*, 4, Mulani, Narendra, ed., Montgomery Research, San Francisco, CA, 2002, 176–178.

25. See Kuglin, Fred A. and Rosenbaum, Barbara A., *The Supply Chain Network @ Internet Speed: Preparing Your Company for the E-Commerce Revolution*, AMACOM, New York, 2001, 129 and Schryver, Rob, "The Trade Tsunami: Traditional 3PLs Expand Roles," *Inbound Logistics*, 21, 9, 2001, 71–76.

26. For more on this type of LSP see Kopczak, Laura Rock, "Trends in Third Party Logistics," in *Achieving Supply Chain Excellence Through Technology*, 1, Anderson, David L., ed., Montgomery Research, San Francisco, CA, 1999, 268–272.

27. See the methodology in Bade, Douglas, Mueller, James, and Youd, Bryan, "Technology in the Next Level of Supply Chain Outsourcing — Leveraging the Capabilities of Fourth Party Logistics," in *Achieving Supply Chain Excellence Through Technology*, 1, Anderson, David L., ed., Montgomery Research, San Francisco, CA, 1999, 260–263.

28. Kuglin and Rosenbaum, 138.

29. Delaney.

30. These points have been summarized from Sabath, Robert E., "Getting Outsourcing to Work in the Supply Chain," in *Achieving Supply Chain Excellence Through Technology*, 1, Anderson, David, ed., Montgomery Research, San Francisco, CA, 1999, 276–280.

31. Garber, Randy and Gould, Stephen, "Your Supply Strategy Means Sink or Swim," *CLO*, April, 2002, 10.

9 Architecting the e-SCM Environment: Organizational and Technical Requirements for e-SCM Success

Over the past several years, much debate has raged over the role and efficacy of *information technology* (IT) in the conduct of business management. Computers have enabled significant productivities by automating business functions, eliminating errors in the performance of routine tasks, and empowering communities of knowledge workers to create radically new products, services, and whole new businesses. Still, there is and has always been an open discussion as to just how important IT really is to our continuous march toward progress. Three groups can be said to have emerged. One segment, the optimists, portray IT tools as driving unparalleled advances in productivity that can only be expected to grow exponentially through time. The most radical members of this group consider the advent of e-business as heralding a new age where the tired paradigms of the twentieth century industrial economy are swept away by the relentless spinning out of a dialectic of existing business architectures and the possibilities posed by a ceaselessly expanding technology-driven environment.

In the middle stand the agnostics who, while acknowledging the impact IT has had on the collective efficiency and productivity of business in general, are, nevertheless, skeptical of the extravagant claims made by the true believers. While they are clearly excited about the possibilities of new IT tools like the Internet, their enthusiasm is dampened by realities of businesses struggling on a day-to-day basis just to use basic IT tools. Instead of the promised integration and collaboration, all they find is silo management styles, software applications poorly adapted to business processes, and powerful centrifugal forces found in corporate cultures that continuously, sometimes unconsciously, move to deconstruct both the mechanics and the logic of their business solutions.

On the far end stand the pragmatists who consider the entire "Information Age" as drastically overblown, overhyped, and out-of-touch with the realities of the ability of most businesses to apply much of today's technology and the capability of the technologies themselves to deliver on the promised rewards. As proof, they point to the decades-old complaint that companies have not received any real return on investment for the MRP II and enterprise resource planning (ERP) systems on which they have expended so much capital and manpower. The abysmal collapse of the dot-coms and B2B craze has simply added to the skepticism. The trauma of 9/11, a stubborn recession beginning in 2001, the obnoxious greed, blatant arrogance, and failure of stewardship of executives at Enron, WorldCom, Arthur Andersen, and Xerox, the arrogance of Wall Street stock analysts, and international unrest have only added to the strength of this position. Overall, spending on IT in 2001 fell for the first time in a decade and is expected to erode further in 2002. While companies still intend to spend money on IT in the period ahead, they will be scrutinizing expected ROI as never before. "Show me the money!" in contrast to dreams of world-wide webs of buyers and sellers is what companies are asking of their IT vendors as business moves into the post-dot-com era.

This final chapter is focused on finding a cohesive strategy linking these three apparent centrifugal forces. The stagnant economic environment of 2001–2002 have found advocates of a "back to basics" and "wait to next year" approach gaining ground as discussion relating to e-business falls to a faint whisper. Still, academics, consultants, and analysts are cautioning companies to continue their search for and implementation of e-SCM technologies. While a period of scaling back of IT efforts was inevitable, businesses must be cautious not to loose ground in the fight for competitive advantage. In fact, in weak economic times it is imperative that companies be more aggressive, and not less, in the search to build capabilities that increase customer service, cement customer loyalties, and enhance market share. According to Mulani and Lee,[1]

> In hard times, the strong lay claim to new territory and prey upon weaker competitors — they move forward, not backward. In the business world, great companies take advantage of a challenging economic environment by increasing customer intimacy, improving product quality, decreasing time-to-market, identifying and offering more value-added services, and reducing overall costs. They also focus on solutions that are critical to their long-term customer strategy and operating model — not just short-term fallback positions with only stand-alone merit.

Such a challenge is a risky one indeed. Many companies find themselves pressed just to survive with much of the basics still not in place. According to a survey conducted by *Supply Chain Systems Magazine*[2] published at the beginning of 2002, one out of every four respondents will be purchasing their first bar code label package and roughly one out of every five said they need to install a warehouse management, inventory control, advanced planning and scheduling (APS), or e-commerce system for the first time. Many are still floundering with implementing existing ERP and SCM software acquired in 2000, and the decaying economy and shrinking work-forces appear to have given all but the most aggressive an excuse to put all technology projects on hold. More than half of the respondents reported decreasing budgetary and staffing resources for supply chain technology initiatives. While the priorities given reflect the uncertain political and economic environment of the times the survey was conducted (the last week of October 2001), by mid-year 2002 it appeared that the overall reluctance of companies to spend on technology had deepened and not lessened. The survey indicated that almost two-thirds of the respondents ranked "preserve cash" as the most important supply chain priority behind better planning and collaboration tools and planning for feared terrorist-related supply chain disruptions.

While companies today are definitely reluctant to purchase technologies that require big risks and are more interested in making modest investments that can show rapid ROI and minimal exposure, the survey also indicated that the types of SCM technology projects they expect to undertake in the next few years exhibit a continuity with the past. According to the responses, the top five applications to be tackled for the first time were B2B e-commerce, inventory control, APS systems, warehouse management, and asset management, respectively. The top applications businesses expected to upgrade were similar, with inventory control and warehouse management as the two top technologies.

Grappling with the content and selection decisions surrounding today's Web-enabled technologies is the subject of this chapter. Discussion opens with a review of the internal, interorganizational, and technology architecture requirements for implementing e-SCM. An e-SCM focused internal organizational architecture requires companies to make the transition from company-centric to supply chain process-centric organizations, that they become customer-focused, flexible, and capable of metamorphosing to be more responsive to the needs of trading partners and customers, and that they are driven by an empowered cross-functional, cross-enterprise workforce. The analysis next moves to the construction of inter-enterprise architecture. The argument voiced is that internal organizational reengineering is insufficient, and that the only way in today's business environment to build sustainable competitive advantage is to architect a collaborative community of trading partners collectively driven to deliver the highest level of customer service possible. The third area discussed, technology architecture, attempts to describe the hardware and software frameworks necessary to ensure the necessary interoperability and integration of the business applications found at each trading partner node in the supply channel. The chapter ends with a review of the future of e-SCM, new technology developments like ASPs and wireless, and the steps necessary to transform the organization to the e-SCM environment.

I. FOUNDATIONS OF e-SCM TECHNOLOGY ARCHITECTURE

There can be little doubt that the single most important concept and application in today's business environment is *supply chain management* (SCM), and at the heart of SCM can be found the enabling power of information technologies. In fact, almost all of the management and technology topics discussed throughout this book — the networking of geographically dispersed channel trading partners, the real-time integration of network strategies and operations, planning systems that facilitate inventory management across the supply chain pipeline, and others — would be impossible without the connective, information-sharing power of today's broad band of information technologies. IT tools enable companies to manage the explosion of data that continuously emanates from every plane in the supply chain galaxy, integrate it with internal business systems, perform sophisticated analysis of the information, and employ the results to develop a more accurate picture of individual enterprise and supply chain partner performance.

While it is true that the economic and political troubles of the early 2000s have indeed temporarily dampened the application of information technology and forced executives to focus closely on cost and efficiency metrics, the challenges of connecting and synchronizing supply chain trading partners has perhaps never been more demanding of creative action. *Externally,* these challenges require companies to architect supply channels that are collaborative, agile, scalable, fast flow, and Web-enabled. The goal is to present customers with a single, seamless response to their wants and needs by creating a unique network of value-creating relationships. Connectivity and synchronization at this level require the end of channel information silos and the construction of collaborative, channel-wide communication and information management directed at a single point — total customer satisfaction. *Internally,* these challenges require companies to development databases and technology applications that can collect, analyze, and generate information about customers, processes, products, services, markets, and company and partner distribution channels to guide purposeful decision-making. Building a real-time knowledge bank can create the pathway necessary to seamlessly link and coordinate the capabilities of individual companies, their customers, and their trading partners. The impact of information connectivity and integration, however, extend beyond merely facilitating internal and operations functions: they provide a launch point for the generation of new sources of products and services, whole new businesses and marketplaces, and radically new forms of competitive advantage.

e-SCM requires companies to review internal, interorganizational, and technology architectures as a fully integrated set of components as portrayed in Figure 9.1. A detailed discussion of each component is as follows.

A. Enterprise Business Architecture

In today's business environment, enterprises and the supply chains in which they are inextricably entwined are not monolithic structures, but rather must be considered as fragile, yet dynamic connections of customers and trading partners constantly maneuvering for competitive advantage. In turn, these smaller galaxies of business relationships are evolving within a much wider context of the industries and economies that comprise the totality of global business. Far from being isolated, self-contained systems, each is growing in internal complexity while at the same time being drawn increasingly into positions of greater dependence on other systems. This movement of rapidly changing and continuously converging systems is SCM, and the force empowering this movement is today's Internet technologies. Unlike the physical universe, where constellations are racing away from perhaps a common point of unity, today's corporations are finding the space separating them from each other shrinking and the need for communion expanding.

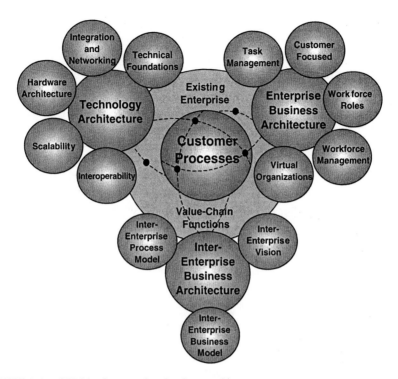

FIGURE 9.1 e-SCM business and technology architecture.

The response of businesses to these twin principles of internal evolution and increasing dependence is found in the continuous deconstruction and reinvention of the enterprise architecture. The term *enterprise architecture* can have a very wide meaning. It consists of the components of the firm that are responsible for the performance of ongoing transactions involved in buying, making, and selling products. It also refers to the corporate cultural that has evolved over time and drives current and future attitudes, expectations, and value judgments about what is the mission of the firm. It consists of the particular configuration of human and computerized resources that accumulate, analyze, and utilize the enterprise's repository of information. An finally, it consists of the core competencies of its human resources that breath life into and serve as the directing instruments of the totality of the firm's business components. "The *enterprise architecture*," according to Fingar, Kumar, and Sharma, "provides the blueprints, the structural abstractions, and style that rationalize, arrange and connect business and technology components to achieve a corporation's purpose."[3] Without an effective architecture an enterprise's evolution to more successful models would cease, and its ability to adapt to change in the face of new business paradigms and technologies would rapidly disintegrate.

A critical theme of this book is the belief that companies today must be careful, yet proactive, to design internal business architectures that will allow them to leverage the tremendous power made available with the application of SCM and Internet concepts and technologies. Before SCM and the Internet, the nature of computing and information technologies severely limited the ability of companies to move beyond the four walls of the enterprise. While technologies such as the telephone, fax, and EDI provided an information outlet to the trading partners ringing the business, data and knowledge transfer was one-to-one and limited by space and time. In addition, databases were monolithic, considered highly proprietary, and difficult to segment into useful categories. The organizational architecture that was constructed around this information model was marked by these limitations and, like all human endeavors, became highly institutionalized.

The structure of a company was designed as a particular configuration of *responsibility centers*. A responsibility center is defined as a work or task unit headed by a manager who was responsible for its performance. These responsibility centers were, in turn, arranged in a hierarchy. The assumptions governing this operating model were simple. To begin with, productive processes were best managed by dividing and subdividing them into small work/task components. In order to maximize productivity, these components were measured and controlled by narrowly defined job descriptions and task standards. The role of the employee was to conform and optimize the work unit performance standards developed for each possible task. Although each work unit had its own particular objectives, presumably these objectives were in alignment with and supportive of the overriding strategy of the whole organization. The role of management was to resolve conflicts between responsibility centers and encourage and guide goal congruence, thereby ensuring that the objectives of individual functions were consistent with the strategies of the organization as a whole. Management control was further enforced by the maintenance of specific rules and codified procedures that governed business practices, job processes, operating customs, and codes of ethics and formalized the control environment and specified the work culture and values of all employees.

Perhaps the ultimate extension of this effort to control and optimize the organization was the growth of two movements begun in the late 1980s — JIT/TQM and business process reengineering. The first movement was focused on generating on the part of everyone in the firm a commitment to the continuous incremental improvement of all business processes. The goal was to redirect responsibility centers away from a concern with local departmental performance and toward a broader understanding of how the productive processes that spanned the entire company could be continuously improved. The second response, known as *business process reengineering* (BPR), was more radical and was centered on "the fundamental rethinking and radical redesign of business processes to achieve dramatic improvements in critical contemporary measures of performance."[4] Instead of slow but steady improvement, BPR sought nothing less than the total deconstruction of all business processes and rebuilding them from the ground level up.

While these two movements had a dramatic effect on competitive advantage, they both suffered from the fact that they were designed to function *within* the confines of the business and had minimal impact when applied across the supply chain. Instead of being revolutionary business philosophies, they were, in fact, the logical culmination of the old organizational model that considered the boundaries of the organization as the limit beyond which organizational design could proceed no further. The rise of SCM and the Internet, however, requires companies to architect organizational environments that view process design and information, not solely as an internal, but rather as a cross-channel networking function. SCM and the Web began as new distribution channel and customer touch-points. Today, these two tools have become recognized for what they real are: strategic business philosophies and technologies that touch every aspect of the supply chain network through channel process engineering, continuous improvement, and total trading partner integration.

Making this transition from BPR and JIT/TQM to SCM and Internet interoperability requires an understanding of the changes to be made to the following elements of business architecture.

1. Organizational Task Management

In the traditional organization, responsibility centers performed the tasks assigned to their departments and then passed the work serially to the next node in the process. In contrast, SCM/Internet-driven organizations are organized around whole processes that extend vertically and horizontally across company divisions. These process-centered organizations will increasingly become highly fluid structures composed of teams that come together to work on a particular project or productive process and then as quickly disband to form new process teams. Because the flow of work is no longer compartmentalized into distinct, self-contained work units, the traditional organization loses its meaning and functional importance and gives way to "virtual" organizations linked together by extranet and Internet communications capabilities.

2. Customer-Focused

Unlike the static organizations of the age of mass production, today's dynamic and constantly changing business landscape requires companies to cultivate cultures that can leverage SCM/Internet technologies to continuously capture the customer. The first applications of e-SCM were focused on establishing point solutions that were often founded as functions separate from the mainstream organization. Today, e-SCM is increasingly being used as the central operating structure of the business, replacing past organizational models. Such structures must be considered as pragmatic, flexible, constantly metamorphosing in order to be responsive to the needs of trading partners and customers. As the speed of shortening product life cycles, manufacturing and distribution lead times, and ability of the customer to increasingly participate in the business process accelerates, organizations will be increasingly responsible for entire process flows, requiring a wide range of competencies and resources that must be assembled quickly from internal functions or from outside company boundaries.

3. Reengineering of Workforce Roles

The requirements to run SCM and Internet technologies require radically new organizational roles for the workforce and management. Because the needs of process organizations will dictate the often oscillating content of work, the workforce and management must possess the skills and capability to migrate rapidly from one process task to another. On the part of the workforce, such a requirement will mean developing employee knowledge and skills that extend beyond the narrow task training of departmentalized organizations. On their part, managers must migrate from being taskmaster and scorekeepers to process owners and coaches responsible for identifying the best resources to apply to a project as well as mentoring the workforce to ensure the long-term availability of knowledgeable and innovative people. This model calling for cross-organizational cooperating has existed in developing Internet initiatives from the very beginning, and now executives will need to escape from previous standards to craft e-SCM strategies based on new forms of e-ROI and e-measurement.

4. Managing the Workforce

e-SCM requires companies to rely more than ever on the knowledge and skills of their workforces and to design compensation and incentive programs that meet the expectations of employees. Perhaps management's greatest challenge in e-SCM is to continually develop avenues that enable people and organizations to remain focused in a fluid work environment where teams are constantly being configured and disbanded, depending on the challenges of the processes and tasks before them. In such an environment, companies must revolutionize their view of their workforces as expanding human repositories of specialized skills and knowledge rather than as being purely task performers. Bringing these productive factors together through information networking and knowledge integration facilitates the task of skills mastery, architecting new process structures and ensuring that the workforce possesses the right combination of skills and knowledge not only to execute necessary business functions, but also to drive the organization along new paths toward innovation and competitive advantage.

The empowerment of the workforce should also be met by new views regarding compensation and incentives. In the past, the workforce was paid and motivated by metrics that focused on high productivity and minimization of costs. This fundamental model, however, is no longer applicable in the e-SCM environment. While productivity and costs are important, the real health and growth potential of an enterprise comes not through incentives or new technologies, but rather from how well the workforce is realizing overall strategic objectives. Compensation, therefore, should be based on the cumulative success of how well the organization is meeting its strategic goals.

5. Developing the "Virtual" Organization

The challenges of competing in the twenty-first century marketplace have increasingly forced companies to utilize the knowledge, competencies, and resources to be found in their supply chain networks. Architecting "virtual organizations" composed of collaborative process teams from across the supply chain provides businesses with unique opportunities to maximize on resources and achieve order-of-magnitude synergies of significant productive and innovative power. The task of constructing and effectively managing these e-SCM forms of organization is perhaps today's most critical management challenge.

Past organization structures focused on individual profit centers. Information proceeded up the organization hierarchy where decisions were made, and then proceeded downward for execution. In contrast, networked organizations utilize information and information transfer, through such tools as the Internet, to empower organizations and to push decision-making down the organizational structure. Information is no longer to be considered as proprietary, but rather to be shared among strategic partners for mutual advantage. The mission of management in these inter-organizational models will be to balance the integration between cross-channel process teams, to define information structures that can be shared without endangering company integrity, and to enable innovation and added value without creating dangerous dependencies on trading partners.

The differences between yesterday's task-focused responsibility centers and today's Internet-driven collaborative process teams are dramatic. The speed of change and the tremendous risks associated with the loss of competitive advantage have forced companies to abandon decades-old internal management styles in favor of fluid organizations empowered by interactive information technology tools capable of leveraging knowledge teams composed of people from any place, at any time in the supply chain continuum.

B. INTER-ENTERPRISE BUSINESS ARCHITECTURE

Much has already been said in the previous chapters about the collaborative nature of today's e-SCM environment. While it is absolutely critical for today's enterprise to architect tightly integrated internal business organizations empowered by information technology, simply reengineering functions and removing redundancies will barely provide the necessary fuel to propel competitive advantage. The really significant gains in productivity are about reengineering the processes that link companies to their channel trading partners. The process change described here is not simply about outsourcing a peripheral function: it is about architecting a collaborative community of trading partners collectively driven by a mission to deliver the highest level of customer service possible. This movement from a company and product-centric strategy to a customer-centric, value-chain strategy will require the constant aligning and optimizing of the value delivered by a company's trading partners and its existing business processes. The new technologies and new roles expected of management and workforce will have to be adapted, expanded, and transitioned to meet the requirements of an effective inter-enterprise architecture.

Although this book has looked at each component in the suite of e-SCM business management functions — IT, e-marketplaces, CRM, manufacturing, SRM, LRM — as separate entities, in reality, the boundaries have been artificial. The same can be said of the distinctions between enterprise and supply partnerships, between demand chain and supply chain. In fact, the basis of business today is the application of repositories of common information and resources, whether its source be customers, trading partners, market information, or products, to present a unique face to every entity that plugs into them. The promise of the Internet is that it provides for the cross-enterprise unification of databases that can be used in an almost infinite variety of ways to provide a different rich context to every accessing entity. "In the unified enterprise," according to Sawhney and Zabin,[5]

> there is no distinction between employee portals, partner portals, and customer portals. They are all windows into the same repository of information, differing only in the roles that are defined for each user, the interactions that are associated with each role, and the level of access permitted for each role. Again, the Internet, intranet, and extranet simply become different levels of secure access to the applications and content objects that constitute the enterprise infrastructure.

Such a vision of inter-enterprise unity requires that all members of the supply chain be closely integrated and their databases and information flows closely synchronized to eliminate distortions and the "bullwhip effect" in the communication of information.

Architecting inter-enterprise structures capable of synchronous information flows requires channel planners to develop and constantly attended to effective e-SCM strategies. Such a program involves the following critical processes.

1. Architecting a Shared Inter-Enterprise Vision

The development of an e-SCM strategy in isolation from channel trading partners is destined to failure. While it is true that the shared vision emanating from inside the organization provides companies with a cohesive force enabling common direction, focus, and personal and team motivation, strategists must be careful to include a vision of how the internal functions of the company are to fit into a much wider supply chain vision. Such an undertaking requires a comprehensive knowledge of internal and partner core competencies, technology capabilities, and commitment to supply chain collaboration. The goal is not only to structure a functional system of cross-channel business, but also to use the framework as a method to leverage the entire business ecosystem to discover breakthrough propositions made possible by the common shared information platform. The process[6] used to guide this analysis is straightforward: an optimized or "green field" architecture is envisioned and documented. Next, the existing "as is" structure is matched against the optimized architecture. Strategists then perform a gap analysis, uncovering where resources and competencies in the existing supply chain occur. Finally, a model of the inter-enterprise architecture should emerge that can be used as the basis for all subsequent e-SCM strategy enhancements.

2. Inter-Enterprise Business Modeling

Once the inter-enterprise vision and strategy has been completed, companies can then begin the task of establishing the enterprise-facing portion of the e-SCM business model. The business model provides a high-level description of how the enterprise is constructed, including the location of inter-enterprise integration points.

The objective of the business model is to detail the firm's architecture in regard to the following base functions:

- Target market/market segment, including expected share, profitability, service goals, customer retention, and new customer acquisition
- Products and services, including product line profitability, life cycle management, new product/service introduction, and manufacturing strategies
- Financial elements, including ROA management, ROI management, potential revenue growth, and internal productivity cost measurements
- Product distribution, including logistics management, depth of channel integration, cost structure, levels of automation, and cost management

A critical element in the business model is the information architecture. It is the responsibility of the firm's information architects to create and maintain the repository of computerized process components. By effectively engineering these process components, solution developers can integrate existing work rules, roles, event management, tasks, and policies that govern the functioning of the business with planned internal and supply channel business environmental changes.

3. Inter-Enterprise Process Modeling

Once the inter-enterprise vision and the business model have been formulated, the next step is to detail the process model that describes the external/e-SCM processes that govern daily functions. Developing the process map requires strategists to know precisely which business functions are going to be inter-enterprise processes, what technology architecture must be in place, and how the organizational infrastructure should be constructed. Constructing effective inter-enterprise processes is a critical project consisting of the following steps.[7]

- *Engineer trading partner processes.* The task of generating the desired inter-enterprise linkages must involve the full participation of customers and suppliers, regardless of the desired complexity of the proposed connectivity. For example, the interaction of information driven through an EDI system will be different than the use of a Web-based system. In regard to *customer processes*, the customer is the driver of the degree of connectivity and the level of response expected from the enterprise. While a significant degree of process standardization is the target, architects must be prepared to fashion process components that permit or are customizable to meet individual customer buying service requirements. Much the same focus must exist when it comes to *supplier processes*. The B2B process components, such as the workflows associated with internal RFQ, sourcing, approval, and order management, must be able to interact with complimentary work components resident in the supplier's information and infrastructure architecture.
- *Degree of process interaction.* An effectively architected system will provide companies with multiple levels of connectivity, depending upon the

business requirements of their trading partners. At the lowest level can be found the loose-coupled model. This level of connectivity between trading partners utilizes information technologies, such as EDI and the Web, simply as a medium to replace paper-based information documents. At the next level, *process handoff*, the inter-enterprise system connectivity has been architected to permit transactions to trigger processes in the systems of trading partners. For example, a sales transaction posted in a retailer's system will trigger a replenishment notice in the planning system of a first-tier supplier. At the highest level, *virtual enterprise*, the process components are used jointly and operate in real-time. This level of architecture provides each linked node in the supply chain full access to information across the channel network galaxy. For instance, information concerning a customer would be available to every trading partner, thereby removing unnecessary supply chain–level redundancies and sub-optimizations.

- *Internal infrastructure and system reengineering.* Much has already been spoken about the challenges to infrastructure provoked by the adoption of e-SCM functions. Regardless of the level of connectivity deployed, the workforce will be required to function in a cross-enterprise mode, and not simply according to the needs of a single company. Technology-wise, supply chain interoperability will require enhancements to existing systems or the purchase of point solutions, such as B2B, to supplement legacy system deficiencies. Normally, this process will require customization of the "wrapper programs" of existing EBS/ERP systems to accommodate the linkages needed to work with new packaged software, portals, and other interoperability solutions.

- *e-Application architecture.* The final technology architecture that emerges should support the inter-enterprise business strategy. According to Hoque,[8]

> e-application architecture involves determining individual integration points between the application and data sources, the application and back-end installed software, and between multiple back-end systems. Every decision should be made with a good deal of attention toward not only the functionality of the application the day it is rolled out, but also the ability of the platform to scale up to support heavy usage, added business attributes, new users, and additional functionality in later revisions.

In summary, the e-application architecture should determine which inter-enterprise processes components will constitute the final platform. The completed architecture should contain the definition of what the networked infrastructure should look like, how networked resources will be accessed, the source and type of the data the networked resources will utilize, resolution of data, hardware, process, and human resource ownership.

- *Pilot, go live, and iterate.* The challenges of developing and implementing a comprehensive inter-enterprise, e-SCM solution are fraught with difficulties, potentially enormous expenses, and significant trauma to even the best of organizations. Most experts caution against trying to do too much in the first round. Implementers should view the process as iterative: utilize a minimalist approach and begin with the easiest processes or the ones that provide the biggest payback. The goal is to keep expectations, costs, and trauma to the organization realistic and "do-able," while ensuring the company is pursuing a path that keeps it at the forefront of the competition.

C. INTER-ENTERPRISE TECHNOLOGY ARCHITECTURE

As a principle, it can be stated that the strategic and operational capabilities of a business are directly related to the enabling power of its information technologies. Simply put, the ability of a company to effectively execute the management of customer, supplier, manufacturing, logistics, and financial functions is in direct proportion to the velocity by which the organization can create, collect, assimilate, access, and transfer information. Before the computer, information processes could move only as fast as human efforts, assisted by crude forms of automation, could manage it. These limitations stood as the foundation for the hierarchical organizations of the "industrial age." With the advent of the computer, capable of handling information and communications data in volumes and at speeds previously thought unimaginable, the limitations on information management were dissolved, revealing whole new avenues for business management and obsoleting past theories regarding the role of infrastructure and relationships with trading partners.

Over the succeeding decades, computerization of enterprise functions and decision-making has expanded dramatically. Beginning as a tool for automating mundane and repetitive processes, information strategists by the mid-1980s were formulating a new and radical role for the computer and the enabling power of information. Up to that period, computers were perceived as proprietary systems focused inclusively on managing core enterprise applications. The result was a multiplication of proprietary systems, a situation that led to fragmented, inefficient computing architectures characterized by limited interoperability and restricted cross-functional and inter-enterprise integration of key business processes. With the arrival in the mid-1990s of new concepts and technologies, such as SCM and the Internet, enterprise computing was forced to move beyond internal boarders toward a more open and broadly deployable computing model.

Two critical dimensions are driving this development. The first is the requirement for a technical architecture that enables the linkage of computer systems and people. The word commonly used for this process is *integration*. Integration means to merge with something else, to form a whole greater than the constituent parts. Organizationally, integration means leveraging information tools that merge operational functions, both on the enterprise and supply network level, by facilitating ever-closer coordination of the performance of joint business processes. The second dimension at the core of modern computing is *networking*. In the past, computing architectures permitted only hierarchical, serial communication between information nodes. In contrast, today's server-based open architectures now permit the connecting of different computers and their information databases together in a network. The advantage is that now people can communicate information directly to other people in the network, enabling the formation of interfunctional and inter-enterprise functional teams focused on a common process. *Integration* is the process of linking business functions together; *networking*, on the other hand, is the activation of the linkage by enabling and empowering people to cut across departmental and enterprise barriers and interweaves common and specialized knowledge to respond to a wide range of common business processes.

Today, the ultimate mission of enterprise technology architecture is to transform the corporate competitive vision into a fully functional set of cross-network business process application components capable of expanding to meet intra- and inter-enterprise integration and networking requirements. Such a challenge is indeed a large one. Most business infrastructures are not designed to function in a pan-channel networking mode. EBS/ERP backbones tend to be proprietary, closed systems that require extensive modification to be able to encompass true enterprise-wide interoperability. Simply understanding the process components, the actual technology, and the data to be accessed at each integration point can be an enormous task. Whether it is a simple sharing between systems of a common data repository or the use of API/method-level integration that utilizes existing or added software connection points or "wrappers" that permit shared common processes as well as data, crafting the necessary architecture to achieve the targeted inter-enterprise objective will require new toolsets and significant infrastructure changes.

1. e-SCM Technical Vocabulary

Before launching into the world of e-business technology architecture, it might be worthwhile to begin by examining the main concepts behind Web-based computing. The following list should serve as a foundation for the discussion to follow.

    i. *Best-of-breed.* From the very beginning of software, companies have been confronted with the possibility of choosing software solutions from multiple vendors. Since no one supplier can possibly build the ultimate system, executives have been faced with the problem of integrating "home-grown," packaged backbone, and specialized point solutions. This problem has been compounded in the Internet environment, which requires integration of software platforms, or open systems, across the entire supply chain network.

    ii. *Interoperability.* This important concept refers to the ability of the matrix of software solutions composing a technical environment to be fully compatible and capable of being integrated with each other. In addition, this heterogeneous environment must be able to evolve to support new technology standards as they emerge. In the Internet environment, the architecting of interoperable business components that must be shared by trading partners is one of the most important challenges before system designers.

iii. *Agility.* A cardinal problem of past software solutions is their rigidity and inability to accept change. Agility is the ability of system architects to make changes or even replace components as technologies and standards change through time. The goal is to develop applications that share information and resources without irreversibly cementing them together, thereby hampering component interfaces and requiring extensive "wrapper code" to enable them to work together.

iv. *Reusable assets.* Today's business systems are composed of software components either closely or partially linked, or are independent standalone solutions. Whether it be an internal or a Web-based solution, it is critical that these "components" are capable of being used again and again with the absolute minimum of redesign. This repository of software assets enables system architectures to easily share information, workflows, reporting/analysis tools, and other features with each other and with requests from systems exterior to the business.

v. *Scalability.* When an application is designed, technical architects can only determine through past metrics or a heuristic what the demand and, therefore, the performance will be once processing begins. Scalability means that the capability of the application can be easily augmented or decreased depending upon the processing and data requirements. This dynamic is particularly important in Web-based business management, where applications can experience large spikes in usage. For the most part, this is a computing hardware issue.

vi. *e-Commerce integration.* Internet-enabled companies must develop technical architectures that enable them to work fluidly and effectively with inter-enterprise business functions. These e-business engines include: user access and role-based profiles, network event and notification management, data and business-object integration, e-market exchange services, business policies and rules, and process and workflow management.

vii. *Web services.* This set of capabilities provides for the movement of data from one application to another over the Internet without the requirement for a direct connection between the two applications and without regard for the operating systems the individual applications run on. Built on a growing set of XML standards, Web services permit interoperability across heterogeneous platforms. For example, German auto manufacturer Quattro uses a Web service to pass real-time information back and forth between their ERP backbone, which runs on Microsoft's Windows NT and a Java-based production planning application. The linkage provides real-time information for Quattro, which makes custom sports cars, to quickly assemble materials to meet the exact configuration requirements of the customer. Although this technology is currently in use, it is still in the formative stage.

2. Technology Foundations for Next-Generation Interoperability

In today's technology environment, businesses are busy designing the strategies for enterprise and inter-enterprise application integration to meet the demands of an increased focus on collaborative relationships and processes. During the first two years of the new century, companies shifted their focus from Web-driven functions to application integration initiatives designed to reduce costs, shrink cycle times, and reduce redundancies by automating business functions. While it is expected that efforts to utilize integration to reduce costs will continue, analysts are predicting that leading-edge companies will seek to merge internal integration projects with external Internet initiatives to increase collaborative networking capabilities and trading partner relationships and improve productivity.

In tackling the task of trading partner integration, technology architects are confronted with several issues. To begin with, while many companies today have embraced the value propositions of technology application suites such as ERP, SCM, CRM, and e-commerce, unfortunately, in too many cases management has viewed each technology as an isolated initiative. The result has been that integration of the entire portfolio of enterprise software applications has been sadly lacking. In addition, IT organizations during the first years of the 2000s have been increasing confronted with the pressure to anticipate changes in business strategies and assemble and disassemble often-heterogeneous sets of applications and technologies to support emerging business ventures. Finally, technology architects are being asked to establish a logical, unified view of information, processes, and applications that extend out into the supply chain and are focused on enhancing trading partner relationships, information integration, and cost-savings.

In general, IT projects focused on internal and supply chain integration are being facilitated with the availability of next generation standards, such as the emerging Web-services specifications, XML, and Java, that are incorporated into the latest versions of enterprise application integration (EAI) and application development tools. According to industry analysts,[9] "Web services provide a common language for integration, which should hasten companies' abilities to integrate enterprise applications, create cross-company workflows, and share common business processes with partners and customers." In addition, today's development platforms that support these standards are facilitating the ability for architects to link applications to business processes, such as moving inventory from the CRM request all the way through to a warehouse-management system. While CRM integration has grabbed most of the integration dollars to date, as companies move toward the mid-2000s, the effort to integrate SCM systems, product data management, and ERP data warehouses with trading partners is expected to dramatically expand.

To assist in conceptualizing the next generation of collaborative business systems, AMR Research[10] has created a conceptual blueprint for inter-enterprise system development. Termed *enterprise commerce management* (ECM), the goal of the methodology is to provide a pathway where integrators can combine applications and services in an Internet-driven environment that can act as a form of universal translator, converting data from customers, suppliers, and the workforce into a common format. Essentially, the model consists of three critical sets of services and the technology that integrates them together. The first layer, *information services,* is responsible for the database (customers, products, suppliers, etc.) necessary for effective decision-making, transaction management, and content management and provides a single logical view of the corporate system of record. The second layer, *interaction services,* defines the business rules, enables enterprise-wide activity aggregation, and provides for a unified view of a company's system of processes. A set of integration services, which maintains the bidirectional integrity of the information layer while delivering in real time the data necessary for process management, act as the connection between these first two levels. The final layer, *collaboration services,* enables a company to activate new ventures, whether short or long-term, with external trading partners by being able to quickly assemble competencies and resources through the Web. In today's environment, it is the role of exchange services, such as a PTX, to act as the platform connecting the interaction and levels collaboration.

In order to effectively utilize the ECM blueprint for SCM integration, AMR has developed a set of seven key technology tools.[11] The goal of these tools is to facilitate a successful implementation of enterprise commerce with customers and trading partners. These seven tools can be summarized as follows:

- *Analytical Data Model.* To ensure the accuracy of data as it radiates from possible multiple systems (SCM, ERP, CRM, etc.), an analytical data model providing key metrics is necessary. The data model is used to measure the success of business ventures, ensure the integration of summary analytical data and EBS detail transaction data, and permit drilldown from summary information in the analytical model with detail transactions resident in the originating system.
- *Application Server.* Whether it resides with the technology standards established with the use of *Java* architecture from Sun or the *.NET* architecture from Microsoft, the application server drives the ability to manage the e-SCM processes of networked partners through a common framework. This framework enables cross-enterprise software applications to participate in e-marketplace exchanges. Currently, XML is considered as the leading interoperability facilitator for interapplication communication.
- *Application Integration.* An integration framework that is intrinsic to the application architecture must exist to act as a mechanism for enabling shared information between customers, suppliers, partners, products/design, assets, and the workforce. The objective of this toolset is to ensure data coordination and integrity across separate internal and trading partner business applications. Integration at this level should preserve investment in legacy systems while making available the suite of application processes at the *interaction services* level necessary to participate in e-marketplace exchanges.
- *Business Process Management* (BPM). The often highly heterogeneous nature of today's computing environment requires a common application that can coordinate the information flows, data, and processes between

supply chain partners, regardless of their origins. It is the role of BPM to coordinate internal and external cross-application business processes, which in turn, enables companies to create agile and flexible processes capable of being dynamically assembled to respond to new supply chain-driven opportunities.

- *Private e-Market Exchanges.* Whether a PTX or a CTX, private e-market exchanges facilitate the integration of trading communities. Normally assembled from several distinct internal and external technology components, a private exchange provides for the mapping and integration of disparate business process from across the supply chain, establishment of interactive content shared by trading partners, definition of process workflows governing how collaborative processes will work, and capability to capture exchange performance metrics.

- *Common Portal Framework.* With the acceleration of data movement in the supply chain network, integration architectures will require a common portal network that provides personalized and secure access to transaction systems and analytical applications by any trading partner. A key requirement is the ability of the portal framework to access content (such as customer, order, product, and inventory information) from internal, proprietary systems and to make it available to independent, external applications with differing methods of presentation.

- *Integrated Systems Management.* Utilization of the ECM blueprint has dramatically expanded the responsibilities of overall systems management. Effectively managing today's inter-enterprise integration architecture requires the performance of a range of tasks from security management, validating the functioning of e-market exchange servers, coordinating process/application components across a heterogeneous computing environment, ensuring data storage capabilities, enabling unbroken, real-time access to local and shared data and performance monitoring of multiple networks.

AMR's ECM approach has become so widely accepted an approach for integrating computing environments consisting of independent solutions that even the biggest business system software companies, such as SAP, Oracle, PeopleSoft, and Sun Microsystems are voicing their support.[12] The alternative is the complete replacement of legacy systems by a single pre-integrated set of applications that provides a complete backbone, portal, exchange and other collaborative applications.

3. Today's e-SCM Technical Architecture

The actual architecture that will emerge depends on the objectives of the inter-enterprise project. Some firms will focus on area solutions enabling intranets and extranets or networking-facing CRM or SRM functions. The model described below (Figure 9.2) illustrates a full-blown e-SCM network that integrates the enterprise backbone with suppliers, customers, and partners. As discussed above, the model follows the ECM blueprint for integrating a heterogeneous computing environment.

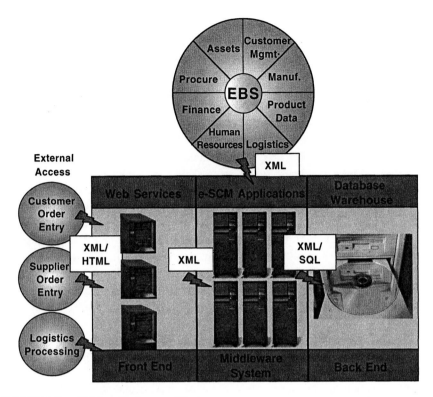

FIGURE 9.2 e-SCM technology architecture.

The goal is the application of interoperable process components that provide the flexibility to encapsulate both EBS/ERP backbones and best-of-breed-software resources.

   i. *Front-End Functions.* The technology used for e-SCM front-end processing must be flexible, scaleable, reliable, and capable of withstanding any level and size of Web-initiated access. Technology in this area can consist of a front-end Web server farm, load balancers, and caching tools. It is critical that components are available to service the volume of incoming messages, especially with the more data-rich presentation and processor-intensive security toolsets of today's inter-application Web serves. Hardware in this area should possess redundant hot-swap disks and power supplies. In today's environment, Web-facing front-ends must be capable of handling a wide volume of data. On the low end, HTML will permit service to the relatively static data such as catalog pages. On the high end, XML is used to integrate Web and server-based components, as well as to pass information between EAI middleware servers and back-end databases.

  ii. *Middleware Functions.* If an external request that requires further processing is received by the front end, it is forwarded to the middleware application servers. Most XML, SQL, and application logic processing is performed at this tier. For example, for a Web-driven front-end, servers in the mid-tier would handle the XML messages generated by shopping cart and e-procurement applications. In an e-SCM environment, this tier is usually characterized by a distributed application structure that actualizes the requirement for business-process extensibility and performance scalability, especially when a very large number of transactions or SKUs are involved. Normally, each server can have its own database or it can be linked to the back-end database.

iii. *Back-End Functions.* The requirements for the availability and scalability for database warehousing is mission-critical in today's increasingly fast-paced and data-rich Internet environment. As supply chain systems grow in use and complexity, data warehousing functions can expect to experience an increase in requirements for real-time data mining, large in-memory databases, and an explosion in the volume of analytical processing needs. The hardware architecture should permit the clustering of storage solutions that provide for dynamic application load balancing, scalability, flexibility, and the highest levels of reliability and virtual non-stop service availability.

The demands of today's open computing environment for extensive inter-enterprise connectivity and highly interactive e-business services require a technical architecture that is capable of continuously increasing performance, availability, and reliability. Besides the elements detailed in AMR's ECM blueprint, the architecture should be capable of deploying end-to-end computing resources to meet demand, whether it be from a Web-enabled front-end application, a third-party SCM system, or analytical requests on the back-end database.

II. THE FUTURE OF e-SCM

In an article entitled "The Metamorphosis of Information,"[13] Downes details how Wal-Mart and its supply and logistics partners are attempting to move the concept of SCM to its next evolutionary step. In a store outside Tulsa Oklahoma, Wal-Mart has installed the latest in SCM computing and data-communications technologies, whereby an Electronic Product Code, which is similar to a bar code but which does not need to be scanned and contains its own power source and antenna, broadcasts by means of radio frequencies to receivers in the warehouse and on store shelves the location of pallets of individually labeled Bounty paper towels. The tracking data is also transmitted up the supply chain to distributors and, finally, the manufacturer. While the cost of these miniature computers today severely limits their application to experiments only, if Moore's Law is true, perhaps in the next few years it will not be surprising to find that manufacturers from Procter & Gamble to the Gap will be able to label all their products with such information devices. "Imagine," concludes Downes, "a trillion new intelligent devices, each with its own Internet address, sending and receiving data through their life spans, creating increasingly complete snapshots of every transaction in every supply chain."

While the prospect of trillions of computerized product codes generating enormous, complex matrices of information may seems generally unreachable today, it, however, is only a single instance of what are perhaps hundreds of computerized applications that analysts are predicting will reshape the nature of business computing in the world of tomorrow. What this will mean to the concept of e-SCM is nothing short of revolutionary. Even with the technology now available, there are numerous "no-man's lands" scattered throughout the supply chain where information and processes disappear from the light of day. It is in these cloudy regions that decisions regarding manufacturing planning, product marketing, advertising, even product development are made outside the mainstream of normal channel management. In contrast, tomorrow's SCM computerized toolsets will create a parallel *information supply chain* (ISC), which will be the mirror image of the physical supply chain where the product resides. The stream of information from the ISC will not only provide companies with a means of tracking a product's positioning and other related physical attributes, but, more importantly, it will enable a company to define future products, services, markets, and competitive advantage. The information, and not the product, will constitute the key value in the supply chain.

A. Changing Face of Information Management

The most attractive component about the Electronic Product Code story detailed above is not the wizardry of the technology, but the *information* the technology makes available. Information provides companies with a window to reality, and the more accurate and the more timely, the better businesses can make the decisions that will assist them to better service their customers, develop their workforces, invest their resources, control their costs, and remain competitive. Today, business concepts and applications like SCM, the Internet, open computing environments, and the focus on trading partner collaboration should be viewed, first and foremost, as methods to increase information availability. Unfortunately, during the dot-com and B2B bubble, everyone, including seasoned analysts, consultants, and practitioners lost sight of what the new Internet technologies should have been focused on, and that was increasing the utility and visibility of information in the supply chain. Now that the hype has finally cleared, companies can begin the task of sorting out what they need to do to transform their businesses by incorporating today's technologies before their competitors beat them to the finish line.

While obvious business applications such as ERP, CRM, SRM, Internet-enabled e-marketplace exchanges, and other computerized toolsets remain as the basis for information management, several new developments are reshaping the face of business computing today.

1. New Generation of Business Applications

Just a few short years ago, technology purchasers were presented with functionality-rich mega systems that were also difficult and costly to implement, difficult to integrate with other technology components, and difficult to add non-native functionality. A perfect example is the dramatic rise and descent into the doldrums of

CRM applications.[14] High-powered systems from Front Range (GoldMine), Onyx, Oracle, PeopleSoft, Pivotal, SAP, and Siebel crushed less worth competitors and bombarded customers with the sheer power of their robust functionality. Unfortunately, by mid-2002, would-be customers had wearied of the enormous effort in time, money, organizational stress, and the often large portions of the software that lie unimplemented. As the economic noose tightened, companies wanted a better return for their investment and wanted CRM products that fit their business strategies, workflows, workforce capabilities, and their native system environments. Instead of bundles of prepackaged functionality, CRM users were asking for smaller, more easily managed components accompanied by more robust toolsets.

As a rule, software companies of all flavors can expect today to experience the following range of requirements from prospects before they will purchase any form of software.

  i. *Technology architecture.* As companies look to their application suites to expand interoperability and inter-enterprise integration capabilities, the utilization of Sun's *Java* or Microsoft's *.NET* framework for Web services development is a critical litmus test for next-generation ERP and B2B applications. Several key reasons emerge. To begin with, there are large pools of technical talent in the marketplace to work with these languages. Second, these platforms make it easy to develop powerful Web application servers. Third, the adoption of either as a standard would facilitate integration with trading partners out in the channel network. Such a standard would permit companies to publish their Web components as services and access components from Internet partners without writing custom interfaces. Fourth, these platforms make database access more flexible by converting data to XML documents that can be easily passed to EBS backbones, wireless devices, or other applications. In summary, who will win the platform battle — Java or Microsoft — is to be determined. Gartner feels that by 2005 each will possess about 40% of all e-business application development.[15]
 ii. *Adaptability.* Past software developers focused on building systems that provided users with robust toolsets that enabled them to configure or build functionality. However, a focus on building giant systems meant that there was also a lot of built-in structure that made the components difficult to change. While today's marketplace considers robust toolboxes a requirement, it wants less built-in structure and a greater focus on company-specific, native business processes.
iii. *Cost.* Today's systems often require huge expenditures for hardware, software, and training. In addition, a substantial budget will be necessary to accommodate modification or enhancement requirements. In contrast, the newer wave of software is built on open architectures and, therefore, requires less expense for hardware, training, and modification.
 iv. *Implementation.* Today's application systems have become so function-rich that implementers often have a hard time embarking on system configuration. Users can get lost in functionality that adds minimal value,

while crucial applications are given insufficient attention. In addition, because of functionality robustness, it is difficult to modify to meet native requirements. While the new wave of software today is less rich in options, it is easier to add native functions to delivered applications and presents fewer barriers to modification.

v.   *User adoption.* A common complaint is that today's business systems are too expansive and too complex for users. Today's new wave of software is easier to use, has less interface clutter, is more focused on native functions, and is more likely to gain user acceptance and validation quicker.

2.   Application Service Providers (ASP)

The dramatic changes impacting technology today have spawned a new industry directed at relieving companies of the cost and organizational burden of implementing cutting-edge software by providing IT services for rent. In the past, the IT function was considered a back-office function. Today, managing IT is a much more complex affair. A company's information systems drive competitive strategy and profitability. IT is often about managing a diverse application infrastructure with overlapping applications. System upgrades and new technologies seem to arrive on the scene every day and they all threaten to obsolete existing solutions and decrease IT asset value. These and other pressures can place excessive demands on even the best run and most successful IT departments. These problems are even more acute for small and medium-sized businesses that lack the people and financial resources just to keep up with changing technologies.

In order to meet the demands of today's highly competitive information technologies, many companies have been turning to ASPs to shoulder the task of implementing and running their IT systems, so they can stay focused on managing their businesses. Computer systems, application software, networks, and the Internet — all are fundamental tools that every business must utilize. Maintaining these tools, however, is normally outside the core competencies of most businesses. What an ASP basically does is to provide companies with the ability to lease software over a secure Internet-accessed network. Often there is little or no up-front investment required by participants. The user does not own, license, or even keep a copy of the software on its in-house systems. The ASP hosts the software and the related IT services, including upgrades and maintenance. In addition, the ASP can provide the network linking the client's offices, homes, and operating locations to the data center. Finally, the ASP provides the licenses, implementation, training, management, and user support to ensure customer value. In return, the ASP charges a single monthly fee for all products and services.

While the cost-benefit of using an ASP is compelling, general acceptance of ASPs has not been forthcoming. Since the idea's inception about four years ago, the ASP model has been drastically overhyped. Research company Gartner Dataquest predicted that the ASP marketplace would reach $10.3 billion by 2004. Currently, other reports predict that more than 60% of today's ASPs will fail within the same time. Several reasons explain the discrepancy. To begin with, the ASP model, while ostensibly simple, has proven more complex than originally believed. The model works best when both parties can agree to a very narrowly defined array of application components that run highly quantified operations, such as payroll and finance, and do not need much modification. The model has extreme difficulties with new or complex areas such as CRM or manufacturing. Again, there is always the issue of security. Not only are ASPs given access to company data, but by using a hosted application, companies potentially can also expose sales leads, marketing information, and customer profiles to Internet-based eyes. Finally, according to an *Information Week* survey, what mattered most to companies was not the cost savings but the requirement that the ASP became a true business partner and not simply a noncommitted, cafeteria-style supplier of software services.[16]

Although the ASP model took a major body blow after the dot-com crash, it is showing signs of recovery. As the economy continues in recession, the prospect of outsourcing software seems to be gaining ground, and specialized ASP providers such as Salesforce.com, a CRM ASP, is projecting their revenues to double in 2002. In selecting an ASP companies should use the following touch points:

- *Determine requirements.* What are to be the outsourced application(s)? How many users and locations will there be, and what level of performance and support is needed?
- *Determine technical environment.* What types of network connections and client devices are needed? Is there any integration needed with existing systems and applications? What implementation and integration services will be necessary?
- *Evaluate ASP.* Evaluate potential partners with regard to their strategic direction, experience, technology infrastructure, and extent of their customer base, cash flow, and investors.
- *Level of ASP services.* Is the ASP vendor certified, and does it have a track record in the desired applications? What types of services are provided, including remediation policies for downtime, quality of security, network and bandwidth options, and backup and recovery capabilities?
- *Determine level of technical support.* Are there limits on the number and type of support calls? What is the ASP's escalation policy? What are the days and hours of available service?
- *Scalability and control of assets.* Can the ASP provider respond to periods of peak load? Does the ASP provider have control over its own assets, and if not, what guarantees does it offer? Does the ASP have the potential to grow along with their clients?
- *Validate ASP's strategy.* Assess the ASP's overall sales and service strategy and commitment to the industry.

3. Wireless

During the past few years, companies have begun to realize the benefits of wireless technology. While the time-honored process of gathering data and then manually inputting it into a computer application dominates computing, its days are numbered.

The application of wireless data technologies in today's computing environment is creating whole new realms of productivities: information can be gathered in the field and transmitted to a database in real time; customer and sales information is instantly available; and coworkers can share information instantly at the point of need. Wireless applications are appearing everywhere — in hotels and stock brokerages, at sales meetings, and most recognizably when UPS comes to the door. Ready or not, wireless technology will become a critical component of IT strategies.

Wireless can be defined, at its most rudimentary form, as the transmission of data between devices that are not physically connected. A wireless device may be anything from a *personal digital assistant* (PDA), to a laptop, a two-way pager, a global positioning satellite antenna, or a remote sensor. The data communication can occur at short range using infrared technology, at a wider range using high-speed wireless LANs located at a fixed structure, or globally using satellites. The goal of wireless technologies is to provide mobile workers access and input to any database, any time. It enables collaborative information exchange where physical collocation is not feasible. It also assists in tracking, locating, and managing movable assets such as cargo, containers, laboratory equipment, and delivery trucks.[17]

The possibilities for the application of wireless technologies are virtually endless. Industries pioneering wireless today range from healthcare to transportation to manufacturing. Everyone is familiar with UPS's use of wireless tracking and shipment verification devices that began in 1992. Wireless CRM devices permit the mobile sales force to view customer information and place orders. Today's shop floor has a variety of wireless data collection devices ranging from terminal emulation keypads to wireless computers and handhelds. New types of bar codes are enabling *radio frequency identification* (RFID) functions that permit the real-time posting of data by mobile operators. Through *radio frequency* (RF) the most up-to-date information can be sent to customers on their PDA devices.

There can be little doubt that, as wireless technology expands and becomes even closer linked to the Internet, it will become an essential building block of e-SCM. Wireless technology provides another medium for e-SCM to extend its influence and increase its value to the supply chain. Wireless enables a wider audience of participants within the organization and outside in the supply network to bring automation and efficiency to a new range of processes by making information ubiquitous and real-time. While there are still many issues to resolve, such as security, bandwidth, device size, standards, and compatibility, wireless technology is destined to have as much of an impact on business and technology architectures as the arrival of the Internet. In the meantime, the evolutionary nature of the wireless revolution will enable companies to implement and experiment with the technology by focusing on high-payback applications currently available to the marketplace.

B. Transforming the Organization to the e-SCM Environment

Through this chapter, the underlying theme has been how companies can leverage their technical environments to provide increasingly granular levels of information to supercharge their SCM business architectures. Success in tomorrow's marketplace requires companies to know with as much precision as possible the answers to such critical questions as who their customers are and what do they want, what are the capacities of supply partners on the other side of the supply chain, what is the actual inventory balance at a local warehouse. Simply, the faster the intelligence is transmitted and received, the more effective will be the decisions made impacting costs, service, and ultimately, competitive advantage. Companies are in a life and death struggle with their competitors, not on a yearly or monthly, but on a day-to-day basis. The same computerized tools that can provide a span of competitive advantage can be easily duplicated by competitors; the instantaneous speed of the Internet can just as easily lose a valued customer to a rival supplier as it can gain new customers.

As it has always been, rarely does the adoption of a new technology or business concept radically change the course of the business environment without a long and often painful period of trail and error. The merger of SCM and the Internet is just such a technology. This book has been an attempt to discuss the broad outlines of the movement of today's business global community toward closer collaboration and integration as defined by e-SCM. While the ultimate shape of this movement is yet to be fully defined, the process is more than under way. To realize the full benefits of the e-SCM model, the following three-staged approach is recommended.

1. Supply Chain Efficiency

As companies emerge out of the era of isolated computing environments toward supply chain connectivity, the focus will be centered squarely on using technology to more closely integrate, standardize, and make more transparent internal business processes. The goal will be to leverage applications like ERP, CRM, data warehousing, procurement systems, and the Internet to abstract critical information that can be used to improve productivity and cost initiatives while opening new pathways to the marketplace. Relationships with supply chain trading partners in this stage will be primarily focused on short-term, operational benefits and will often lack a coherent overall strategy. This is the stage most companies are in today.

2. e-SCM Integration

Once companies have fully integrated enterprise functions, executives will turn in earnest to their supply chains and inter-enterprise technologies for new sources of competitive advantage. As the efforts to reduce internal costs and reengineer productivities reach a level of diminishing returns, firms will search for supply chain interoperability to pull information from channel-facing application components such as forecasting, inventory management, product development, supply chain planning, and procurement processes to further competitive advantage. Utilization of e-CRM and SRM e-market exchanges will increase in importance as organizations search for greater agility, scalability, and customization in working with customers and to further outsource non-core functions. Relationships with supply chain trading partners in this stage begin to evolve from a concern with operational short-term gains to the creation of strategic ventures with critical customers, suppliers, and technology partners.

3. Collaborative Convergence

In stage three of the implementation of the e-SCM concept, the direction of information streams are reversed from flowing into the individual enterprise to freely flowing between the partner nodes constituting the supply chain. Toolsets such as Web services, open application components, XML, information generation devices like the Electronic Product Code used by Wal-Mart discussed earlier, and wireless devices enable whole supply chains to respond concurrently as a seamless virtual customer-satisfying entity to any marketplace challenge and to provide the seedbed for the simultaneous generation of new products and services. In this business environment the *information supply chain* will replace the physical supply chain.

The three stages of e-SCM development discussed above are the culmination of the SCM philosophy as described in the first chapter of this book. SCM was described as a

> tactical and strategic management philosophy that seeks to network the collective productive capacities and resources of intersecting supply channel systems through the application of Internet technologies in the search for innovative solutions and the synchronization of channel capabilities dedicated to the creation of unique, individualized sources of customer value.

Actualizing this definition of SCM is a difficult process indeed, and it can have as many paths as there are businesses. Some industries are struggling just to meet the requirements of stage-one e-SCM. Other companies find themselves grappling with developing infrastructure and inter-enterprise technology to meet the emergence of all three. Succeeding at each stage will require companies to create not just one, but multiple strategies to handle the changes to the organization driven by each stage.

III. SUMMARY

In the past, companies thought that industry leadership would be achieved by offering better quality, greater speed, and lower costs than the rest of the competition. Today, "best practices" have increasingly become a commodity, simply the price of admission to get into the game. According to a group of researchers,[18] it was found that leading companies were moving beyond just best practices and were beginning to embrace "next strategies" that would provide them with a springboard to pursue sustainable advantage. In executing these strategies, firms are setting new standards for excellence by utilizing their supply chains and Internet technologies to enable agile, scalable processes that optimize cost and service levels while minimizing waste in resources and activities across the length of the supply chain network.

Creating an environment dedicated to using their business partners and technology connectivity to architect visionary strategies that lock in competitive advantage requires establishing at the core of the company the following leadership and organizational attributes.

- *Leadership.* Strategy-focused organizations are directed by the most senior levels of the firm's management staff. Executives must have a clear strategy concerning the role of SCM and the Internet, be able to effectively communicate that vision to the organization, be capable of translating that vision into a business model that clearly defines internal focus, supply chain relationships, and key performance metrics measuring the business's success.

- *Expanding supply chain participation.* Success in business today requires companies to abandon their focus on internal performance in favor of engineering closer relationships with channel trading partners. This reengineering of corporate vision involves reformulating marketing, sales, service, product design, production, and logistics functions from a company-centric to a supply chain-centric perspective. Accelerating value-chain participation will require companies to increase their investment in innovative backbone, Internet-driven, and hardware technology toolsets.

- *Focus on operations efficiencies.* Effective e-SCM requires companies to redouble their efforts to remove internal and supply chain-facing cost redundancies, increase quality, shorten all forms of cycle time, and develop responsive, agile operations that can anticipate and rapidly adapt to changes in the marketplaces. While manufacturers have for years focused on developing lean operations that reduce waste, facilitate throughput, and minimize working capital, this initiative needs to be expanded to supply chain management.

- *The process-focused organization.* A fundamental assumption of e-SCM is that today's most competitive form of organization is the "virtual organization" composed of multiple teams that span enterprise functions and that have the capability to also include the human resources of channel partners existing outside the boundaries of the enterprise. Although the process-focused organization can take many forms (partnership, joint venture, strategic alliance, supplier-contractor, cooperative agreement, outsourcing contract, and integrated channel process team) based on the nature of the competitive strategy pursued, they all contain several similar characteristics. To begin with, they are driven by comprehensive strategic plans. Second, they depend on the existence of inter-enterprise process teams assembled from across the network. Third, utilizing today's Internet technologies, these teams should be considered as "virtual teams" where internal and external resources can be linked without dependence on the physical and temporal proximity of team members.

- *Careful architecting of information requirements and integration tools.* e-SCM requires companies to vigorously explore the array of possible application component integration points out in the supply chain. Since each trading partner could have differing integration needs and technologies, supply chain and application component road mapping can be used as tools to assist in deciding the nature of channel relationships, partner selection, and technology interoperability requirements.

Today's business enterprise must pursue these baseline requirements as they develop and mature their e-SCM systems. A critical requirement is getting all channel network constituents to buy into the approach, or the e-SCM project will be stillborn. Strategic e-SCM will continue to struggle until channel members understand that, when information is shared openly between them regarding total network demand and supply and resource availability and capacity limitations, companies can use effective decision-making to truly exploit the power of the convergence of SCM and the Internet.

ENDNOTES

1. Mulani, Nardenda P. and Lee, Hau, "New Business Models for Supply Chain Excellence, in *Achieving Supply Chain Excellence Through Technology,* Mulani, Nardenda P., ed., Montgomery Research, Inc., San Francisco, CA, 2002, 14.
2. Sharp, Kevin R., "What's Hot: Supply Chain Spending in 2002," *Supply Chain Systems Magazine,* 22, 1, 2002, 36–40.
3. Fingar, Peter, Kumar, Harsha, and Sharma, Tarun, *Enterprise E-Commerce: The Software Component Breakthrough for Business-to-Business Commerce,* Meghan-Kiffer Press, Tampa, FL, 2000, 221–222.
4. This definition is from Hammer, Michael and Campy, James, *Reengineering the Corporation,* HarperBusiness, New York, 1993, 32.
5. Sawhney, Mohan and Zabin, Jeff, *The Seven Steps to Nirvana: Strategic Insights into e-Business Transformation,* McGraw-Hill, New York, 2001, 199.
6. This process is detailed in Fingar, Kumar, and Sharma, 228–229.
7. The three levels of inter-enterprise integration are detailed in *Ibid.* 235–236.
8. Hoque, Faisal, *e-Enterprise: Business Models, Architecture, and Components,* Cambridge University Press, Cambridge, UK, 2000, 153.
9. Gonsalves, Antone, "Integration Projects Take Aim at Partner Collaboration," *Information Week,* January 7, 2002, 49–51.
10. For a detailed discussion on ECM see Parker, Bob, "Enterprise Commerce Management: The Blueprint for the Next Generation of Enterprise Systems," AMR Research, June, 2001.
11. A complete discussion of the seven technologies can be found in Austvold, Eric and the ETS Staff, "The Seven Technology Pillars of Enterprise Commerce Management," AMR Research, July, 2001.
12. Hill, Sidney, "Find a Solution that Fits," *Manufacturing Systems,* 20, 2, 2002, 26–28.
13. Downes, Larry, "The Metamorphosis of Information," *Optimize Magazine,* June, 2002, 37–43.
14. See the interesting analysis about CRM in Lee, Dick, "Running Out of Gas?" *Customer Relationship Management,* 6, 7, 2002, 26–29.
15. Baer, Tony, "At Each Other's Throats," *Manufacturing Systems,* 20, 2, 2002, 16–20.
16. Weiss, Peter, "ASPs: They Do More Than Just Save Money," *Information Week,* November 5, 2001, 111.
17. For more details see Hayes, Ian S., "Upwardly Mobile: a Wireless Primer," *Software Magazine,* 21, 4, 2001, 40–48.
18. Lowe, Paul G. and Markham, William J., "Perspectives on Operations Excellence," *Supply Chain Management Review,* 15, 6, 2001, 52–60.

Index

Printed in the United States
134026LV00002B/52-60/A